Modern photographic films are truly rem[illegible] you consider how effectively they record the events of our lives. The uses of film in our society are almost endless. Because film is such a vital part of the photographic process and so profoundly affects the quality of your pictures, you need a film that gives results of consistently high quality. Kodak films meet these requirements.

Kodak films are manufactured with a wide variety of characteristics so that you can choose the best film for the type of photographs you want to take. In order for you to select the best film to suit your needs, you should be familiar with the characteristics of the films available. The purpose of this book is to acquaint you with Kodak films for general use.

The book has two sections—a text portion and a section of Data Sheets at the end of the book. The text portion explains what you'll want to know about selecting the right film, how to expose it properly, how to get it processed, and how you should store your films. The Data Sheet section gives you all the details for each film, such as film speeds, recommended filters, flash exposure guide numbers, and processing requirements. The information presented in this book will help you make photographs that you will be proud to show to your friends.

For data books on professional roll and sheet films, you may want to purchase *KODAK Color Films for Professional Use* (E-77), $4.00, and *KODAK Professional Black-and-White Films* (F-5), $3.00. These books are available at stores that sell photographic products (see inside back cover).

Picture on front cover.

NEIL MONTANUS

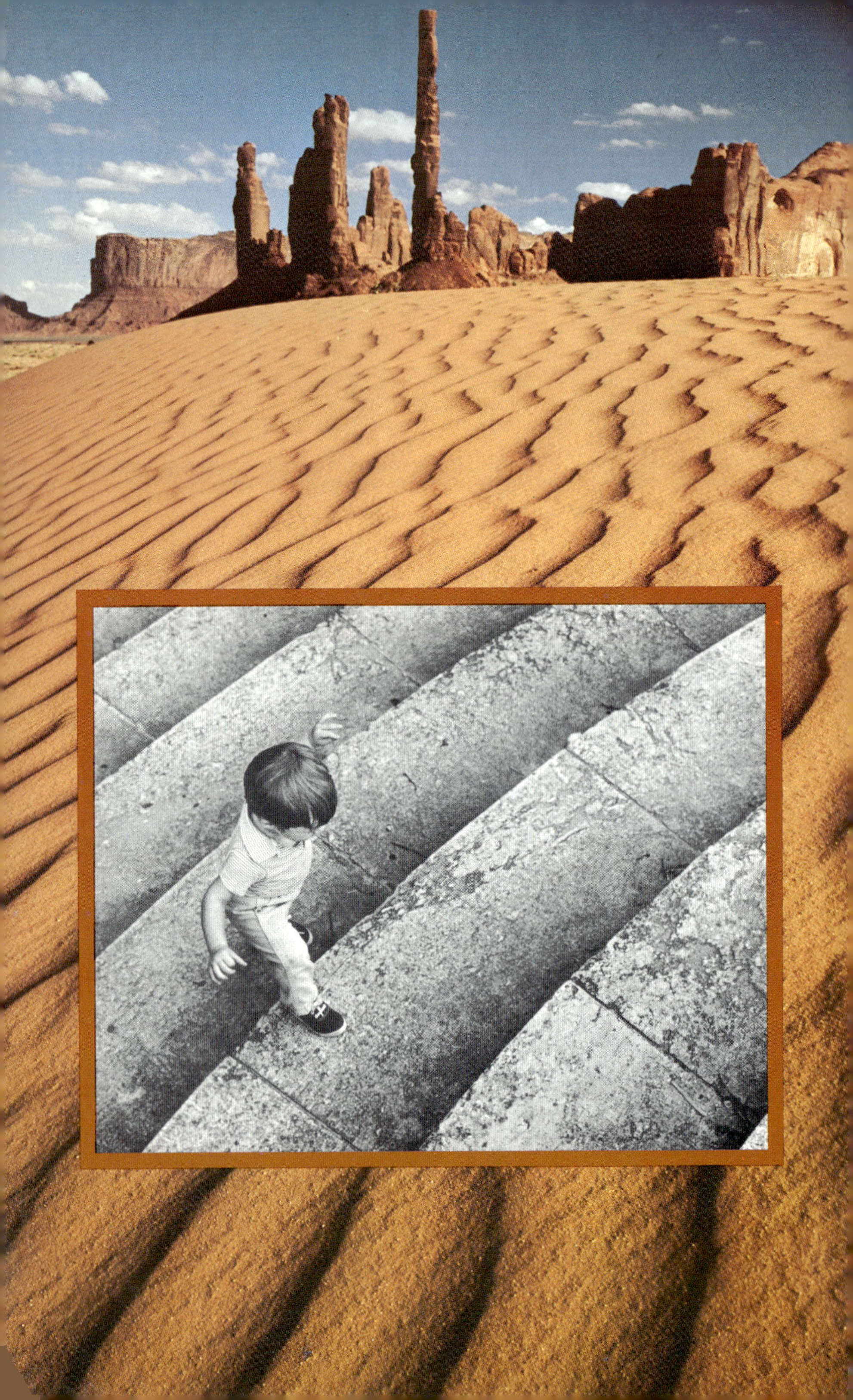

CONTENTS

Second 1978 Printing

ISBN 0-87985-161-9

Desert picture—DAVID MUENCH/H. A. ROBERTS

Picture of boy on steps—HOWARD M. BESOSA, KINSA*

*Courtesy Kodak International Newspaper Snapshot Awards.

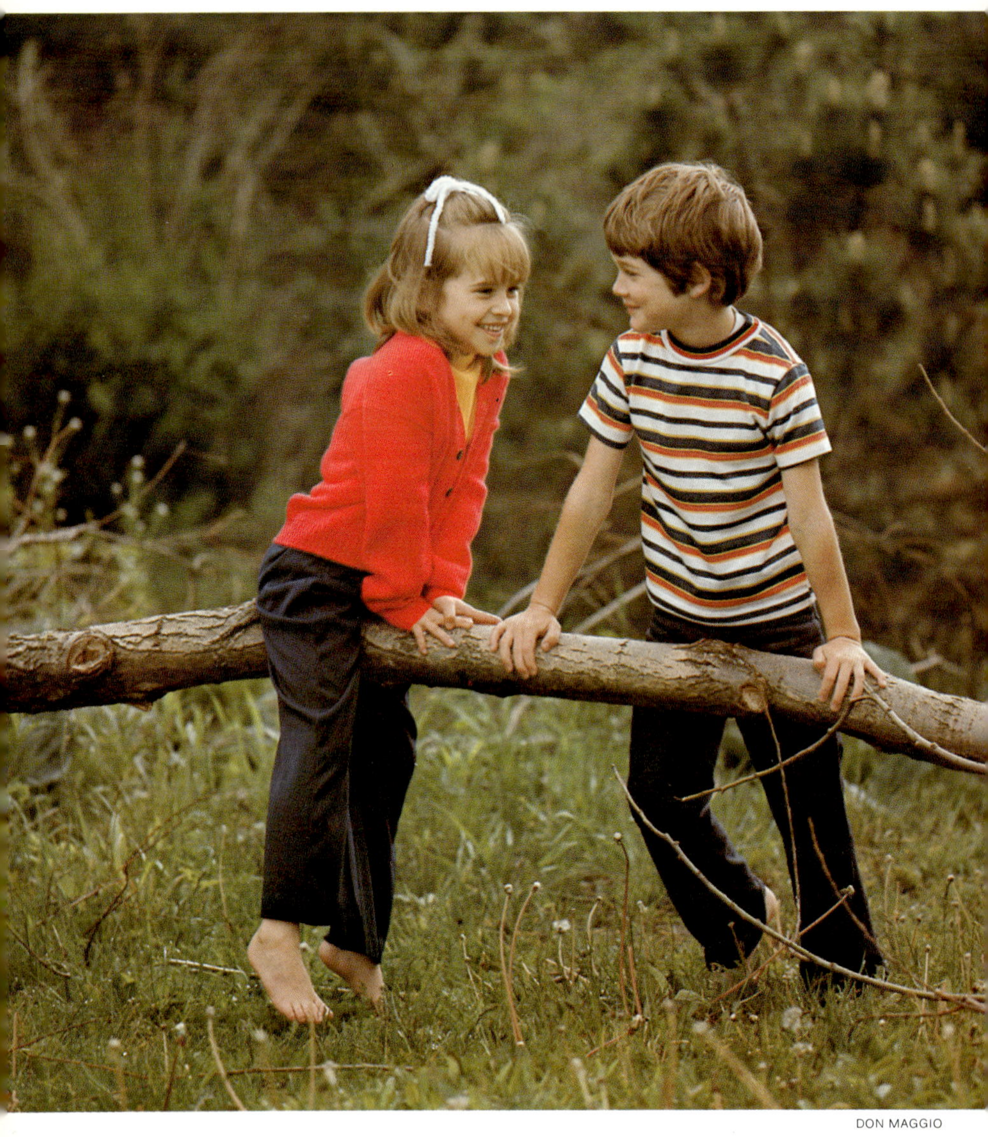

DON MAGGIO

Choosing a Film

Your first consideration in selecting a film is the kind of camera you have—conventional or instant. If you have a KODAK Instant Camera, Kodak makes an instant print film for use in these cameras which gives you instant color prints. If you have a conventional camera, your next consideration is the type of pictures you want—color prints, color slides, or black-and-white prints. Kodak makes several films with different characteristics for each type of picture for use in conventional cameras. The information in this book will help you select the best film for your needs.

You'll also want to know what films are available in the size that your camera accepts. Kodak films for general use are manufactured in four general forms—135 magazines, 110 and 126 cartridges, rolls, and PR10 instant film packs.

The 135 films are rolled on spools in magazines. These films are 35 mm wide and have no backing paper. They are available in 20-, 24-, or 36-exposure lengths, depending on the kind of film.

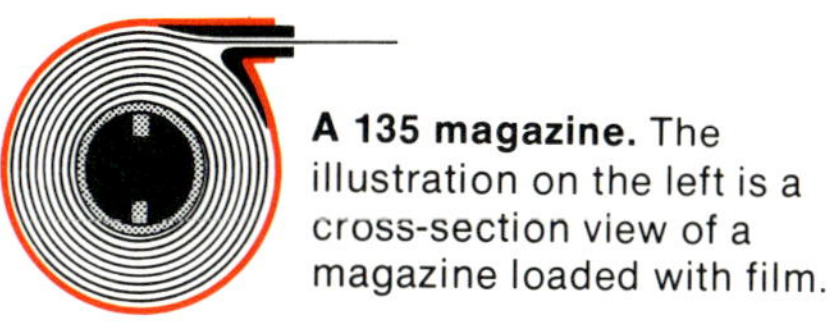

A 135 magazine. The illustration on the left is a cross-section view of a magazine loaded with film.

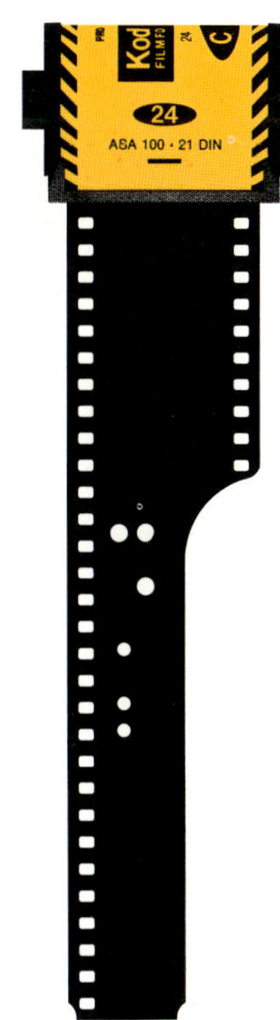

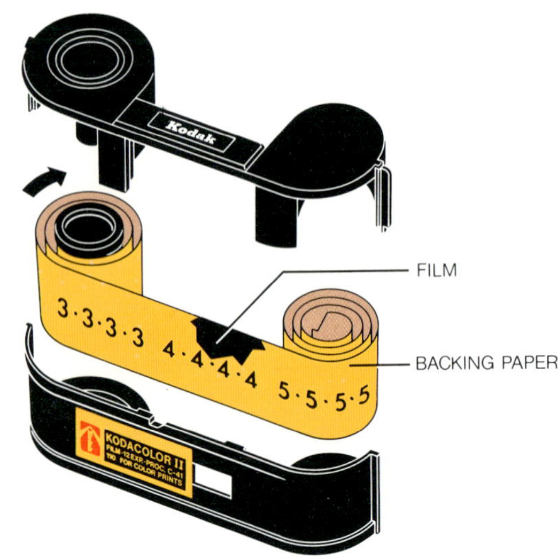

110 Cartridge

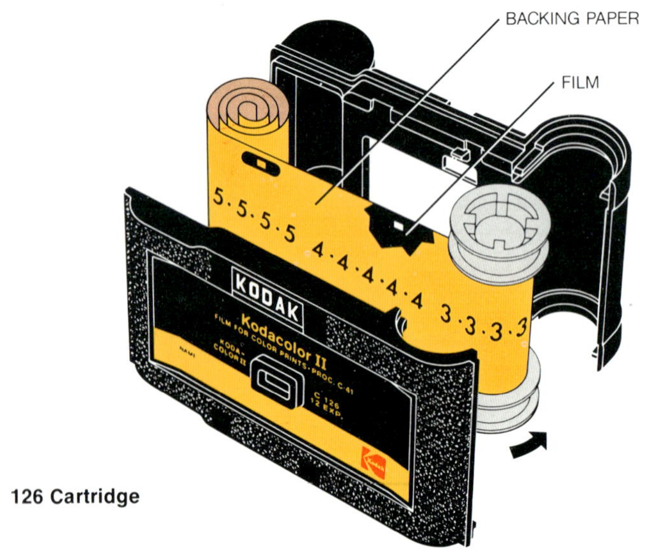

126 Cartridge

An inside view of a 110 and a 126 film cartridge. Do not break open the cartridge unless you process the film yourself. Otherwise the film will be ruined by light-fogging.

Cartridge films have a backing paper to protect the film from light and are supplied in plastic cartridges designed for drop-in loading of KODAK INSTAMATIC® Cameras and similar cameras. Cartridge film is identified by the number 110 or 126. Some 110- and 126-size films come in 12-exposure lengths, others come in 20-exposure lengths, and some are available in both lengths.

Roll films also have a backing paper and are rolled on spools. They are available in a variety of sizes and are designated by such numbers as 120, 127, and 620. The number of exposures is determined by the camera format; there are 8 to 16 exposures for rectangular pictures, depending on the camera, and usually 12 exposures for square pictures.

KODAK Instant Film packs each hold 10 instant color picture units. The pack is disposable plastic and includes a film cover to protect the film from light before the pack is loaded in the camera.

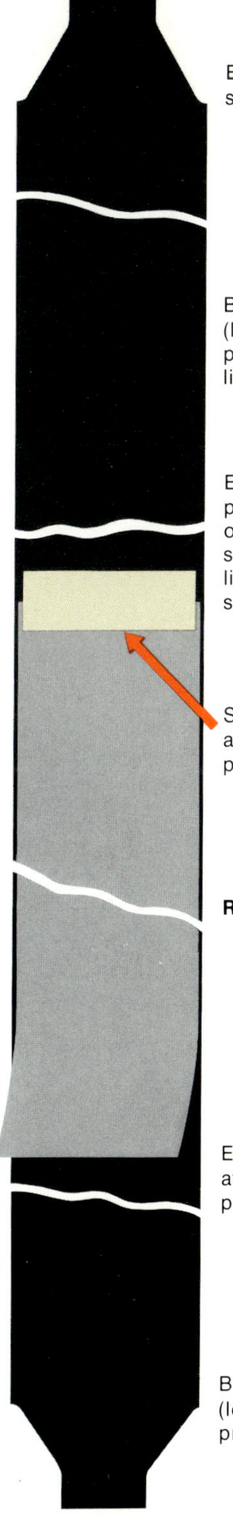

Roll Films

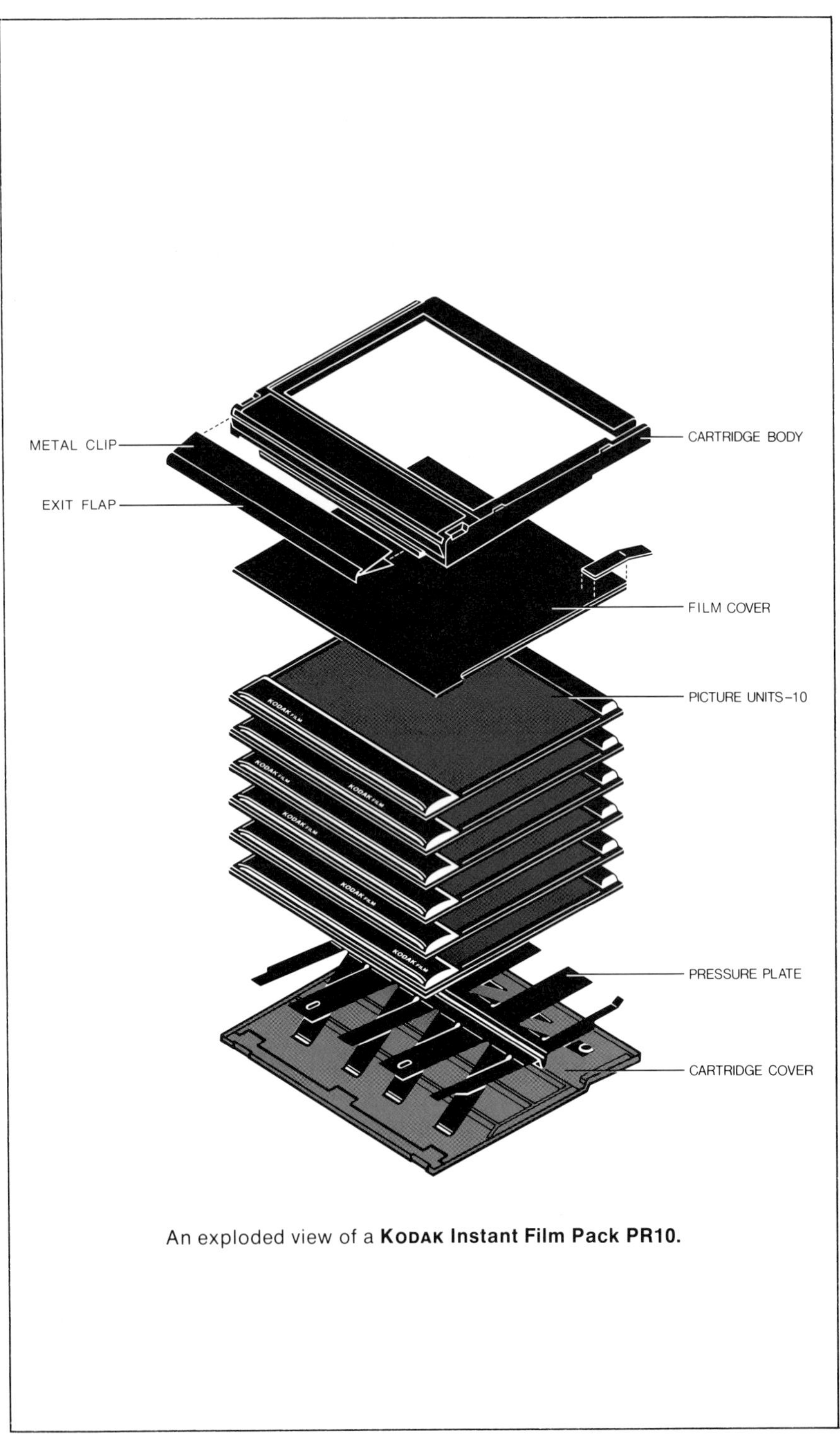

An exploded view of a **KODAK Instant Film Pack PR10.**

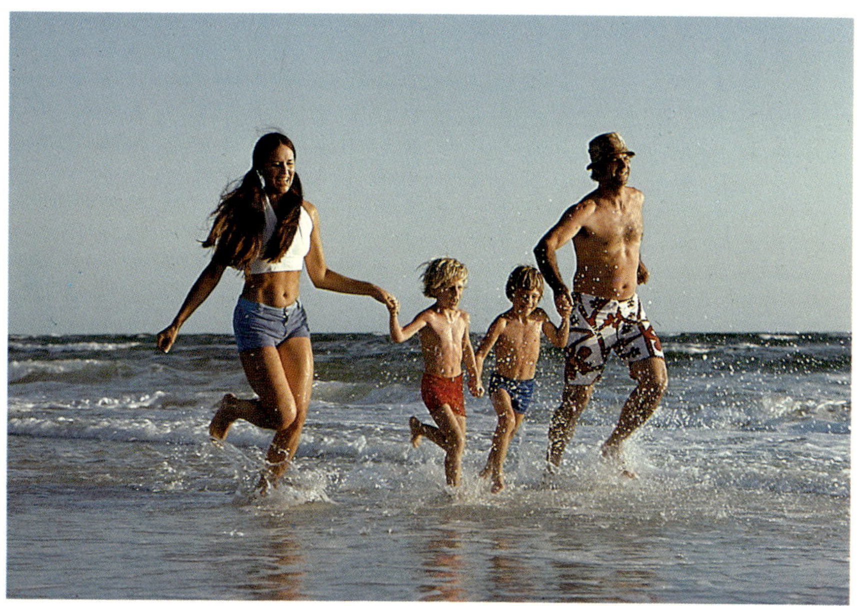

KODACHROME 64 Film (Daylight). NEIL MONTANUS

To choose a color film, you'll want to know, in addition to the kind of pictures it makes and the film sizes available, the film speed and the light sources recommended for the film. Also, you'll want to have some idea of the color quality and the definition (see page 50) of the pictures it produces. If you do your own darkroom work, you'll want to know if you can process the film yourself.

To choose a black-and-white film is simpler than selecting a color film. Unless you need one of the few films particularly designed for special purposes, the main considerations for general-use black-and-white films are film speed and the quality of definition you'll get in your pictures. Definition is explained on page 69.

Nonadjustable cameras and some basic automatic cameras will not expose high-speed films correctly. See your camera manual for the films recommended for these cameras.

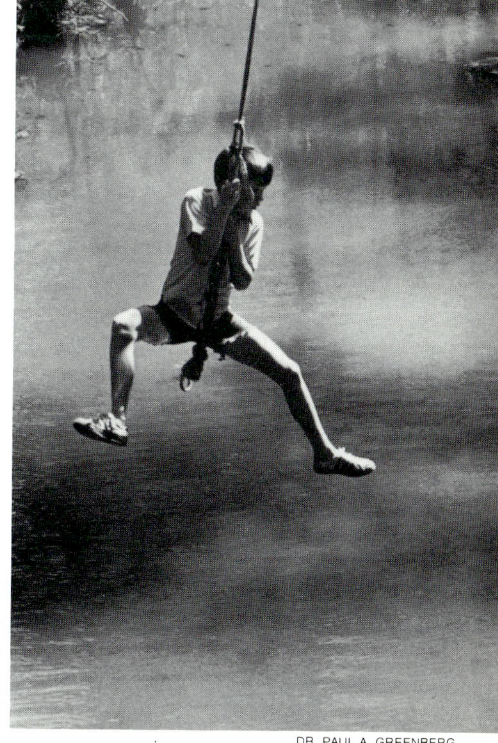

KODAK TRI-X Pan Film. DR. PAUL A. GREENBERG

CHOOSING A FILM

Each kind of Kodak film is designed primarily to produce only one of these four kinds of pictures. Each film carton tells you the kind of pictures that particular film makes. For the sizes available in each kind of Kodak film, see pages 120 and 121. Processing services are available so that you can also obtain other kinds of pictures from your negatives, slides, or prints. See page 53.

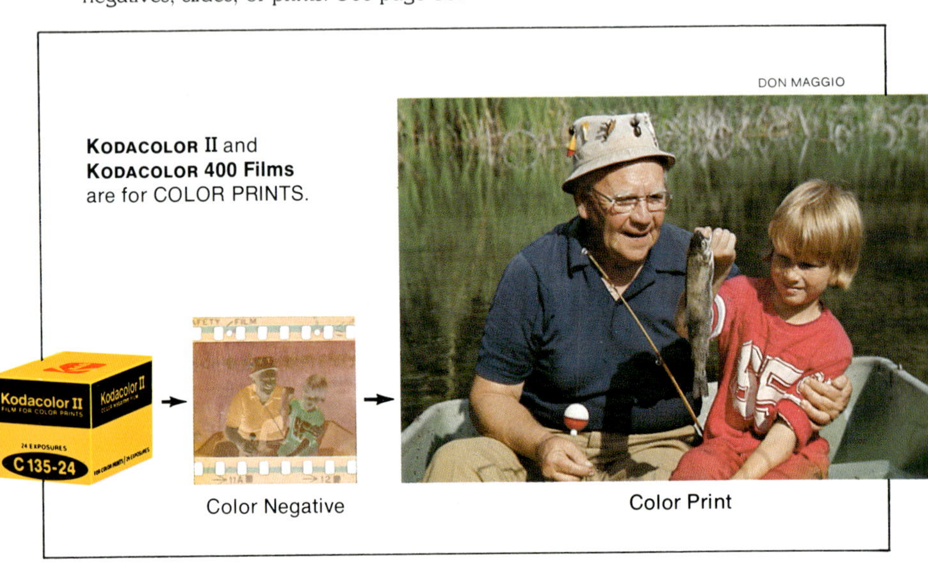

DON MAGGIO

KODACOLOR II and
KODACOLOR 400 Films
are for COLOR PRINTS.

Color Negative

Color Print

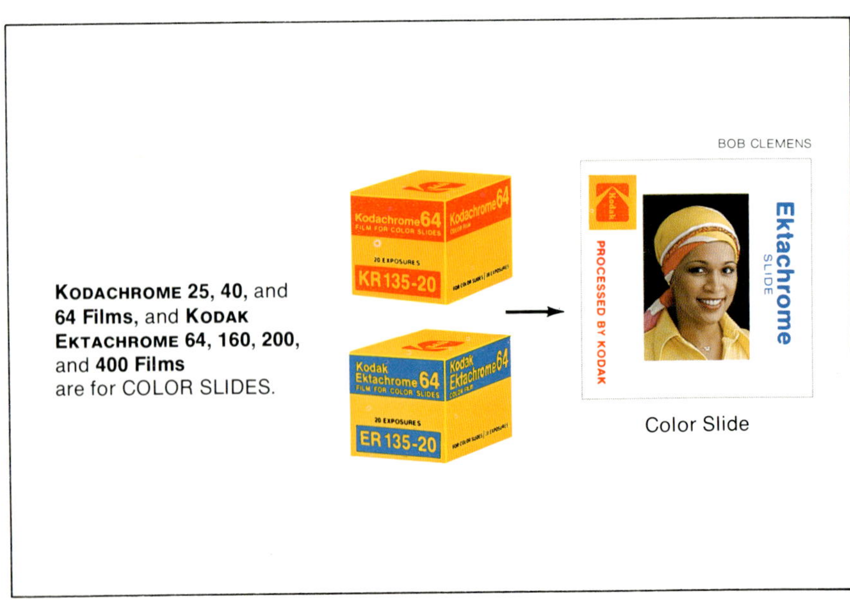

BOB CLEMENS

KODACHROME 25, 40, and
64 Films, and **KODAK**
EKTACHROME 64, 160, 200,
and **400 Films**
are for COLOR SLIDES.

Color Slide

Kodak Verichrome Pan, Plus-X Pan, Panatomic-X, and **Tri-X Pan Films** are for BLACK-AND-WHITE PRINTS. Other black-and-white films for special purposes are described on page 67.

JOY C. BUTZ, KINSA

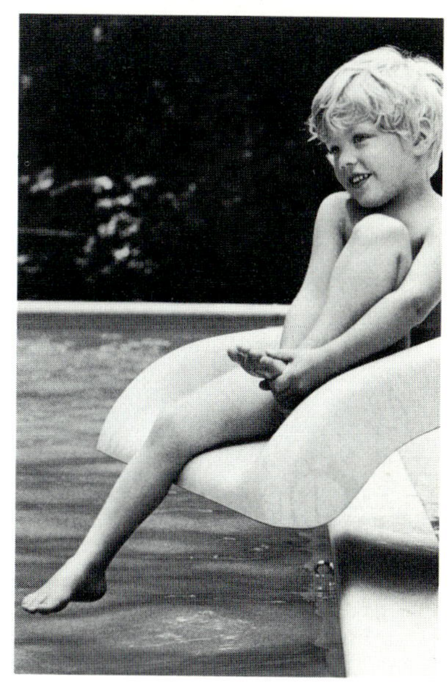

Black-and-White Negative

Black-and-White Print

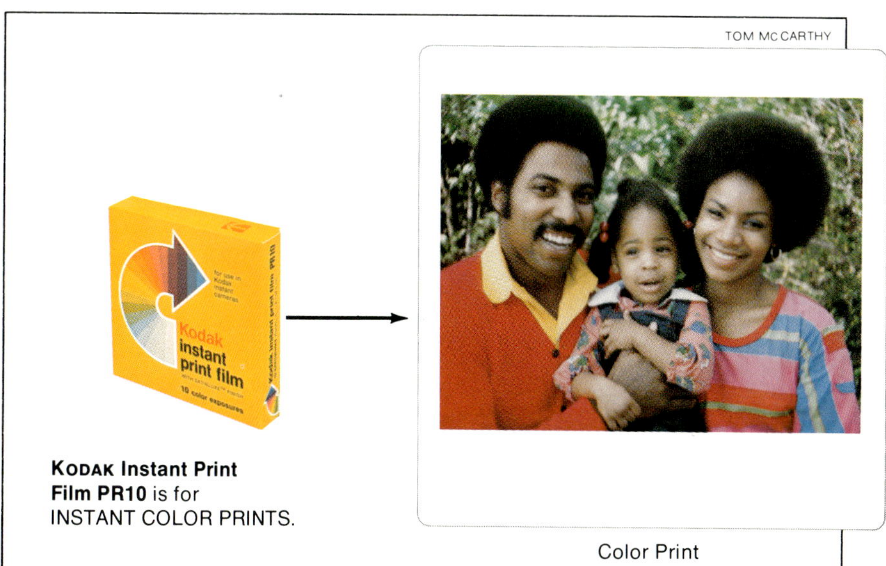

TOM MC CARTHY

Kodak Instant Print Film PR10 is for INSTANT COLOR PRINTS.

Color Print

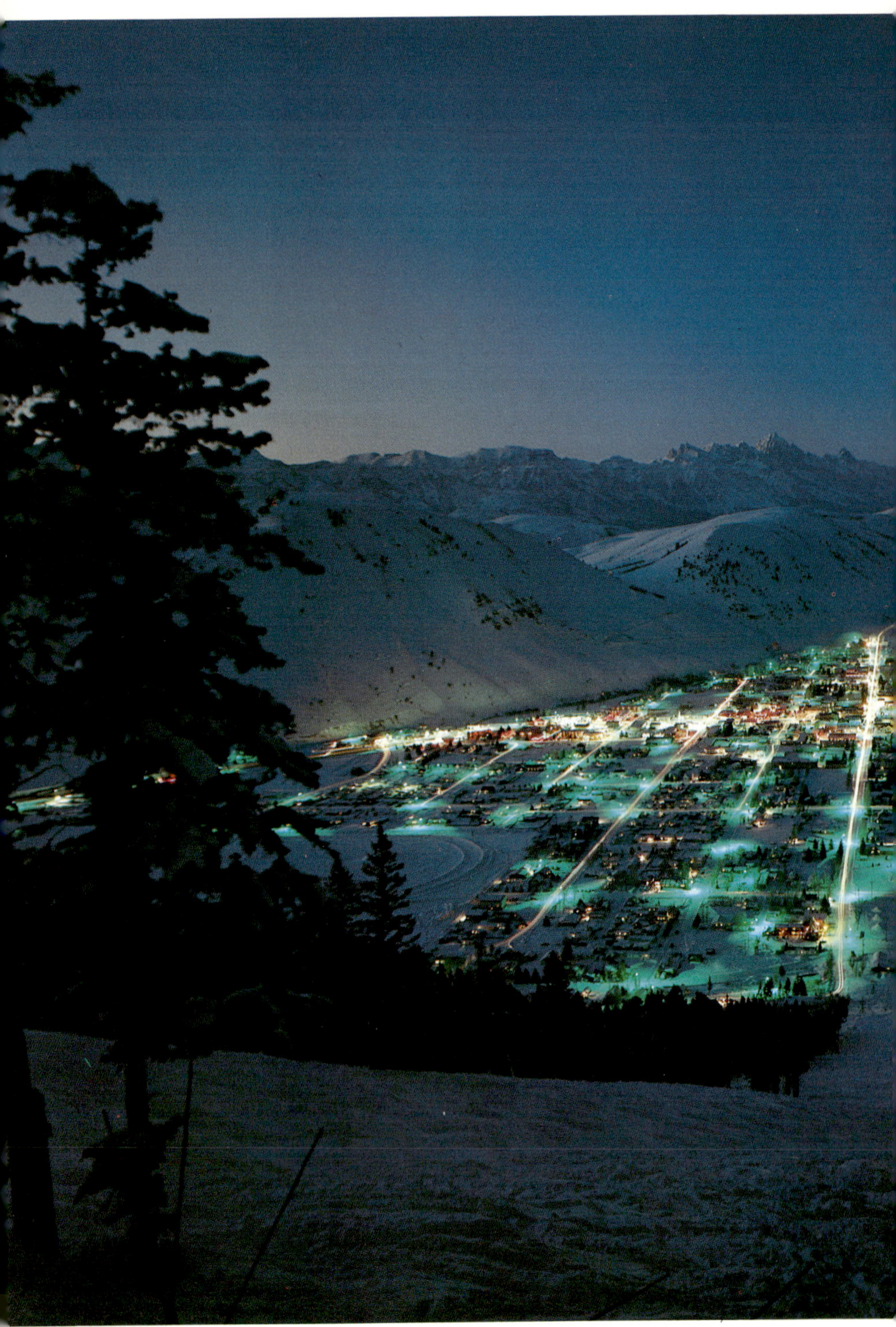

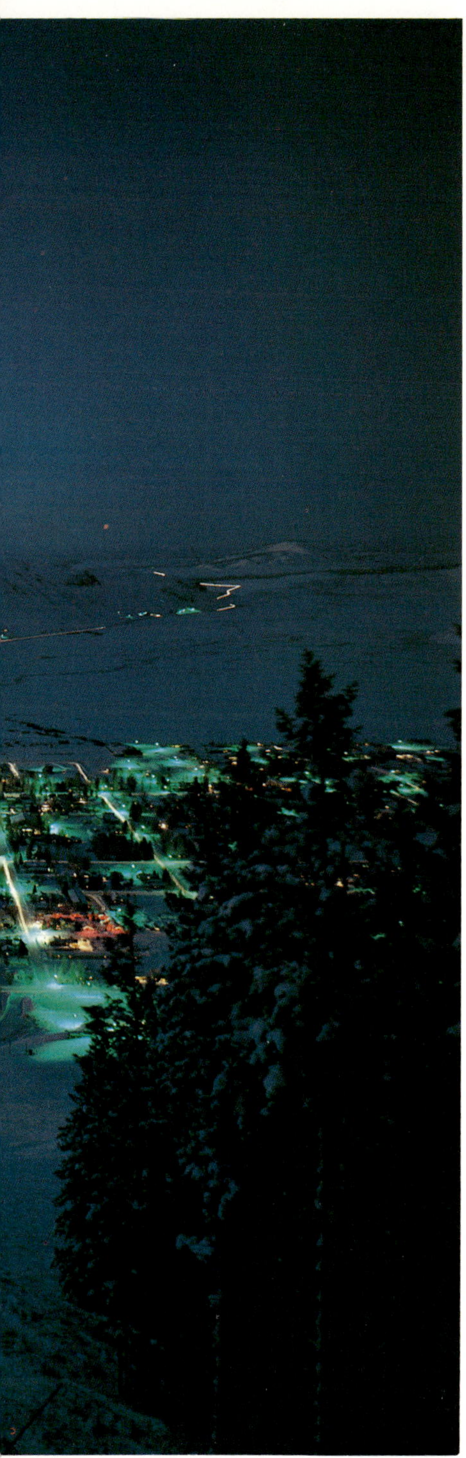

NEIL MONTANUS

Kodak Color Films

Color films for still cameras are available in three general kinds. One kind produces color negatives which are primarily used to make color prints; another kind of film produces color slides; and the third kind produces instant color prints.

In color negatives, all the tones and colors of the original scene are reversed: Light tones are recorded dark, dark tones are recorded light, and the colors are the complements of the colors you saw when you took the picture. Kodak color-negative films have a built-in mask that helps improve the quality of prints made from them. This mask gives the negatives an overall color cast of light orange-tan. All the color relationships are properly reproduced when the negatives are printed on color photographic paper. You can also have color slides made from your color negatives; see "Getting Prints or Slides Made—from Your Negatives, Prints, or Slides" on page 53.

While the interesting colors of twilight last only a few moments, a picture taken on color film will preserve a visual experience that would be only a fleeting memory. Jackson Hole, Wyoming.

The second kind of color film gives you color slides directly. During processing, the image on the film is reversed from a negative to a positive, resulting in a color slide or transparency that you can either project onto a screen or look at with a viewer. The same film that was exposed in your camera is processed, mounted, and returned to you as slides (or as unmounted transparencies if you prefer). You can order prints or duplicate slides from your slides or transparencies; see page 53.

The third kind of color film, instant print film for use in instant cameras, produces finished color prints in a matter of minutes. There is no usable negative. You can have additional color prints or color slides made from both instant and conventional, finished original color prints.

Kodak color-negative films and Kodak color-slide films are both available in films designed for general use and in films designed for professional use. Kodak color films for professional use have "professional" in their names. The main difference between films for general use and those for professional use is the more rigid requirements for storing and handling professional films. See the section on storage of Kodak films beginning on page 107.

You'll find a comprehensive table of condensed information for Kodak color films on page 120.

FILMS FOR COLOR PRINTS

There are two Kodak color-negative films for general use in conventional cameras that are for color prints—a fast, general-purpose film and a high-speed film. Some simple cameras are not designed for use with high-speed films. See the discussion in the section on "Exposure" beginning on page 83.

Kodak makes one film for use in KODAK Instant Cameras—KODAK Instant Print Film PR10.

The descriptions that follow will help you select a film for color prints.

KODACOLOR II Film is a fast, general-purpose, color-negative film which has extremely fine grain, high sharpness, excellent color reproduction with saturated colors, and good versatility. The film was modified to raise its speed to ASA 100 and to improve its color reproduction. It has wide exposure latitude—the ability to produce pleasing results even though moderate exposure errors are made. You can take pictures with daylight, electronic flash, or blue flashbulbs. You can also use this film to take pictures by the existing lighting. However, KODACOLOR 400 Film, a faster film, is a better choice for existing-light photography (see page 42). KODACOLOR II Film, though, has finer grain. This film is available in many sizes. See the table on page 120.

When you want color prints and you can use a general-purpose film, choose **KODACOLOR II Film** for your camera.

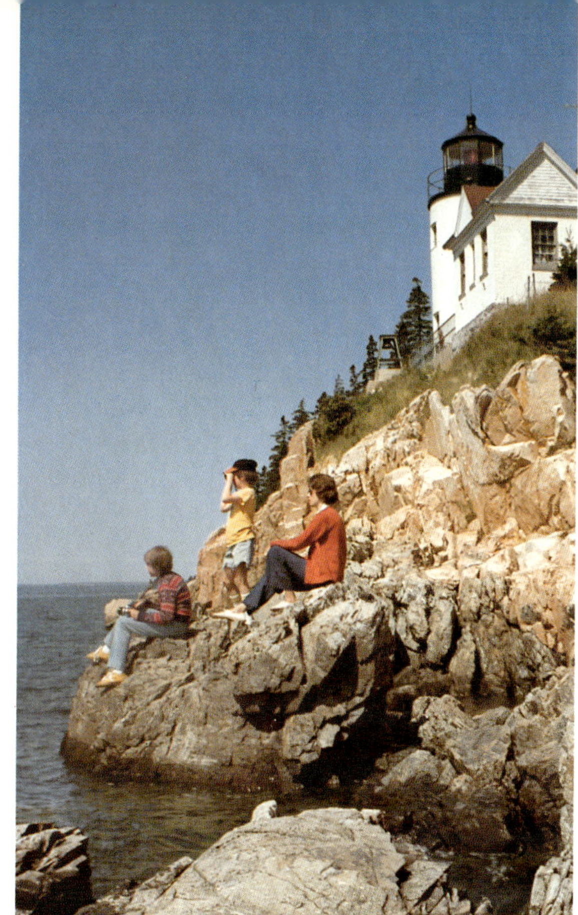

JOHN FISH

KODACOLOR II Film has a speed of ASA 100, which is just right for most picture-taking situations. To take pictures in the shade, such as this one, you need an adjustable or automatic camera.

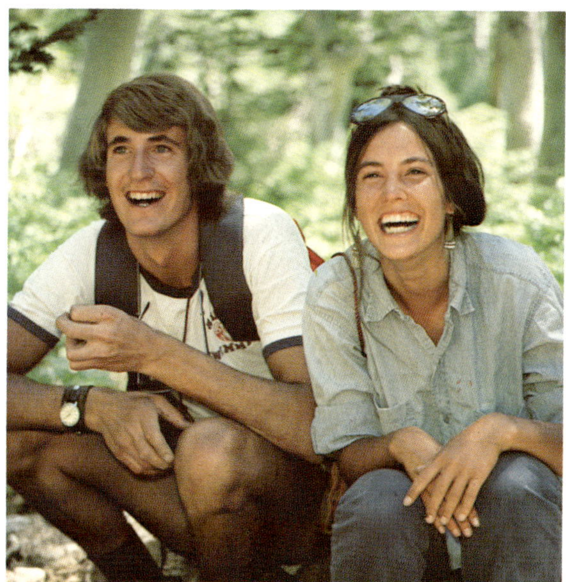

NORM KERR

KODACOLOR 400 Film is a high-speed, color-negative film for photographing subjects in dim lighting, such as existing light; fast action; and subjects requiring good depth of field and high shutter speeds; and for extending the flash distance range. This film extends your picture-taking opportunities; it lets you take pictures you couldn't get with a slower-speed film. KODACOLOR 400 Film has great versatility because you can use it to photograph subjects under lighting conditions ranging from bright sunlight to very dim light, depending on your camera. However, the film is intended primarily for picture-taking situations where you need high film speed. It has a speed of ASA 400 and good graininess characteristics for such a high-speed film.

KODACOLOR 400 Film is color-balanced for daylight, electronic flash, or blue flash. It also has special sensitizing characteristics that let you obtain pleasing pictures under a variety of other light sources, such as household light bulbs and fluorescent lamps, without using camera filters. The film can handle mixed light sources without using filters, as well. This film offers wide exposure latitude. It's available in 135, 110, and 120 sizes.

You can send KODACOLOR Films to Kodak or other photofinishing laboratories for processing and printing, or you can process these films and print the negatives yourself.

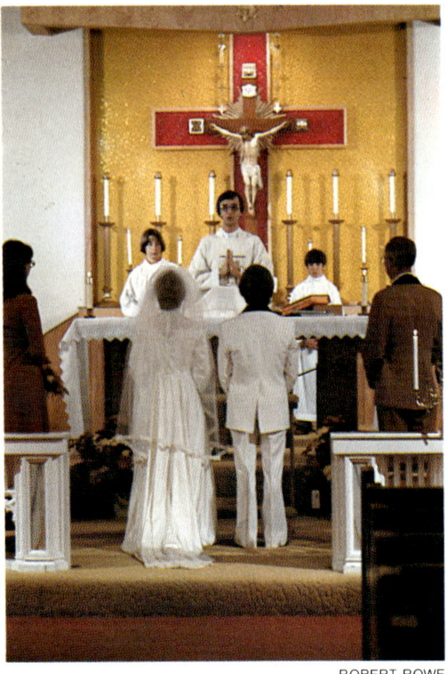

ROBERT ROWE

When your subject is in subdued lighting conditions and you want color prints, a high-speed film—**KODACOLOR 400 Film**—lets you capture the picture if your camera has a fast lens: *f*/5.6 or faster. 1/125 second *f*/4.

In order to use a high shutter speed to stop motion in dim lighting, you need a high film speed. **KODACOLOR 400 Film,** with a speed of ASA 400, gives you the necessary film speed. 1/250 second *f*/4.

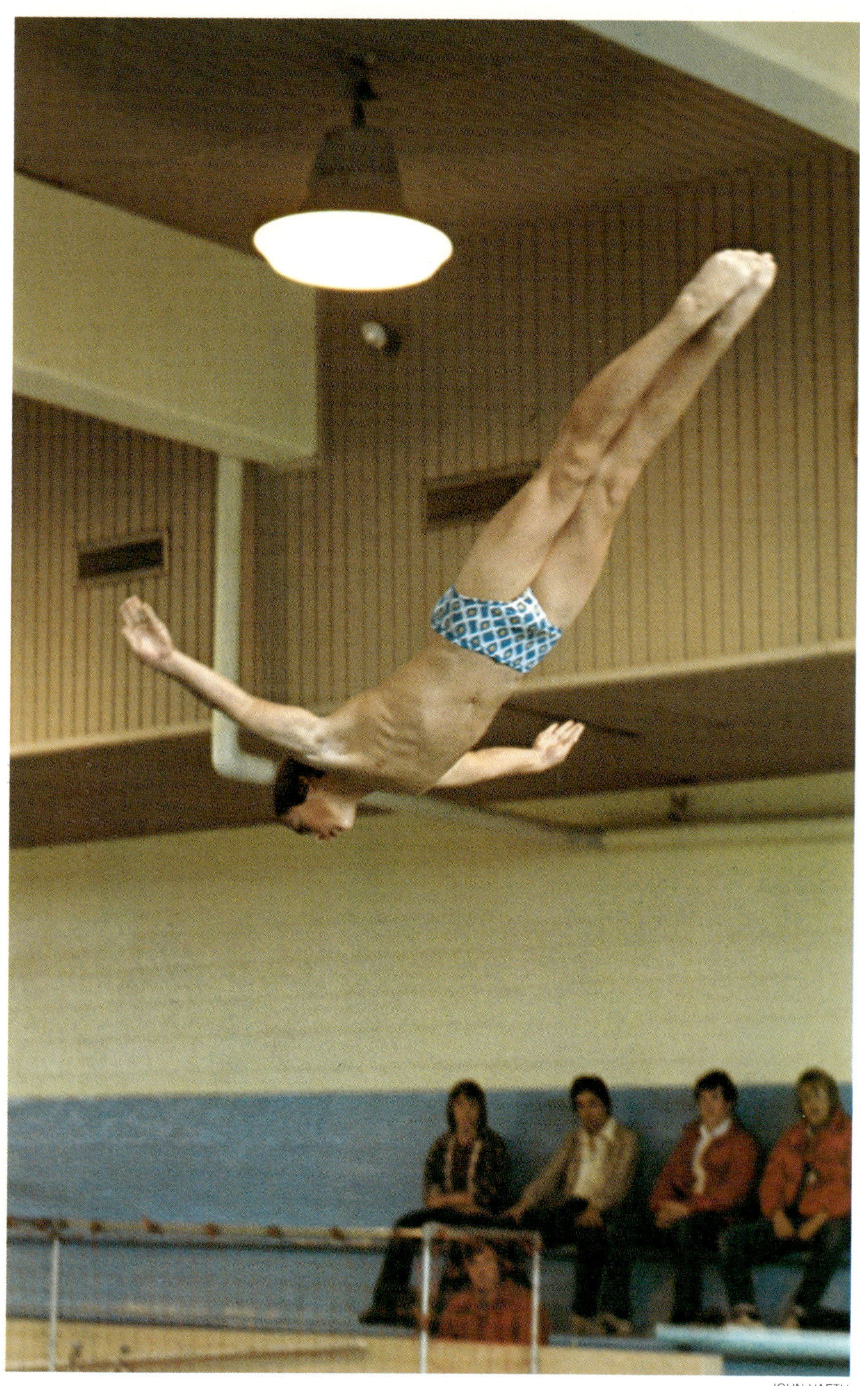
JOHN VAETH

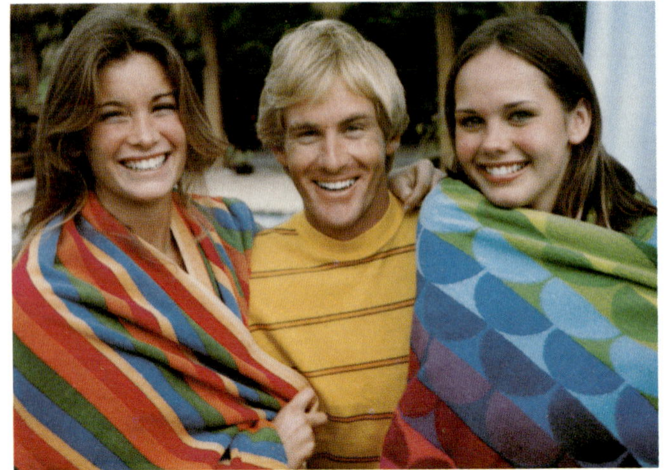

TOM MC CARTHY

You can enjoy the fun and instant satisfaction of color prints when you use **KODAK Instant Print Film PR10.**

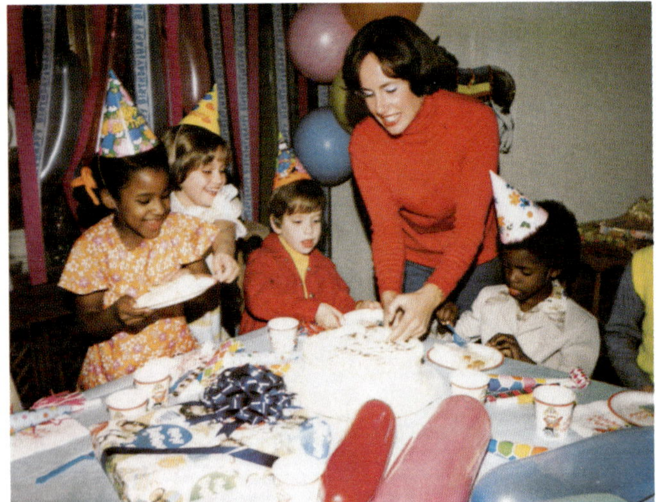

JIM DENNIS

You can take sharp, brilliant instant pictures with color by Kodak. **KODAK Instant Print Film PR10** gives you beautiful color prints with the elegant KODAK SATINLUXE™ Finish.

KODAK Instant Print Film PR10, for use in KODAK Instant Cameras, produces brilliant, rectangular, color prints directly from the camera. You can compose the picture for either a vertical or a horizontal format. After you take the picture, the development process starts as the print is ejected from the camera. The picture develops right before your eyes without peeling, timing, or litter. An image begins to form in approximately 1 minute and the color picture is essentially complete in about 8 minutes under normal temperature conditions.

Prints from KODAK Instant Print Film have an elegant, textured KODAK SATINLUXE™ Finish which gives a pleasing appearance and helps protect the prints from smudges and fingerprints. The film produces beautiful color rendition. It's designed for taking pictures in daylight or with electronic flash or blue flash.

FILMS FOR COLOR SLIDES

Kodak offers several color-slide films, each with different characteristics. One of the most obvious differences is film speed. Some of the other characteristics, such as color rendition, sharpness, and graininess, are more subtle—a critical comparison would be required to see the differences between films. Actually, personal preference is usually the most dominant factor in selecting a color-slide film. The following descriptions will help you choose a film to suit your needs.

KODACHROME 25 Film (Daylight) is a popular color-slide film noted for high sharpness and extremely fine grain. The film features excellent color quality—pleasing flesh tones, clean whites and yellows, bright reds, greens, and blues, and realistic sky reproduction. KODACHROME 25 Film has good exposure latitude and tone reproduction. It retains good detail in highlights and shadow areas. This film with a speed of ASA 25 is for use with daylight, electronic flash, or blue flashbulbs. It's available in 135 size only.

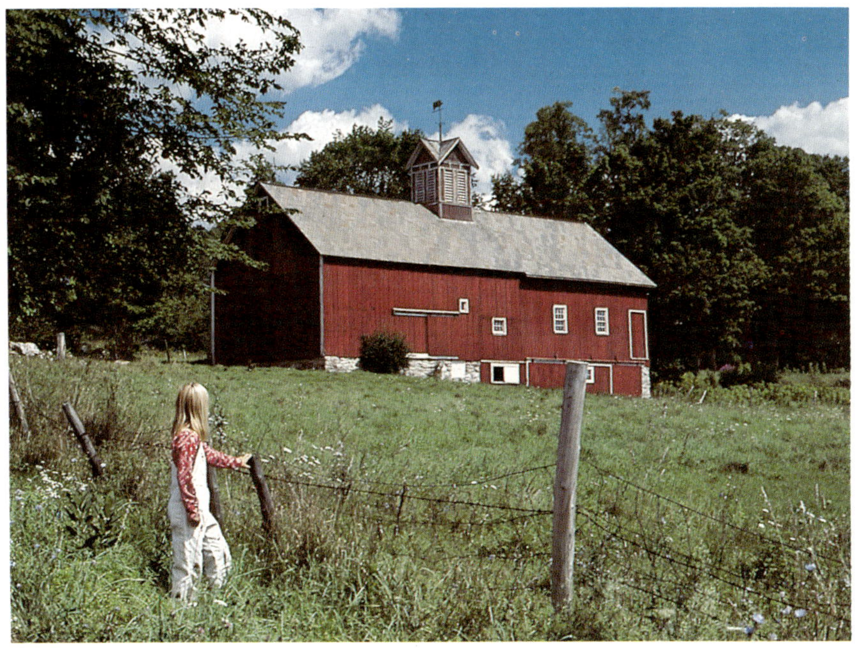

ROBERT KRETZER

KODACHROME 25 Film (Daylight) is an excellent general-purpose film for color slides. It is well known for its superb sharpness and extremely fine grain. 1/125 sec *f*/8.

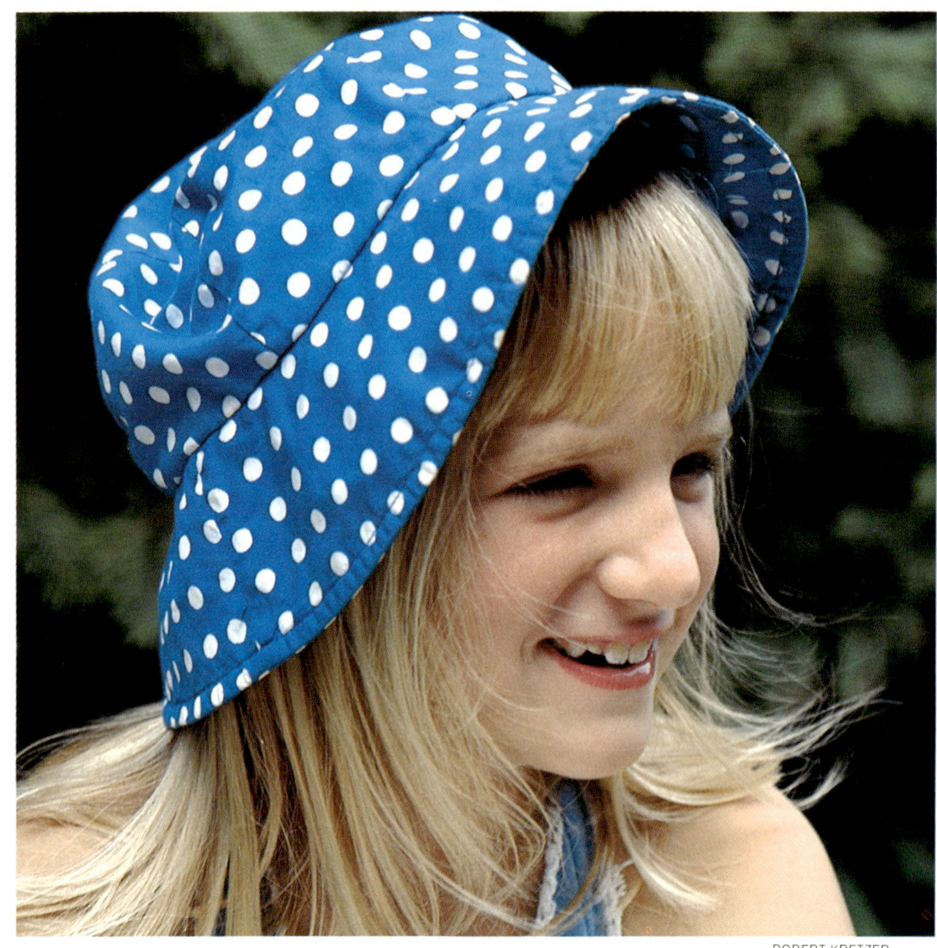

ROBERT KRETZER

Choosing a color film by the way it records various colors is a matter of personal taste. The flesh tones produced by **KODACHROME 25 Film (Daylight)** make it a favorite film for many people.

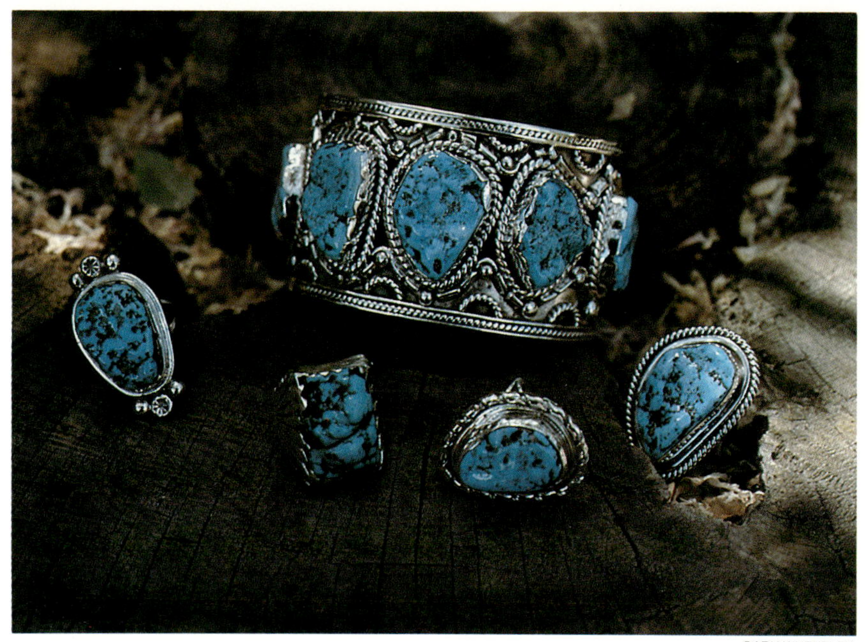

GARY WHELPLEY

The delicate colors and intricate detail of Indian jewelry have been superbly reproduced by **KODACHROME 64 Film (Daylight).**

KODACHROME 64 Film (Daylight) is a good choice for all-around picture-taking when you want color slides. Its ASA 64 speed lets you use higher shutter speeds or smaller lens openings under normal lighting conditions and extends picture-taking capability on overcast days, in the shade, or in somewhat subdued lighting. The film produces excellent color rendition—bright reds, greens, and blues; clean whites and yellows; good blue skies; and pleasant flesh tones. In addition, the film shows adequate detail in both highlight and shadow areas. It has good exposure latitude that helps yield pleasing results even with moderate underexposure or overexposure.

KODACHROME 64 Film is almost as sharp and fine-grained as KODACHROME 25 Film. At normal screen viewing distances, most viewers can't see any difference in sharpness or graininess. KODACHROME 64 Film is for use in daylight or with electronic flash or blue flash. It comes in sizes 135, 110, and 126.

Have your KODACHROME Films processed by Kodak or another commercial laboratory. You can't process these films in your own darkroom because the process is highly complex and requires commercial photofinishing equipment.

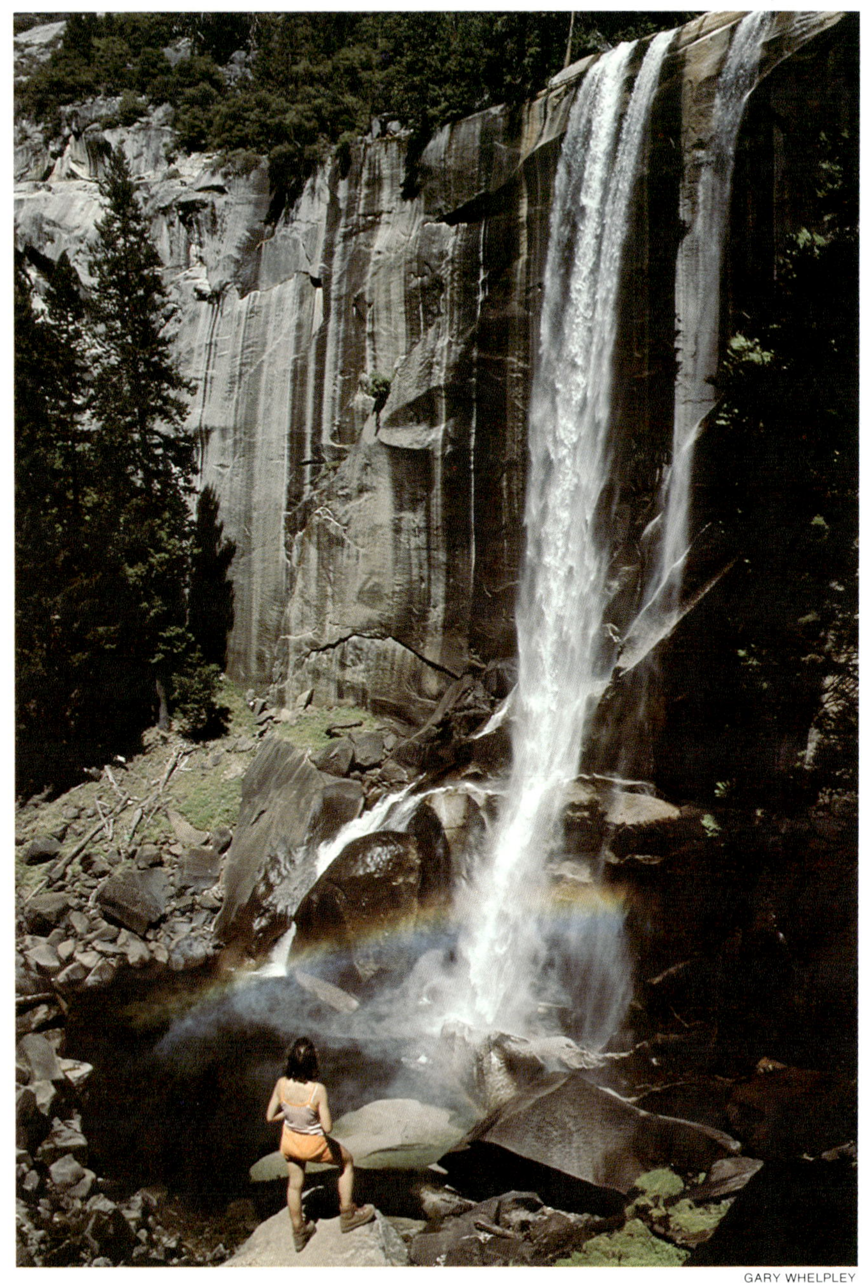

GARY WHELPLEY

KODACHROME 64 Film (Daylight) has many of the same fine qualities as KODACHROME 25 Film (Daylight) but more than twice as much speed—ASA 64. The high-quality color rendition produced by KODACHROME 64 Film helps make it a great film for general picture-taking.

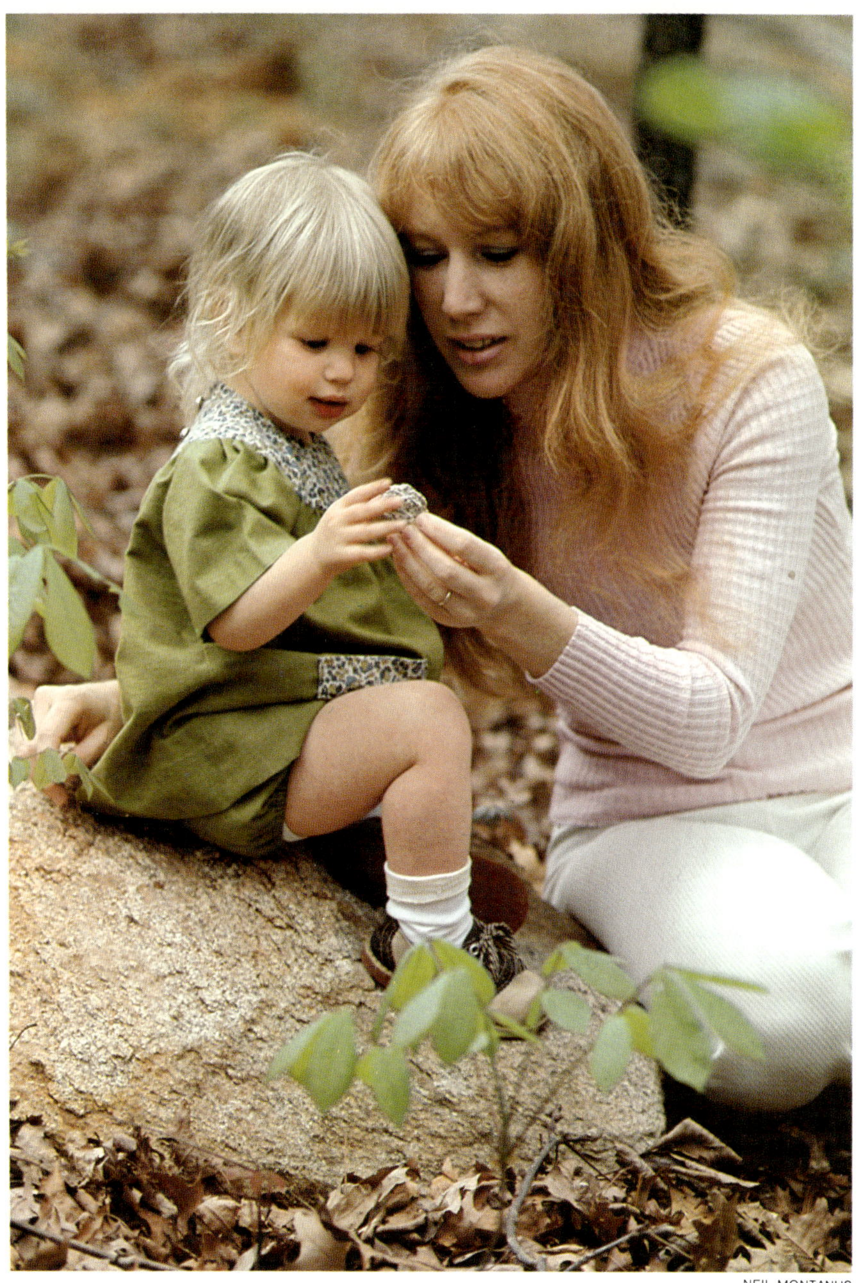

NEIL MONTANUS

The extra speed of **KODACHROME 64 Film (Daylight)** is especially helpful when the light level is reduced, as it was in this picture made on an overcast day. 1/250 sec *f*/4.

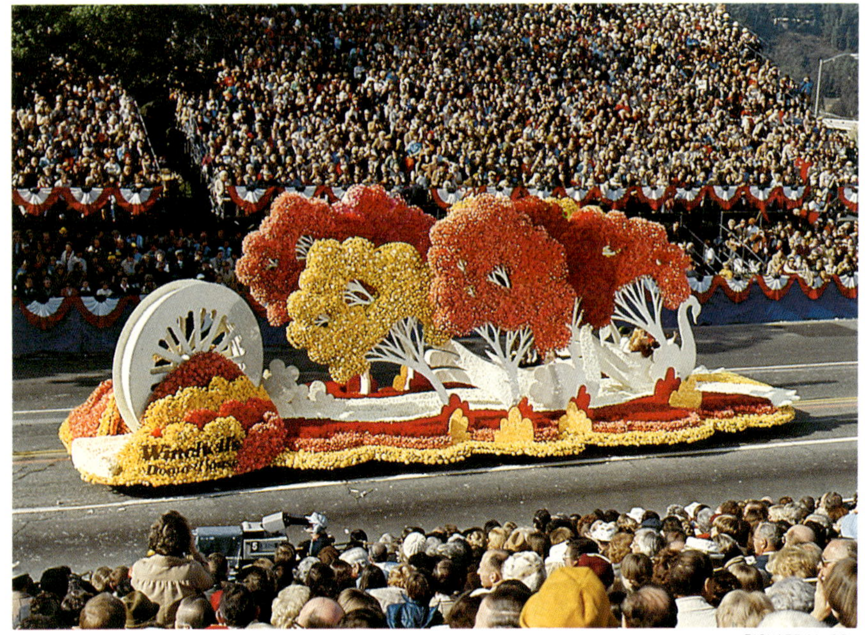

RICHARD MC COY

Many people prefer **KODAK EKTACHROME 64 Film (Daylight),** but here again it's a matter of personal taste. This is an excellent film for general picture-taking when you want color slides. Tournament of Roses Parade, Pasadena, California.

KODAK EKTACHROME 64 Film (Daylight) is an excellent general-purpose color-slide film with a speed of ASA 64. EKTACHROME 64 Film replaced KODAK EKTACHROME-X Film. EKTACHROME 64 Film has improved color reproduction for better flesh tones, vivid blue skies, bright reds and yellows, clean highlights, and good shadow detail. The film distinguishes well between similar colors, such as red and orange.

EKTACHROME 64 Film has improved sharpness and very fine grain which give high image quality. This film is not quite as sharp or fine-grained as KODACHROME 64 Film, but it's difficult to see the difference in sharpness or graininess on the projection screen. EKTACHROME 64 Film is a daylight-type film. For flash pictures, use electronic flash or blue flashbulbs. This film is available in several sizes. Refer to the table on page 120.

An additional feature of all KODAK EKTACHROME Films is that you can process these films in your own darkroom if you want to.

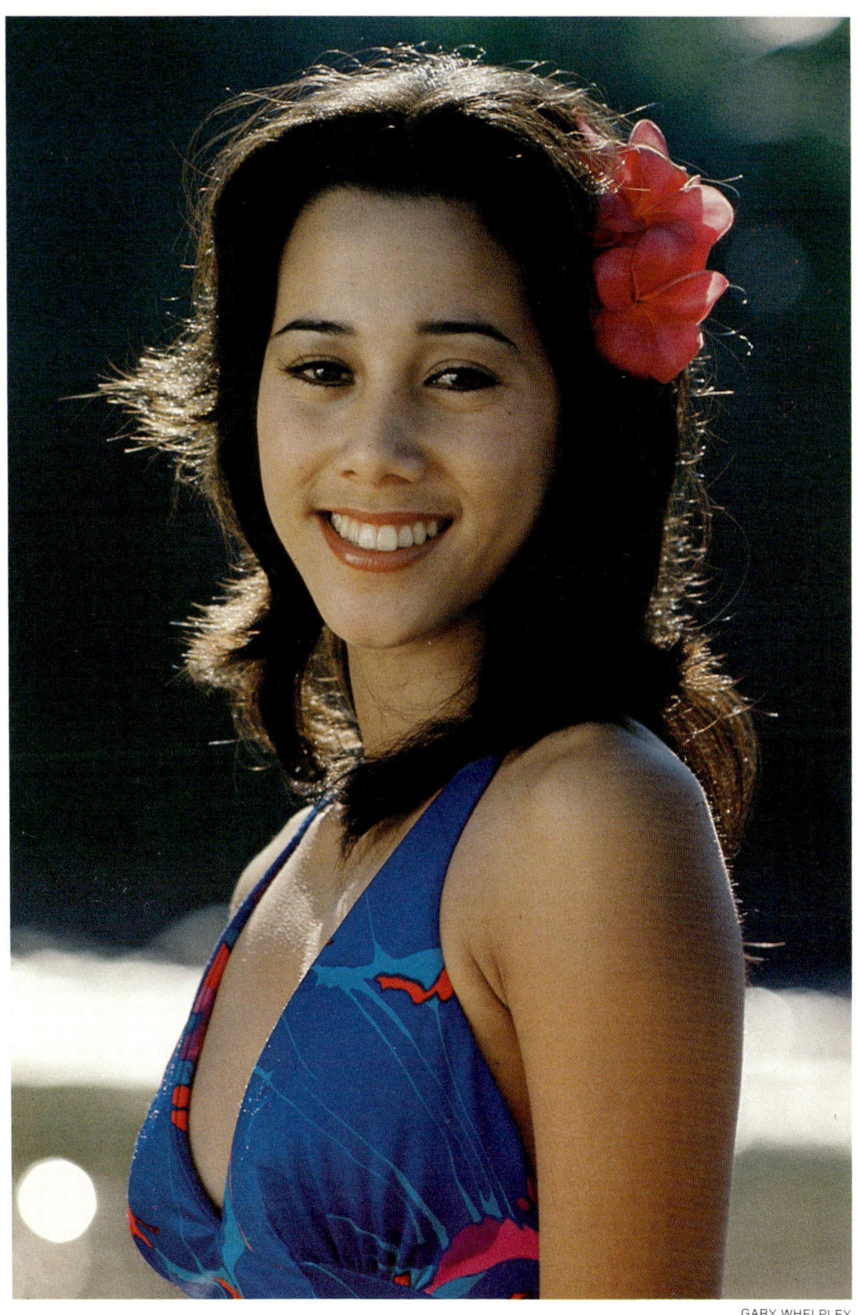

GARY WHELPLEY

One of the many fine features of **KODAK EKTACHROME 64 Film (Daylight)** is its outstanding color reproduction.

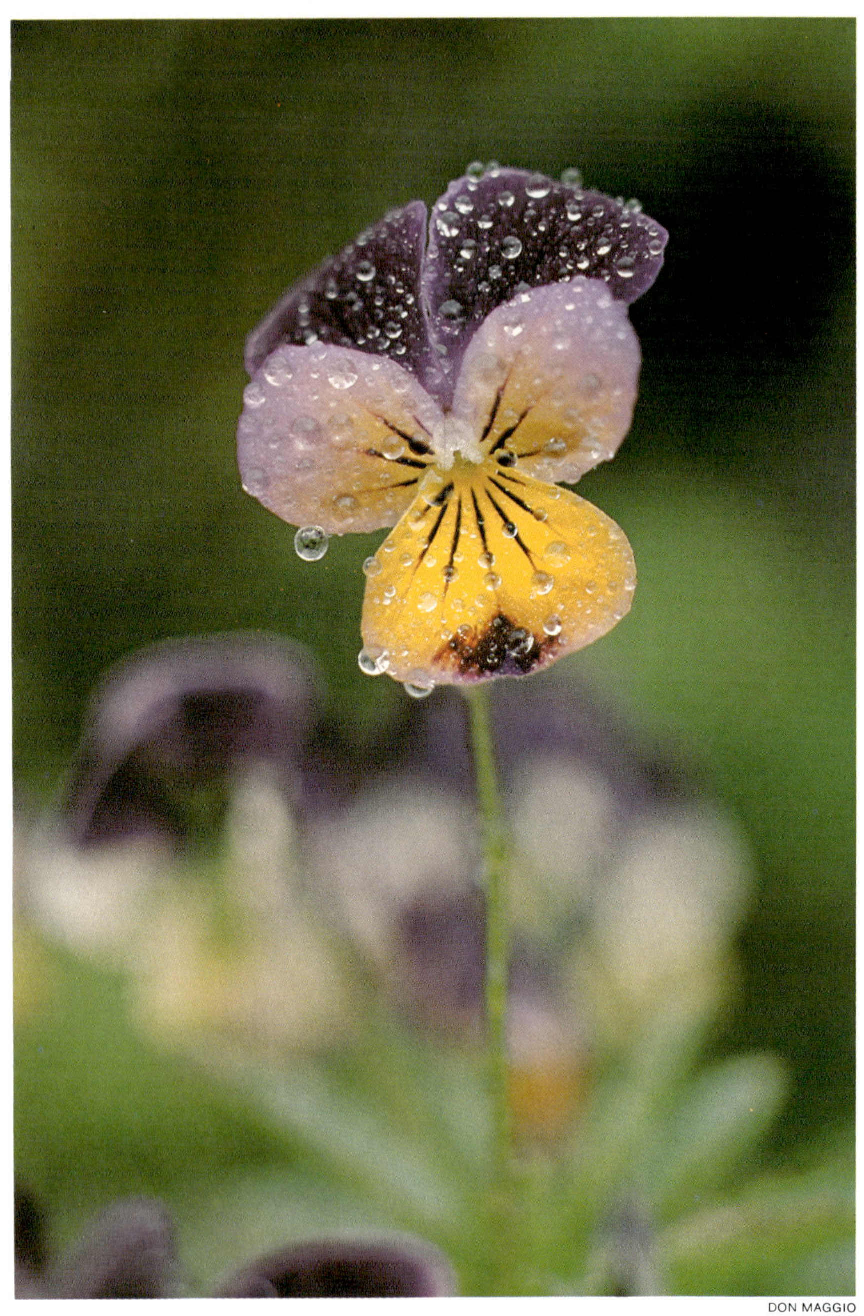

DON MAGGIO

In this picture, the high fidelity of **KODAK EKTACHROME 64 Film (Daylight)** gives you the feeling that you can almost reach out and touch the blossom.

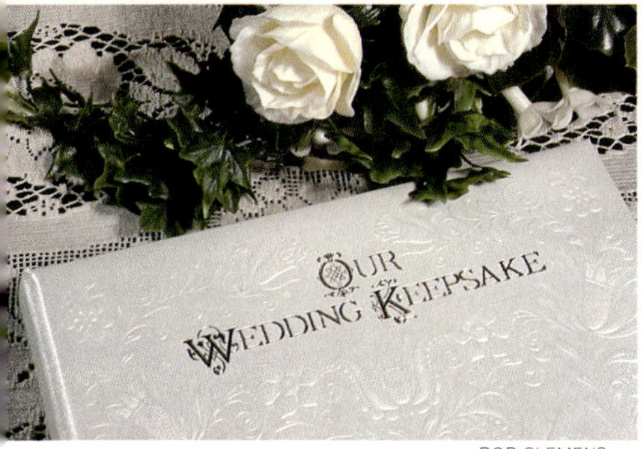

BOB CLEMENS

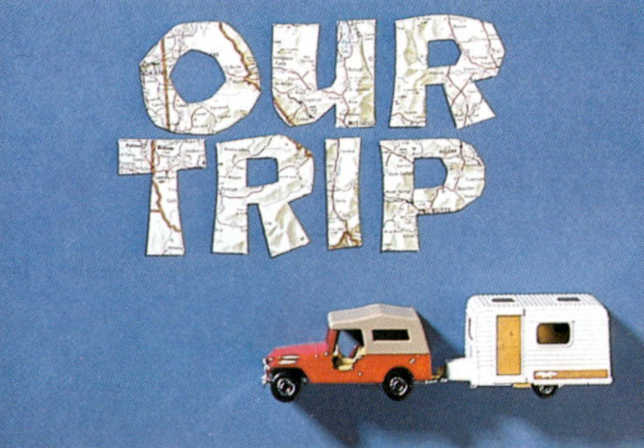

FRANK SOLOMAN, JERRY KILBORN, JOHN HOOD

KODACHROME 40 Film 5070 (Type A) is a color-slide film designed for taking pictures with 3400 K photolamps. It has a speed of ASA 40 with this illumination. This film, which replaced KODACHROME II Professional Film (Type A), has finer grain, improved color quality, and revised processing recommendations. KODACHROME 40 Film is processed in the same commercial process as KODACHROME 25 and 64 Films (Daylight).

The color balance of KODACHROME 40 Film for photolamp lighting together with its snap, brilliance, and color fidelity make it an excellent film for informal portraits, close-ups, title slides, and for copying color originals. The film with its high sharpness, extremely fine grain, and ability to record fine detail will provide high-quality color slides. You can take pictures in daylight when you use a No. 85 filter over your camera lens with a film speed of ASA 25. You can purchase this film in 135 size.

If you use title slides, they will help make your slide show more effective and enjoyable. **KODACHROME 40 Film 5070 (Type A)** is a good choice for making your title slides. It produces excellent results with 3400 K photolamp lighting, which is easy to control.

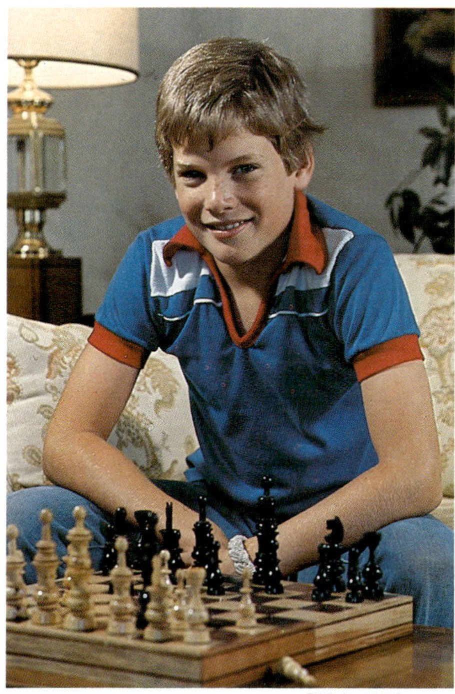

BOB CLEMENS

KODACHROME 40 Film 5070 (Type A) is an excellent color-slide film to use for informal portraits of subjects lighted by 3400 K photolamps.

KODAK EKTACHROME 200 Film (Daylight) is a high-speed color-slide film for photographing dimly lighted subjects, such as those in existing light; subjects that require good depth of field and high shutter speeds; fast action; and for extending the flash distance range. The film has a speed of ASA 200. It is designed for use with daylight, electronic flash, or blue flashbulbs. You can also use it to photograph subjects illuminated by carbon-arc spotlights. This is a versatile film which lets you photograph in a large range of lighting conditions from bright sunlight to dim existing light, depending on your camera.

EKTACHROME 200 Film (Daylight) replaced KODAK High Speed EKTACHROME Film (Daylight). EKTACHROME 200 Film has higher speed, improved color rendition, and improved sharpness and graininess. The improvement in graininess in EKTACHROME 200 Film is quite significant because this film has nearly as fine grain as that of EKTACHROME 64 Film. The difference in graininess between the two films is usually not evident in projected slides viewed from a normal viewing distance. In comparison with the 64-speed film, EKTACHROME 200 Film gives slightly less saturated colors. The 200-speed film is available in 135 and 126 sizes.

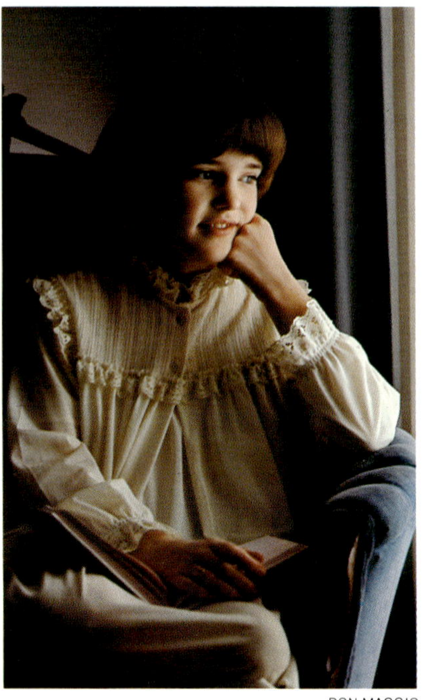

DON MAGGIO

KODAK EKTACHROME 200 Film (Daylight) with its high speed of ASA 200 is especially suited for taking color slides in the home by existing daylight. This film gives you very fine grain and pleasing color rendition as well as the high film speed.

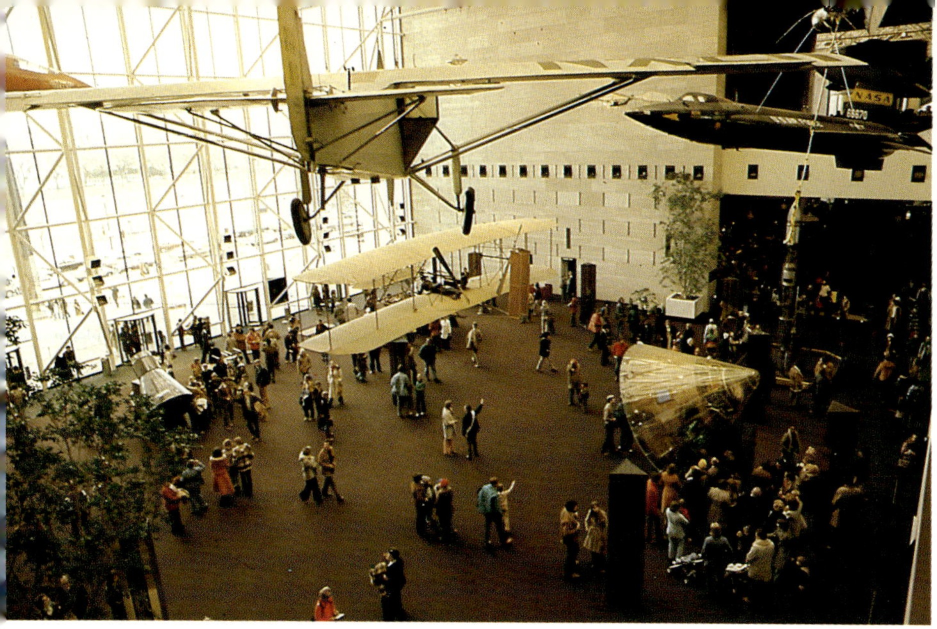

BARBARA JEAN

Kodak Ektachrome 200 and 160 Films have been designed for taking pictures under existing lighting conditions, such as those in the Air and Space Museum, Washington, D. C. The Daylight film produces a natural appearance in this scene illuminated by the daylight coming through the windows. If Tungsten film had been used, this picture would be too blue.

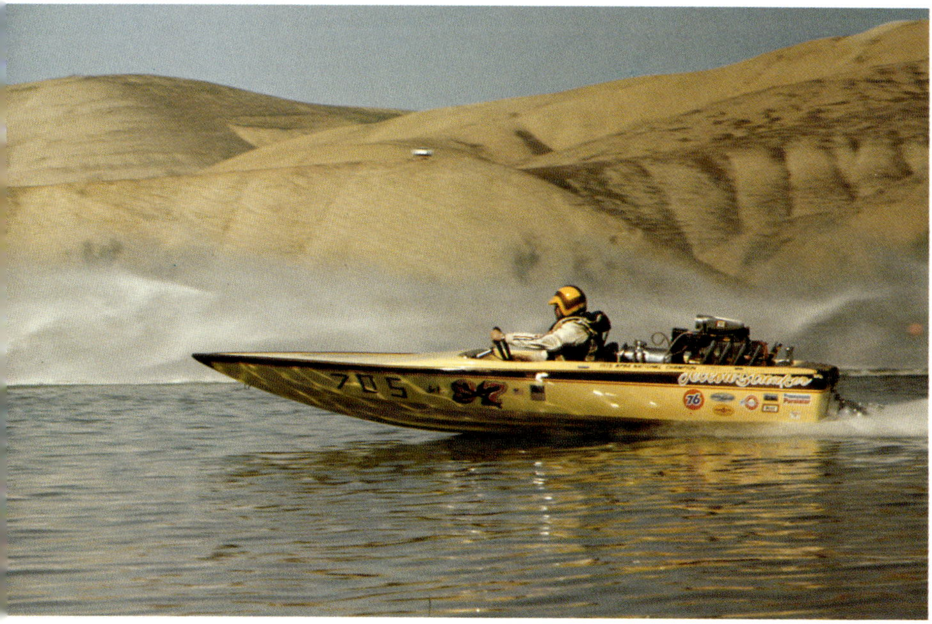

PETER GALES

When you want to photograph action in color slides and perhaps use a telephoto lens, a high-speed film will allow you to use the high shutter speeds you'll need. **Kodak Ektachrome 200 Film (Daylight)** has the speed—ASA 200—and high quality to give you excellent results.

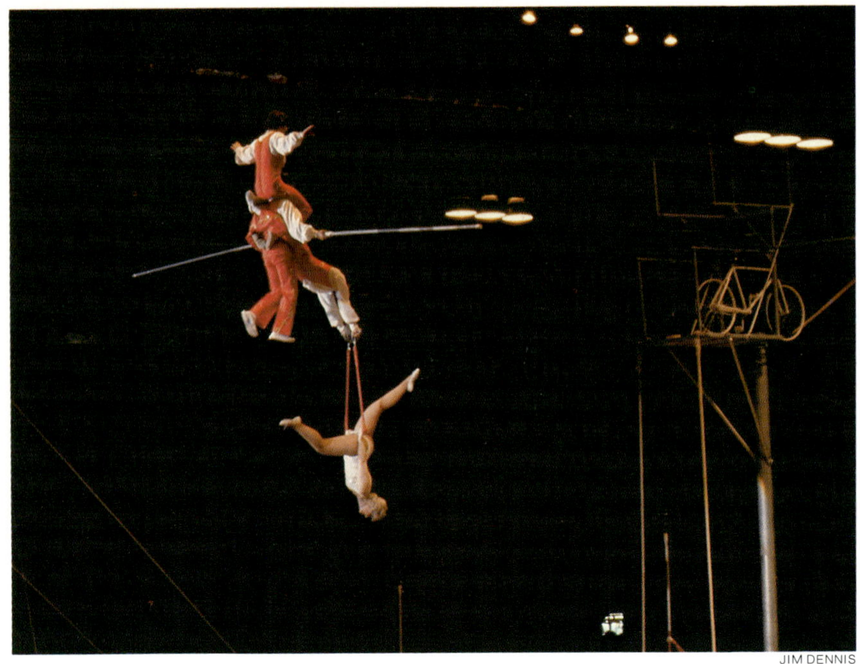

JIM DENNIS

KODAK EKTACHROME 400 Film (Daylight) is a great film for taking color slides under the existing lighting conditions where you often need a high-speed film. The high-wire act at the Damascus Temple Shrine Circus was illuminated by carbon-arc spotlights.

KODAK EKTACHROME 400 Film (Daylight) is a very high-speed color-slide film for use when you need a lot of film speed such as in existing light where subjects are often dimly lighted; for subjects where you want both good depth of field and high shutter speeds; and for stopping fast action in your pictures, such as sports. The film is good for pictures with long telephoto lenses which don't have large lens openings and where you'll want to use a high shutter speed to avoid camera motion effects. EKTACHROME 400 Film lets you take flash pictures at greater distances than other Kodak color-slide films. The film has a speed of ASA 400. It is color-balanced for daylight, electronic flash, or blue flashbulbs. With this film you can also photograph subjects lighted by carbon-arc spotlights.

EKTACHROME 400 Film has fine grain although it is not quite as fine as that of EKTACHROME 200 Film. Grain characteristics of the two films are comparable when EKTACHROME 200 Film is push-processed for a film speed of ASA 400. EKTACHROME 400 Film has good sharpness for a high-speed film. When this film is push-processed, it offers the outstanding feature of an extremely high film speed of ASA 800 with high quality. You can also have other EKTACHROME Films push-processed for increased speed. See page 37.

When you need a color-slide film with maximum speed for tungsten illumination, for example in low-light conditions, you can use EKTACHROME 400 Film without using a light-balancing filter. This will produce warm or yellow-red results. Many people find such slides acceptable because tungsten lighting has a natural, warm quality. This film is sold in 135 and 120 sizes.

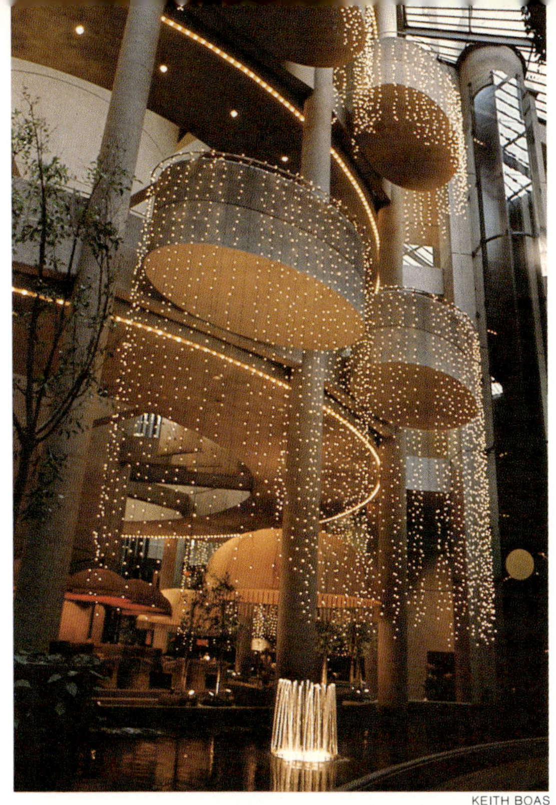

KEITH BOAS

This interesting hotel lobby, lighted by a combination of daylight and tungsten light, was realistically recorded on **KODAK EKTACHROME 400 Film (Daylight).**

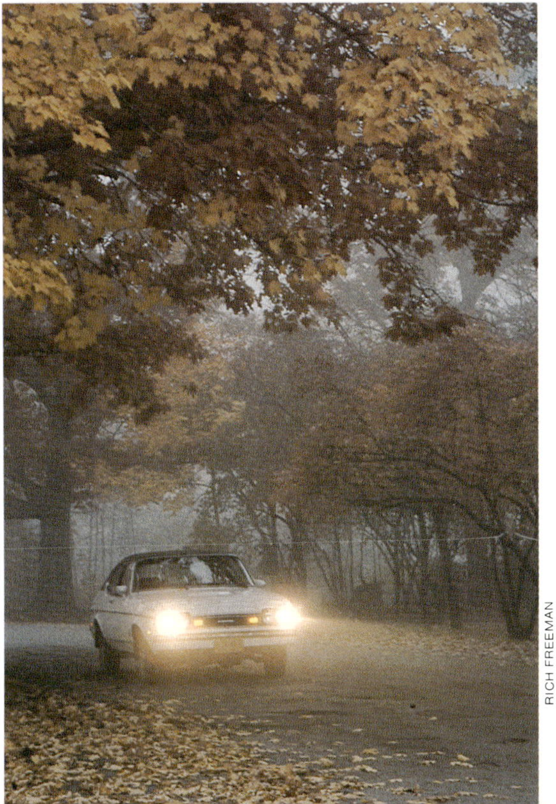

RICH FREEMAN

The high speed of **KODAK EKTACHROME 400 Film (Daylight)** was beneficial for photographing this low-light scene. The high film speed let the photographer use a small lens opening for good depth of field even though the lighting was dim.

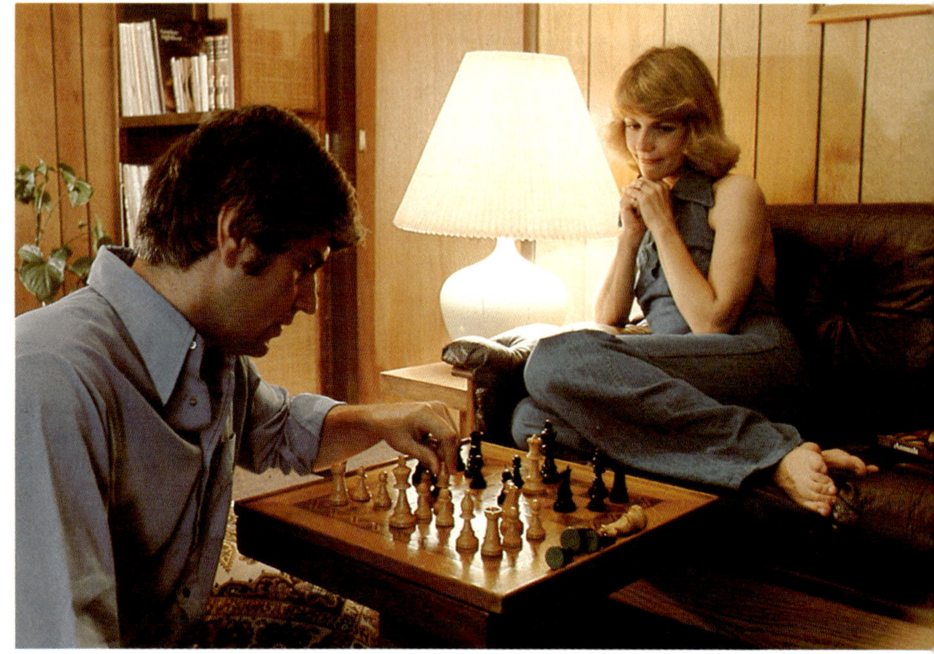

BOB CLEMENS

For taking the most natural-looking pictures at home, use the existing lighting. When the lighting is provided by tungsten household lamps and you want color slides, you can use **KODAK EKTACHROME 160 Film (Tungsten),** which is designed for this kind of picture-taking. It has a speed of ASA 160.

KODAK EKTACHROME 160 Film (Tungsten) is a color-slide film designed for use with 3200 K tungsten lamps or with existing tungsten light, such as the light from household lamps and other general-purpose lamps. This film, which replaced KODAK High Speed EKTACHROME Film (Tungsten), has a higher speed, ASA 160, and improved color rendition and sharpness. Its color quality and sharpness are similar to those of EKTACHROME 200 Film (Daylight). You can also take pictures in daylight with the Tungsten film when you use a No. 85B filter over your camera lens, reducing the film speed to ASA 100.

For taking pictures under dim tungsten existing-light conditions where you may need more film speed, you can have this film push-processed to increase its speed by 2 times to ASA 320. See page 37. The film is sold in 135 size.

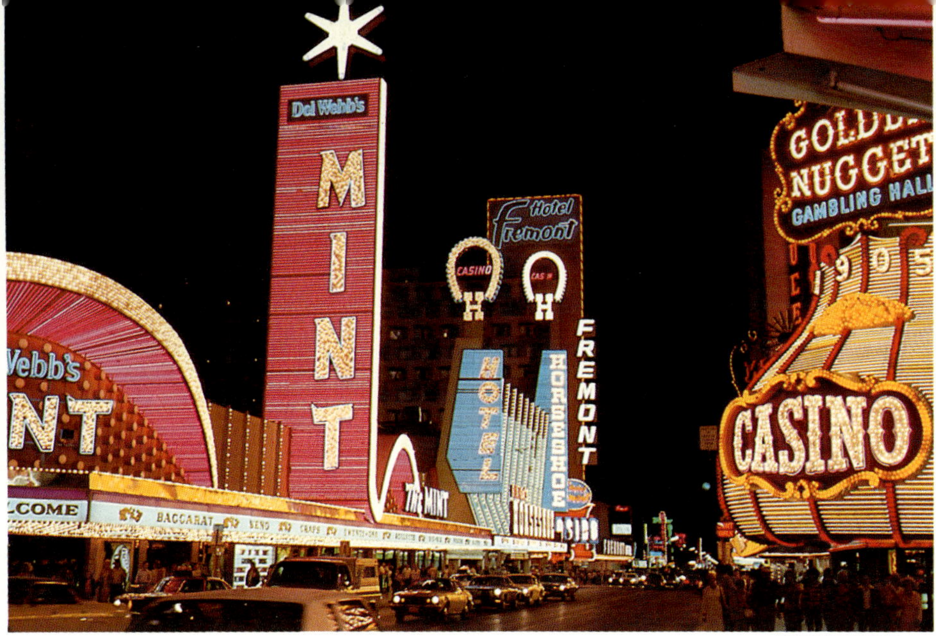

CAROLINE GRIMES

KODAK EKTACHROME 160 Film (Tungsten) is a splendid color-slide film for night scenes. This view captures the exciting lighting of signs in Las Vegas, Nevada.1/30 sec *f*/4.

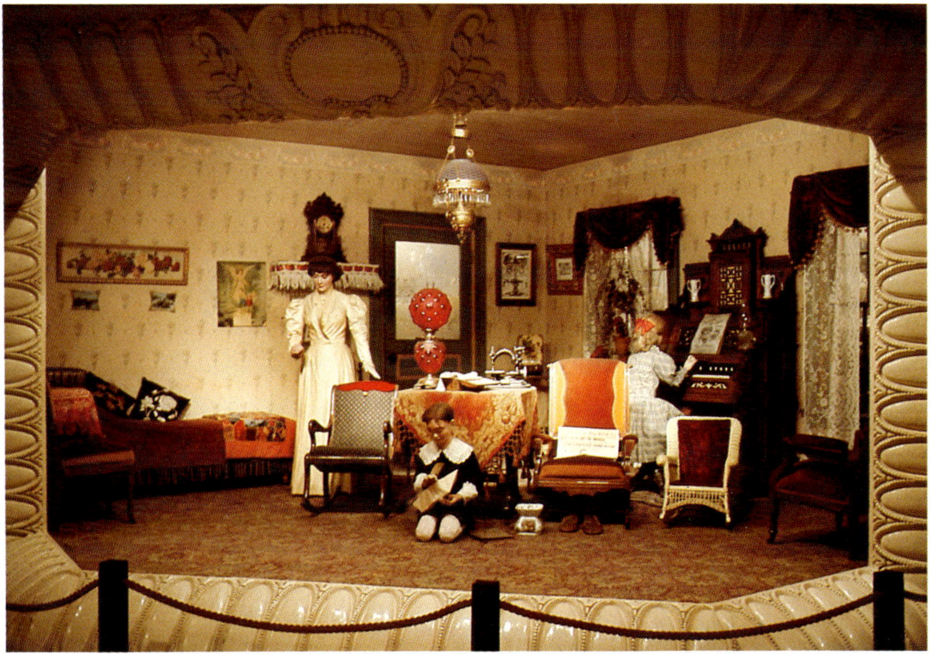

CAROLINE GRIMES

When you want to take color slides in public places lighted by tungsten lighting, you need a high-speed tungsten film. **KODAK EKTACHROME 160 Film (Tungsten)** is well-suited for this purpose. Museum of Science and Industry, Chicago, Illinois.

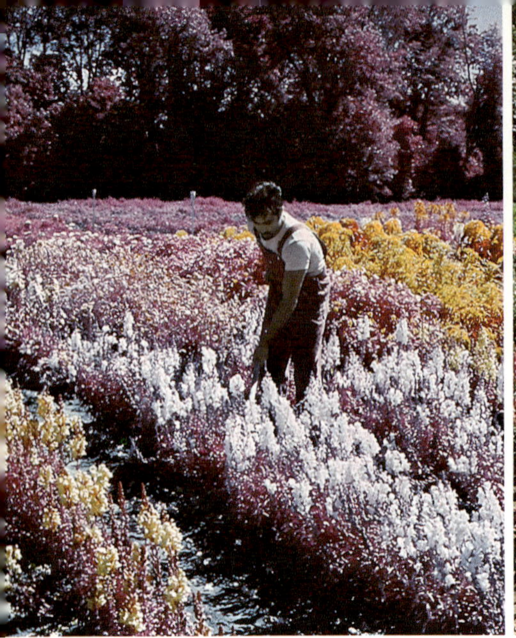

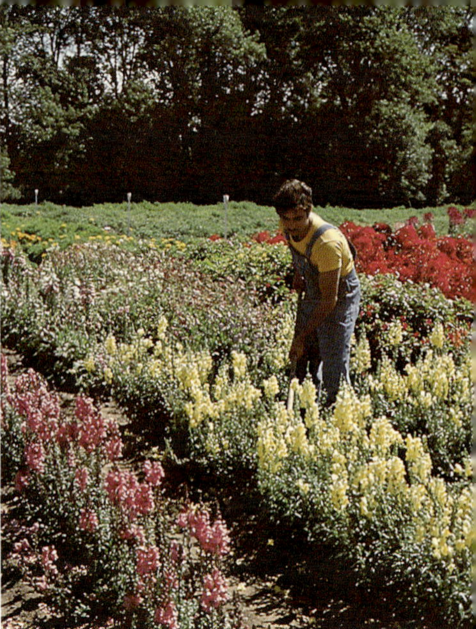

DON MAGG

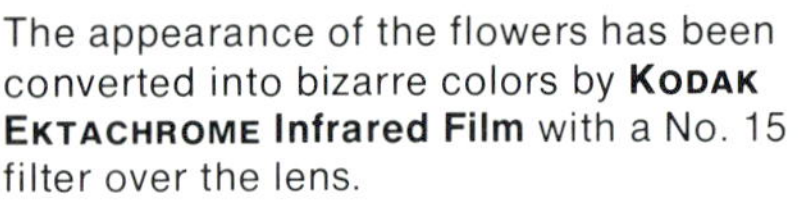

The appearance of the flowers has been converted into bizarre colors by **KODAK EKTACHROME Infrared Film** with a No. 15 filter over the lens.

Conventional color rendition. KODAK EKTACHROME 64 Film (Daylight).

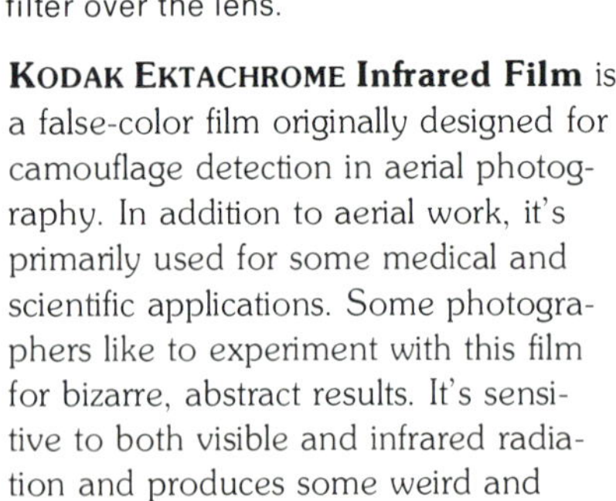

KODAK EKTACHROME Infrared Film is a false-color film originally designed for camouflage detection in aerial photography. In addition to aerial work, it's primarily used for some medical and scientific applications. Some photographers like to experiment with this film for bizarre, abstract results. It's sensitive to both visible and infrared radiation and produces some weird and interesting effects, such as red grass and trees and flowers with strange colors. Some objects are recorded in much the same way as with conventional color films, while others change colors completely. The film is designed for use with a No. 12 or No. 15 filter. With the filter, the film has a speed of 100. It's available only in 135 magazines, 20 exposures.

When you want to experiment with color slides, try **KODAK EKTACHROME Infrared Film** for abstract results. Photographed through a No. 15 deep-yellow filter. Conventional rendition is on the right.

DON MC DI

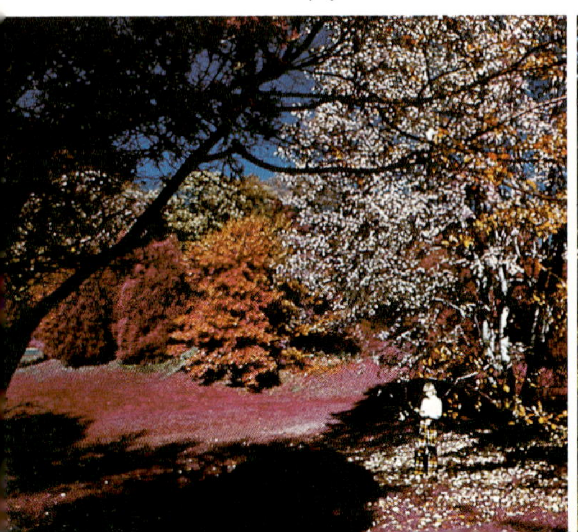

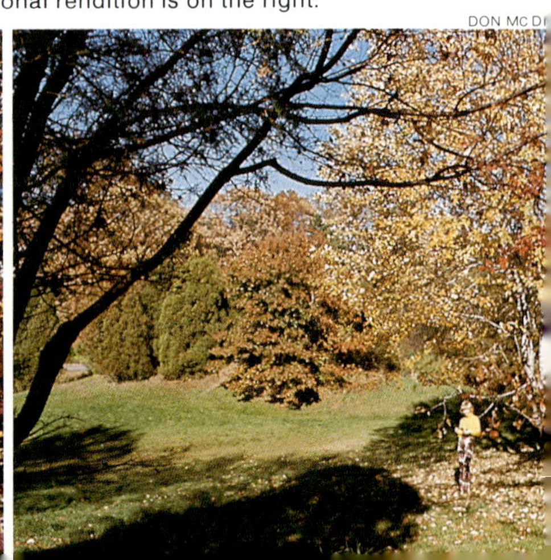

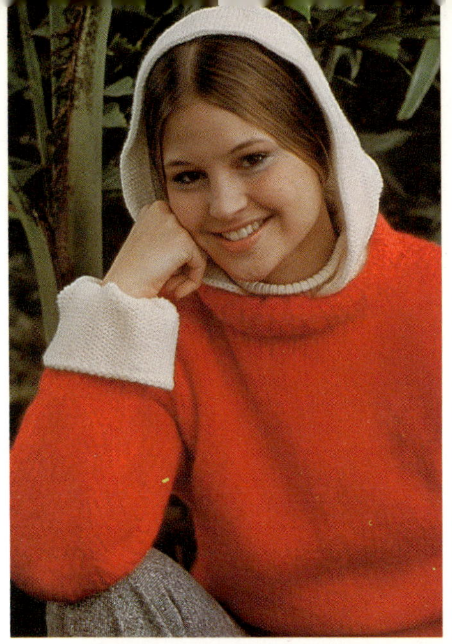

Kodak Ektachrome Slide Duplicating Film 5071 (Process E-6) is a superb film for making duplicate color slides from original color slides. Sometimes you can make the duplicate slide better than the original. Here the duplicate was cropped for improved composition.

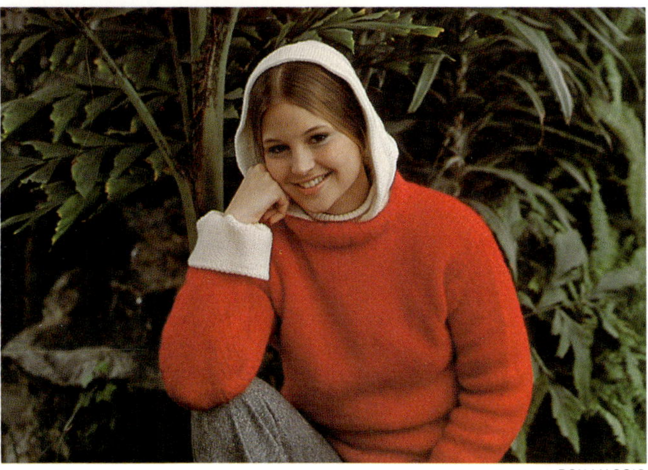

Original slide.

DON MAGGIO

Kodak Ektachrome Slide Duplicating Film 5071 (Process E-6) is a color-slide film for copying original color slides. The film is designed for tungsten illumination 3200 K, but you can use it with daylight or electronic flash with the proper filters. (Results with electronic flash may be less than optimum. See page D 24.) The contrast and color reproduction characteristics make this an outstanding film for making excellent duplicates which are difficult to distinguish from the original slides.

Sometimes when the original slides are less than ideal, you may be able to make improvements when you make the duplicates, such as cropping for better composition, correcting for exposure, correcting or changing color, and combining two or more images in one duplicate slide. The potential for creating new interpretations from your original slides are considerable. The film is sold in 135 magazines, 36 exposures.

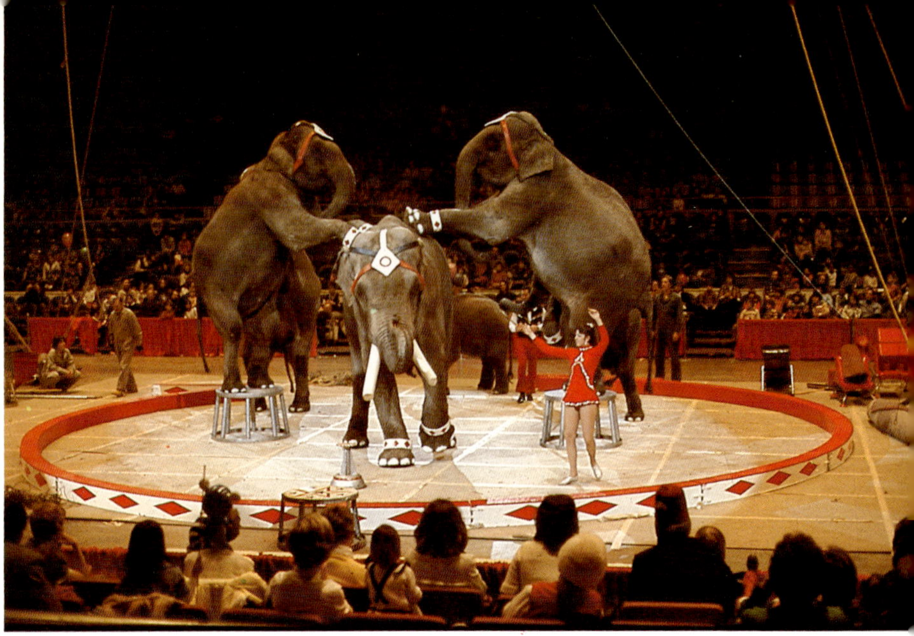

CAROLINE GRIMES

EKTACHROME 400, 200, and 160 Films have an exceptional feature. You can expose the 135-size films at 2 times their normal speeds when you have the films specially processed. EKTACHROME 200 Film (Daylight) with ESP-1 Processing—ASA 400, 1/125 sec *f*/4. Damascus Temple Shrine Circus.

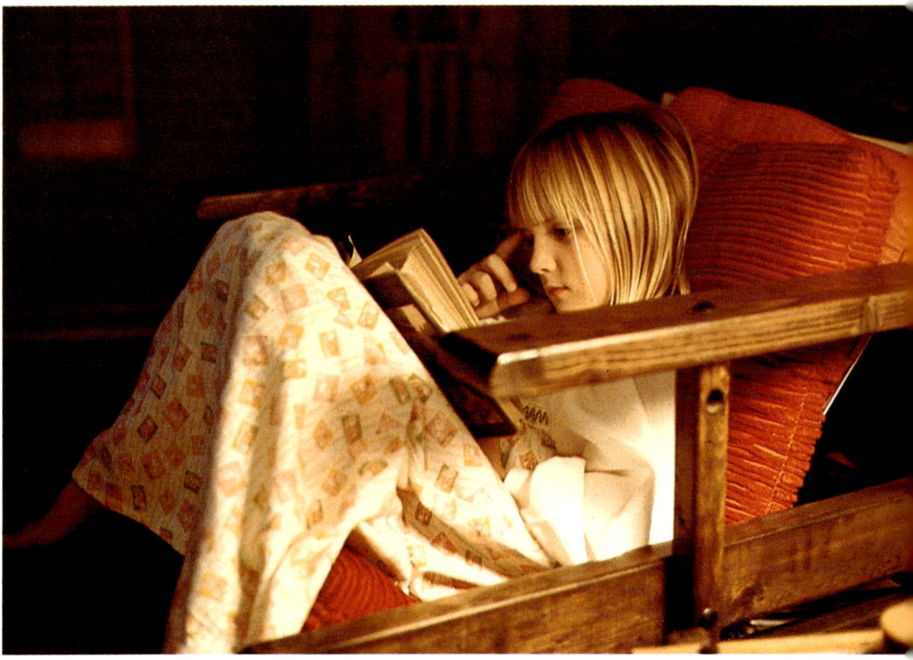

ROBERT KRETZER

Home lighting at night is relatively dim so you need a very high film speed. EKTACHROME 160 Film (Tungsten) with special processing—ASA 320, 1/30 sec *f*/2.

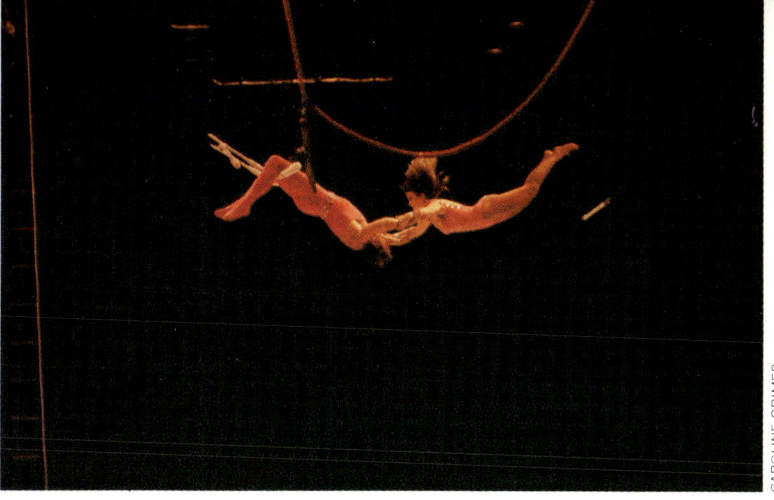

CAROLINE GRIMES

EKTACHROME 400 Film (Daylight) with ESP-1 Processing offers an exceptionally high speed of ASA 800 to help you stop action in low-light pictures. Damascus Temple Shrine Circus, 1/250 sec *f*/2.8.

Increased Film Speed with KODAK EKTACHROME 400, 200, and 160 Films. An exceptional feature of EKTACHROME 400, 200, and 160 Films (and of KODAK EKTACHROME 200 and 160 Professional Films, see page 39) is that you can expose them at higher-than-normal speeds when you obtain special processing. Kodak offers a special processing service for these films, in 135 and 120 sizes, which increases the effective speed to 2 times the normal speed (1 stop). The speeds are increased to ASA 800 for EKTACHROME 400 Film (Daylight), ASA 400 for EKTACHROME 200 Film (Daylight), and ASA 320 for EKTACHROME 160 Film (Tungsten).

When necessary, you can specify the special processing for KODAK EKTACHROME 64 Film (Daylight) [also KODAK EKTACHROME 64 Professional (Daylight) and KODAK EKTACHROME 50 Professional (Tungsten) Films]. The speed of EKTACHROME 64 Film is increased to ASA 125. (The speed of EKTACHROME 50 Professional Film is increased to ASA 100.) However, since quality is reduced slightly with special processing, it's seldom practical to pay the additional cost of the special processing for these films when you can use EKTACHROME 400, 200, and 160 Films at their normal speeds of ASA 400, ASA 200, and ASA 160.

The processing section on page 52 tells how you can obtain special processing of your film.

You'll obtain the best quality with EKTACHROME 400, 200, and 160 Films when you expose the films at their normal speeds and have them processed normally. However, the very high film speed and high quality of these films with special processing make possible many opportunities for color pictures that would be impossible or impractical with slower-speed films. The increased speed is very helpful under dim lighting conditions—in existing light, for example. It's also helpful when you want to use high shutter speeds and small lens openings. Special processing increases contrast and graininess to some extent. However, these changes are not too noticeable on the screen. The overall quality is very good.

When you take pictures with KODAK EKTACHROME 400, 200, and 160 Films at high shutter speeds combined with small lens openings, there is an additional exposure factor to be aware of in determining exposure. This is discussed on page 100.

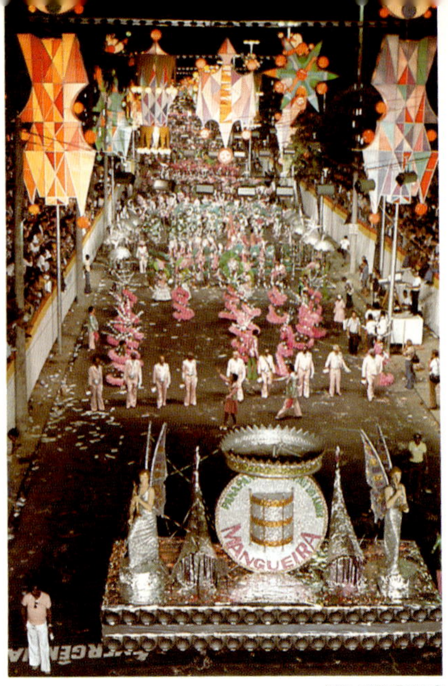

NEIL MONTANUS

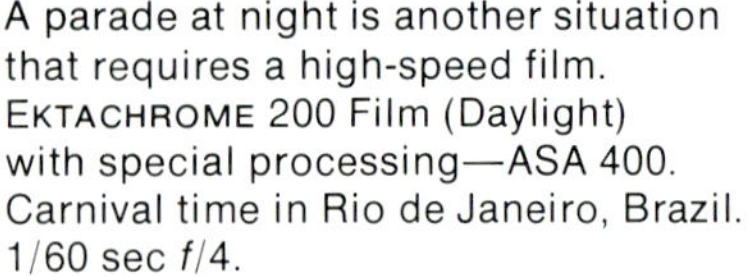

A parade at night is another situation that requires a high-speed film. EKTACHROME 200 Film (Daylight) with special processing—ASA 400. Carnival time in Rio de Janeiro, Brazil. 1/60 sec *f*/4.

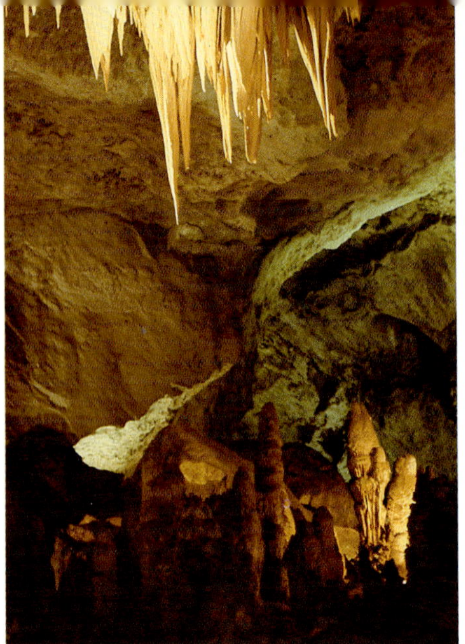

ROGER SMITH

Since the existing lighting in caverns is quite dim, you need a lot of film speed to take pictures without flash and record the natural appearance of the lighting. EKTACHROME 200 Film (Daylight) with special processing—ASA 400. Carlsbad Caverns, 1/15 sec *f*/1.4.

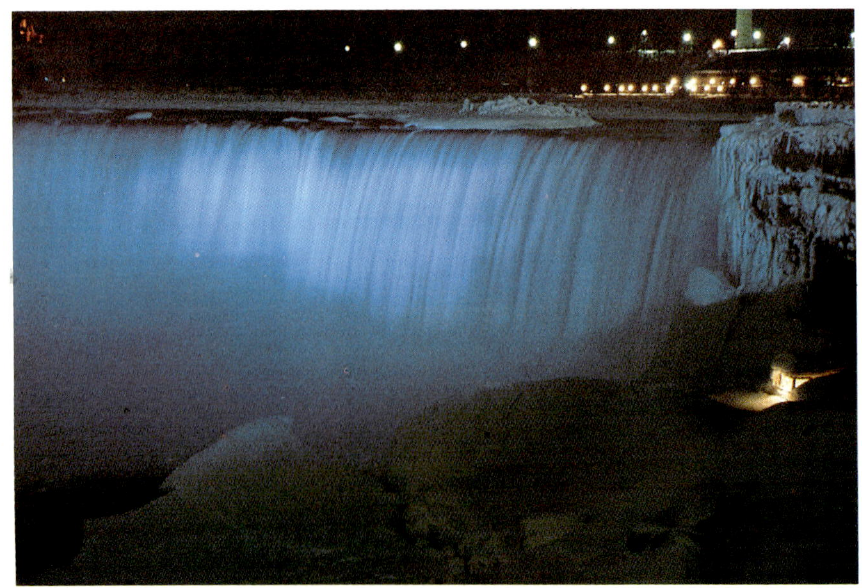

MARTIN TAYLOR

To photograph Niagara Falls at night it helps to have all the film speed you can get. EKTACHROME 400 Film (Daylight) with ESP-1 Processing for a film speed of ASA 800.

OTHER *KODAK* COLOR FILMS

The following films are designed for the professional; therefore, only brief descriptions are given in this book. If you have questions about these films, write to Eastman Kodak Company, Photo Information, Department 841, 343 State Street, Rochester, New York 14650. The data book *KODAK Color Films for Professional Use* (E-77), $4.00 (see inside back cover of this book, AF-1), includes technical data and other information for the films described here.

Since these films are intended for critical photography by professional photographers, they are manufactured with more rigid requirements for storage and handling than Kodak color films for general use. Store unexposed professional color films under refrigeration—55°F (13°C) or lower. After exposure, it's important to have these films processed promptly. See "Storage and Care of KODAK Films," page 107.

KODAK VERICOLOR II Professional Film, Type S, is a color-negative film intended primarily for professional use and professional photofinishing equipment and procedures. This film is designed for portraiture and commercial work. It has slightly lower contrast and less saturated colors than KODACOLOR II Film. VERICOLOR II Professional Film, Type S, is color-balanced for use without a filter in daylight or with electronic flash or blue flash. It has a speed of ASA 100 and excellent graininess characteristics. With this film you must use an exposure time of 1/10 second or less. It's available in sizes 135, 120, 620, and 220 and in sheet-film sizes.

KODAK VERICOLOR II Professional Film, Type L, is the tungsten-light version of VERICOLOR Film. The Type L Film is available only in 120 size and in sheet-film sizes. This professional film is designed for exposures of 1/50 second to 60 seconds with tungsten lamps 3200 K. Its speed at 1/50 second under these conditions is ASA 80. You can also use the film in daylight with a No. 85B filter at a speed of ASA 50.

KODAK EKTACHROME 64 Professional Film (Daylight) is the professional version of EKTACHROME 64 Film (Daylight). Both films are very similar except that the professional film is designed for professional use, storage, and handling. It has the same ASA 64* film speed. The professional film is available in 135 and 120 sizes and in sheet-film sizes.

KODAK EKTACHROME 200 Professional Film (Daylight) is the professional version of EKTACHROME 200 Film (Daylight). The professional film is optimized for critical photography requiring professional handling techniques. It has the same speed* and other characteristics which are similar to the general-use film. The professional film comes in 135 and 120 sizes.

KODAK EKTACHROME 160 Professional Film (Tungsten) has the same ASA 160* speed as the general-use EKTACHROME 160 Film (Tungsten). Both films are similar in most other respects. The professional film is available in 135 and 120 sizes.

KODAK EKTACHROME 50 Professional Film (Tungsten) is a color-slide film designed for taking pictures with 3200 K tungsten lamps. It has a film speed of ASA 50* with this illumination. The fine color quality of this Tungsten film makes it an excellent film for informal portraits, close-ups, and title slides. You can also use this film to take pictures in daylight by using a No. 85B filter over your camera lens, reducing the film speed to ASA 32. You can purchase this film in 135 and 120 sizes.

*For increased accuracy for the professional photographer, the effective speed of a specific emulsion for KODAK EKTACHROME Professional Films is printed on the instruction sheet packaged with the film. The effective speed may be the same as, or plus ⅓ stop, or minus ⅓ stop from the nominal speed. For example, for the 64 speed film, the effective speed can be ASA 64, 80, or 50.

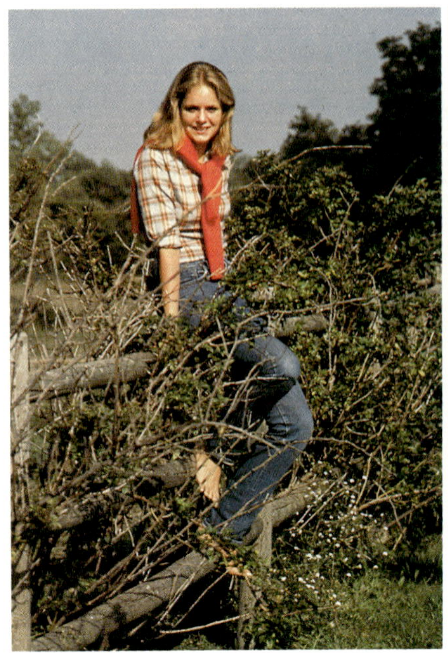

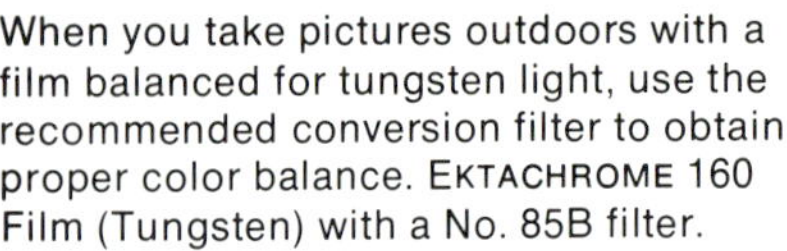

When you take pictures outdoors with a film balanced for tungsten light, use the recommended conversion filter to obtain proper color balance. EKTACHROME 160 Film (Tungsten) with a No. 85B filter.

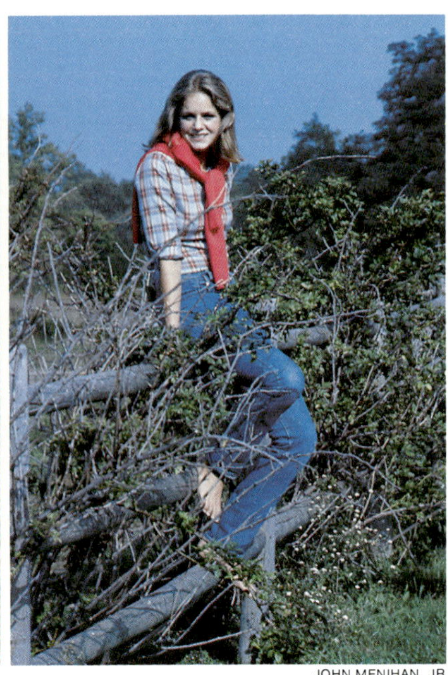

JOHN MENIHAN, JR.

If you don't use the recommended filter with Tungsten film outdoors, this is the kind of result you'll get.

COLOR BALANCE

Color balance refers to the ability of a film to reproduce the colors of a scene as the eye sees them. Color films are balanced in manufacture for exposure to light of a certain color quality, such as daylight, 3400 K photolamps, or 3200 K tungsten lamps.

You'll get the best results when you use a film with the kind of illumination for which it's balanced. Usually under these conditions you don't need a filter to obtain correct color rendition. If you use a light source with a color quality different from that for which the film is balanced, you'll need to use the conversion filter recommended in this book or on the film instruction sheet. You can get good results with filters, but most of them absorb light and reduce the effective speed of the film.

Since the film in a slide is usually the original film you expose in your camera, the color rendition depends primarily on the light source and the filter you use when you take the picture. The color balance of prints made from color negatives exposed with the wrong light source usually can be improved somewhat when the prints are made. But if the film was exposed with light sources significantly different from that for which the film is balanced, satisfactory corrections may not be possible.

FLASH PICTURES WITH COLOR FILMS

Electronic flash, blue flashbulbs, flashcubes, magicubes, and flipflash are recommended for taking flash pictures with daylight-type Kodak color films.

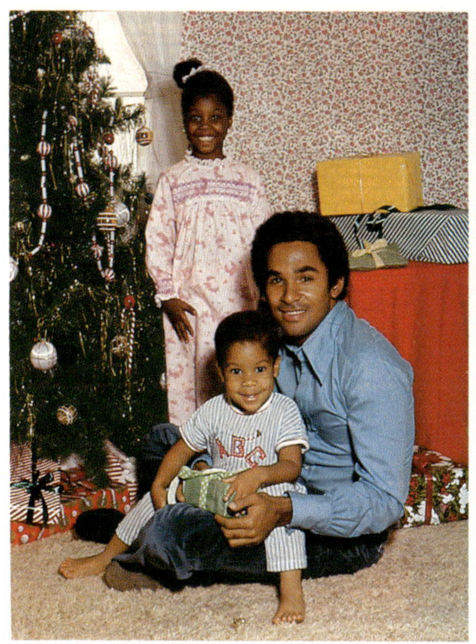

G. ABRAMOWITZ

Electronic flash, blue flashbulbs, flashcubes, magicubes, and flipflash are recommended for taking flash pictures with most Kodak films for general use.

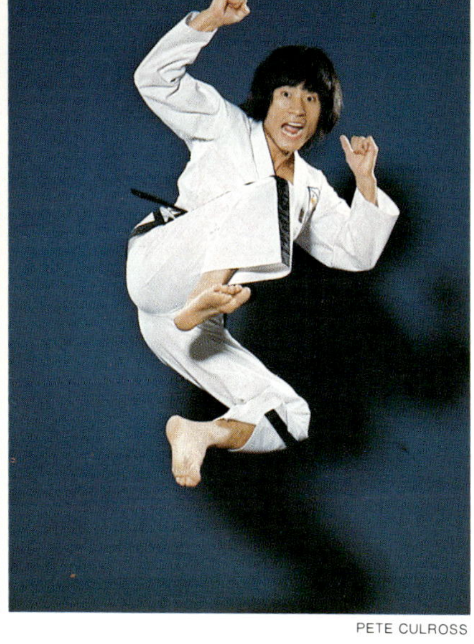

PETE CULROSS

Usually you don't need a filter for taking color pictures with electronic flash. However, if your pictures are consistently too blue, use a No. 81B filter on your camera lens or over the flash reflector to improve the color rendition.

RECOMMENDED FILTERS FOR FLASH

Color Film	Electronic Flash	Blue Flashbulbs, Flashcubes, Magicubes, Flipflash	Clear Flashbulbs	
			5, 25, 6, 26	AG-1, M-3
KODAK Daylight-Type Color Films KODACOLOR II KODACOLOR 400	None*	None	80C	80D
KODAK EKTACHROME 160 (Tungsten)	85B	85B	81EF	85C
KODACHROME 40 5070 (Type A)	85	85	81C	81EF
KODAK EKTACHROME Infrared	12 or 15	12 or 15	—	—

*If your pictures are consistently too blue, use a No. 81B filter.

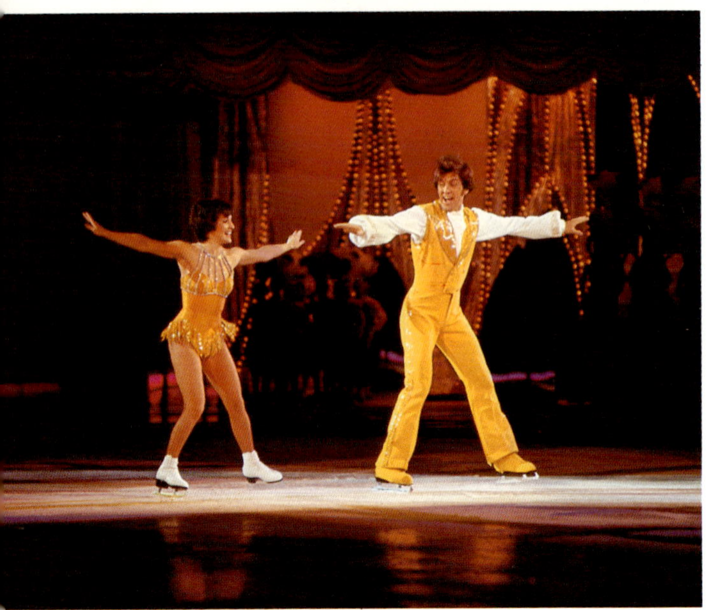

JOHN MENIHAN, JR.

For taking existing-light color slides with daylight illumination or with carbon-arc spotlights such as those illuminating this scene at the Ice Follies, use a film balanced for daylight. EKTACHROME 200 Film (Daylight) is excellent for existing light because of its high speed and superb quality.

The color quality of these light sources is similar to that of daylight, and you don't normally need a filter. Electronic flash units do vary, though, and some flash units may produce pictures that are too bluish. If your pictures are consistently too blue, use a No. 81B yellowish filter and increase exposure by ⅓ stop. If you prefer to use clear flashbulbs with daylight film, you'll need a blue conversion filter; see the table on page 41.

When you want to take flash pictures on EKTACHROME 160 Film (Tungsten) or KODACHROME 40 Film 5070 (Type A), you can use electronic flash, blue flashbulbs, or flashcubes with the proper conversion filter. See the table. If you prefer, you can use clear flashbulbs with the proper filter.

FILMS FOR EXISTING-LIGHT PHOTOGRAPHY

Existing light, sometimes called available light, includes artificial light which naturally exists in the scene, daylight indoors, and twilight outdoors. Technically, daylight lighting conditions outdoors, including bright sunlight, are existing light. But in defining existing light for photography, we are referring to lighting that is characterized by lower light levels than you would encounter in most daylight conditions outdoors. Outdoor scenes after dark or at twilight are considered to be existing-light situations.

Actually you can use all Kodak color films for general use for taking pictures by existing light, except KODAK Instant Print Film, if you don't mind putting your camera on a tripod or some other firm support and using slow shutter speeds or time exposures in some situations. But your picture-taking will be made much more versatile and convenient if you can handhold your camera and use shutter speeds of 1/30 second or higher. This requires an *f*/2.8 or faster lens and a high-speed film for most subjects, because existing lighting is often quite dim.

This is the modern way to take existing-light pictures—take advantage of today's high-speed lenses and high-speed films by taking candid pictures while handholding your camera. Excellent high-speed films to use are

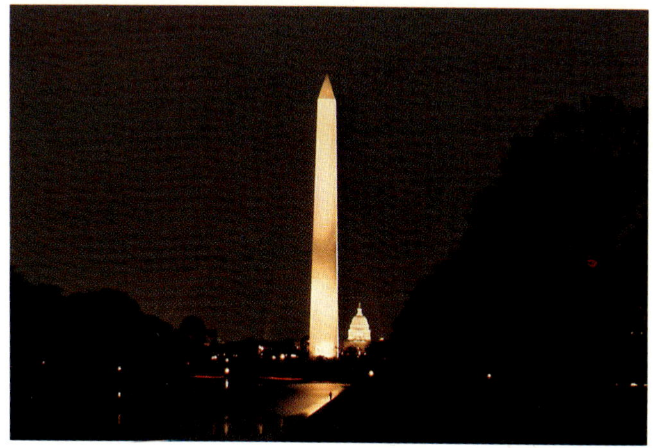

JEANNETTE KLUTE

A good choice for outdoor night pictures when you want color slides is EKTACHROME 400 Film (Daylight). Its high speed came in handy for photographing the Washington monument in Washington, D.C. The exposure for this subject would be 1/30 sec *f*/1.7.

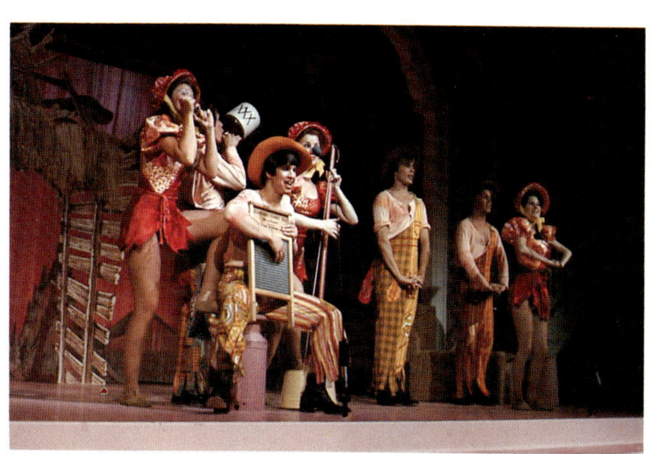

KEITH BOAS

KODACOLOR 400 Film, with a very high film speed of ASA 400, is an excellent film for existing-light pictures when you want color prints. Stage show at the family fun park, Six Flags, Atlanta, Georgia. 1/250 sec *f*/2.

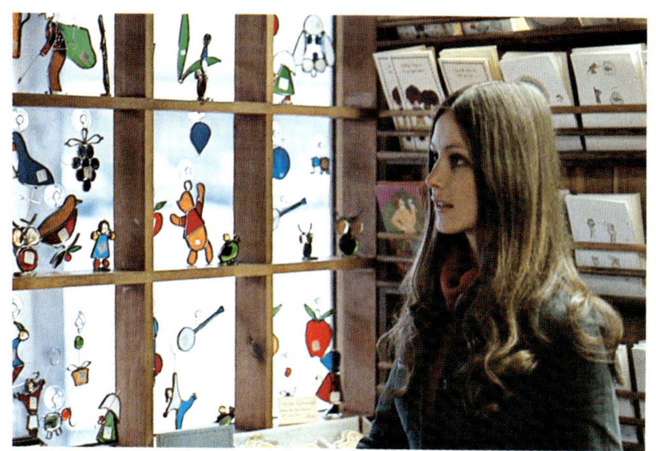

JOHN VAETH

You can get pleasing results in your color prints without using camera filters in a variety of existing-light conditions, such as tungsten household lighting (regular light bulbs), fluorescent illumination, and daylight indoors when you use KODACOLOR 400 Film. 1/60 sec *f*/4.

KODACOLOR 400 Film for color prints and EKTACHROME 400, 200, and 160 Films for color slides.

Since KODACOLOR 400 Film has special sensitizing characteristics and color rendition can be partially controlled when the prints are made, you can take pictures of good quality in various kinds of existing light without using filters. If you're using color-slide films, such as EKTACHROME Films, the choice between the Daylight film and the Tungsten film depends on the type of lighting and your personal taste.

The Daylight film, of course, is better for indoor scenes illuminated by existing daylight. You can also use it to photograph performers illuminated by carbon-arc spotlights. When you're photographing subjects indoors with fluorescent lighting, Daylight film will give the best results; however, the color rendition of the slides will usually be greenish, depending on the type of fluorescent lamps used. See "Filters for Fluorescent Illumination" on page 46. You can use the Daylight film for existing-light photography outdoors at night, too. The results will be warmer or more yellow-red than if the pictures were made on the Tungsten film. With mercury-vapor lamps used at some sports stadiums and for some street lighting, you'll get the best results on Daylight film. However, your pictures will have a blue-green appearance because mercury-vapor lamps are deficient in red. You can usually identify mercury-vapor lighting by its slightly blue-green appearance in comparison with tungsten light.

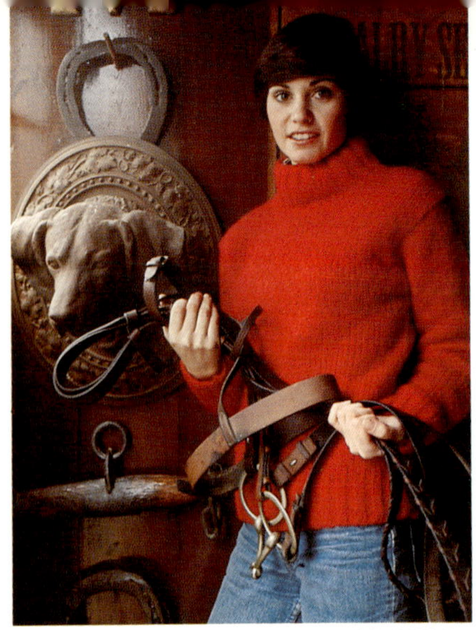

DON MAGGIO

Since existing daylight is usually brighter than other kinds of existing light, you can use a medium-speed film, such as EKTACHROME 64 Film (Daylight), depending on your camera.

EKTACHROME 160 Film (Tungsten) is excellent for existing tungsten light, such as the light from household lamps and other general-purpose tungsten lamps, when you want color slides. Outdoors at night you can use the Tungsten film for pictures of illuminated buildings, fountains, statues, signs, street scenes, and similar subjects. Slides of such subjects taken on Tungsten film may look

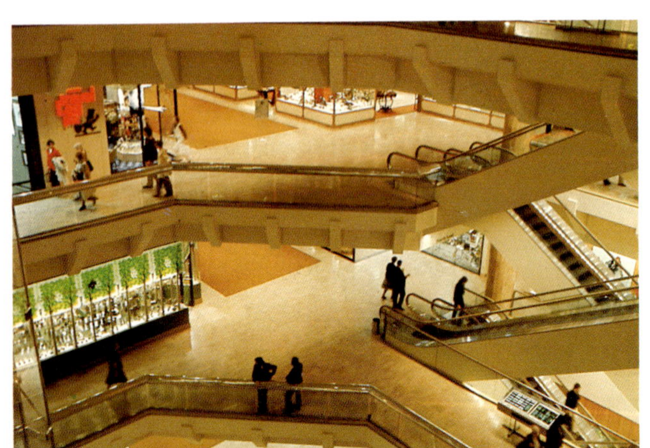

When the existing lighting is provided predominantly by tungsten lamps, you'll get more natural-looking color slides by using film balanced for tungsten light. EKTACHROME 160 Film (Tungsten) at Water Tower Place, Chicago, Illinois.

CAROLINE GRIMES

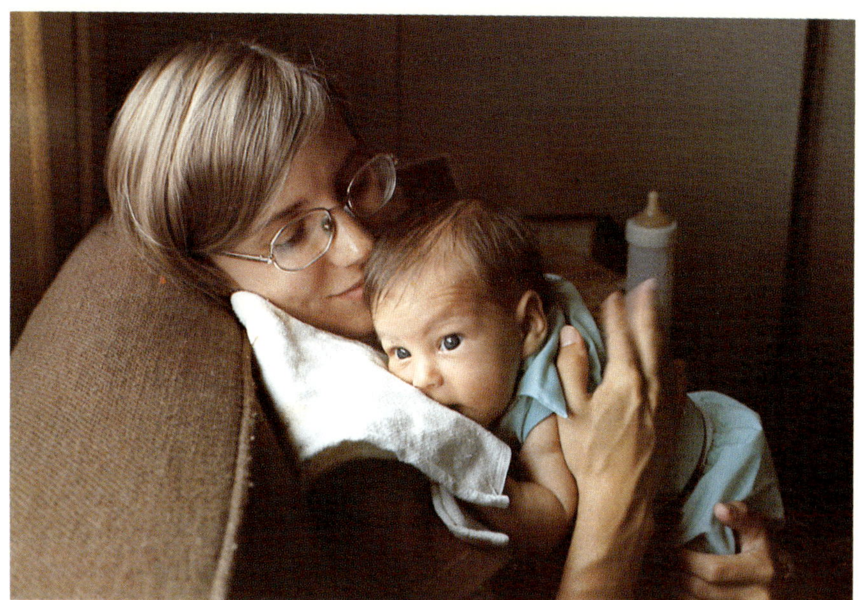

ROBERT L. LEAF, JR., KINSA

With an adjustable camera, you can take pictures in existing daylight on KODACOLOR II Film. 1/30 sec $f/2$.

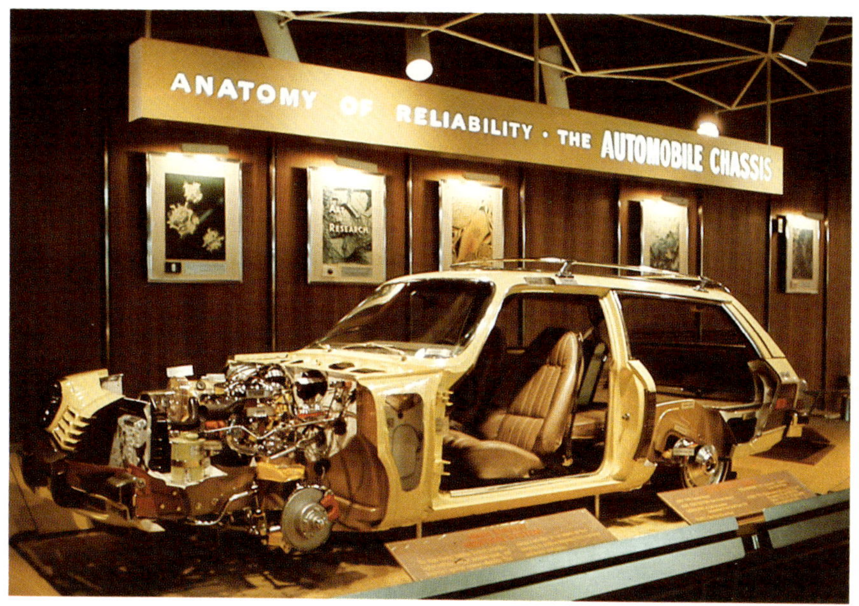

CAROLINE GRIMES

Tungsten lighting on EKTACHROME 160 Film (Tungsten). Museum of Science and Industry, Chicago, Illinois.

more natural than those taken on Daylight film. The type of color-slide film you use for outdoor pictures at night is a matter of personal taste. Both types produce pleasing results.

Sometimes you'll find more than one kind of illumination in the same scene. If one type of light source is predominant, use color-slide film balanced for that light source. For example, in a scene which includes both daylight and tungsten light, daylight is usually the predominant light source and Daylight film would give more pleasing results. If the kinds of illumination in the scene are about equal in intensity and distribution, the choice of color-slide film is a matter of personal taste. If you like warmer-looking, or more yellow-red, pictures, use Daylight film; if you prefer colder-looking, or more blue, pictures, use Tungsten film. Of course, in many situations the choice depends on the type of film that happens to be in your camera.

Since most existing light is dim, you'll often need all the film speed you can get. With KODACOLOR 400 and EKTACHROME 400 Films you have a high film speed of ASA 400 which is very helpful in existing-light photography. When you are using EKTACHROME 400, 200, and 160 Films and you need more speed, a real boon to the existing-light photographer is the special processing service for increasing the speed of EKTACHROME Film which was mentioned earlier. See page 37 for more information on special processing.

In brighter levels of existing light, such as existing daylight, you can use a fast- or medium-speed film—KODACOLOR II, KODACHROME 64, or EKTACHROME 64 Film.

FILTERS FOR FLUORESCENT ILLUMINATION

Pictures made on daylight-type film without a filter in fluorescent light may be acceptable, although the pictures sometimes have a greenish cast depending on the film and the type of fluorescent tubes in use. Tungsten film without filters usually produces pictures that are much too blue. Generally speaking, it's not practical to use filters in existing-light photography because they absorb too much light and reduce the effective speed of the film. However, when the reduced film speed is acceptable for the type of pictures you want to take, you can improve the color quality of pictures taken under fluorescent illumination by using filters over your camera lens.

Selecting filters for fluorescent illumination is sometimes difficult because the lamps are often inaccessible and therefore hard to identify. There are several kinds of fluorescent lamps, and each kind produces light of a slightly different color. If optimum color rendition is important and you can find out the kind of lamps in use, you can improve the color in your pictures by using the KODAK Color Compensating Filters recommended in the table on page 47. These filters are available from photo dealers.

Since you may have difficulty finding out what kind of fluorescent lamps are in use, you can use a compromise filter. Lamp manufacturers' sales figures show that a large majority of the fluorescent lamps sold are white, warm white, or cool white. Therefore, you can reasonably assume that the lamps in use are one of these three kinds. If you're using a daylight-type film, the compromise filter recommendation is a CC30M filter. Increase exposure by ⅔ stop with this filter. If you're using Tungsten film, the compromise filter to use is a CC50R filter with a 1-stop increase in exposure.

For critical work with color-slide film, you should take test pictures using your

KODAK COLOR COMPENSATING FILTERS (CC) FOR FLUORESCENT LIGHT

KODAK Color Film

Type of Fluorescent Lamp	KODACHROME 25 (Daylight) KODACHROME 64 (Daylight) EKTACHROME 64 (Daylight) EKTACHROME 200 (Daylight) KODACOLOR II, KODACOLOR 400*	EKTACHROME 160 (Tungsten)	KODACHROME 40 5070 (Type A)†
Daylight	40M + 30Y + 1 stop	No. 85B + 30M + 10Y + 1⅔ stops	No. 85 + 40M + 40Y + 1⅔ stops
White	20C + 30M + 1 stop	40M + 40Y + 1 stop	40M + 30Y + 1 stop
Warm White	40C + 40M + 1⅓ stops	30M + 20Y + 1 stop	30M + 20Y + 1 stop
Warm White Deluxe	60C + 30M + 1⅔ stops	10Y + ⅓ stop	No Filter None
Cool White	30M + ⅔ stop	50M + 60Y + 1⅓ stops	50M + 50Y + 1⅓ stops
Cool White Deluxe	30C + 20M + 1 stop	10M + 30Y + ⅔ stop	10M + 30Y + ⅔ stop

Note: Increase exposure by amount shown in table.
*Suggested starting point for critical use. †Tentative data.

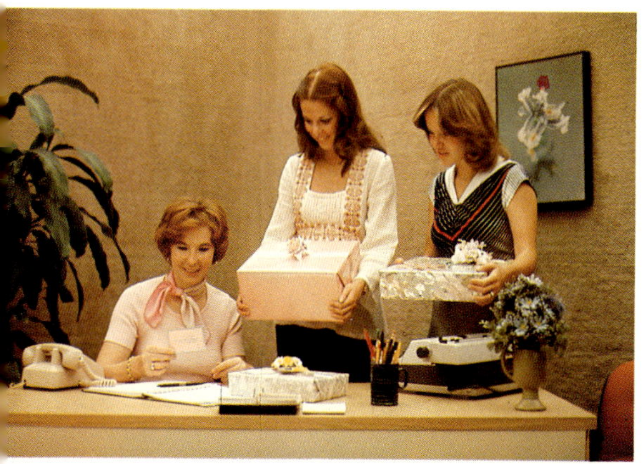

For taking color pictures under fluorescent illumination without using a filter, you'll get the best results on daylight film. Although the pictures are usually acceptable, they may have an overall color cast depending on the kind of lamps. EKTACHROME 200 Film (Daylight), no filter.

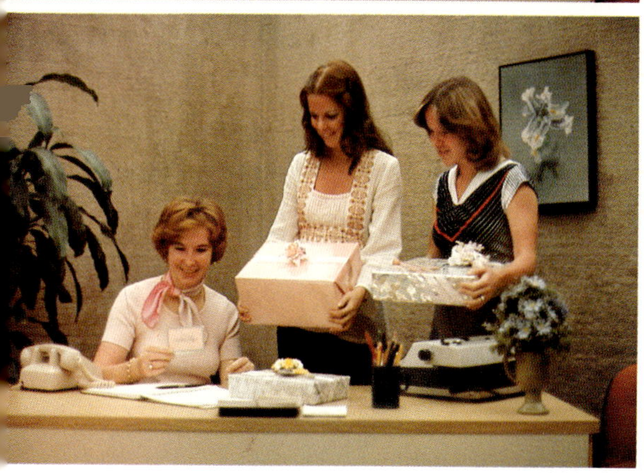

DON MAGGIO

For better color rendition in photographs of subjects brightly illuminated by fluorescent light, use the filters recommended in the table above. EKTACHROME 200 Film (Daylight) with CC30C + CC20M filters.

film with the filters recommended in the table for each type of lamp, and with filters that vary at least plus and minus CC10M and CC10Y from the filters listed. Color-negative film, such as KODACOLOR Film, is a good choice for taking pictures under fluorescent illumination because color rendition can usually be improved when your negatives are printed. KODACOLOR 400 Film with its special sensitizing characteristics is especially good for fluorescent lighting. With this film, you do not normally need to use filters with fluorescent light unless the results are for critical use.

In general with fluorescent lamps, use a shutter speed of 1/30 second or slower to avoid uneven exposure or underexposure due to the flicker in brightness of the lamps. This is caused by the 60-cycle alternating current and is not apparent to the eye.

For more information on taking pictures by existing light, you can purchase the Kodak book *Adventures in Existing-Light Photography* (AC-44), $3.00, from your photo dealer. See inside back cover.

FILMS FOR PHOTOLAMP ILLUMINATION

You may want to take some indoor portraits of your family or friends, photograph small objects close up, or make title slides for your slide shows. Excellent light sources for these subjects are the various types of photolamps sold by photo dealers. Generally, lamps are available in two color temperatures designated 3400 K and 3200 K. The advantage of using photolamps is that it's so easy to control the light. You can see the lighting before you take the picture and you can use your exposure meter to determine exposure.

When you want the highest quality and you don't need a high-speed film, KODACHROME 40 Film 5070 (Type A) is the best choice for color slides. You can use this slide film with 3400 K photolamps without a filter. To use 3200 K tungsten lamps with the Type A film, see the table that follows this section for the recommended filter and film speed.

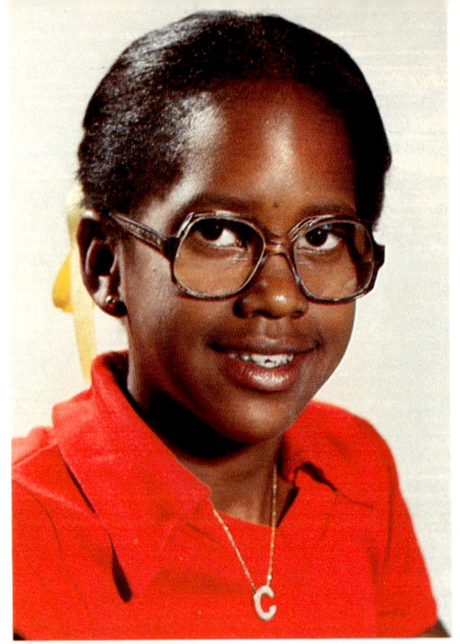

BOB CLEMENS

Photolamps let you see the lighting and adjust the lights before you take the picture, so it's easier to obtain high-quality results. KODACHROME 40 Film 5070 (Type A) with 3400 K photolamps.

If you need a high-speed color-slide film, an excellent choice is KODAK EKTACHROME 160 Film (Tungsten), which requires no filter when you expose it by 3200 K illumination. You can also take pictures using 3400 K lamps when you use the proper filter; see the table.

You can take pictures on daylight-type film under photolamp illumination, but the conversion filters absorb a lot of light and reduce the speed of the film considerably, as shown by the table. So when you want color slides, it's better to use Type A or Tungsten film under these conditions. If you want color prints of subjects lighted by photolamps, KODACOLOR II Film exposed with the filter recommended in the table will give you excellent results.

FILTERS AND FILM SPEEDS FOR PHOTOLAMPS

KODAK Color Film	3400 K Photolamps	3200 K Tungsten Lamps
KODACHROME 40 5070 (Type A)	None ASA 40	82A ASA 32
EKTACHROME 160 (Tungsten)	81A ASA 125	None ASA 160
KODACOLOR II	80B ASA 32	80A ASA 25
KODACOLOR 400	80B ASA 125	80A ASA 100
KODACHROME 25 (Daylight)	80B ASA 8	80A ASA 6
KODACHROME 64 (Daylight)	80B ASA 20	80A ASA 16
EKTACHROME 64 (Daylight)	80B ASA 20	80A ASA 16
EKTACHROME 200 (Daylight)	80B ASA 64	80A ASA 50
EKTACHROME 400 (Daylight)	80B ASA 125	80A ASA 100
EKTACHROME Infrared	12 or 15 + CC50C-2 Film Speed 50	—

FILMS FOR COPYING

For copying originals such as photographs (prints), drawings, documents, and paintings, choosing a color film is much the same as for conventional subjects. The choice depends on whether you want prints or slides and on the type of illumination.

You can use any of the light sources recommended for the film, such as daylight, flash (used off the camera if there are reflecting surfaces), or photolamps. However, since most copies are close-ups, photolamps are usually the best choice because they make it easier to control the illumination and you can use your exposure meter to determine exposure. See "Using Exposure Meters in Copying," page 101. If you use photolamp illumination, film recommendations for copying are the same as those under "Films for Photolamp Illumination."

If your original is black-and-white, you can obtain good copies on color film. However, if you want a monochromatic image that is a more accurate reproduction of the original or if you have many copies to make, it may be better or more economical to use black-and-white film (see page 77).

FILMS FOR DUPLICATING COLOR SLIDES

When you want to make duplicate slides of color-slide originals made on such films as KODACHROME and KODAK EKTACHROME Films, you'll usually get the best results when you use a film specifically designed for duplicating. KODAK EKTACHROME Slide Duplicating Film 5071 (Process E-6) is made for this purpose. It has low contrast and color rendition characteristics suitable for producing excellent slide duplicates.

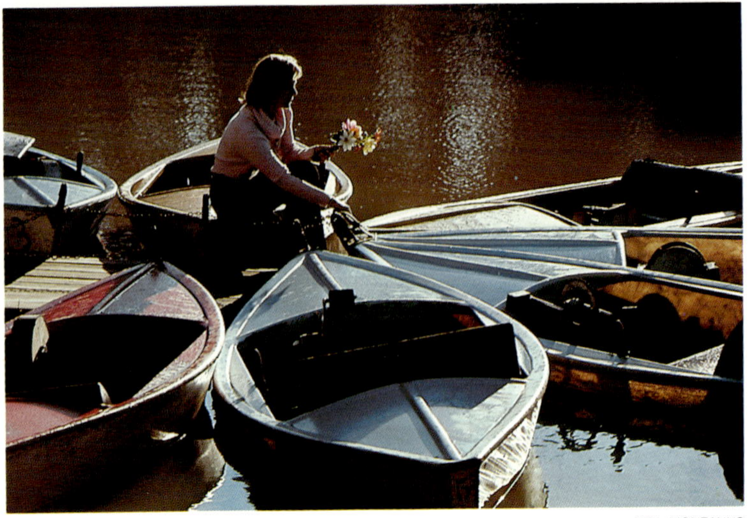

NEIL MONTANUS

KODACHROME Films are well known for their outstanding definition characteristics. KODACHROME 64 Film (Daylight). 1/125 sec *f*/8.

You can use conventional color-slide films for making duplicate slides, but the duplicates made with such films are generally less than satisfactory due to contrast that's too high and unsaturated colors. Sometimes if you have an original slide that would be better with increased contrast, you can duplicate it on a conventional color-slide film such as KODACHROME 25 Film (Daylight) and get good results. A duplicate slide made on this film will usually have increased contrast.

DEFINITION

Definition is the clarity of detail seen by a person when viewing a photograph. Several factors give you the impression of definition. The degree of graininess, resolving power, and sharpness are usually used to describe a film's definition characteristics. Classifications for each of these definition factors have been assigned to Kodak films for general use. See the Definition Tables in the Data Sheets. A more thorough discussion of definition is given on page 69 in the chapter "KODAK Black-and-White Films."

Since the "Degree of Enlargement" classification described on page 72 applies to prints, this classification is not given in the Data Sheets for color-slide films. When color prints are made from color slides, the degree of enlargement depends on the method used to make the prints; i.e., through internegatives or directly on reversal color-printing paper. Definition classifications are not provided for KODAK Instant Print Film because they would not be meaningful for comparing this film with a negative or slide film.

RECIPROCITY CHARACTERISTICS

Most color films are designed for the typical short exposure times used in general picture-taking. At exposure times of 1 second or longer, the speed of most films will begin to decrease and color rendition will shift away from normal. These changes are referred to as the "reciprocity characteristics" of the film.

You can correct for the reciprocity effect by using filters and increasing the exposure. Recommended corrections for critical work are given on the Data

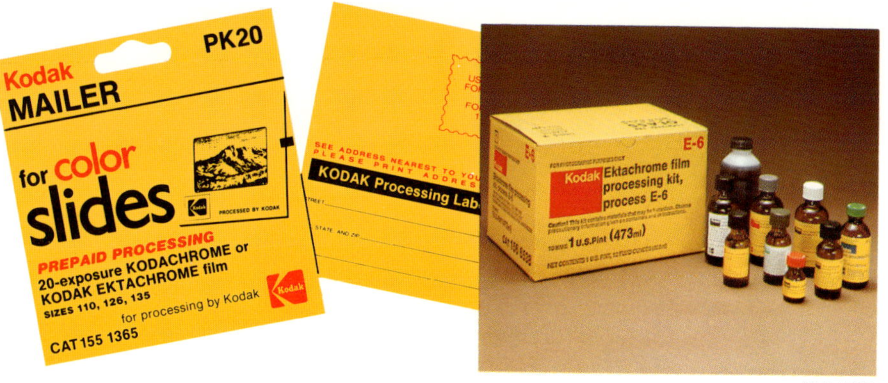

JOHN HOOD

KODAK Mailers are convenient to use because you can mail your Kodak color film directly to Kodak for processing. After your pictures are processed, they are mailed to any address you specify.

Kodak chemicals for processing KODAK EKTACHROME and KODACOLOR Films are available from photo dealers in handy kit form. Each kit contains the chemicals you need plus complete instructions.

Sheet for each Kodak color film. In most existing-light situations it's not practical or essential to use filters, but you can increase exposure to compensate for the decrease in film speed. You can avoid the effect simply by using shutter speeds shorter than 1 second when it's practical (shorter than 1/100 second with EKTACHROME Infrared Film).

PROCESSING

Have your film processed promptly after exposure. Return Kodak color film to your photo dealer for processing by Kodak or another laboratory, or mail it directly to Kodak in the appropriate KODAK Mailer for prepaid processing. The processing comments made here do not, of course, apply to KODAK Instant Print Film. For developing this film, see page D 7.

You can process KODACOLOR and KODAK EKTACHROME Films yourself in processing kits sold by photo dealers. All the necessary chemicals and instructions for processing the film are included in the kits. For information on processing and printing Kodak color films, see your photo dealer or write to Eastman Kodak Company, Photo Information, Department 841, 343 State Street, Rochester, New York 14650, and request the pamphlet *Introduction to Processing and Printing KODAK Color Films* (AE-12). For prompt delivery of the pamphlet, please send a self-addressed business-size envelope with the publication title and number written on the back. We'll pay the postage.

To process KODACOLOR Films, you can use the KODAK FLEXICOLOR Processing Kit for Process C-41 or the equivalent. The C-41 process requires 7 steps which take 24¼ minutes (plus drying time). Complete instructions come with the processing kit.

After your color negatives are processed, you can have prints made through your photo dealer or you can make them yourself. If you want to make your own color prints and have questions about the procedure, write to Kodak at the address given above. You can purchase Kodak books on making color prints—*Bigger and Better Enlarging* (AG-19), $10.95, and *Basic Developing, Printing, Enlarging in Color* (AE-13), $3.75—from your photo dealer.

To process EKTACHROME 64, 160, 200, and 400 Films and EKTACHROME Slide Duplicating Film 5071, you can use the KODAK EKTACHROME Film Processing Kit, Process E-6, or equivalent. Process E-6 has 11 steps and takes 37 minutes.

If you want to process EKTACHROME Infrared Film, you have to use a different process. For the Infrared film, use the KODAK EKTACHROME Film Processing Kit, Process E-4, or equivalent. The E-4 process has 13 steps and takes 56 minutes. It is important that you use the specific process recommended for the kind of EKTACHROME Film you're using. Do not process EKTACHROME Films for Process E-6 in Process E-4 or vice versa.

Handling color film during processing is much the same as handling black-and-white film (see page 77). The main differences are that different processing chemicals are required for color, there is a greater number of steps in the color process, and some of the processing solutions must be very close to the recommended temperature: within ±¼ or ½°F (±0.15 or 0.3°C). Color processing has to be precise for satisfactory results, so carefully follow the instructions that come with the chemicals. The Kodak book AE-13, mentioned previously, provides information on how to process Kodak color films.

SPECIAL PROCESSING FOR INCREASED SPEEDS

When lighting conditions are dim, as in many existing-light scenes, you may need higher film speed for taking pictures while handholding your camera, stopping action, using a telephoto lens, or using a small lens opening to gain greater depth of field. You can increase the speed of KODAK EKTACHROME 400, 200, and 160 Films (or KODAK EKTACHROME 64 Film when necessary) by obtaining special processing from Kodak, by sending your film to another laboratory, or by extending the development if you process the film yourself. The effective speeds of the films are increased to 2 times the normal speeds. The speed of EKTACHROME 400 Film (Daylight) is increased to ASA 800, the speed of EKTACHROME 200 Film (Daylight) to ASA 400, and the speed of EKTACHROME 160 Film (Tungsten) to ASA 320. The speed of EKTACHROME 64 Film (Daylight) is increased to ASA 125.

To obtain the special processing from Kodak, purchase a KODAK Special Processing Envelope, ESP-1, for *each* roll of EKTACHROME 400, 200, or 160 Film (or EKTACHROME 64 Film), 135 and 120 sizes. The charge for special processing is in addition to the regular cost of KODAK EKTACHROME Film processing. Expose the entire roll of film according to the instructions that come with the ESP-1 Envelope. Put the roll of exposed film into the ESP-1 Envelope, and then either take the film to your photo dealer for processing by Kodak, or mail it in the appropriate KODAK Mailer to a Kodak Processing Laboratory in the United States.

If you want to process the film yourself to obtain increased speed, simply increase the normal first-development time by the amount given in the table on the next page. For all the other steps, follow the normal processing times given in the instructions that come with the chemicals. When you process your own films, you can change their effective speeds over a wide range, as shown in the table. Exposing and processing the film at speeds other than the normal speed will result in some reduction in photographic quality. The more the speed of the film is varied from normal, the greater the reduction in quality.

PROCESSING ADJUSTMENTS FOR DIFFERENT SPEEDS WITH *KODAK EKTACHROME* FILM CHEMICALS, PROCESS E-6

ASA Film Speed				
KODAK EKTACHROME 400 Film (Daylight)	KODAK EKTACHROME 200 Film (Daylight)	KODAK EKTACHROME 160 Film (Tungsten)	KODAK EKTACHROME 64 Film (Daylight)	Change the time in the first developer by
1600	800	640	250	+ 5½ minutes
800	400	320	125	+ 2 minutes
Normal 400	Normal 200	Normal 160	Normal 64	Normal
200	100	80	32	− 2 minutes

GETTING PRINTS OR SLIDES MADE—FROM YOUR NEGATIVES, PRINTS, OR SLIDES

COLOR PRINTS

When you want color prints or enlargements made from your color negatives, see your photo dealer. The dealer can order the prints for you. When they're made by a Kodak Processing Laboratory, the color prints from these negatives are called KODAK Color Prints, and the enlargements are called KODAK Color Enlargements.

You can also have color prints and enlargements made directly from finished color prints. This service is especially suitable for obtaining extra prints from instant color prints. When made by Kodak, the prints are called KODAK Color Copyprints; the enlargements, KODAK Color Copy Enlargements.

Your photo dealer can have color prints or enlargements made from your color slides, too. When they're made by a Kodak Processing Laboratory, the prints are called KODAK Color Prints and the enlargements, KODAK Color Enlargements.

COLOR SLIDES

When you want duplicates of your slides or transparencies, you can have them made by Kodak or another laboratory. See your photo dealer. They are called KODAK Color Slide Duplicates when made by a Kodak Processing Laboratory.

You can have color slides made from your Kodak color negatives, except for size 110. These slides are called KODACOLOR Slides when made by Kodak Processing Laboratories. You can also have color slides made from your color prints. When Kodak makes these slides, they are called KODAK Color Copy Slides.

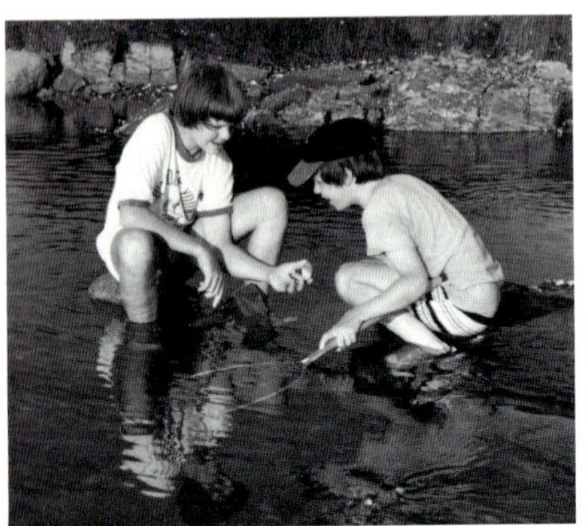

JOHN FISH

When you want to make your own black-and-white prints from your color negatives, you can use KODAK PANALURE Paper. This picture was printed on PANALURE Paper.

BLACK-AND-WHITE PRINTS

If you want black-and-white prints from your color negatives, you can make them on KODAK PANALURE Paper, which is specially designed for this purpose. Instructions are included with the paper. To make black-and-white prints from color slides, you'll need to make a black-and-white negative from each slide first. If you have questions about this procedure, write to the address given inside the back cover.

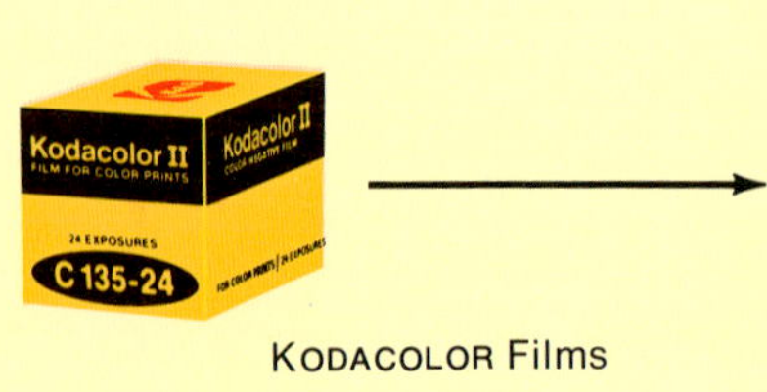

KODACOLOR Films

Kodak COLOR FILMS for Prints, Slides, and Enlargements

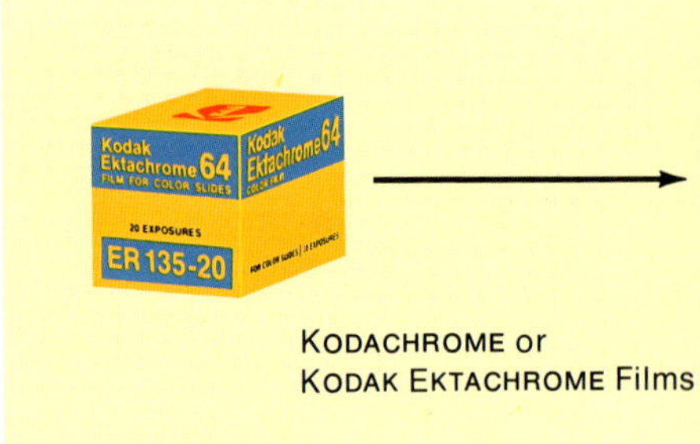

KODACHROME or KODAK EKTACHROME Films

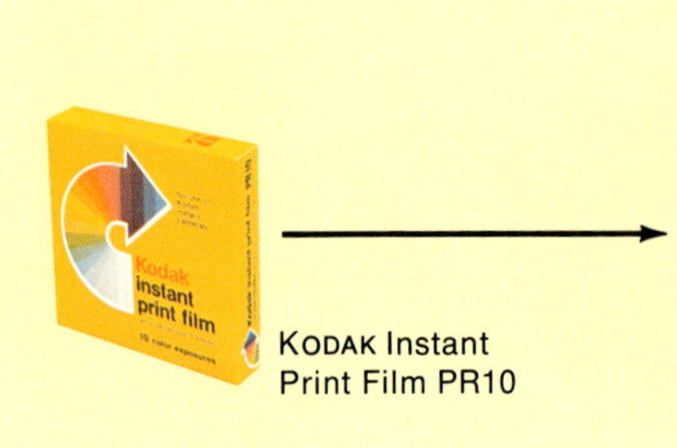

KODAK Instant Print Film PR10

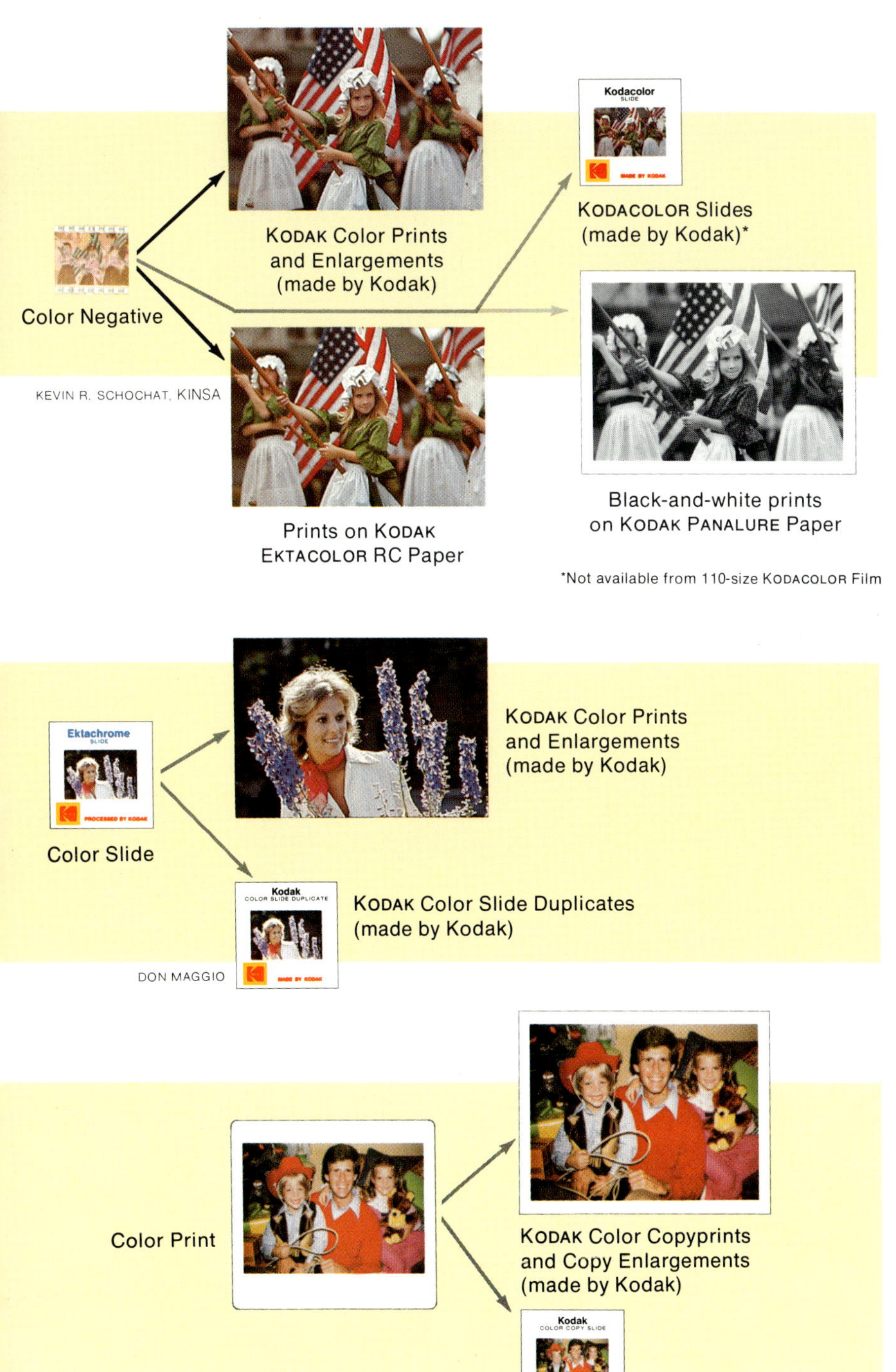

Photo page 56 —PAUL W. LEBHARDT

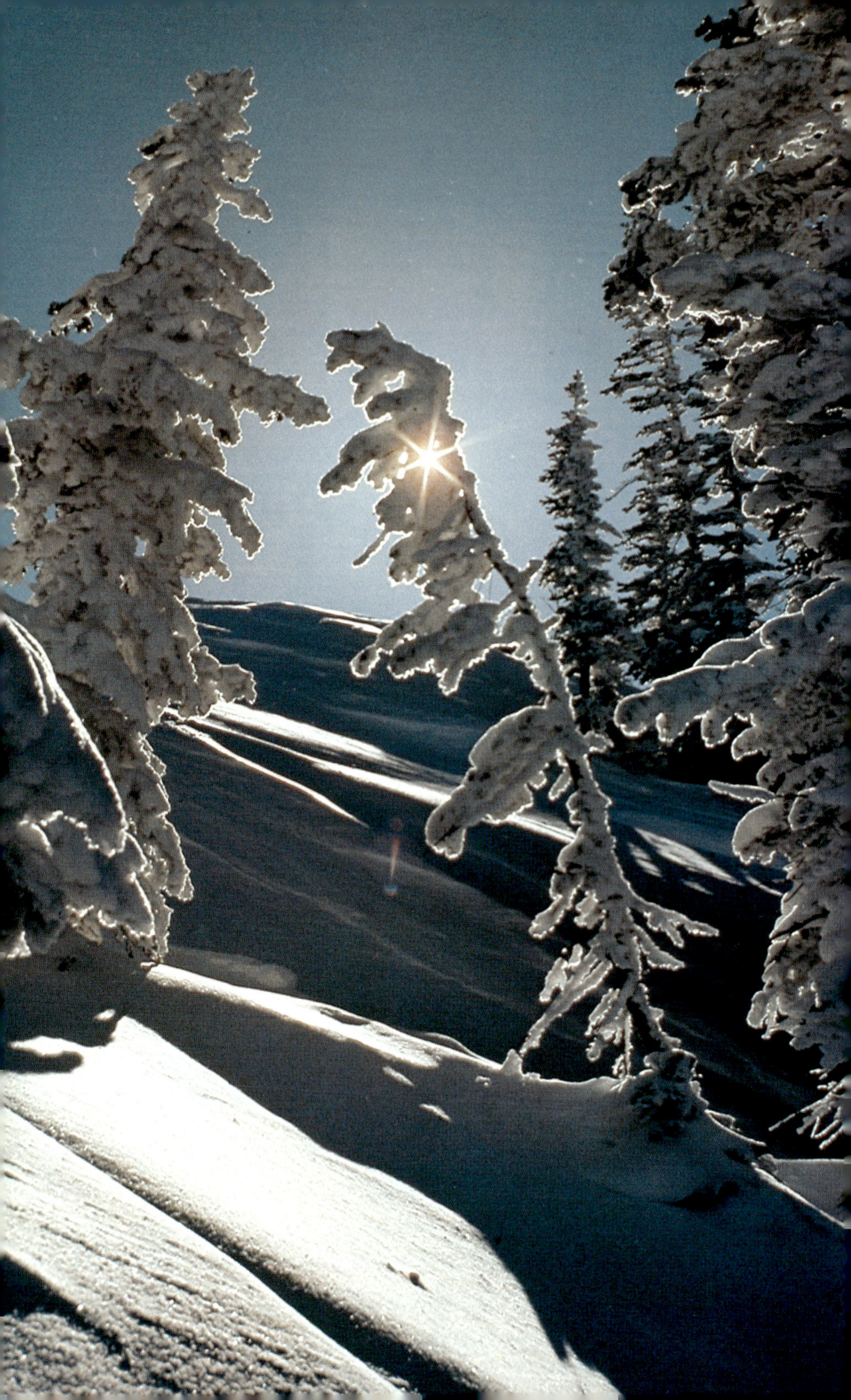

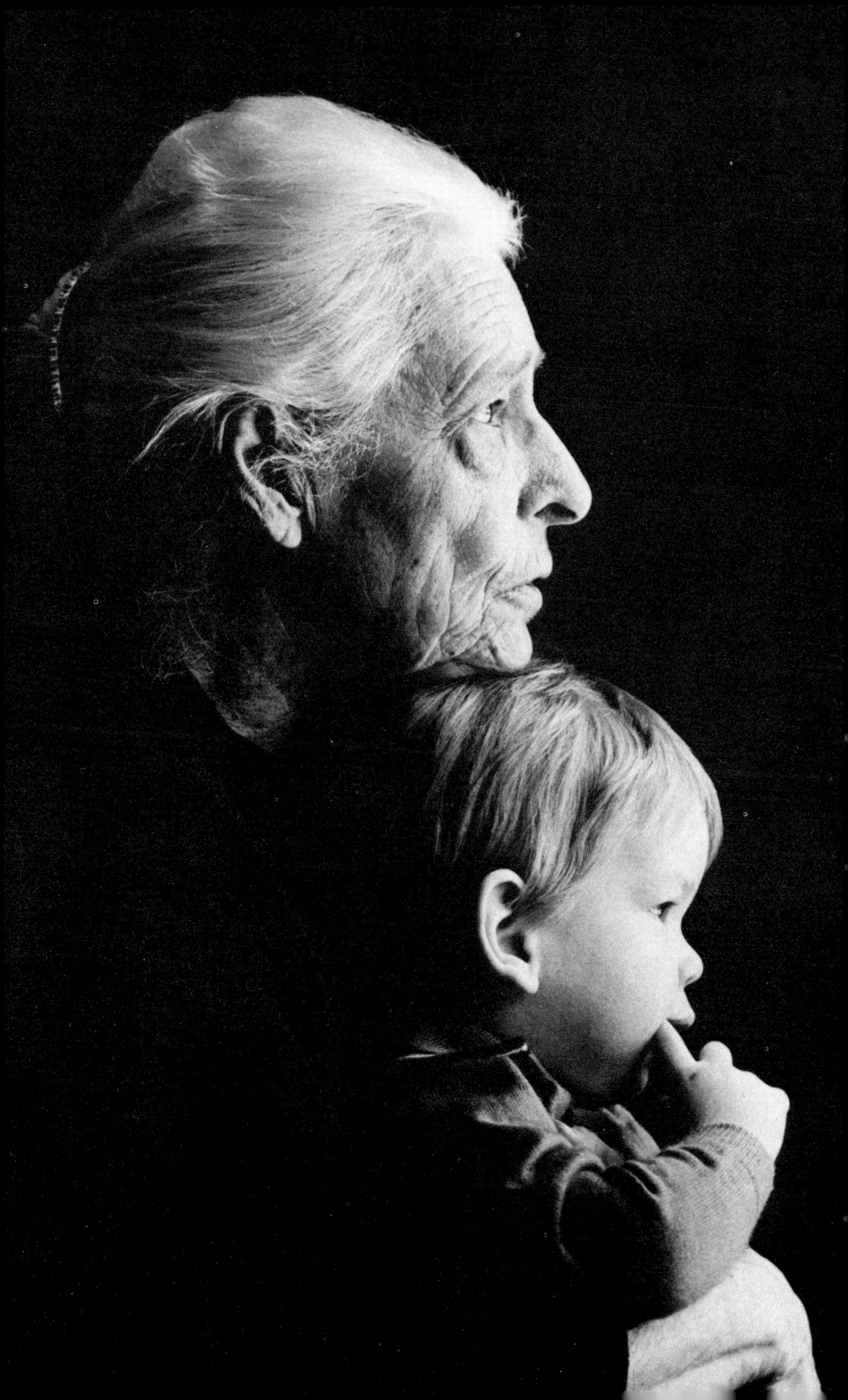

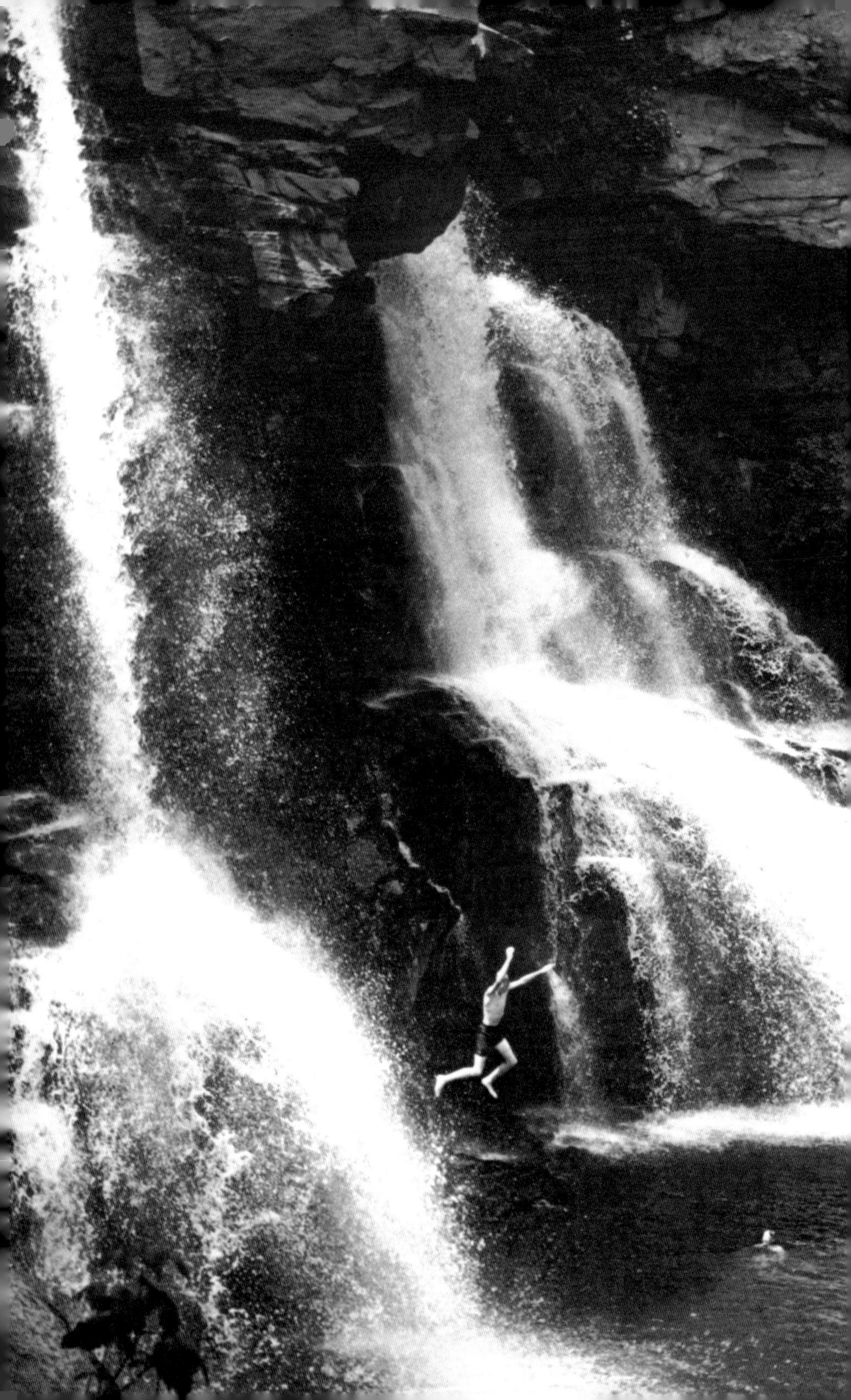

Kodak Black-and-White Films

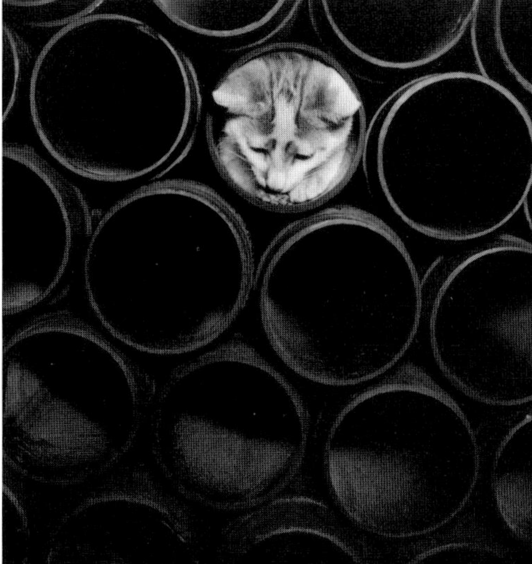

MICHAEL J. LACWITA, KINSA

As we said earlier, the most important considerations in selecting a black-and-white film for conventional photography are the film speed that's best for the kind of pictures you want to take and the definition quality you'll obtain. A few films are designed for special purposes, such as recording infrared radiation and copying printed material.

A table listing Kodak black-and-white films is given on page 121.

FILMS FOR GENERAL USE

KODAK VERICHROME Pan Film is a fast panchromatic film with extremely fine grain. It is a good choice for general picture-taking in all types of roll-film and cartridge cameras. This film is not available in 135 size. Its speed of ASA 125 is high enough for most situations, and its definition is excellent. You can use this film in simple, nonadjustable cameras. Most other Kodak black-and-white films require an adjustable camera for proper exposure.

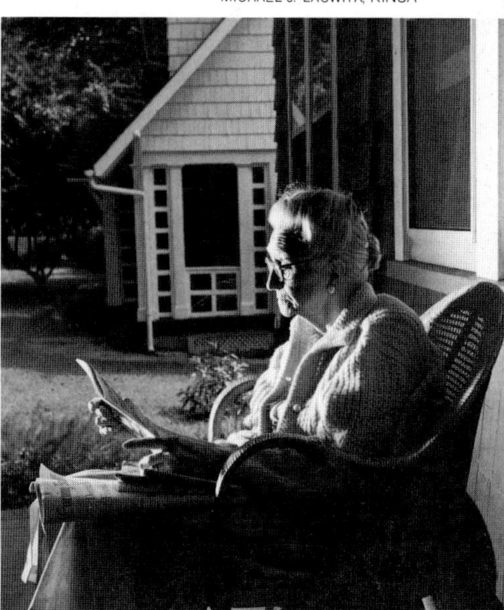

LOUIS MANCUSO, SKPA*

KODAK VERICHROME Pan Film, with a speed of ASA 125 and extremely fine grain, is an excellent general-purpose film. It will suit your needs ideally for most black-and-white pictures.

*Courtesy Scholastic/Kodak Photography Awards

ODAK PLUS-X Pan Film, 1/500 sec *f*/8.
WALLENCHECK, KINSA

Photo page 57, **KODAK TRI-X Pan Film.**
PAUL J. GOLDMAN, KINSA

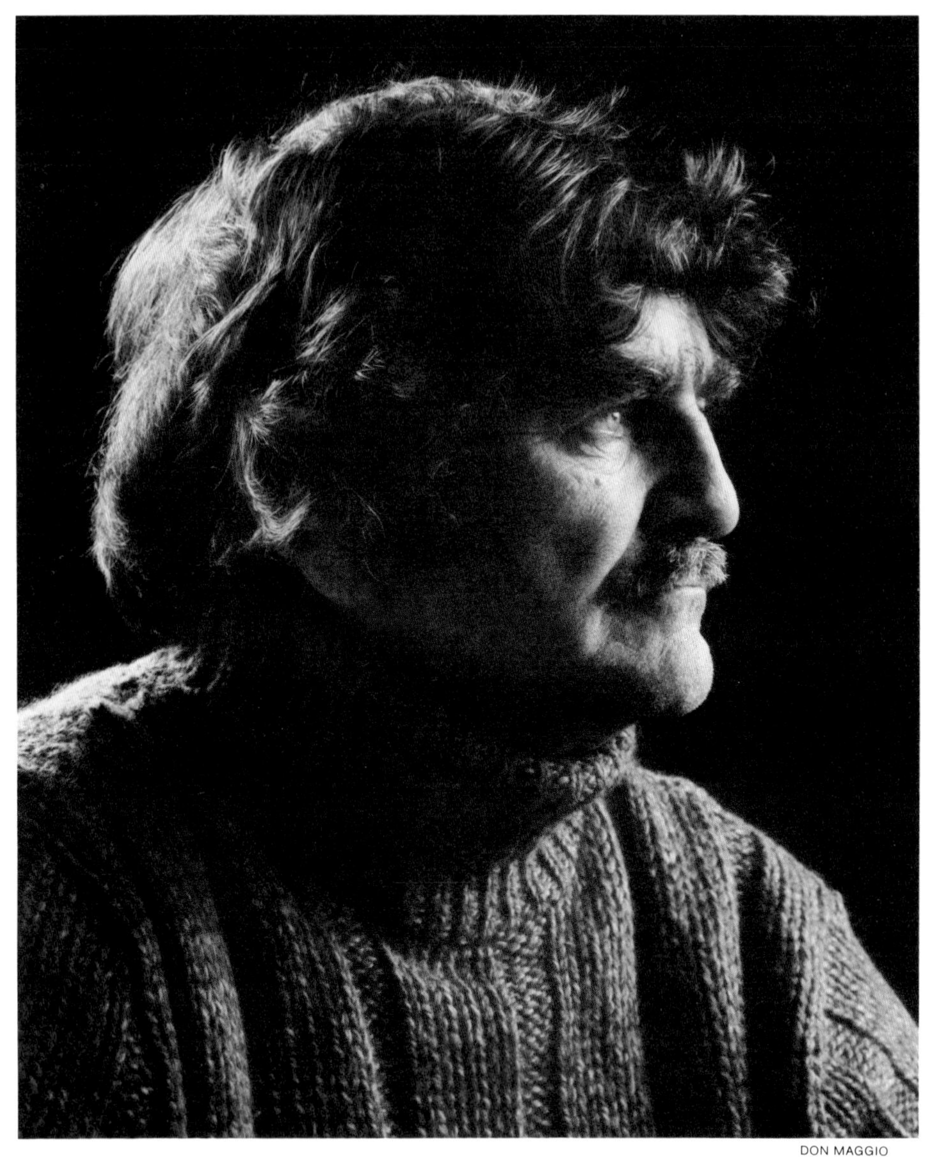

DON MAGGIO

KODAK PLUS-X Pan Film has many of the same fine characteristics as KODAK VERICHROME Pan Film. It's for use in 35 mm cameras.

KODAK PLUS-X Pan Film has characteristics similar to those of KODAK VERICHROME Pan Film except that it's for use in 35 mm cameras. PLUS-X Pan Film is a general-purpose film with a speed of ASA 125. It has finer grain than KODAK TRI-X Pan Film.

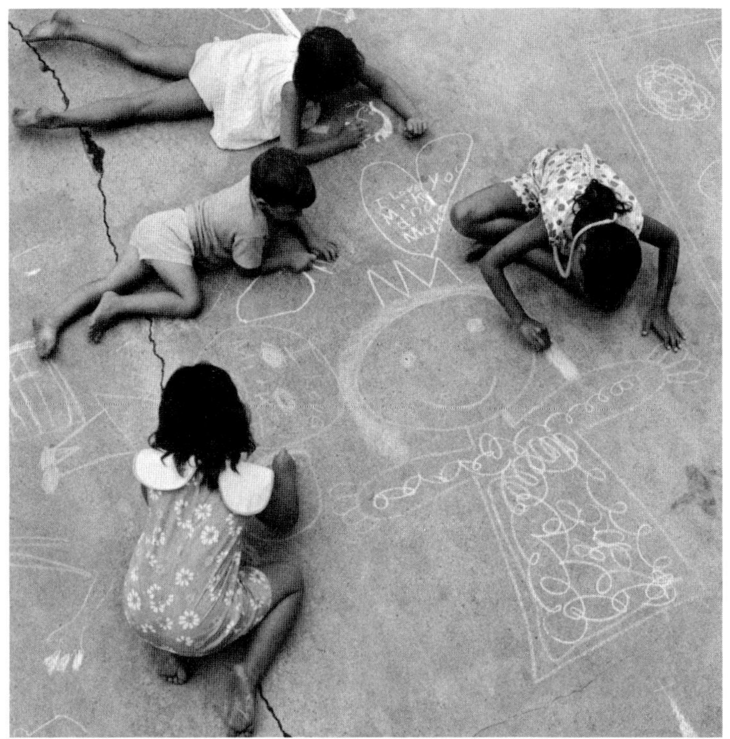

WILLIAM J. FIORE, KINSA

KODAK PANATOMIC-X Film. This film, which has excellent definition characteristics, is designed for making prints with a very high degree of enlargement.

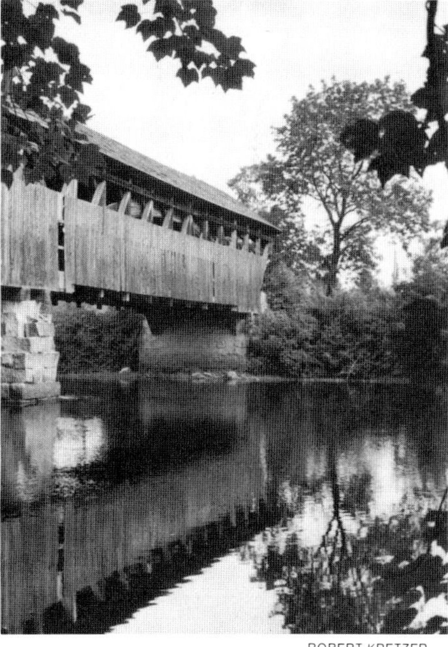

ROBERT KRETZER

KODAK PANATOMIC-X Film is an extremely fine-grained panchromatic film with very high sharpness. It has a speed of ASA 32, which is adequate for many picture-taking situations. This is an excellent film to use when you want to make big enlargements. With special reversal processing, the 135-size film will produce black-and-white positive slides. In 120 size, the film is called KODAK PANATOMIC-X Professional Film.

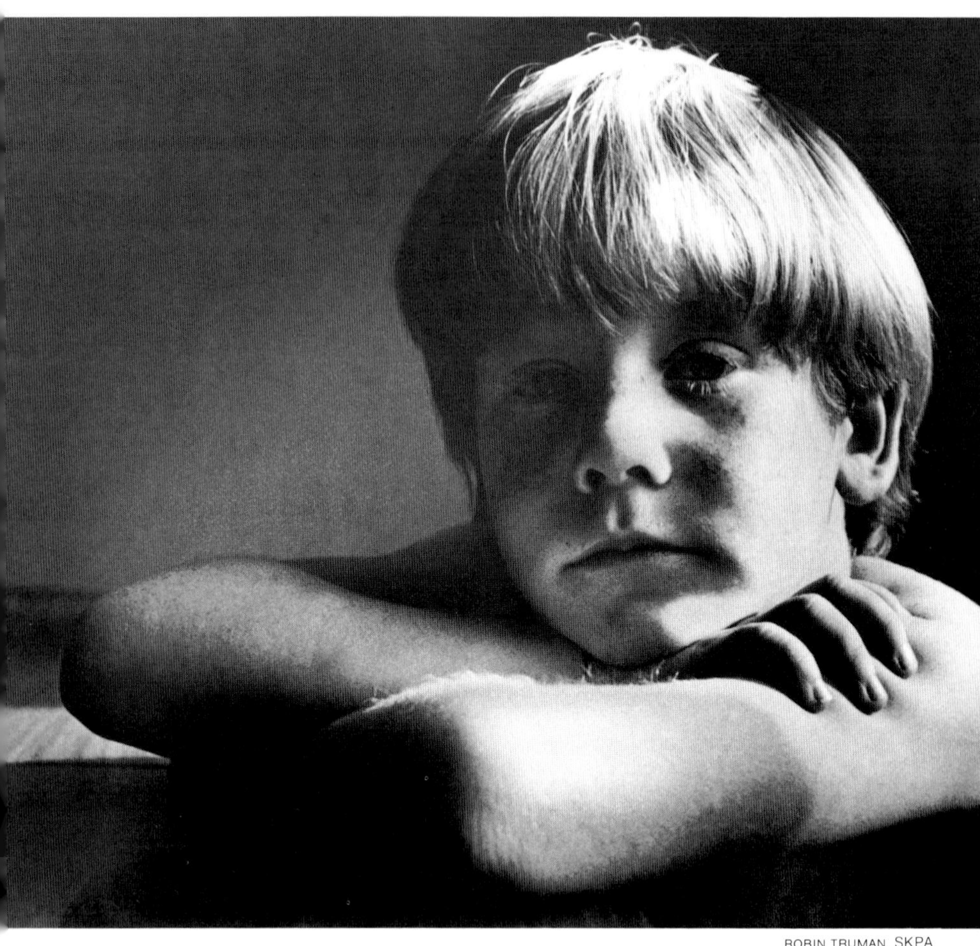

ROBIN TRUMAN, SKPA

KODAK TRI-X Pan Film is well known as a top-notch film for existing-light pictures. Its high speed of ASA 400 is especially helpful in the comparatively dim lighting conditions usually found in homes.

KODAK TRI-X Pan Film is a high-speed panchromatic film with fine grain and excellent sharpness. The combination of very high speed—ASA 400—and very good definition characteristics makes TRI-X Pan Film an excellent choice for photographing dimly lighted subjects, fast action, and subjects requiring good depth of field and high shutter speeds. It also extends the distance range for flash pictures. This film has great flexibility because it lets you take pictures under a wide range of subject and lighting conditions, depending on your camera.

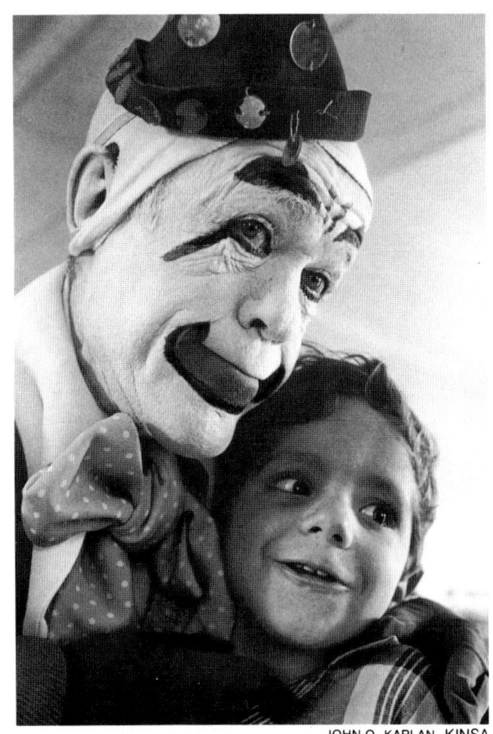

JOHN O. KAPLAN KINSA

KODAK TRI-X Pan Film features excellent tone reproduction and high-quality definition in addition to its high speed. These qualities make it a very popular and outstanding film.

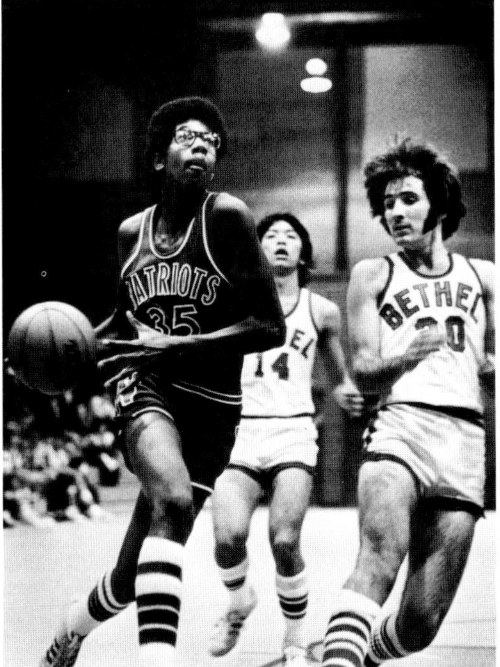

MARK CHRISTIAN PEDERSON, SKPA

The high speed of **KODAK TRI-X Pan Film** lets you use the high shutter speeds necessary to stop motion in existing-light pictures. 1/250 sec *f*/1.8.

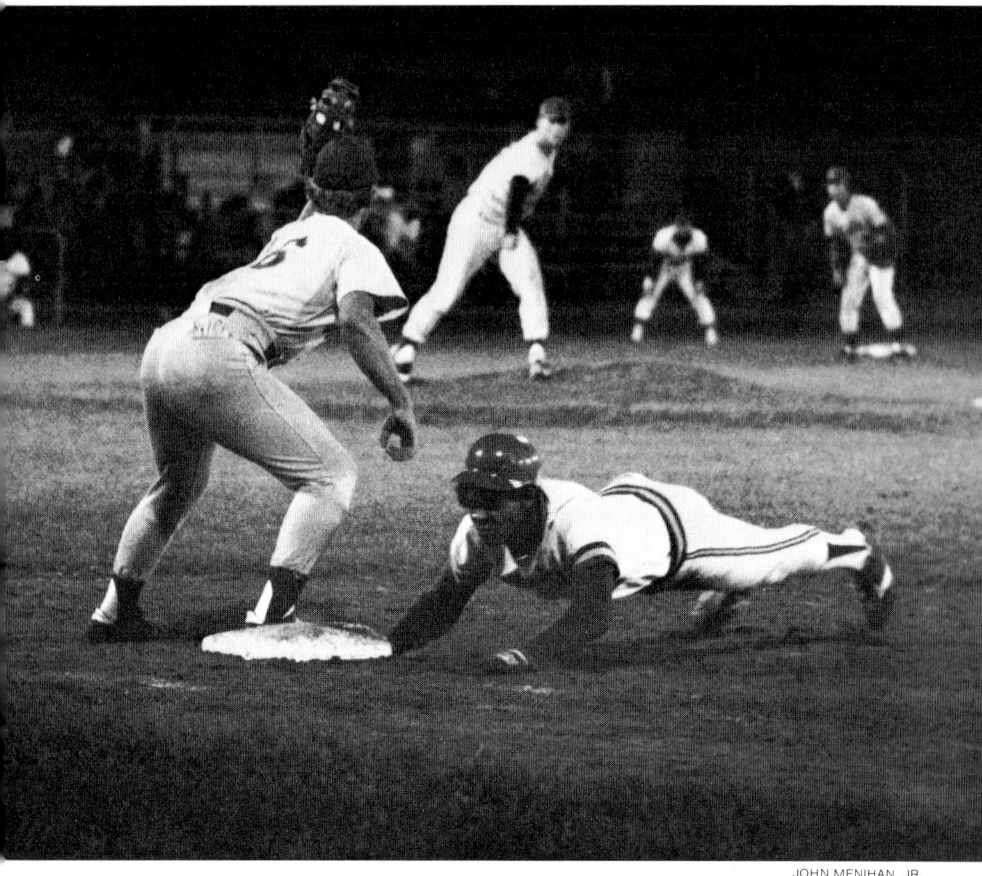

JOHN MENIHAN, JR.

KODAK ROYAL-X Pan Film with its extremely high speed is a good choice for sports photography at night. 1/250 sec *f*/4.

KODAK ROYAL-X Pan Film is an extremely high-speed panchromatic film. This film, for 120-size cameras only, is designed for situations in which you need the highest film speed, as in taking action photographs by existing light or taking pictures when the light is very poor. This film, because of its extremely high speed—ASA 1250—is grainier than the slower films, but its medium grain is usually acceptable in the type of pictures for which the film is designed.

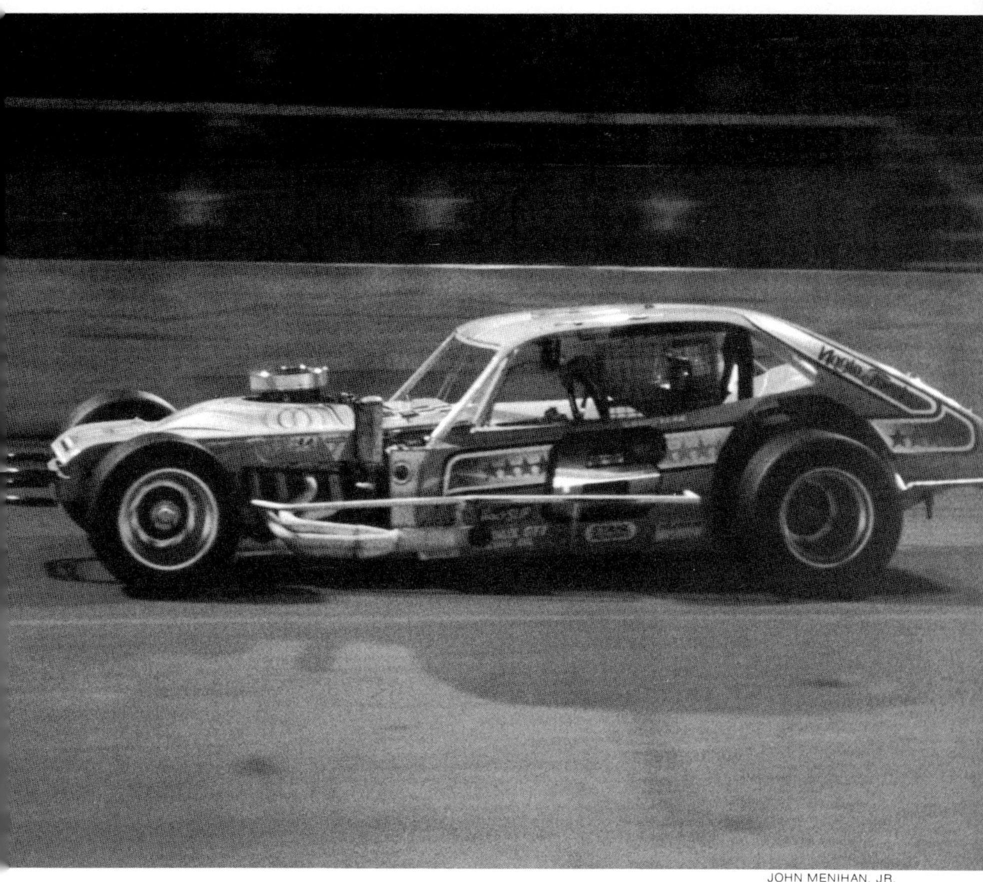

JOHN MENIHAN, JR.

Here's a picture-taking situation with adverse conditions—fast action photographed with a telephoto lens at night. These conditions require an extremely high-speed film such as KODAK ROYAL-X Pan Film or KODAK Recording Film 2475 (ESTAR-AH Base). The choice between these two films depends on the size of film your camera accepts. Photographed on **KODAK Recording Film 2475 (ESTAR-AH Base),** 1/250 sec *f*/2.5.

KODAK Recording Film 2475 (ESTAR-AH Base) is an extremely high-speed film with extended red sensitivity (see page 67). This film is for 35 mm cameras, and you can use it for the same purposes as ROYAL-X Pan Film. It has coarse grain because of its exceptionally high speed—1000. Use this film only in situations where the extra speed is more important than fine grain.

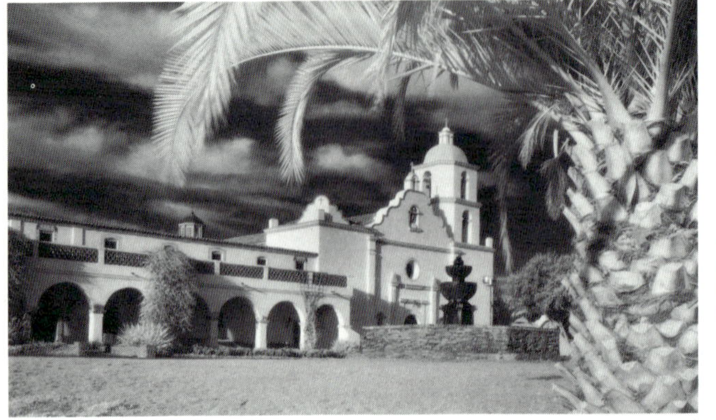

For an eerie, abstract quality in architectural or landscape photographs, take your pictures on **KODAK High Speed Infrared Film** with a No. 25 filter. 1/60 sec *f*/16.

PETER GALES

KODAK High Speed Infrared Film is a fast, moderately high-contrast film that's sensitive to infrared radiation. With this film and the recommended filter, you can create some striking and unusual photographs of subjects such as landscapes and architecture. In infrared photographs the sky appears almost black; shadows are dark, but usually show adequate detail; live grass and leaves appear very light, as though covered by snow; and distant details obscured by haze in the original scene show up with remarkable clarity. By using a flash unit with the proper filter you can photograph subjects in the dark without their being aware of it. This film has many applications for technical and scientific photographs.

This film has an approximate tungsten speed of 125 with a No. 25 filter (see page D 38). The high speed is valuable for taking pictures with a hand-held camera in relatively dim light and for stopping motion in photographs of subjects that require high shutter speeds. This film has fine grain, but it is not intended for high degrees of enlargement. Because of the sensitivity of High Speed Infrared Film, cameras must be loaded and unloaded in total darkness; no safelight should be used. Store 135 magazines of this film in the tightly closed film cans or in total darkness.

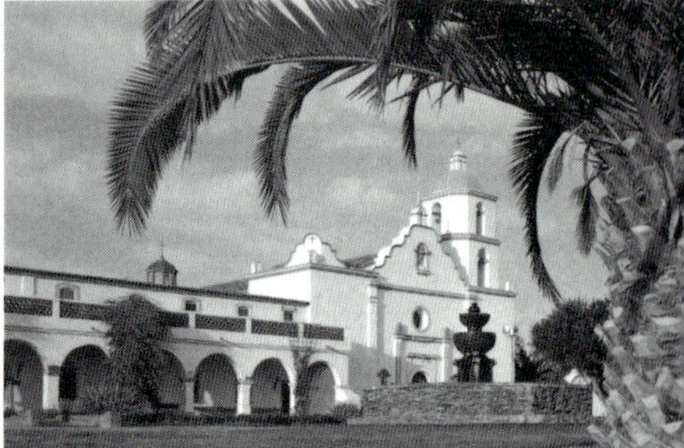

Conventional rendering on KODAK PLUS-X Pan Film, no filter. 1/125 sec *f*/16.

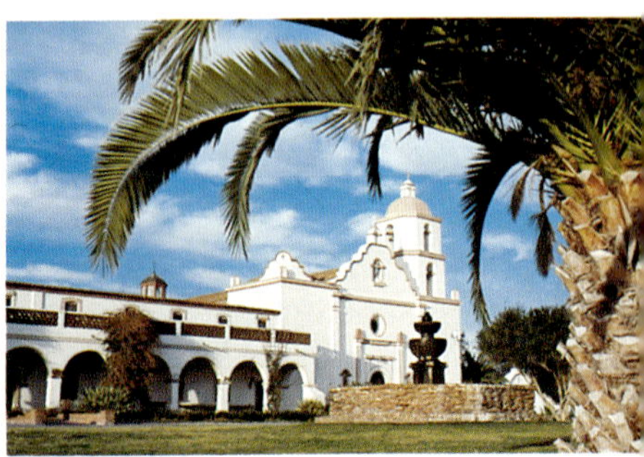

Normal appearance.

KODAK High Contrast Copy Film 5069 is an improved high-contrast film with extremely fine grain and ultra high resolving power. It's designed for copying printed matter, such as books, magazines, maps, and documents. The film has a tungsten speed of 64.

OTHER *KODAK* BLACK-AND-WHITE FILMS

There are several black-and-white 35 mm and roll films designed for professional use. Descriptions of the more popular of these films are given here; if you have questions on these films, write to the address given on the inside back cover. For complete information on professional films, see the books *KODAK Professional Black-and-White Films* (F-5), $3.00, and *Planning and Producing Slide Programs* (S-30), $4.00, available from photo dealers.

KODAK PLUS-X Pan Professional Film is a medium-speed panchromatic film with extremely fine grain and very high sharpness. It has a speed of ASA 125. The emulsion side of the film has a retouching surface. This film, which is available in 120 and 220 sizes and in sheet-film sizes, is the roll-film counterpart of 135-size KODAK PLUS-X Pan Film. Its characteristics are much the same as those of KODAK VERICHROME Pan Film.

KODAK TRI-X Pan Professional Film is a high-speed panchromatic film with fine grain and very high sharpness. It is the roll-film version of KODAK TRI-X Pan Professional Film 4164 (ESTAR Thick Base) in sheets, and it has a speed of ASA 320. This film is for use with all types of lighting, both outdoors and indoors. It has been designed to produce both excellent shadow detail and brilliant highlights, especially in photographs taken under artificial light, such as portraits made in studios. Both sides of the film have surfaces designed for retouching. The roll film is available in 120 and 220 sizes.

KODAK Direct Positive Panchromatic Film 5246 is a medium-speed reversal film with extremely fine grain. It is designed for making black-and-white slides of high quality. Its reversal processing is faster and simpler than using a negative film and then making separate positives. You can make 2 x 2-inch slides with this film by photographing other slides, photographs, and outdoor and indoor subjects. It has a speed of 80 for daylight and 64 for tungsten. Direct Positive Panchromatic Film is sold only in 35 mm 100-foot-long rolls and must be loaded into 135 magazines for use in 35 mm still cameras.

EASTMAN Fine Grain Release Positive Film 5302 is a low-speed blue-sensitive film with extremely fine grain for printing black-and-white slides—positives—from continuous-tone or line negatives. This film is not recommended for general use in your camera. It's available in 35 mm 100-foot-long rolls.

COLOR SENSITIVITY

The color sensitivity of a film describes its response to light of various wavelengths or colors. While the average normal eye is sensitive to all colors, the same is not necessarily true of films. Silver bromide, the fundamental light-sensitive element in all emulsions, is sensitive only to blue and ultraviolet. Sensitizing dyes incorporated in orthochromatic, panchromatic, and infrared emulsions make these classes of films sensitive to certain other colors or wavelengths of light or other radiation. The type of sensitizing is one of the most important photographic characteristics of a film because it affects both the monochromatic rendition of colors

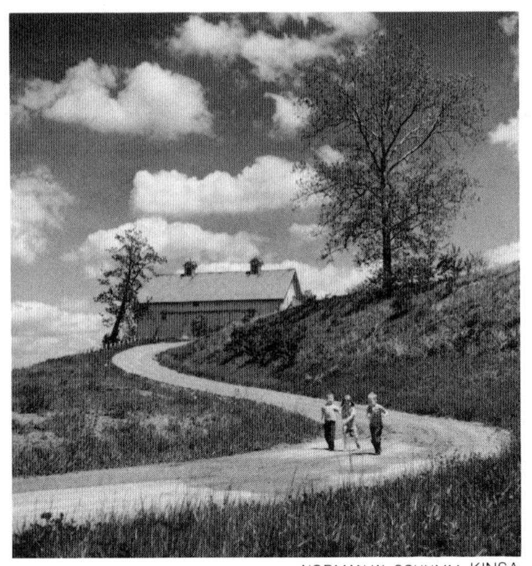

NORMAN W. SCHUMM, KINSA

With a panchromatic film, you can darken the gray-tone rendering of a color in a photograph by using a filter with a color complementary to the color you want to darken. You can use a No. 15 deep-yellow filter to darken the blue sky in the picture and to make the sky and the clouds appear more natural. VERICHROME Pan Film.

in the photographs you obtain and the handling of the film in the darkroom.

Kodak black-and-white films are divided into several sensitizing classes. Except for certain special sensitizings, there are four general classes. Professional films are available in all four classes; films for general use are available in only two of them—panchromatic and infrared. The color sensitivity of each black-and-white film is given on the Data Sheets in this book. The four sensitizing classes are as follows:

Noncolor-sensitized or blue-sensitive films are sensitive only to ultraviolet and blue-violet; this characteristic is inherent in silver halides—the light-sensitive element in the emulsion.

Orthochromatic films are sensitive to green light in addition to ultraviolet and blue-violet.

Panchromatic films are sensitive to all visible colors, including red, as well as to invisible ultraviolet radiation.

Infrared films are sensitive to ultraviolet, and all visible colors, including deep red, as well as to the invisible infrared radiation.

The color sensitivity of a black-and-white film determines the following:

Gray-Tone Rendition of Colored Objects. A film that's not sensitized to green or red light will reproduce these colors as tones of gray that are too dark in the print. Panchromatic films for general use will record colors as gray tones in the print in approximately the same relative brightness as they appear to the eye. For critical work you can obtain gray-tone rendition in a photograph that's very close to the visual brightness of the original scene by using the proper correction filter.

Some panchromatic films have extended, or increased, red sensitivity. Such films will reproduce red objects as tones of gray that appear lighter in the print than the brightness of the objects themselves appears to the eye.

Filters and Filter Factors. The filters that you can use depend on the color sensitivity of your film. For example, a red filter should be used only with a film sensitive to red light, such as panchromatic film. Since filters absorb light, their use requires an exposure increase. This increase in exposure is specified by the filter factor, which depends on the color sensitivity of the film and the color quality of the light source. For example, a film with a large portion of its sensitivity in the blue-violet requires a much greater relative exposure through a yellow filter, which eliminates most of the blue light, than a panchromatic film requires. Panchromatic film is sensitive to all colors and therefore can record the red and green light transmitted by the yellow filter.

How to apply the filter factor for proper exposure is explained beginning on page 97.

If you want to make an object appear darker in the print than it appears to the eye, use a filter that has a color complementary to the color of the object. For example, a yellow filter darkens a blue sky. To lighten the gray-tone rendering of an object, use a filter similar in color to the object. You can also use filters to increase the contrast between colored objects that would normally photograph as nearly the same shade of gray.

Filter Designations. Filter designations, such as K2, A, and G, that were used to identify different filters in the past have been replaced with the present numbering system. Since published literature frequently makes reference to the older designations, both designations are given here.

Current Designations	Discontinued Designations
No. 6	K1
No. 8	K2
No. 11	X1
No. 15	G
No. 25	A
No. 47	C5
No. 58	B

Recommended filters and factors for each film are given in the Data Sheets in this book. There is more information on filters in the KODAK Photo Book *Filters and Lens Attachments for Black-and-White and Color Pictures* (AB-1), $2.25, available from photo dealers.

Safelight Filters. The function of a safelight filter is to provide maximum visibility in the darkroom without fogging the film. For some films, this is achieved by selecting a filter which transmits light in the region to which the film is least sensitive. For example, a noncolor-sensitized film is sensitive only to blue-violet and blue light. You can safely handle this kind of film under a safelight filter transmitting only red light, such as the KODAK Safelight Filter No. 1A (light red).

Since panchromatic films are sensitive to all colors of visible light, you must normally handle them in total darkness. With some restrictions, you can use a dark-green safelight filter. A filter of this color, because it transmits light to which the eye is most sensitive, provides maximum visibility with a minimum amount of light.

Safelight recommendations for each Kodak black-and-white film are given in the Data Sheets in this book.

DEFINITION

The terms definition and sharpness are often used interchangeably, but such usage is only partly correct. Definition refers to the overall appearance of detail, while sharpness is one factor affecting definition and describes the appearance of edge sharpness between details in a photograph.

Definition is the composite effect of several factors, among which are sharpness, resolving power, and graininess. Usually resolving power and sharpness increase as graininess decreases, but this is only a general rule, and there are exceptions.

Graininess. This refers to the sandlike or granular appearance in a film or slide resulting from the clumping of the silver grains, or dye particles in color film. Graininess is caused by the irregular distribution of the silver grains rather than by the individual grains themselves. Individual grains are not visible

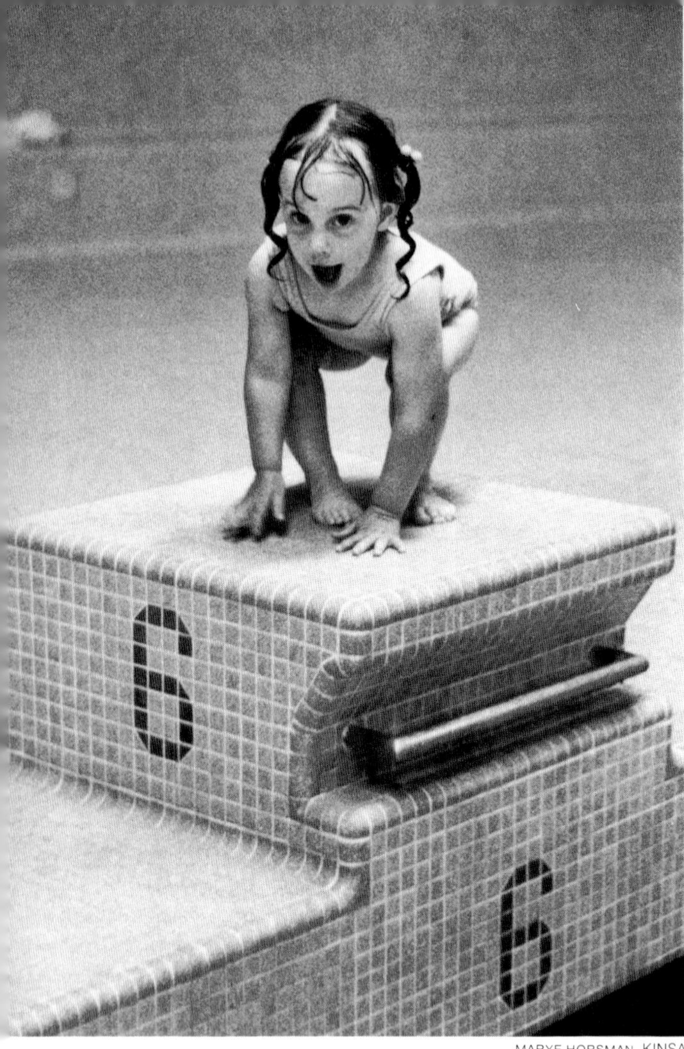

When enlargements are made from a grainy negative, objectionable graininess usually becomes the most important definition factor limiting the degree of enlargement.

MARYE HORSMAN, KINSA

under the magnifications used for ordinary enlargements.

For films of a general type, graininess tends to increase with film speed. When a given black-and-white film is developed in different developers to the same contrast index (see page 82), graininess will vary somewhat, depending on the type of developer used. Some fine-grain developers produce less graininess, but at the expense of some loss of film speed. Several Kodak developers are recommended in the Data Sheets in this book. To help you select a developer for black-and-white film, descriptions are provided on the last page of the Data Sheet section.

Graininess is increased by overexposure or overdevelopment of black-and-white negatives and by underexposure or overdevelopment of color negatives. Overdevelopment results when the temperature of the developer is too high, the development time is extended, or the film receives excessive agitation during development.

The graininess in a print is most apparent in the lighter middle tones, especially in large, uniform areas such as the sky. You can conceal graininess somewhat by softening the focus of your enlarger or by printing on a paper with a rough surface, but with some sacrifice in sharpness. The type of enlarger you use affects the graininess of the print and slightly affects the sharpness. An enlarger with a diffuse light source produces images with slightly softer sharpness and minimizes graininess. A condenser enlarger, which has a more specular light source, produces slightly sharper images but makes graininess more apparent.

The graininess of both negatives and prints increases with increasing contrast. Use the recommended development for your film, and in black-and-white printing, use the contrast grade of paper suitable for the contrast of the negative. Printing paper that's too low in contrast reduces apparent sharpness while paper too high in contrast increases the appearance of graininess.

Kodak films in the Data Sheets have been assigned graininess classifications, such as *Micro Fine, Extremely Fine, Very Fine, Fine, Medium, Moderately Coarse, Coarse,* or *Very Coarse.*

Resolving Power. The ability of a film or print to record fine detail is referred to as resolving power. In measuring resolving power a parallel-line test chart is photographed at a great reduction in size (see the illustration). The lines of the test chart are separated by spaces of the same width as the lines. The image is examined under a microscope at a specific magnification, and the number of lines per millimeter that can be seen as separate lines is determined. Lines closer together than this number (more lines per millimeter) are indistinct from each other on the film and appear as a gray mass.

The resolving power of a film depends only slightly on the degree of development, but resolution falls off considerably with both overexposure and underexposure. This is one important reason for exposing negatives correctly. The resolving-power classifications given

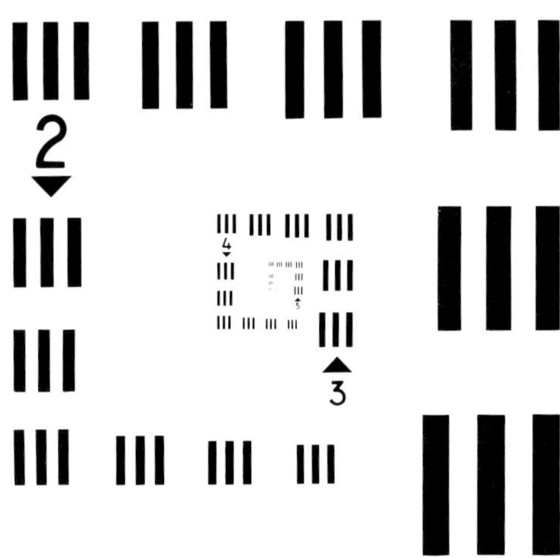

Photograph of a standard resolving-power test object.

in the Data Sheets are based upon the maximum values determined for recommended exposure and processing.

The maximum resolution which you can obtain in your negatives is limited by the camera lens as well as by the film, and is lower than the resolution of either one alone. In order to obtain the maximum resolution of which a film is capable, the resolving power of a lens would have to be at least three times the resolving power of the film.

Since resolving-power measurements are derived visually, they are subject to variation depending on the person making the measurement. For this reason we have not given specific resolving-power values for the films in the Data Sheets. Instead, we have placed them in the following classifications:

RESOLVING-POWER CLASSIFICATIONS

Resolving Power	Lines per mm
Ultra High	630 or Above
Extremely High	250 to 500
Very High	160 to 200
High	100 to 125
Medium	63 to 80
Low	50 or Below

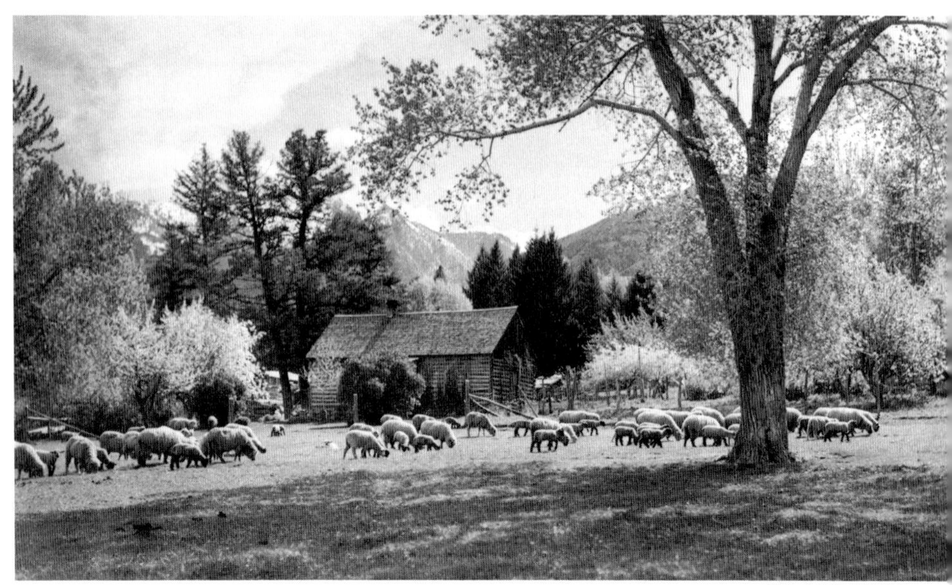

JOHN C. HABERSTROH

This picture shows excellent definition.

Sharpness. The sharpness of a film is the visual impression of good edge sharpness between details in a photograph. The boundary between detail that is dark in a photograph and detail that is light is not a perfectly sharp line. The dark area in the negative tends to bleed over into the light area because of light scatter or diffusion in the emulsion. This effect varies with different types of emulsions, the thickness of the emulsion, and the thickness of the film base, as well as the antihalation properties of the base and its backing. Kodak films have thin emulsion coatings and very efficient antihalation properties, and as a result they produce sharper pictures than many of the older films.

Sharpness measurements are made by the manufacturer. The procedure is a complex one beyond the scope of this book; but briefly, a sine-wave test pattern of varying frequencies is photographed. The test pattern recorded on the film is scanned by sensitive measuring equipment. Then the data is plotted graphically and is analyzed to determine the sharpness classification. Kodak films in the Data Sheets have been placed in one of the following sharpness classifications: *Extremely High, Very High, High, Medium, Moderately Low,* or *Low*.

The sharpness of some films can be enhanced when you develop them in certain developers that have been diluted. Some diluted developers produce edge effects that make boundaries between objects appear sharper. Development recommendations for those films that will produce improved sharpness with diluted developers are given in the Data Sheets.

Degree of Enlargement. Graininess, resolving power, and sharpness have a combined influence on definition. However, under certain conditions, any one of these may be more important than the others in controlling the definition of a photograph.

When a negative made on a coarse-grain film is enlarged, graininess usually increases to an objectionable level.

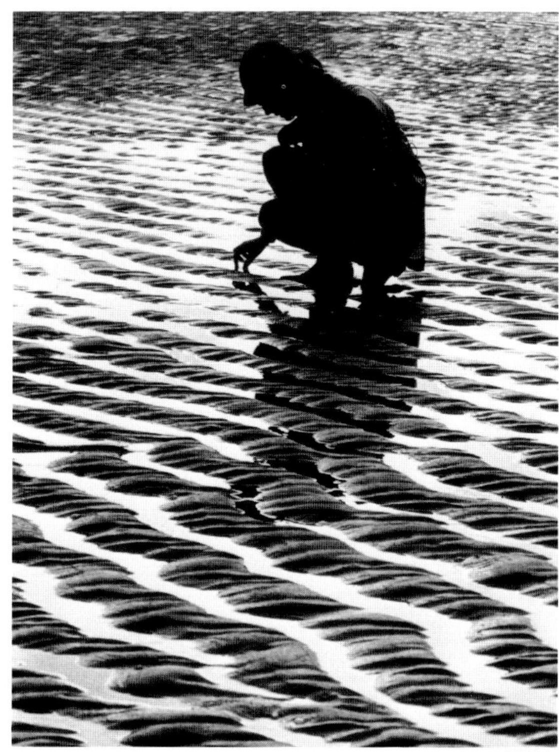

In addition to sharp camera focus, one of the most important factors in obtaining high definition is to hold your camera steady while you press the shutter release. PLUS-X Pan Film, 1/60 sec *f*/4.

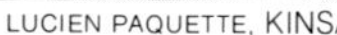

LUCIEN PAQUETTE, KINSA

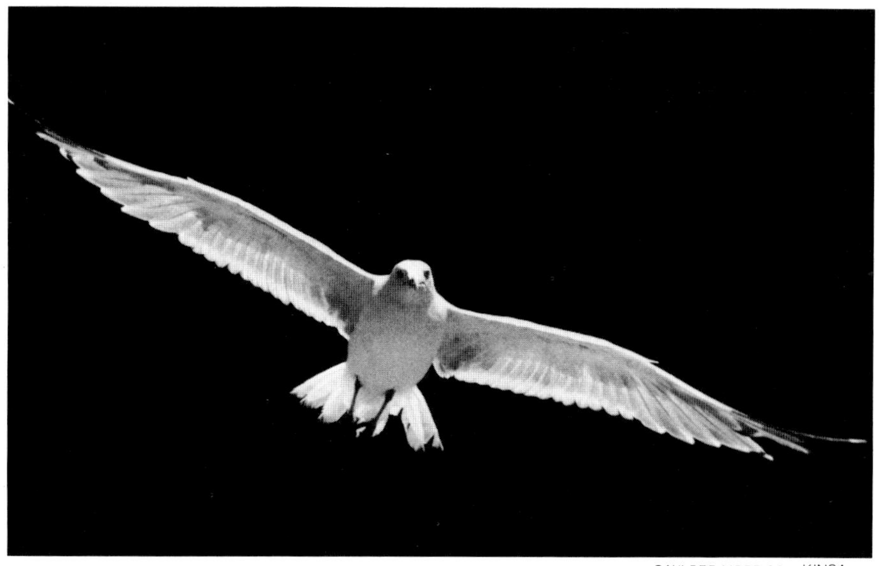

GAYLORD MORRISON, KINSA

For high definition in action pictures, you have to use high shutter speeds to freeze the action. This is especially important when you use a telephoto lens which magnifies both the image and the blur from subject motion. PLUS-X Pan Film, 1/1000 sec *f*/5.6.

before the loss of resolution or sharpness becomes unacceptable. In this situation, then, graininess is the limiting factor in definition.

While the resolving power and the sharpness of the film are related, resolving power alone is not a definite indication of ability to produce sharp pictures. In some cases it may be misleading. When viewing a picture at normal reading distance and under the best conditions, the normal eye can resolve about 10 lines per millimeter. If the resolving power of the film is too low to reproduce details about twice as fine as this in the print, definition will be limited by the resolving power. However, when resolving power is adequate and graininess is not noticeable, the sharpness of the image is the most important factor affecting definition. All these factors were taken into consideration in assigning the "Degree of Enlargement Allowed" for each negative film in the Data Sheets.

TIPS FOR GOOD DEFINITION

When a photographer takes pictures, processes the film, and makes prints, the definition may be limited not by the film characteristics but by the way the photographer handles the equipment and materials. In order to realize the maximum definition the film is capable of producing, observe the following tips:

Picture-Taking Tips

1. Use a high-quality camera lens and make sure it's clean and free of dust and fingerprints.
2. Focus carefully, preferably with an accurate rangefinder or ground glass. If your camera doesn't have either of these, estimate the distance as accurately as you can. For close-up pictures, use a tape measure if your camera does not have ground-glass focusing.
3. When you want sharp images of both near and distant objects in the same picture, consult the depth-of-field scale on your camera or a depth-of-field table in your camera manual for the best focus setting and lens opening to use. Most lenses produce the best definition at a lens opening about midway on the lens-opening scale.
4. Hold your camera steady and squeeze the shutter release slowly. When you can, use a shutter speed of 1/125 second or higher to minimize the effects of camera movement. For maximum steadiness, place your camera on a tripod or other firm support and use a cable release to trip the shutter. For shutter speeds slower than 1/30 second, a tripod or other support is a necessity for sharp pictures.
5. Expose correctly; avoid overexposure and overdevelopment, either of which will produce negatives that are too dense, or dark. Excessive density causes a loss of definition and increased graininess. Use the minimum amount of exposure that will produce an excellent print with good shadow detail. Develop your film using the recommended developer, time, temperature, and agitation.

Print-Making Tips

1. Use a high-quality enlarger lens and check it for cleanliness.
2. If definition is of utmost importance, use a smooth-surface printing paper, such as glossy or smooth lustre.
3. Choose the grade of black-and-white printing paper that will give you a good print from your negative without either excessive or insufficient contrast.
4. When you make enlargements, be sure that your enlarger is free of

vibration and the image is sharply focused on your printing paper.

5. Use the recommended safelight filter and bulb at the proper distance.

RECIPROCITY CHARACTERISTICS

Reciprocity effects are less serious with Kodak black-and-white films for general use than for Kodak color films. You don't have to be concerned with shifts in color balance with black-and-white film. However, film speed and contrast of black-and-white films change when you use long or very short exposure times rather than the typical exposure times used in general picture-taking.

Reciprocity characteristics for black-and-white films are given on page D 41 in the Data Sheets. Reciprocity characteristics are described more fully on page 50.

FLASH PICTURES WITH BLACK-AND-WHITE FILM

You can use electronic flash, blue flashbulbs, or clear flashbulbs for flash pictures with black-and-white film. Guide numbers for electronic flash and blue flashbulbs are given on the Data Sheets in this book. It's more convenient to use blue flashbulbs since they're recommended for both black-and-white and color film. Then you don't have to buy two different kinds of flashbulbs if you switch from black-and-white to color. However, if you prefer to use clear flashbulbs, simply multiply the guide numbers for blue flashbulbs by 1.25 to obtain the proper guide numbers.

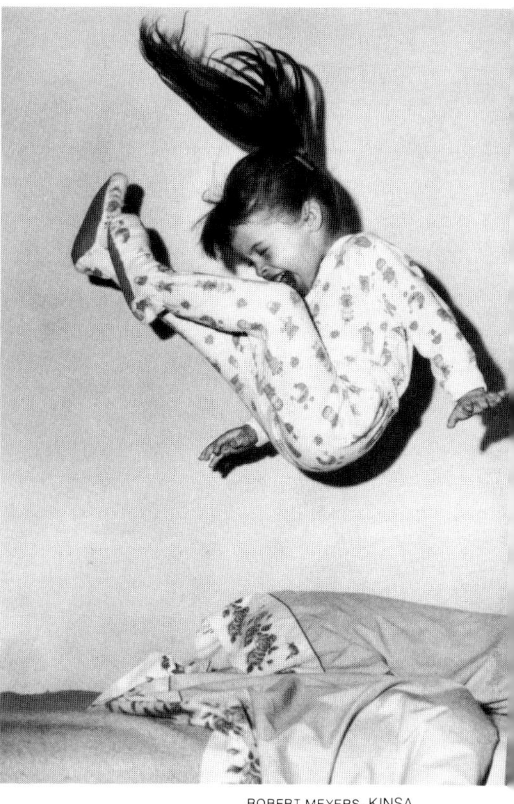

ROBERT MEYERS, KINSA

Electronic flash effectively stopped the action in this picture made on PLUS-X Pan Film.

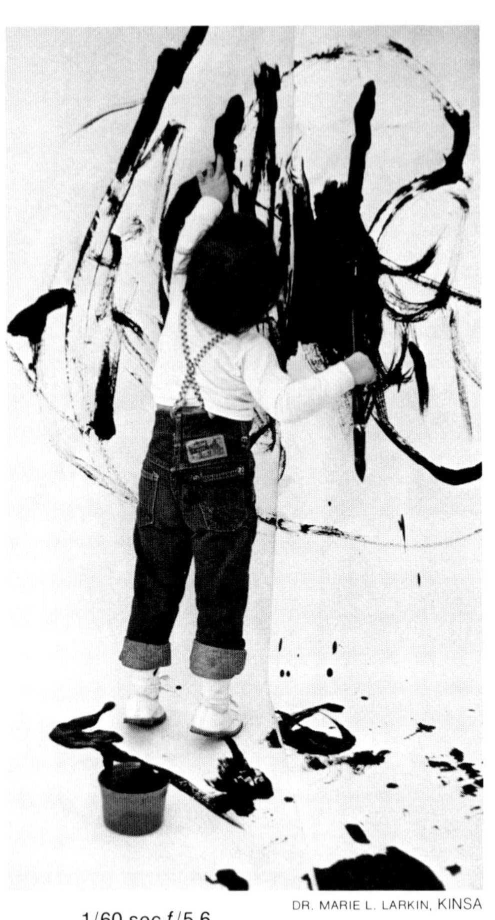

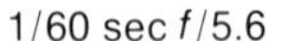
1/60 sec f/5.6 DR. MARIE L. LARKIN, KINSA

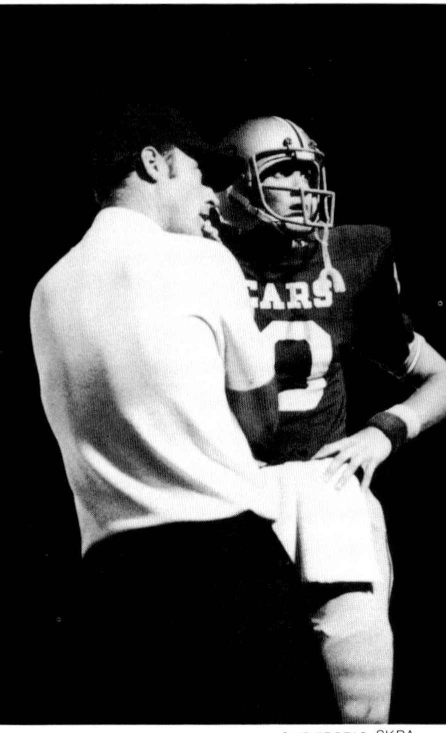

1/125 sec f/1.4 SKIP EROTAS, SKPA

Since the light levels are often low in existing-light photography, you have much more versatility with a high-speed film. KODAK TRI-X Pan Film.

FILMS FOR EXISTING-LIGHT PHOTOGRAPHY

The primary requirements in choosing a film for photographing existing-light subjects are high speed and good quality. KODAK TRI-X Pan Film has these features; it's an ideal film for existing-light photography. If you're photographing subjects in relatively bright existing light, such as existing daylight indoors, or if you don't mind putting your camera on a tripod for subjects in very dim light, you can use a film with a slower speed, such as KODAK VERICHROME Pan Film or PLUS-X Pan Film.

If the lighting is extremely poor, or if you want to photograph action in existing light or use telephoto lenses, you may need a film even faster than TRI-X Pan Film. For 120-size cameras you can use KODAK ROYAL-X Pan Film; for 35 mm cameras, you can use KODAK Recording Film 2475 (ESTAR-AH Base). Since Recording Film 2475 is so fast and 35 mm negatives are small, prints made from this film have coarse grain. But if you need the extremely high film speed, you may find the results acceptable. ROYAL-X Pan Film has medium grain and produces good quality prints.

FILMS FOR COPYING

For photographing continuous-tone originals—for example, photographs, paintings, or pictures in magazines or books—use one of the films recommended for general picture-taking, such as VERICHROME Pan or PLUS-X Pan Film. The speed of these films is ample for originals lighted by photolamps. If the lighting is dim, such as the existing lighting in an art gallery, a better choice would be high-speed TRI-X Pan Film. However, when you can put your camera on a tripod or other firm support, a high-speed film is unnecessary.

If you want to copy printed matter, such as the text portion of documents, magazines, or newspapers, you'll get better results with a high-contrast film specially designed for this work. Copies of printed matter made on KODAK High Contrast Copy Film 5069 will have a cleaner, whiter background and will look more like the original than copies made on conventional films.

PROCESSING

After you have exposed an entire roll of film, you should have it processed promptly for best results. It's easier and more convenient to take your film to your photo dealer for developing and printing. But when you do your own darkroom work, you'll find it's a lot of fun—and a rewarding and interesting extension of your photo hobby as well. You have much more control over the results when you process the film yourself and make your own prints.

To process the film, we recommend that you use a film tank. Several different kinds are available from your photo dealer. Be sure that the one you select will accept the size of your film.

Loading your film into the developing tank requires TOTAL DARKNESS.

To open **135 magazines,** hold the magazine with the long end of the spool down, and use a lid lifter or a hook-type bottle opener to remove the upper end cap from the magazine. Pull the loaded spool out of the magazine, taking care not to let the film unwind. The film is attached to the magazine spool with a strip of tape. Separate the film from the spool. Load the film-tank reel according to the film-tank instructions.

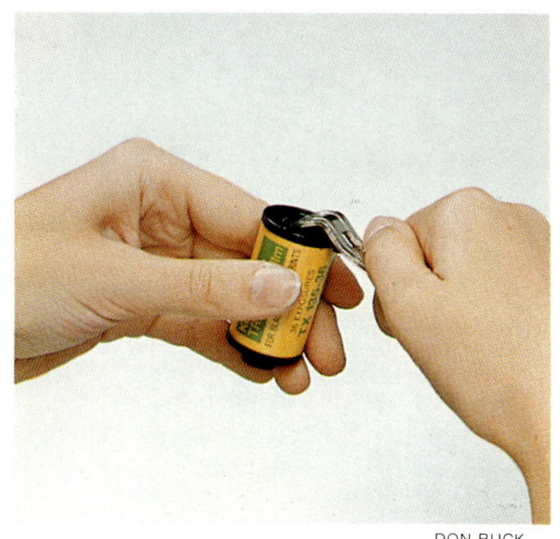
DON BUCK

To process your own 135 film, open the magazine in TOTAL DARKNESS. Hold the magazine with the long end of the spool down, and use a lid lifter or a hook-type bottle opener to remove the upper end cap from the magazine.

To break open an exposed **110 or 126 cartridge,** hold it with the label facing you and your thumbs on the label. Use both hands to bend the two cylindrical chambers toward the label. If it's a 110 cartridge, pull the film, together with its backing paper, from the take-up chamber in a direction so that the *paper* rubs against the inner surface of the cartridge back. This minimizes the likelihood of scratching the film emulsion. If the end of the backing paper (trailer) has been wound into the take-up chamber, you will have to pry open the chamber (after breaking the cartridge) to retrieve the film.

After breaking open a 126 cartridge, remove the film spool from the larger

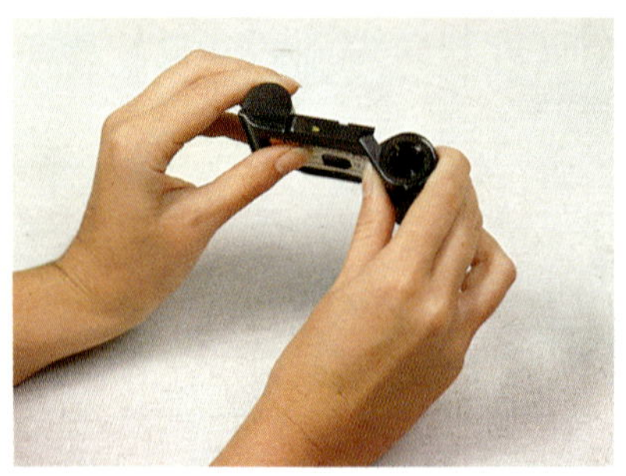

To open a 126 or 110 cartridge for processing, break open the cartridge in TOTAL DARKNESS by bending the cylindrical chambers toward the label.

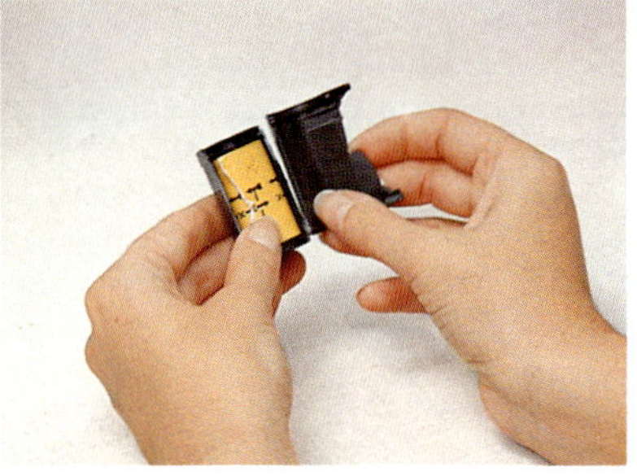

To remove the film after you've opened a 126 cartridge, separate the plastic sections surrounding the spool. If it's a 110 cartridge, pull the paper backing out of the broken cartridge in a direction so that the paper rubs against the cartridge. The film will come out along with the backing paper. Handle the film by the edges only.

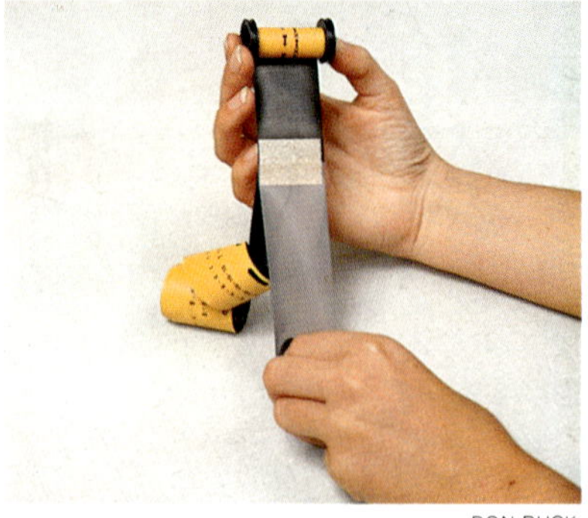

DON BUCK

The film in 126 cartridges is attached to the paper backing with a strip of tape. Detach the film and discard the paper and tape. Handle the film by the edges only.

chamber by separating the plastic sections surrounding the spool. Unroll the film and the paper backing. The film is attached to the paper backing in the same way as roll film.

Rip the "Exposed" sticker on **roll film** and carefully unroll and separate the film from the paper backing. Be careful not to cinch or scratch the film. The film is attached to the paper with a strip of tape at the end near the core of the film spool.

PROCESSING RECOMMENDATIONS

Develop your film for the time given in the development table in the Data Sheet for the film you're using. Be sure to use the recommended agitation procedure. See "Tips on Using Film Developing Tanks."

The developing times given in the Data Sheets for Kodak black-and-white films are for small roll-film tanks. A small tank is defined as one in which the agitation is produced by moving the tank or the reel inside when the reel has a handle. A small tank is for processing roll film of conventional length and size, such as 135, 126, 110, 120, 127, and 620 sizes, with the film held in a reel or apron. The reels are not used in a rack, basket, or on a spindle. The solution volume of a small tank is usually 1 quart (about 1 litre) or less.

Rinse in KODAK Indicator Stop Bath or KODAK Stop Bath SB-5 at 65 to 75°F (18 to 24°C) for about 30 seconds with agitation. With most films you can use a water rinse if an acid stop bath is not available. However, an acid stop bath is better because it stops development instantly by neutralizing the developer. See the Data Sheet for your film.

Fix in KODAK Fixer, KODAK Fixing Bath F-5, KODAK Rapid Fixer, or KODAFIX

Solution at 65 to 75°F (18 to 24°C). *Agitate films frequently during fixing.* See the Data Sheet for your film for the recommended fixing time.

Wash for 20 to 30 minutes in running water at 65 to 75°F (18 to 24°C). After washing, to minimize drying marks, treat in diluted KODAK PHOTO-FLO Solution for 30 seconds, or wipe surfaces carefully with a KODAK Photo Chamois or a soft viscose sponge.

You can use KODAK Hypo Clearing Agent after fixing to reduce washing time and conserve water. First remove excess fixer, or hypo, by rinsing the film in water for 30 seconds. Then bathe the film in KODAK Hypo Clearing Agent solution for 1 to 2 minutes, with moderate agitation. Then wash it for 5 minutes in running water, using a water flow sufficient to fill the washing container in 5 minutes.

You'll obtain the best results when you keep the temperatures of the rinse, fix, and wash approximately the same as the developer temperature.

Dry in a dustfree place.

TIPS ON USING FILM DEVELOPING TANKS

In the dark (see safelight recommendations on the Data Sheets), start the timer and place the loaded film reel or apron into your tank containing the developer. Keep the reel or apron under the surface of the solution, and tap it on the bottom of the tank before you replace the tank cover. This helps dislodge air bells. After you replace the cover, you can carry out the remaining steps in normal room light.

If this procedure is not possible with your tank, begin the process by pouring in the developer with the reel of film inside the tank. Tap the bottom of the tank against the working surface to dislodge air bells.

Recommended Agitation

Proper agitation is as important as the correct temperature and development time. Too little agitation during development will cause mottle and uneven development. Too much agitation can cause overdevelopment and streaks on the film. When you follow the recommended agitation procedures, you'll avoid these undesirable effects.

Methods of Agitation. After the film has been immersed for 30 seconds, agitate the tank for 5 seconds according to the method recommended below for your tank. Repeat this agitation at intervals of 30 seconds for the remainder of the development time.

1. For a tank that can't be inverted, agitate by sliding the tank back and forth over a distance of about 10 inches at a rate of two cycles per second during the agitation intervals. At the same time, turn or rotate the tank back and forth through about one-half turn (see below).

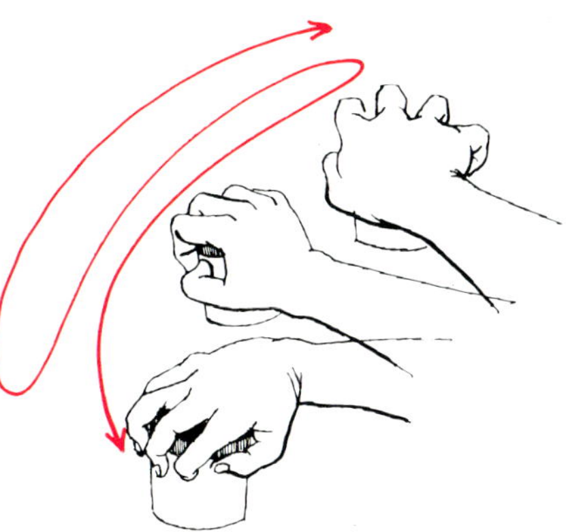

The recommended method of agitation for a film tank that can't be inverted.

2. For tanks that you can turn upside down without spilling the solution, invert the tank once per second during the 5-second agitation intervals.

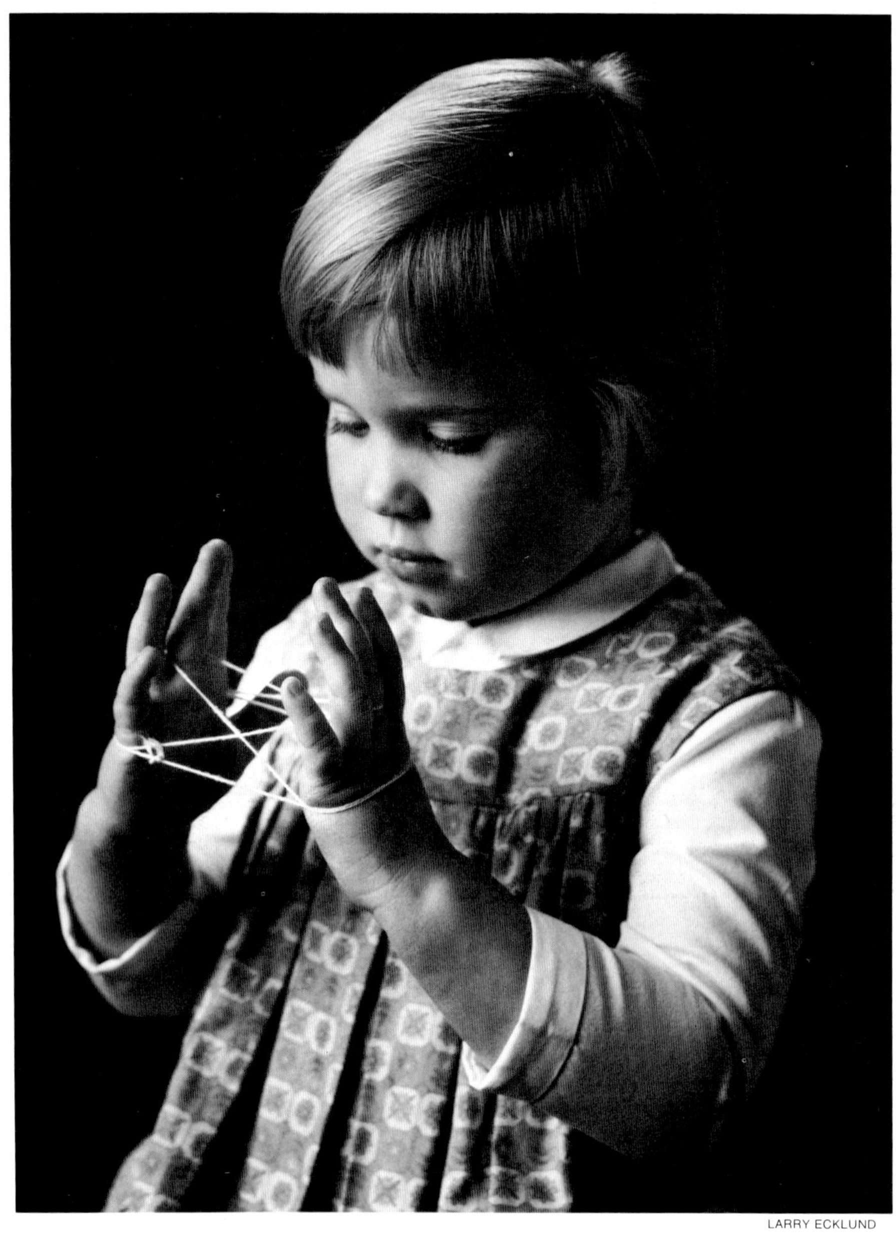

LARRY ECKLUND

In this picture, detail has been retained in both highlights and shadows for good tone rendition—the result of normal exposure and normal development of the film.

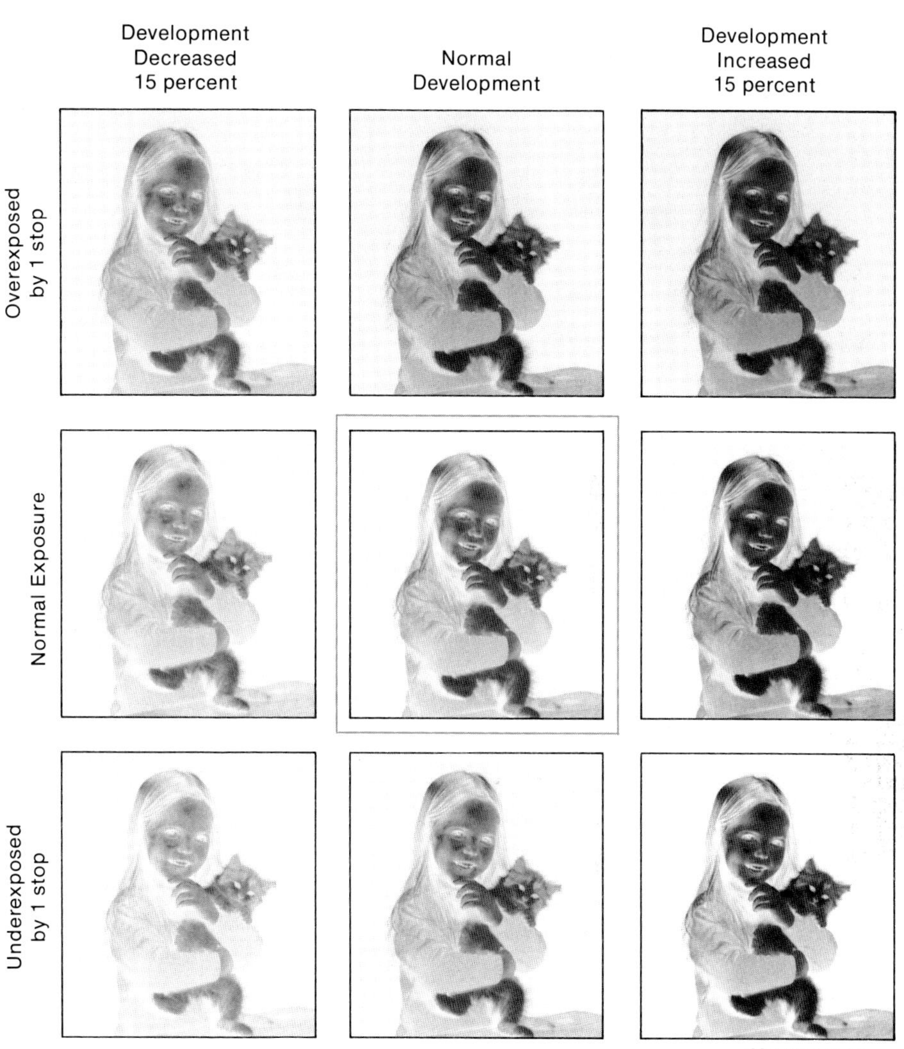

These negatives show the results of changing the camera exposure and the degree of development. The negative in the center received normal exposure and normal development.

These illustrations were made from negative print images for technical reasons. However, each negative print was matched as closely as possible to actual negatives exposed and processed as indicated.

3. With tanks that have a handle for turning the reel, rotate the reel back and forth gently through about one-half turn at a rate of one cycle per second during the agitation intervals.

If the method of agitation described in the instructions for your film tank differs from these, agitate the film for 5 seconds at 30-second intervals according to the method recommended in the tank instructions.

DEGREE OF DEVELOPMENT

The degree to which you develop your film has an important effect on the quality of your finished pictures. Development determines to a large extent the contrast grade of photographic paper you'll need to make the best possible prints from your negatives. The degree of development for a film and developer combination depends on the developing time, the temperature of the developer, and the degree of agitation. Underdevelopment reduces the contrast of the negative and can cause loss of shadow detail. Overdevelopment increases negative contrast and graininess, reduces sharpness, and can block up highlights, making the negatives hard to print. Negatives that have received correct exposure and development should print best on contrast grade No. 2 or No. 3 photographic paper. The development recommendations given in the Data Sheets will produce the proper contrast in prints made with average printing conditions from properly exposed negatives of average subjects.

Since the degree of development depends on time and temperature, several normal development times are given to compensate for changes in temperature. See the development tables in the Data Sheets.

Contrast Index

The degree of development, or development contrast, is specified by contrast-index measurements. Most of the recommended development times given in the Data Sheets are based on a normal contrast index of 0.56. Under average conditions, properly exposed negatives processed to this contrast index should print on medium-contrast photographic paper. If your negatives are consistently too contrasty and require low-contrast paper such as grade No. 1, develop to a lower contrast by reducing development time by about 30 percent. If your negatives are consistently too low in contrast and print on high-contrast paper, such as grade No. 4, develop to a higher contrast by increasing the development time by about 40 percent.

To produce negatives consistent in overall density and quality, you should make an exposure compensation when you adjust development times, particularly with shorter development times. When reducing development times, increase exposure by about ⅓ stop. When increasing development times, reduce exposure by about ⅓ stop.

The effective printing contrast of your negatives is affected by the method you use in making prints. A diffusion-type enlarger produces about the same degree of contrast in the print as a contact printer. A condenser enlarger produces greater contrast than a diffusion enlarger or a contact printer. The difference in contrast may be as much as the contrast difference between No. 2 and No. 3 grades of photographic paper. Complete information on printing papers is given in the book *KODAK B/W Photographic Papers* (G-1), $3.50. If you want to know more about enlarging techniques, a good book on this subject is *Bigger and Better Enlarging* (AG-19), $10.95. Both of these Kodak books are sold by photo dealers.

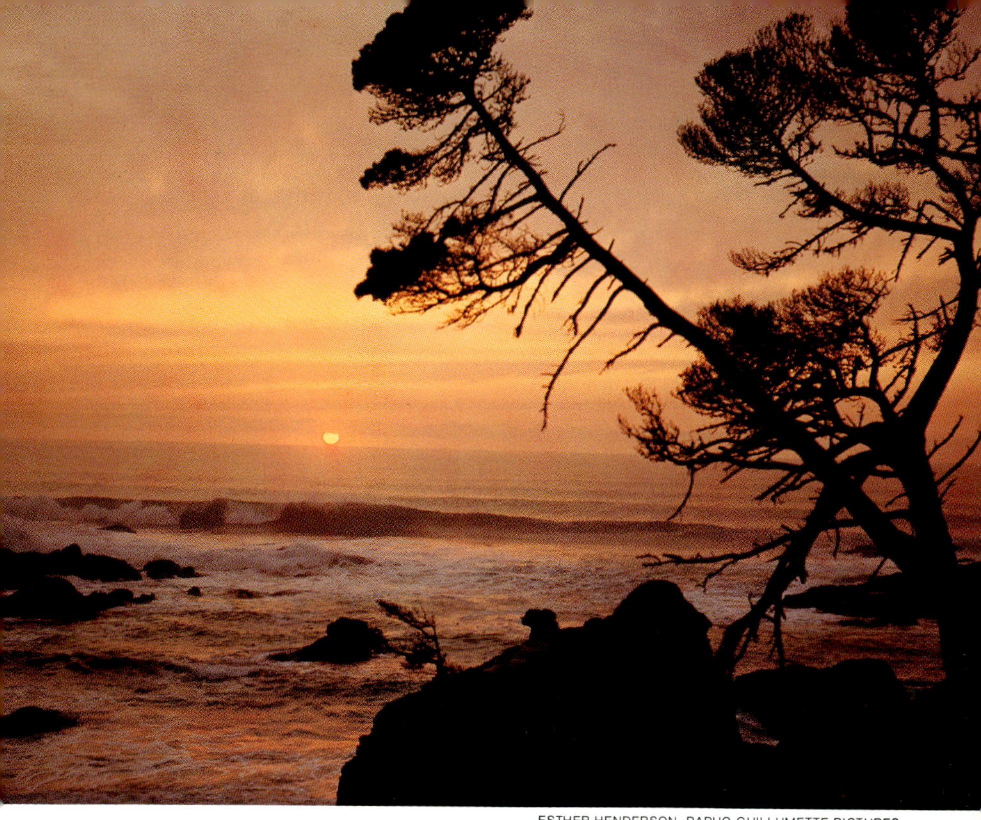

ESTHER HENDERSON, RAPHO GUILLUMETTE PICTURES

Exposure

To determine correct exposure, you need to know the speed of the film you're using. The film speeds in this book are for use with exposure meters or cameras with built-in meters marked for ASA speeds or Exposure Indexes.

Film speed indicates relative sensitivity to light. Film with a high speed number is more light-sensitive, or faster, than a film with a low number. For example, a film with a speed of ASA 200 is twice as fast as a film with a speed of ASA 100. The film speed for each Kodak film is given in the Data Sheets and on the instruction sheet packaged with the film or on the film carton.

If your exposure meter or camera with a built-in meter is marked with a different scale of film-speed numbers, you can convert ASA speeds to the film-speed numbers used on your meter. For example, some exposure meters and cameras manufactured outside the United States use the DIN system. Write to the manufacturer or American distributor of your equipment for a list which converts ASA speeds to the film-speed numbers used on your meter. You can also obtain the KODAK Customer Service Pamphlet *Equivalent Exposure Meter Settings* (AF-18), which gives equivalent ASA, BSI, early

Weston, DIN, and Scheiner film-speed numbers. See your photo dealer for a copy, or write to Kodak at the address given on page 51.

Many of the simpler cameras, such as some of those that take either 110-size or 126-size film, are not designed for use with high-speed film and will not expose it properly. For example, many older 110-size cameras are not designed for use with KODACOLOR 400 Film, and many 126-size cameras are not designed for use with KODAK EKTACHROME 200 Film (Daylight). Read the instruction manual for your camera or write to the manufacturer or the American distributor of your camera to see if you can use such films in your camera.

EXPOSURE LATITUDE

The exposure latitude of a film is the range of camera exposures from underexposure to overexposure which will produce pictures of acceptable quality with that particular film. In other words, exposure latitude is the amount you can be off from the ideal exposure and still get acceptable pictures. Exposure latitude depends mainly on the film you're using, the subject brightness range, and your own requirements for picture quality.

Continuous-tone negative films have greater exposure latitude than slide, or reversal, films. However, you obtain the best quality with any film when your pictures are properly exposed.

Film speeds and exposure guides for Kodak negative films are based on the minimum exposure required to record important shadow detail. Because of the latitude of negative films, slight variations in exposure produce no loss of image quality. Generally, negative films have greater latitude for overexposure than they do for underexposure.

Film speeds and recommended exposures for Kodak color-slide films and black-and-white slide films are based upon the exposure that produces the best picture when highlight detail and shadow detail are of equal importance. Slide, or reversal, films have higher contrast than most negative films. In addition, no corrections can be made after you take pictures because no printing step is used. As a result, camera exposure is more critical with reversal films than with continuous-tone negative films. Since reversal films have limited exposure latitude, carefully follow the exposure guides or your exposure-meter readings unless results with your equipment consistently indicate the need for an adjustment in the indicated exposure.

EXPOSURE GUIDES

Kodak provides exposure tables and dial exposure guides which are based on many practical picture tests and extensive data on illumination, subject brightness, film speed, and print-making requirements. The exposure recommendations have been confirmed by years of experience. For any picture-taking situation specifically covered by a Kodak exposure guide, the camera settings indicated by the guide will produce a high percentage of properly exposed photographs.

The *KODAK Master Photoguide* (AR-21) contains dial exposure calculators covering the use of daylight, flash, photolamps, and existing light with a variety of Kodak films. The text includes information on lighting techniques, filter selection, depth of field, and other essentials. This guide is sold by photo dealers.

Exposure tables are provided in the Data Sheets in this book, in the instruction sheets packaged with Kodak films, and in many Kodak publications.

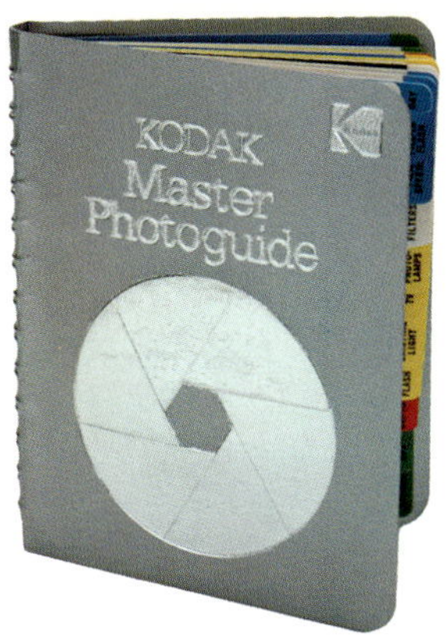

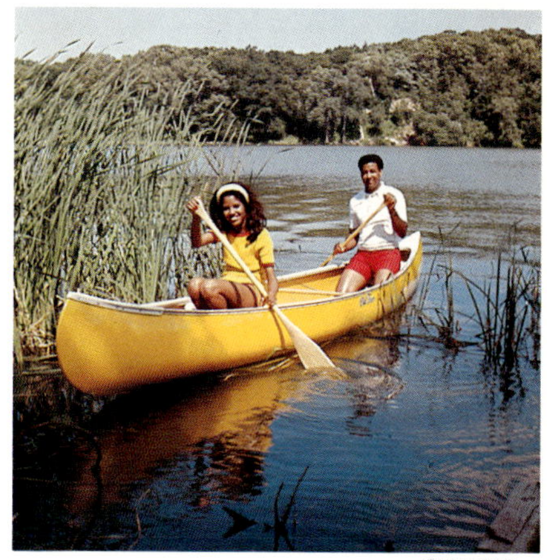

JOHN HOOD

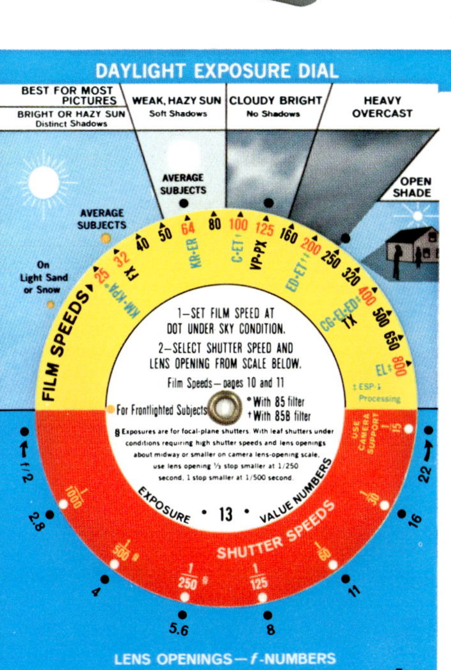

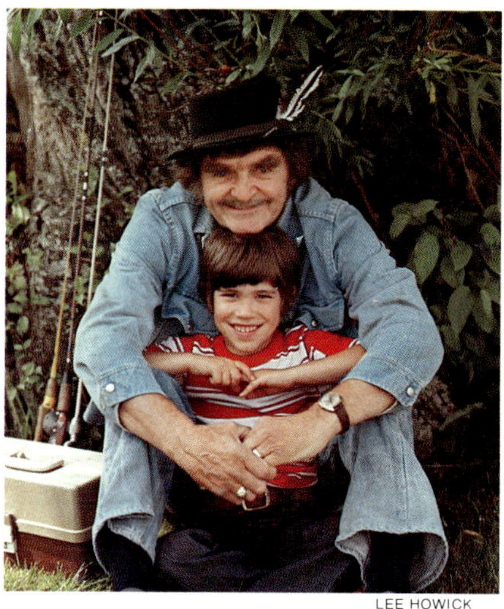

LEE HOWICK

For average scenes such as these, it's a simple matter to determine the correct camera settings. Just make an overall meter reading from the camera position.

You can obtain a high percentage of properly exposed pictures by following exposure guides. This Daylight Exposure Dial is from the *KODAK Master Photoguide* (AR-21), $5.75, available from photo dealers.

EXPOSURE METERS

The big plus of owning an exposure meter or a camera with a built-in exposure meter is that you can determine exposure for almost any kind of scene and lighting situation. If you use your exposure meter according to the procedures recommended by the meter or camera manufacturer, you should get an extremely high percentage of properly exposed pictures.

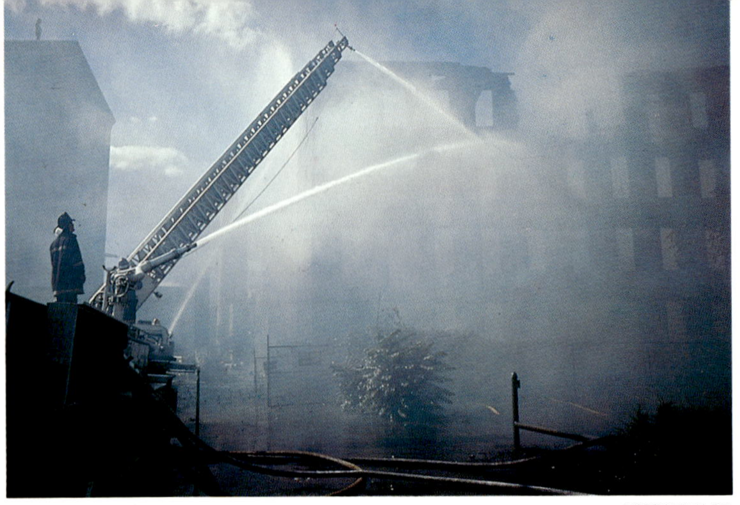

MARTIN TAYLOR

An exposure meter is invaluable when the lighting or atmospheric conditions are unusual. KODACHROME 25 Film (Daylight), 1/125 sec *f*/5.6.

However, an exposure meter doesn't think for itself. If you use your meter in a purely mechanical fashion, chances are that you will not get consistent results. Study your exposure-meter or camera instruction book and learn how to use your meter; familiarize yourself with the flexibility and limitations of the type of exposure meter you have. Then you can use this knowledge to interpret your meter readings and obtain a larger percentage of correctly exposed pictures.

Basically there are two types of exposure meters: reflected-light and incident-light. Some meters have attachments that let you measure either reflected light or incident light. A special kind of reflected-light meter is the spot meter. This kind of meter selectively reads the light reflected from one small area in a scene.

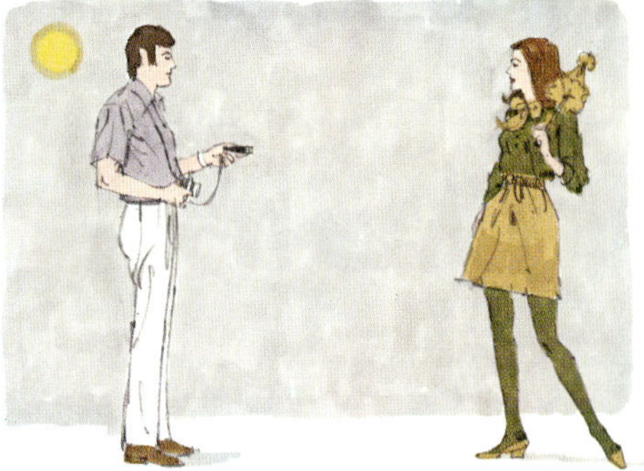

With a reflected-light exposure meter, you point the meter toward the subject to determine the correct exposure.

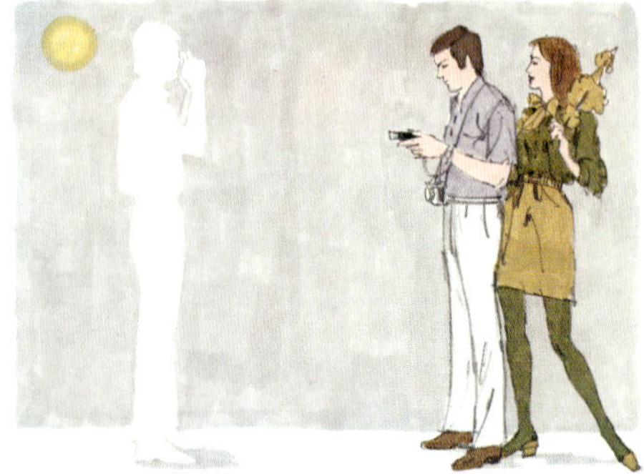

With an incident-light exposure meter, you point the meter toward the camera position to make the reading.

REFLECTED-LIGHT METERS

A reflected-light exposure meter measures the light reflected from all the areas included in the meter field of view. One of the main advantages of a reflected-light meter is that you can make the meter reading from the camera position for most scenes. Because the meter is designed to average the overall light reflected from scenes with normal reflectance characteristics, it gives correct exposure for most pictures.

Since the exposure meters built into cameras are reflected-light meters, you can aim and use the meter from the camera position when you are ready to take the picture. (A few built-in exposure meters in still cameras also have incident-light attachments.) Some cameras are automatic; that is, you don't have to be concerned with exposure because the built-in exposure meter makes the reading and sets the exposure for you automatically. Built-in exposure meters give very good results for most scenes.

However, for some scenes an overall exposure-meter reading will result in incorrect exposure. When you make an overall meter reading from the camera position, your exposure meter is influenced by a predominant light or dark area in the scene. Your exposure meter, though, has no way of knowing what part of the scene is the most important part of your picture. If the scene has light and dark areas of about equal distribution and importance, or if a large light area or a large dark area is the most important part of the picture, your exposure meter will usually indicate the correct exposure. On the other hand, if the most important part of the picture is surrounded by a large area which is much lighter or darker, your meter will indicate an exposure which is incorrect for the important part. The way to determine the correct exposure in such situations is to make a selective meter reading of the principal subject. For example, a close-up reading of the subject will exclude unimportant light or dark surroundings in the scene that can mislead your exposure meter. In making close-up readings, be careful not to

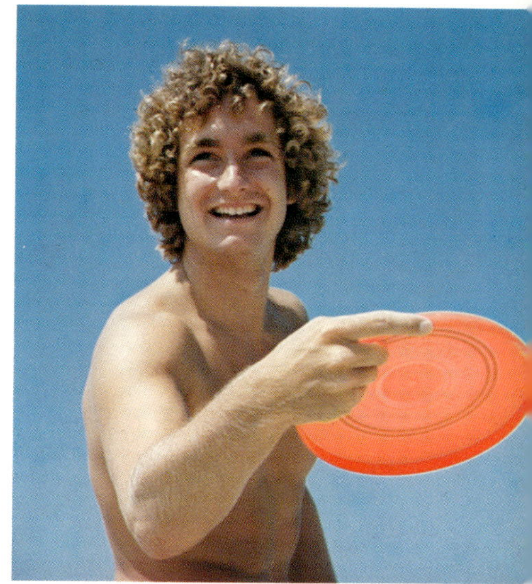

PETE CULROSS

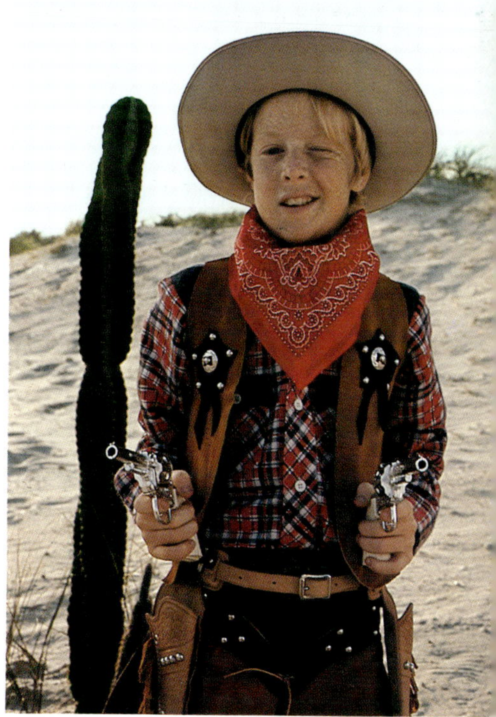

RONALD DE MILT

When there is a lot of sky in the background, make a close-up reading of your subject with a reflected-light meter.

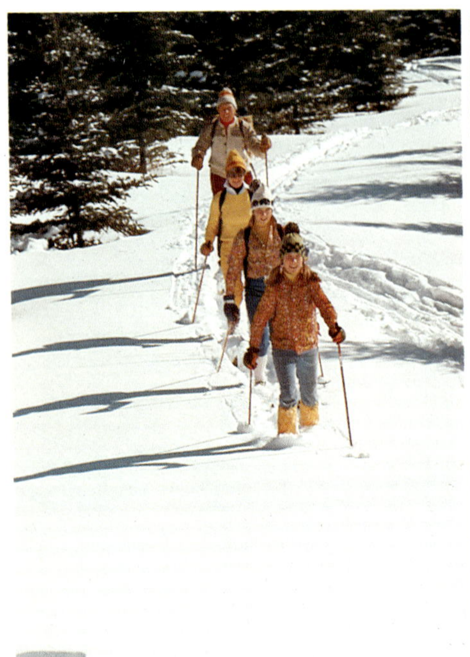

NORM KERR

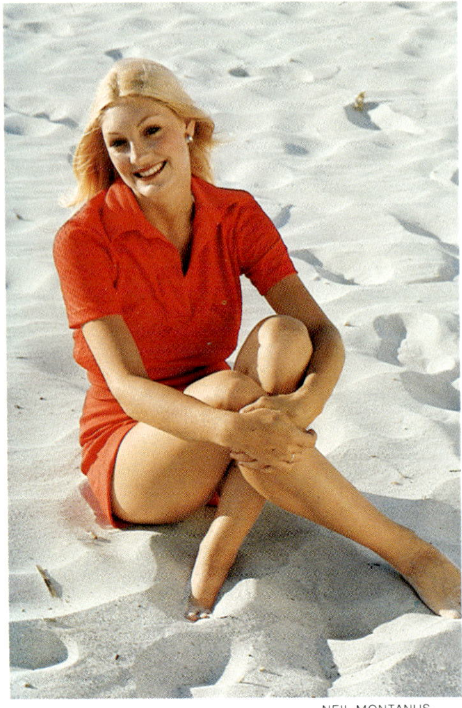

NEIL MONTANUS

A light background, such as bright sand or snow, with average or dark subjects can fool a reflected-light meter. A reading made from the camera position will be too high and the subjects will be underexposed. For correct exposure, make a close-up meter reading of the subjects.

measure your shadow or the shadow from the meter or the camera.

Here are some examples of scenes that require selective meter readings to determine optimum exposure:

The most common situation that can mislead reflected-light meters is a scene that includes a large portion of the sky. The sky is brighter than the other parts of the scene with average reflectance. Therefore, the meter may be overly influenced by the sky and will indicate too little exposure, causing underexposure of the subject. This effect is even greater on overcast days when the sky is whitish. Some manufacturers of reflected-light meters recommend that you tilt the meter downward at a slight angle to avoid undue influence from the sky. Most cameras with built-in exposure meters have interior baffles or other devices to reduce the influence of the sky brightness. It's usually not necessary or practical to tilt cameras with built-in exposure meters downward to avoid the sky. Consult your camera instruction manual for the correct use of your camera exposure meter.

Scenes with large light areas such as snow, light sand, or white concrete may mislead the exposure meter when the most important part of the scene is much darker than the surroundings. This will result in underexposure of the subject. In these situations, take a close-up meter reading of the principal subject for proper exposure. When a large light area is the important part of

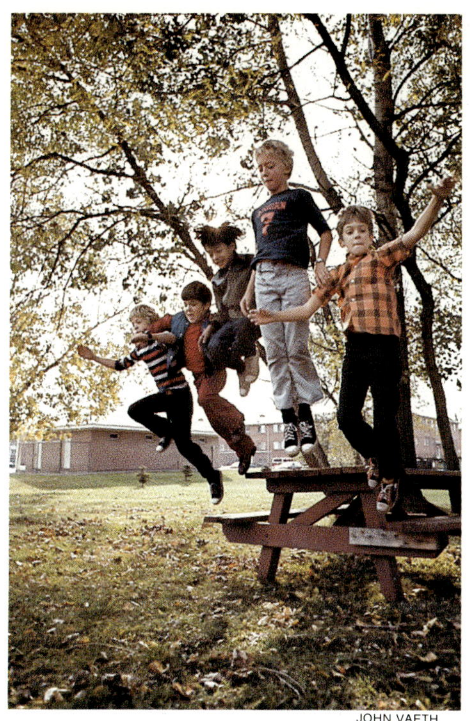

JOHN VAETH

KODACOLOR 400 Film, 1/500 sec f/5.6.

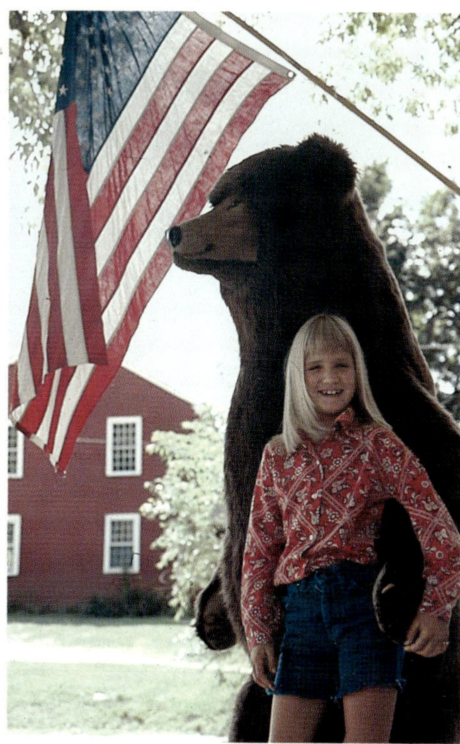

ROBERT KRETZER

KODACHROME 25 Film (Daylight), 1/30 sec f/4.

When subjects are in the shade with a sunlit background, a reflected-light meter reading made from the camera position would respond too much to the bright background so that shaded subjects would be underexposed.

the picture, such as a snow scene but not a close-up of a person, your reflected-light meter may be overly influenced by the bright snow, and the picture will be underexposed, with gray-looking snow. In a situation such as this, compare your meter reading with a Kodak exposure guide, such as the one on the film instruction sheet. If your meter reading indicates much less than the recommended exposure for snow scenes in the exposure guide, you'll probably get better results by following the exposure guide.

When the subject is much lighter than the surroundings, your exposure meter may indicate too much exposure, causing overexposure of the subject. An example is an outdoor scene with a bride in a white wedding dress standing in front of a dark foliage background. Because of the dark surroundings, your meter sees mostly the large dark area and therefore indicates an exposure that is too much for the subject. As a result, the subject is overexposed. Once again, take a close-up meter reading of the principal subject to determine the correct exposure.

In backlighted scenes the background is often sunlit and is therefore brighter than the subject. Also, light can shine directly into the light-sensitive meter cell. Both these factors cause a high meter reading and underexposure results. The solution is to take a close-up meter reading while shading the meter with your hand or some other object to

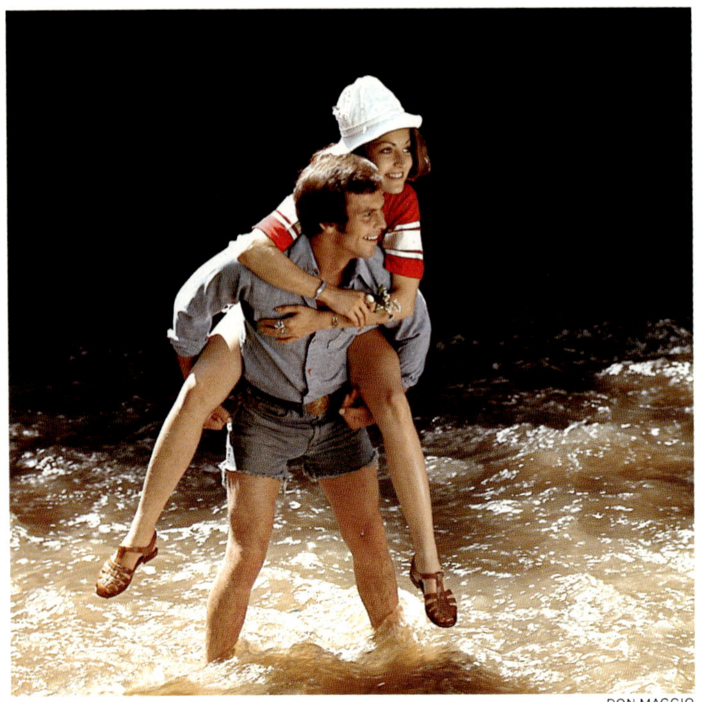

DON MAGGIO

A reflected-light meter reading made from the camera position would be too low because of the dark background, and the subject would be overexposed. A close-up meter reading will produce more accurate exposure.

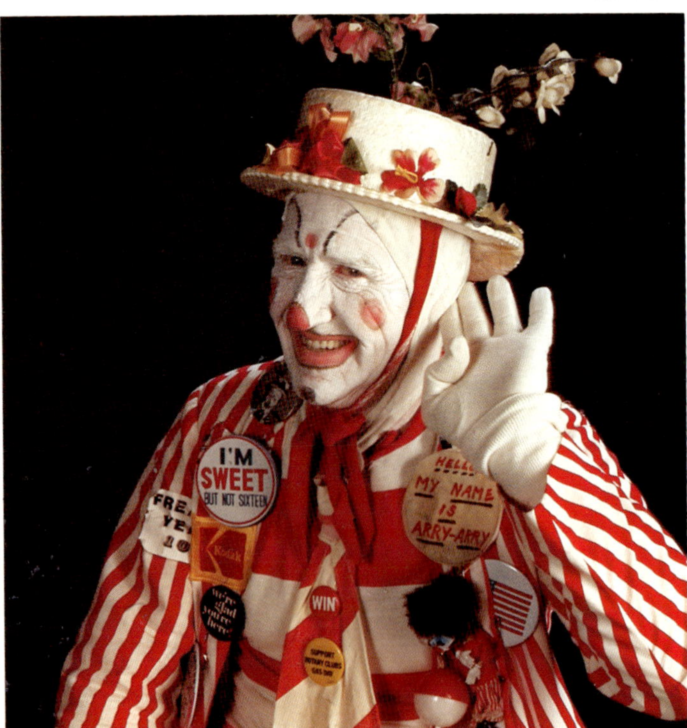

WALTER LEE

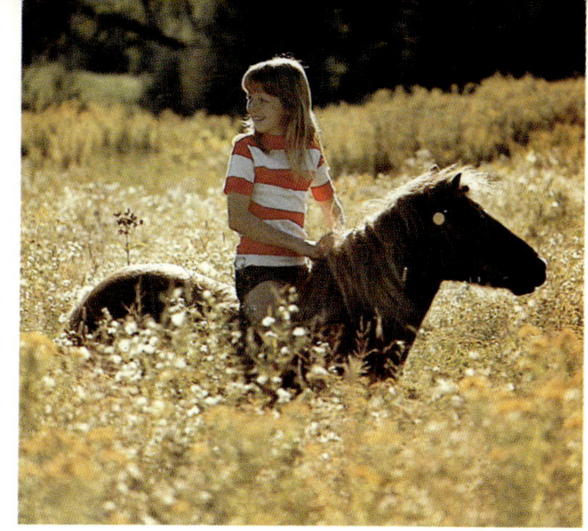

BOB CLEMENS

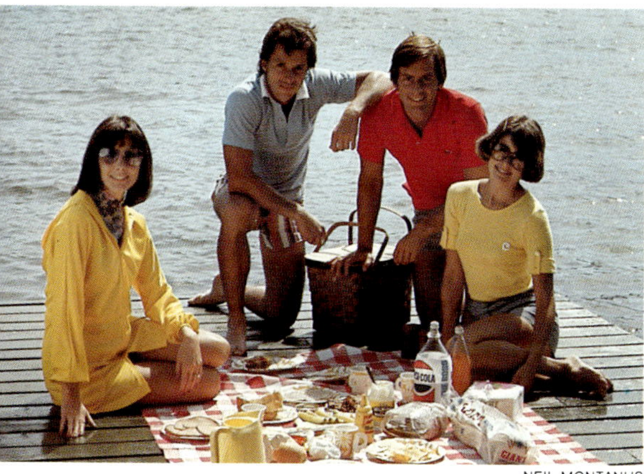

NEIL MONTANUS

In these backlighted scenes, a reflected-light exposure meter would be influenced by the bright background, and the sun might shine into the light-sensitive cell of the meter. Both of these factors would result in underexposure.

block the sun (or lights) that may be directly illuminating the meter cell.

You can make close-up meter readings with some built-in camera meters and then move back to take the picture. If you can't do this with your camera, you may be able to change the film-speed setting to a different number to compensate for unusual lighting or subject brightness. For photographing average or dark subjects in *very light* surroundings, divide the speed of your film by 2 and set the resulting *lower* number on the film-speed dial of your camera. For example, if you were using KODACHROME 64 Film in this type of situation, you would set 32 instead of 64 on the film-speed dial. For photographing average or light subjects in *very dark* surroundings, multiply the speed of your film by 2, and set the resulting *higher* number on your film-speed dial. Since operating procedures vary with different cameras, check your camera instruction manual for the recommended method to use with your built-in camera meter. Remember to reset your film-speed dial to the normal speed setting when you've finished photographing the unusual scene.

Spot meters selectively measure the reflected light of small areas in a scene from the camera position. These meters measure only the small area toward which they are pointed. Therefore, they are not influenced by large light or dark surrounding areas. This type of meter is useful for telephoto pictures, which

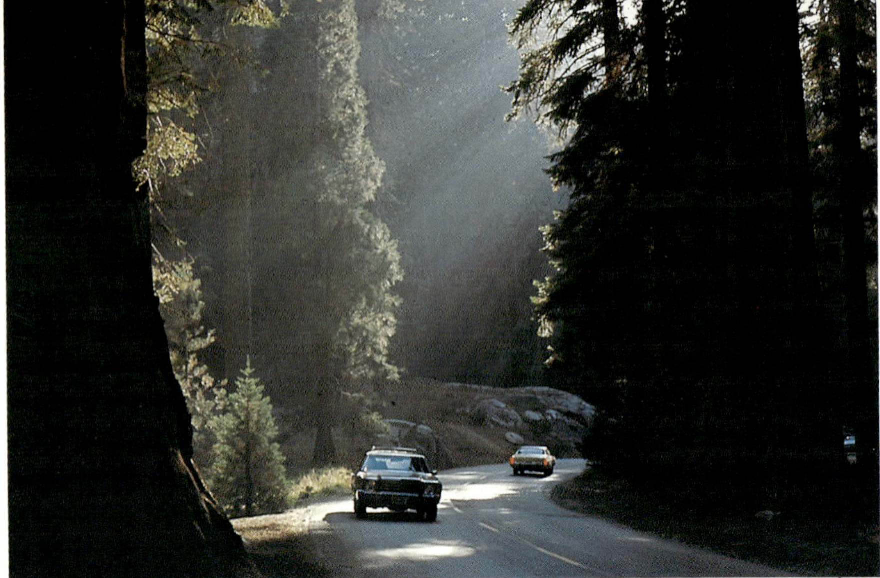

HERB JONES

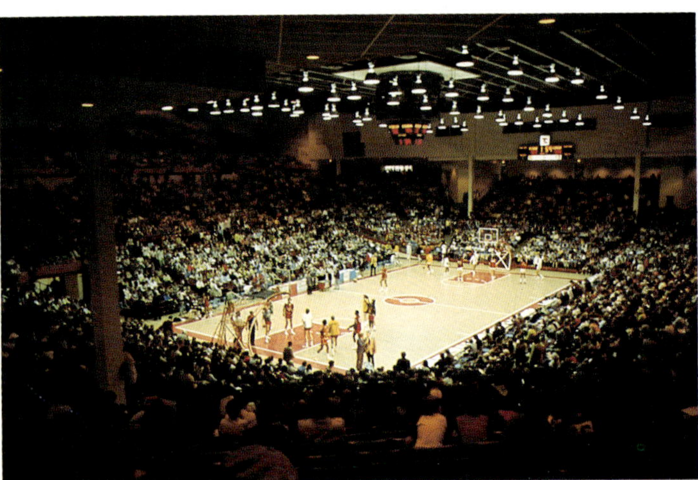

PETE CULROSS

Since a spot meter measures a small area to determine exposure, it would come in handy for pictures such as these. You could make the meter reading of the important areas of the scenes from the camera position.

include only a small portion of the overall scene, and for scenes with uneven lighting or reflectance. However, since a spot meter reads one small area at a time, you must decide which areas in the scene are important to your picture. This is especially true when you're taking pictures with a normal or wide-angle camera lens, which usually includes many different areas of brightness in one picture. The important areas in the scene are the areas that you should measure with the spot meter. To determine correct exposure in this type of situation, take a meter reading of the lightest important area in the scene and the darkest important area in the scene; then set your exposure halfway between the two. For example, if your exposure meter indicates that 1/250 second at *f*/16 is correct for the light area and 1/250 second at *f*/4 is correct for the dark area, then 1/250 second at *f*/8 is the average exposure which is the best compromise for the scene.

Because it is often necessary to make several exposure-meter readings, using a spot meter is more time-consuming and requires more knowledge of what to measure in the scene. Consequently, such meters are used primarily by experienced photographers.

Reflected-Light Readings of a Substitute Test Card

When you are photographing a subject indoors, the subject is frequently brighter than other parts of the scene, such as the background. A person lighted by photolamp illumination requires the same exposure to produce good flesh tones whether the person is in front of a dark background or a light one. But if you make reflected-light meter readings of such scenes from the camera position, the readings will be misleading because the meter will be influenced by a background which is much lighter or darker than the subject you're photographing.

To determine exposure for this type of scene, take a close-up reading with a conventional reflected-light meter, or use a spot meter from the camera position. If you make the meter reading of your subject's face, you must divide the film speed by 2 to compute your exposure. This is necessary because average Caucasian skin has twice as much reflectance as the average indoor scene, and exposure-meter calibration is based upon average scene reflectance.

Another way you can determine exposure accurately for these situations is to make reflected-light readings of a test card of known reflectance. Most indoor scenes have an average reflectance of about 18 percent. If you make a reflected-light reading of an 18-percent gray card held close to and in front of the principal subject, you should obtain accurate exposure for the scene. Photo dealers sell KODAK Neutral Test Cards for this purpose. The test cards come in a package of four, and they are 8 x 10 inches in size. Each neutral test card has a gray side of 18 percent reflectance and a white side of 90 percent reflectance. You can use the white side to get a higher meter reading in low light levels. If you use the white side or any other matte white card of about 90-percent reflectance, divide the ASA speed of the film by 5 and set the answer on the calculator dial of your exposure meter, using the nearest film-speed number.

To make a meter reading of a gray or white card, place the card close in front of your subject and hold it straight up and down, facing halfway between the main light and your camera. Make the meter reading by holding your meter close to the card so that it reads only the card. Be sure that the meter doesn't read its own shadow. When you make the reading, turn on all the lights that will illuminate the subject. Shield your exposure meter from other lights that might shine directly into its light-sensitive cell.

You can also use the KODAK Neutral Test Card for meter readings outdoors. This is particularly helpful when distance or a barrier of some sort makes it difficult to get an accurate reading of the light reflected from the subject or when unimportant light or dark areas can mislead your meter. It's desirable to place the card at or near the principal subject, but when it's impractical to do so, just make sure that the light on the test card is the same as the light on the subject. When you make a meter reading from the test card, your meter is not influenced by light or dark areas in the scene. Since the exposure meter is calibrated for average reflectance, the meter reacts as though the subject has average reflectance.

When you use the card outdoors, exposure adjustments are necessary because the reflectance of the card differs from that of the scene. Complete instructions are included with the neutral test cards.

INCIDENT-LIGHT METERS

An incident-light meter measures the light illuminating the scene. To make an incident-light reading, you position your meter in the same light that's illuminating the subject and point the meter toward the camera (unless the meter instruction book recommends a different technique). When possible, hold the meter at the subject position. To do this you'll have to move close to your subject. This is the reason why automatic cameras don't have incident-light meters. You can make an incident-light reading from the camera position if the light falling on the camera is the same as the light falling on the scene you are photographing. Point the meter in the same direction as you would if you were making the reading at the subject position.

Exposure determined by an incident-light meter assumes that the scene has average reflectance. Fortunately, most scenes have average reflectance, and as a result the exposure indicated by an incident-light meter is correct for most picture-taking situations.

Since an incident-light meter measures the illumination on the scene, scene reflectance does not influence the meter. This means that light or dark areas in the scene will not mislead the meter. If these areas are unimportant in your picture and the principal subject has average reflectance, your picture

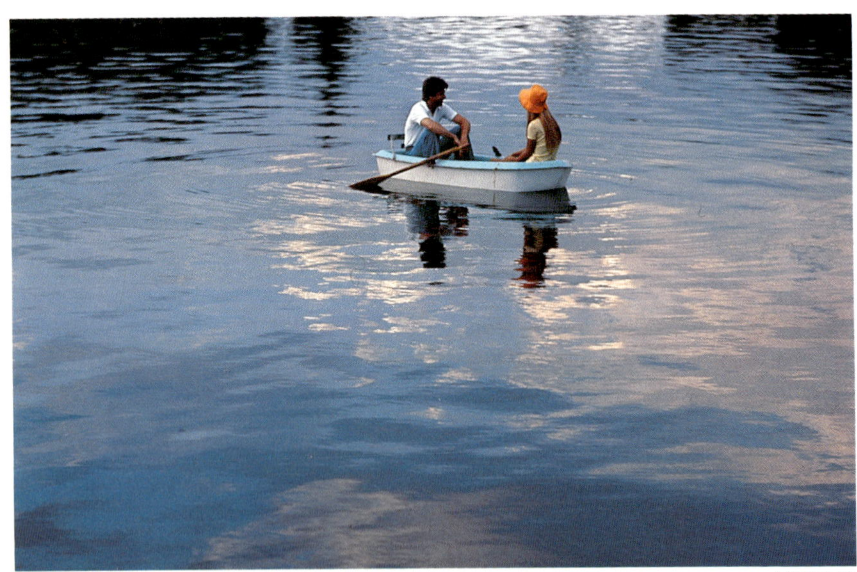

NORM KERR

When you can't get close enough to your subject to make an incident-light meter reading at the subject position, you can make the reading from the camera position if the light falling on the camera is the same as the light falling on the subject. Remember to aim the meter in the same direction as you would if you were at the subject position.

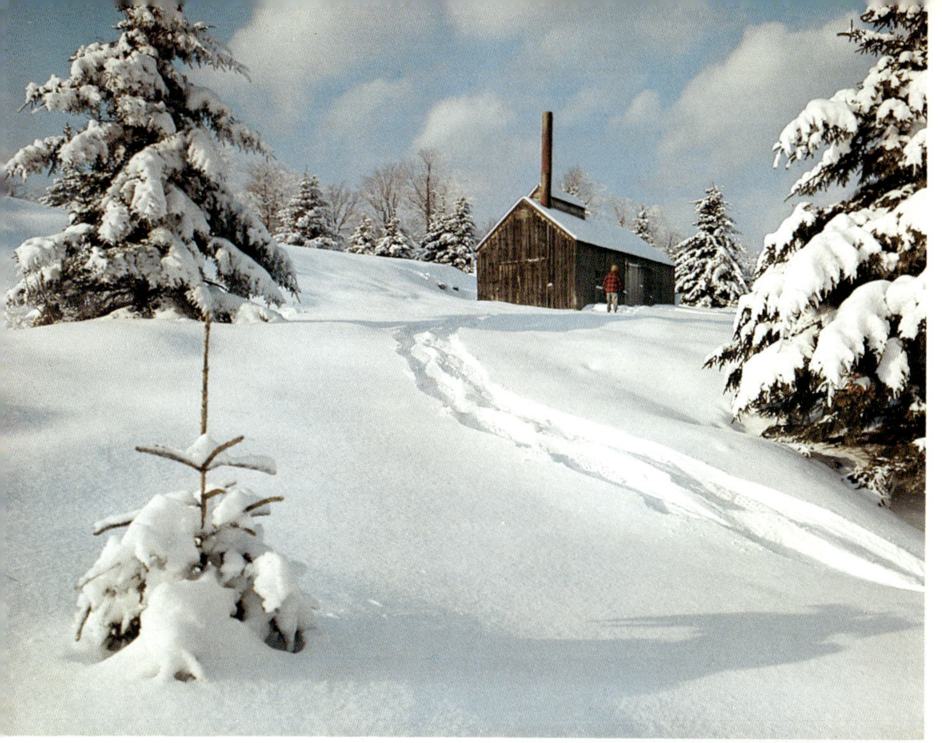

ROBERT HOLLAND

If a bright area, such as snow, is an important part of the picture, use a lens opening 1 stop smaller than your incident-light meter indicates.

should be properly exposed when you use an incident-light meter. Or if you are photographing an evenly lighted scene which has a large brightness range where detail in the light and dark areas is of equal importance, an incident-light meter will indicate a compromise exposure that should be correct.

On the other hand, if either a very bright area or a very dark area is the important part of the picture and you want to record detail in this area, you must modify the exposure indicated by your incident-light meter. If a bright area is an important part of the picture, use a lens opening ½ to 1 stop smaller than your meter indicates. If a dark area is important, use a lens opening ½ to 1 stop larger than your meter indicates.

When the scene has uneven lighting and you want the best overall exposure, make incident-light readings in the lightest and darkest areas of illumination that are important to your picture. Then use the exposure that is midway between the exposure settings indicated for these areas.

Many scenes, especially those outdoors in daylight, have average reflectance. For these scenes an incident-light meter and a reflected-light meter will work equally well and yield a high percentage of good exposures.

When lighting remains constant, as it does for most of the day in bright sunlight, you can use the same exposure for similarly lighted scenes with average reflectance. As a result, for average picture-taking conditions it is unnecessary to make a separate meter reading of each scene.

EXPOSURE BRACKETING

When you encounter scenes that are unusual or that are difficult to determine the correct exposure for and you're not sure of the proper camera settings, it's a good idea to bracket your exposures. Bracketing gives you more assurance of getting a picture with proper exposure. First determine the exposure as accurately as you can with your exposure meter or from an exposure guide, and then take a picture at this setting. Next take another picture at 1 stop less exposure and a third picture at 1 stop more exposure. If you want even more assurance of a properly exposed picture, take two *more* pictures—one at 2 stops under and one at 2 stops over the exposure recommended by your meter or the exposure guide.

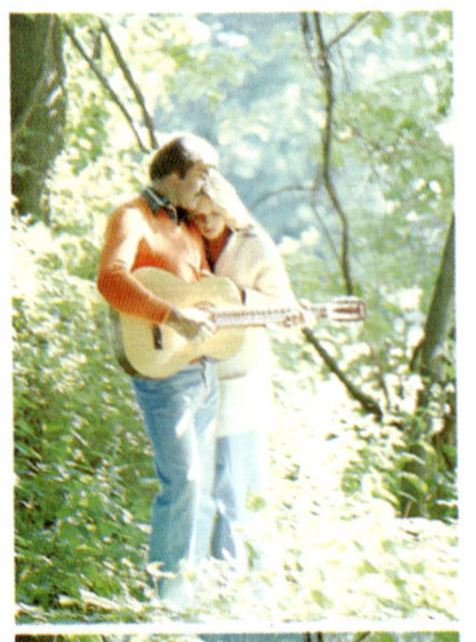

2 stops overexposed—1/125 sec *f*/2.8.

1 stop overexposed—1/125 sec *f*/4.

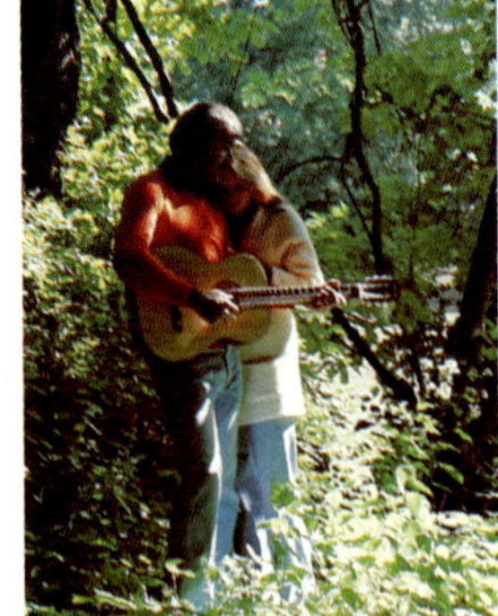

1 stop underexposed—1/125 sec *f*/8.

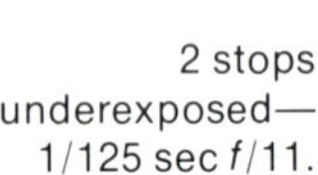

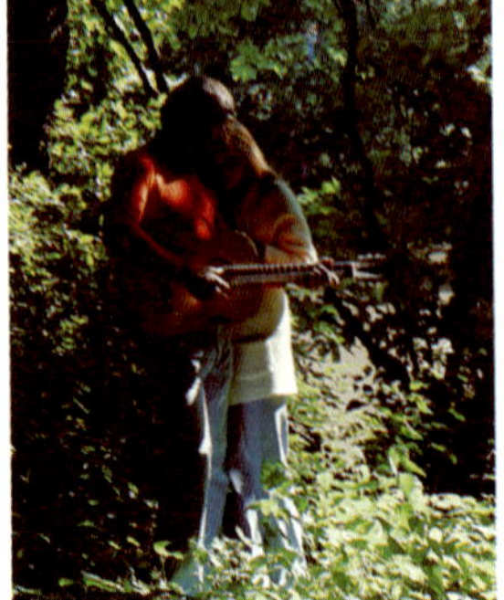

2 stops underexposed—1/125 sec *f*/11.

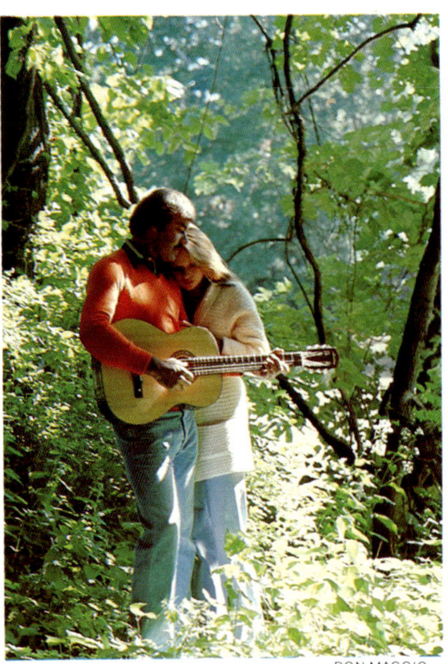

DON MAGGIO

Normal exposure—1/125 sec *f*/5.6. Exposure bracketing gives you more assurance of getting a picture with proper exposure. These pictures were made on KODAK EKTACHROME 64 Film (Daylight).

EXPOSURE WITH FILTERS

Since most filters absorb light, you must make an exposure compensation when you use them. With Kodak color films and the conversion filters recommended for various light sources, the compensation is included in the film speed given for each light source and filter combination. Just use the speeds given on the instruction sheets that come with the films or in the Data Sheets in this book. With Kodak black-and-white films, filter factors are given on the film instruction sheets and the Data Sheets. Divide the film speed by the filter factor to make the exposure compensation. Then set the corrected speed value on the film-speed dial of your camera or exposure meter.

Another way you can apply the filter factor is to set your exposure meter for the speed of the film without a filter and then modify the camera settings indicated by the meter. For example, if the filter factor is 2 and the camera setting indicated by the meter is 1/125 second at *f*/11, you can either double the exposure time to 1/60 second or open the lens 1 full stop to *f*/8. See the filter factor table on this page.

Many cameras with built-in exposure meters measure the light through a filter placed over the camera lens. With most cameras of this type, you should set the built-in meter for the speed of the film *without a filter.* However, with some filters, built-in exposure meters that make the reading through the filter may require a correction in the film-speed setting to indicate the proper exposure.

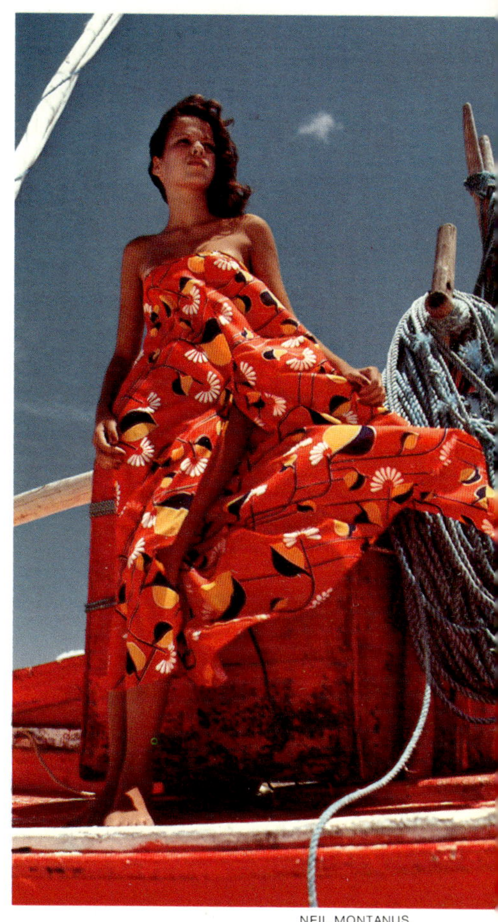

NEIL MONTANUS

Colors are reproduced with more saturation when you use a polarizing screen. KODACHROME 64 Film (Daylight), 1/125 sec *f*/5.6.

EQUIVALENT *f*-STOP CORRECTIONS FOR FILTER FACTORS

Filter Factor	*f*-Stops	Filter Factor	*f*-Stops	Filter Factor	*f*-Stops
1.2	+ ⅓	3	+1⅔	8	+3
1.5	+ ⅔	4	+2	10	+3⅓
2	+1	5	+2⅓	12	+3⅔
2.5	+1⅓	6	+2⅔	16	+4

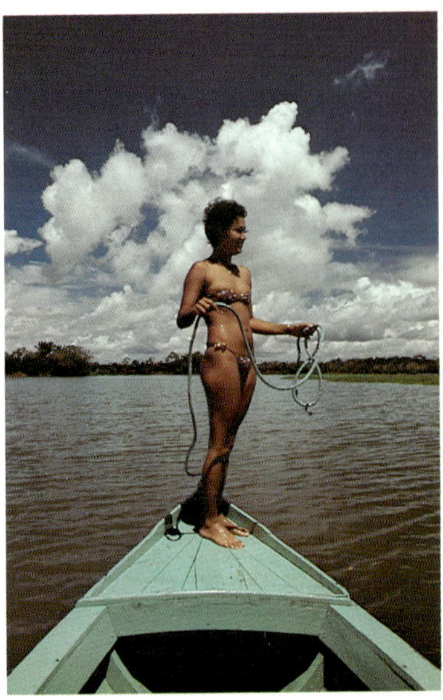

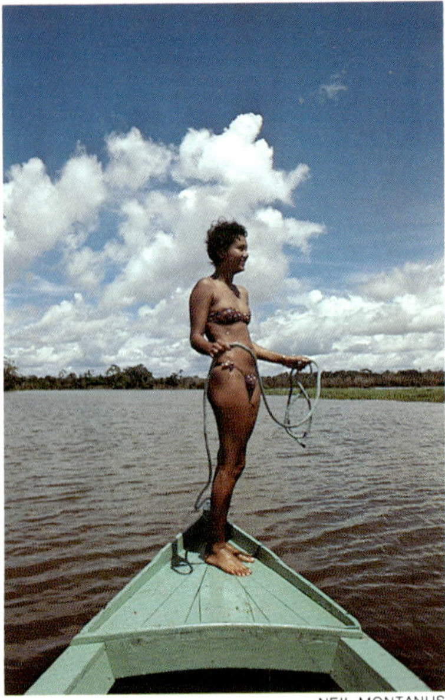

NEIL MONTANUS

A polarizing screen with a filter factor of 2.5 was used to produce the dramatic sky in the top picture. To determine the correct exposure, divide the film speed by 2.5 or increase exposure by 1⅓ stops. KODACHROME 64 Film (Daylight).

Therefore, since camera instructions vary, check your instruction manual for details on how to set your camera.

If your camera manual doesn't adequately cover this situation, you can write for such information to the manufacturer or the American distributor for your camera. Or you can determine your own correction factor for filters by using the following procedure.

Select an average scene that's typical of the type of scenes and lighting you'll photograph using a particular filter. The lighting should remain constant and the subjects should not change while you're making comparative exposure meter readings for this test.

Put your camera on a tripod. For *color film,* set the film speed dial on your camera for the speed of the film *with the filter.* For *black-and-white film,* divide the speed of the film by the filter factor for the filter you're using and set the resulting number on the film speed dial of your camera. Next make an exposure meter reading with your camera *without using the filter.* Note the shutter speed and *f*-number indicated by the meter reading. This tells you what the exposure should be *with* the filter.

Without moving the camera, put the filter over the lens and make an exposure meter reading of the same scene with the same lighting through the filter with your camera. Do not change the exposure settings; keep the same shutter speed and *f*-number as before. Then adjust the film-speed dial on your camera to center the exposure meter needle or, depending on the exposure determination system in your camera, adjust the film speed dial to obtain the same shutter speed and *f*-number combination. For example, with automatic cameras the exposure meter determines either the shutter speed or the lens opening.

Note the new ASA setting on the film-speed dial. This shows you what the

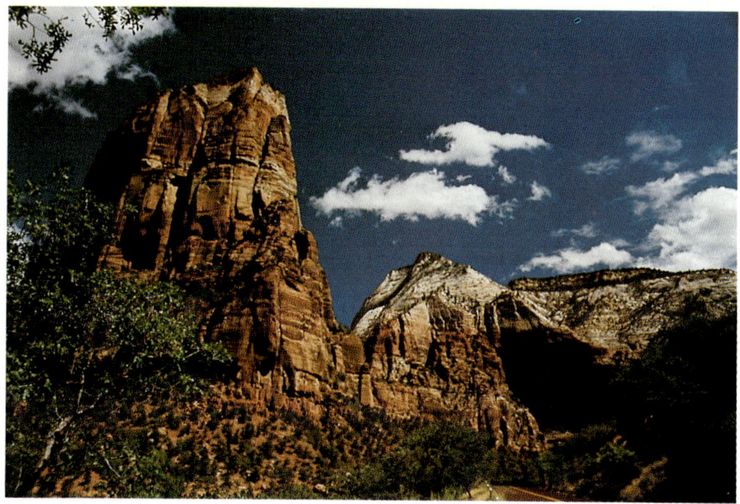

With polarizing screen.

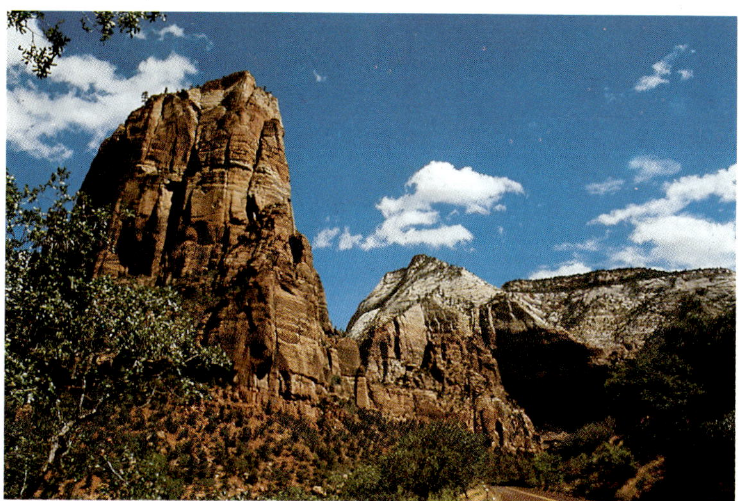

Without polarizing screen.

CAROLINE GRIMES

film speed should be for your camera when making meter readings through the filter.

Compare this new ASA setting with the film speed recommended for the film *without a filter.* This is the correction to use for the film, filter, and lighting conditions you used to make the test. You can make the same correction for other films for use with this filter.

For example, if the film has a speed of ASA 64 *without a filter* and you find from your meter reading test that it should be ASA 50 when you make the meter reading through the filter with your camera exposure meter, then divide 64 by 50. The answer 1.25 is the correction factor by which you should decrease the speeds of other films for use with this filter when you make the meter reading through the filter.

Note that some black-and-white films have different basic filter factors for the same filter. For these exceptions, you'll need to make a separate exposure meter test to find the correction for each film that has a filter factor different from the film you used for your original test.

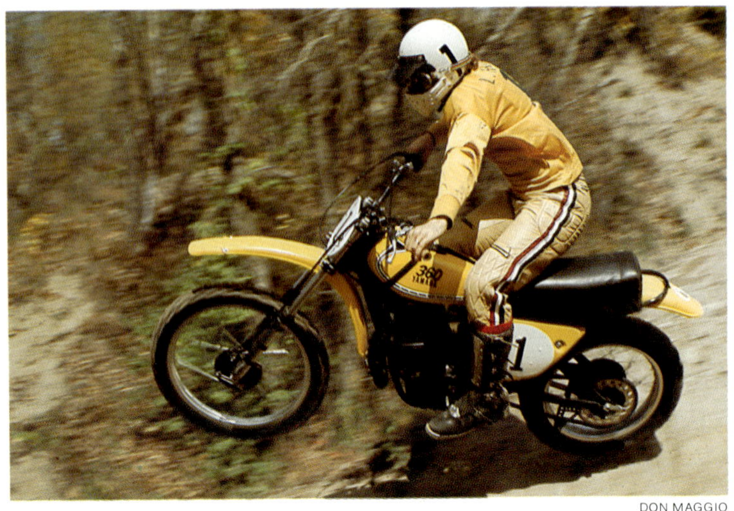

DON MAGGIO

When you use high shutter speeds and medium or small lens openings with a camera that has a *leaf shutter,* you should use a smaller lens opening than normal. This exposure correction is more important for taking pictures on high-speed color-slide film than it is for high-speed negative films because the negative films have more exposure latitude.

EXPOSURE FACTOR FOR SHUTTER EFFICIENCY

When you take pictures on high-speed film under certain conditions, there is an additional exposure factor you should consider. If you're using a camera with a leaf-type shutter under exposure conditions that require high shutter speeds and medium or small lens openings, lens openings beginning about midway on the lens-opening scale of your camera, significant overexposure will result unless you make an exposure correction. This happens because shutter speeds are calibrated at the maximum lens opening of the camera, but shutter efficiency with a leaf-type shutter changes as the lens opening is decreased. At high shutter speeds and medium or small lens openings, the effective exposure times are longer than the shutter-speed settings indicated on your camera. At slow shutter speeds the difference between the effective exposure time and the indicated shutter-speed setting is relatively insignificant, and you can ignore it.

The exposure error may be equal to a half stop at 1/250 second and a full stop at 1/500 second. Because of the short exposure latitude of color-slide films, the exposure error is more critical for high-speed color-slide films than for high-speed color and black-and-white negative films. To correct for the exposure error, you should reduce the lens opening 1/2 stop at 1/250 second and 1 full stop at 1/500 second when exposure-meter readings indicate medium or small lens openings. *No such correction is necessary when you use a camera with a focal-plane shutter.*

These exposure corrections are given in the daylight exposure table on the Data Sheets and the instruction sheets for KODAK EKTACHROME 200 and 400 Films (Daylight) and on the instruction sheet supplied with the KODAK Special Processing Envelope, ESP-1.

USING EXPOSURE METERS IN COPYING

It's important that you adjust the lights so that the illumination over the copy area is even. To determine exposure for copying, you can either use an incident-light meter held in the plane of the original you are copying or use a reflected-light meter and take the reading from a gray card with 18-percent reflectance that you have substituted for the original. You can use the gray side of the KODAK Neutral Test Card for this purpose. If you don't have the proper gray card, you can make a reflected-light reading from a matte white surface of 90-percent reflectance, such as the back of a sheet of double-weight white photographic paper. Your meter reading, of course, will be much higher. Compensate by setting the meter calculator at 1/5 the normal film-speed number.

The film speeds for copying linework are intended for trial exposures. The exposure for linework is affected by the reflectance of the lines or dark areas of the original and the inherently short exposure latitude of high-contrast films. To obtain the best contrast between the background and the lines, you should use the maximum exposure that you can without causing filling-in or grayness of lines on the negative.

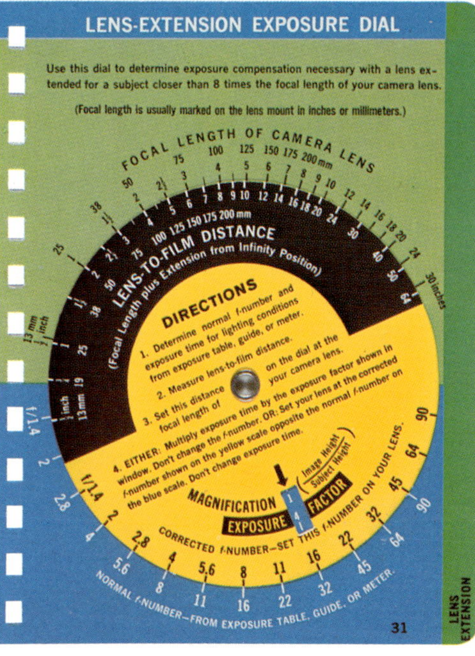

The *KODAK Master Photoguide* (AR-21) includes a handy Lens-Extension Exposure Dial for determining the effective *f*-number quickly and easily when you're using a lens-extension device.

CORRECTION FOR LENS EXTENSION

In computing the exposure for copying or other close-up work for which you extend the camera lens by using extension tubes or bellows, make sure you allow for the effective increase in the indicated *f*-number. Otherwise, your pictures will be underexposed. For example, if you ignore this factor when determining exposure for taking a close-up picture of an object that will be the same size in your picture or a ratio of 1:1, your film will be underexposed by 2 *f*-stops. You should make an

$$\text{Effective } f\text{-number} = \frac{\text{Indicated } f\text{-number} \times \text{Lens-to-film distance}}{\text{Focal length}}$$

exposure compensation whenever the subject distance is less than 8 times the focal length of your lens. Close-up lenses require no exposure compensation unless you use a lens-extension device. The *KODAK Master Photoguide* (AR-21) provides a convenient calculator dial for determining the effective *f*-number quickly and easily. You can also calculate the effective *f*-number by using the formula on page 101.

The lens-to-film distance is approximately equal to the focal length of your camera lens plus the distance the lens is extended beyond its position at infinity focus.

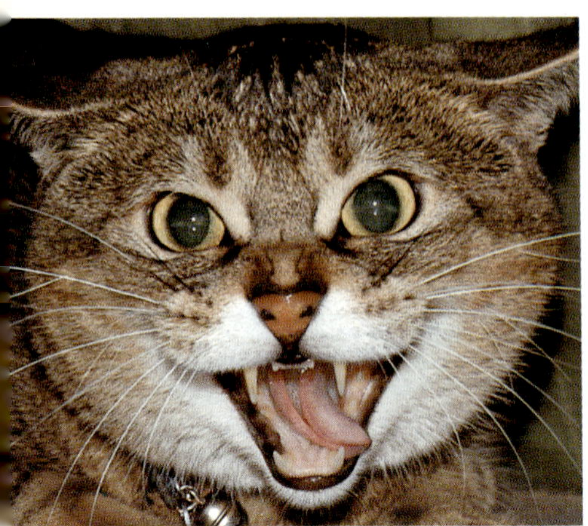

CHARLES A. CARNAGHI, KINSA

Many electronic flash units determine the correct exposure automatically.

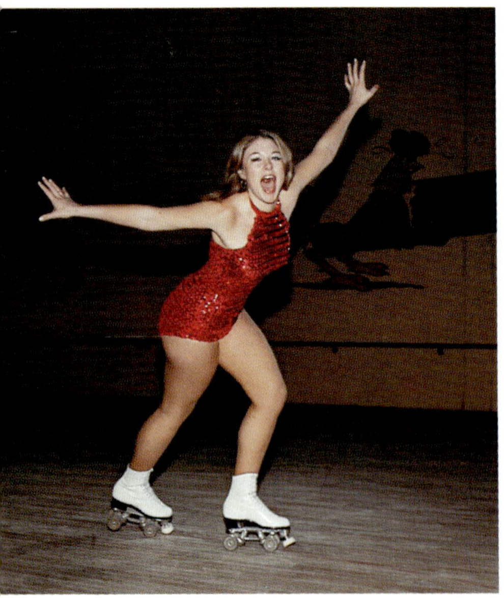

PETER GALES

Flash guide numbers provide a reliable method for determining exposure with nonautomatic electronic flash units and flashbulbs.

MODIFYING FILM-SPEED NUMBERS

Film speeds published by film manufacturers are an excellent basis for obtaining optimum exposure. Optimum exposure is the minimum exposure required to produce a picture of excellent quality. Underexposure results in less density, or blackness, in your negatives or more density in your slides and loss of shadow detail in both. Overexposure increases negative density or decreases slide density and results in a loss of highlight detail in both. Furthermore, overexposure in negatives increases graininess (with black-and-white films), reduces sharpness, increases printing time, and makes focusing the enlarger more difficult.

To produce the quality you want in your pictures with your own equipment and procedures, it's sometimes necessary to modify recommended film-speed numbers. However, before you depart from the film speed recommended for a particular film, be sure that you are making careful exposure-meter readings, using the technique recommended in your meter or camera instruction book. Then if your pictures are consistently unsatisfactory and indicate that you should change the film-speed setting on your meter, change it as follows. With normal development, if your films are consistently underexposed, increase exposure by using a lower film-speed number; if your films are consistently overexposed, reduce exposure by using a higher film-speed number. Divide the published film speed by 2 to produce 1 stop more exposure. Multiply by 2 to produce 1 stop less exposure.

FLASH EXPOSURE

The most important factor affecting flash exposure is the distance from the flash to your subject. Subjects close to the flash receive a lot of light, while subjects farther away receive less light. Some electronic flash units automatically adjust the light from the flash for proper exposure, and some cameras automatically adjust the lens opening for the proper flash exposure as you focus the lens. With nonadjustable cameras, flash-to-subject distances of 5 to 9 feet usually produce acceptable exposures. With most adjustable cameras, however, flash guide numbers provide a convenient means for determining flash exposure.

The guide number you should use depends on the film you're using and on the output of your electronic flash unit. If you're using flashbulbs, the guide number depends on the film, the type of flashbulb and reflector, the shutter speed, and the synchronization of your shutter. Flash exposure tables in the Data Sheet for each film give the recommended guide numbers for different combinations of these variables.

Divide the proper guide number by the flash-to-subject distance in feet to find the *f*-number for average subjects. For example, if your guide number is 80 and the subject is 10 feet away from the flash, divide 80 by 10. The answer 8 means that you should set your lens opening at *f*/8. If the answer is between two *f*-numbers marked on your camera lens, set the lens opening at the nearest *f*-number or halfway between the two, whichever is closer to the answer.

Guide numbers are just *guides;* they are for average subjects in average-size rooms. They don't take into account subjects that are lighter or darker than average or small rooms with light-colored walls that reflect a lot of light. If you're photographing a light subject, use a lens opening ½ stop smaller than the guide number indicates; for a dark subject, use a lens opening ½ stop

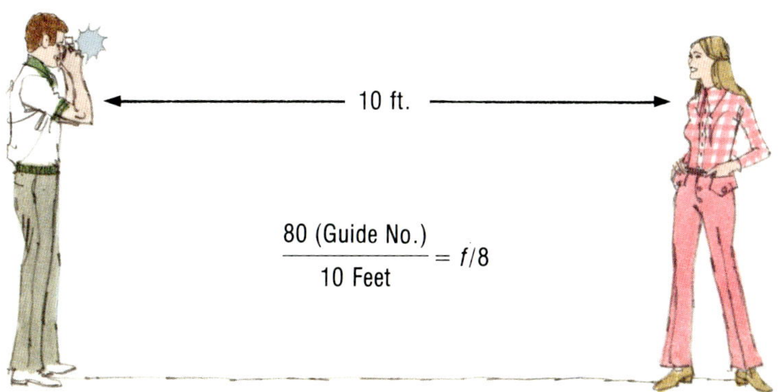

The most important factor affecting flash exposure is the distance from the flash to your subject. To determine the *f*-number for average subjects, divide the proper guide number by the flash-to-subject distance in feet.

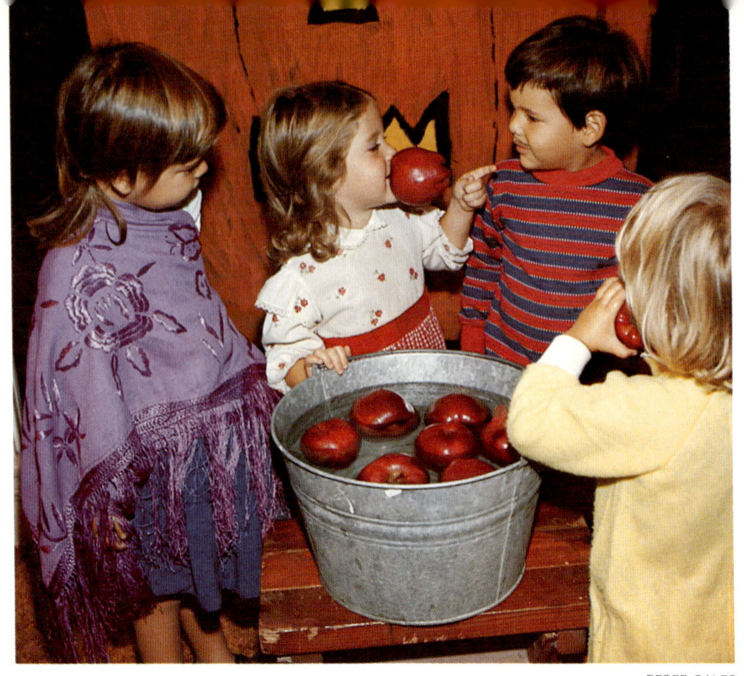

PETER GALES

Some flash units have convenient-to-use exposure dials to tell you the *f*-number to use for the speed of the film you're using and the flash-to-subject distance.

larger. In small rooms with light-colored walls, use 1 stop less exposure than the guide number indicates.

If necessary, you can change the guide numbers to improve your results. If your pictures are consistently underexposed—if your negatives are too light or your slides are too dark—use a lower guide number. If your pictures are consistently overexposed—if your negatives are too dark or your slides are too light—use a higher guide number.

The *KODAK Master Photoguide* (AR-21), described earlier, takes the arithmetic out of calculating flash exposure. It includes a convenient Flash Exposure Dial which indicates the correct *f*-number opposite each subject distance. The flash dial in the *Master Photoguide* provides a quick and easy method for determining the *f*-number setting for both electronic flash and flashbulbs.

Flash pictures of distant subjects, such as sports or other spectator events at distances of about 50 feet or farther away, are not very satisfactory. The foreground is usually shown as a large overexposed area which is distracting and spoils the picture. You can photograph these distant subjects much more effectively by the existing light.

You should *not* use flash to photograph the image on your television screen or projected images such as slides or movies. The bright light from the flash would overwhelm the image you want to photograph and all you would get is a blank area on the film. Here again, photograph these subjects by the existing light. You may want to purchase the book on existing-light photography mentioned on page 48.

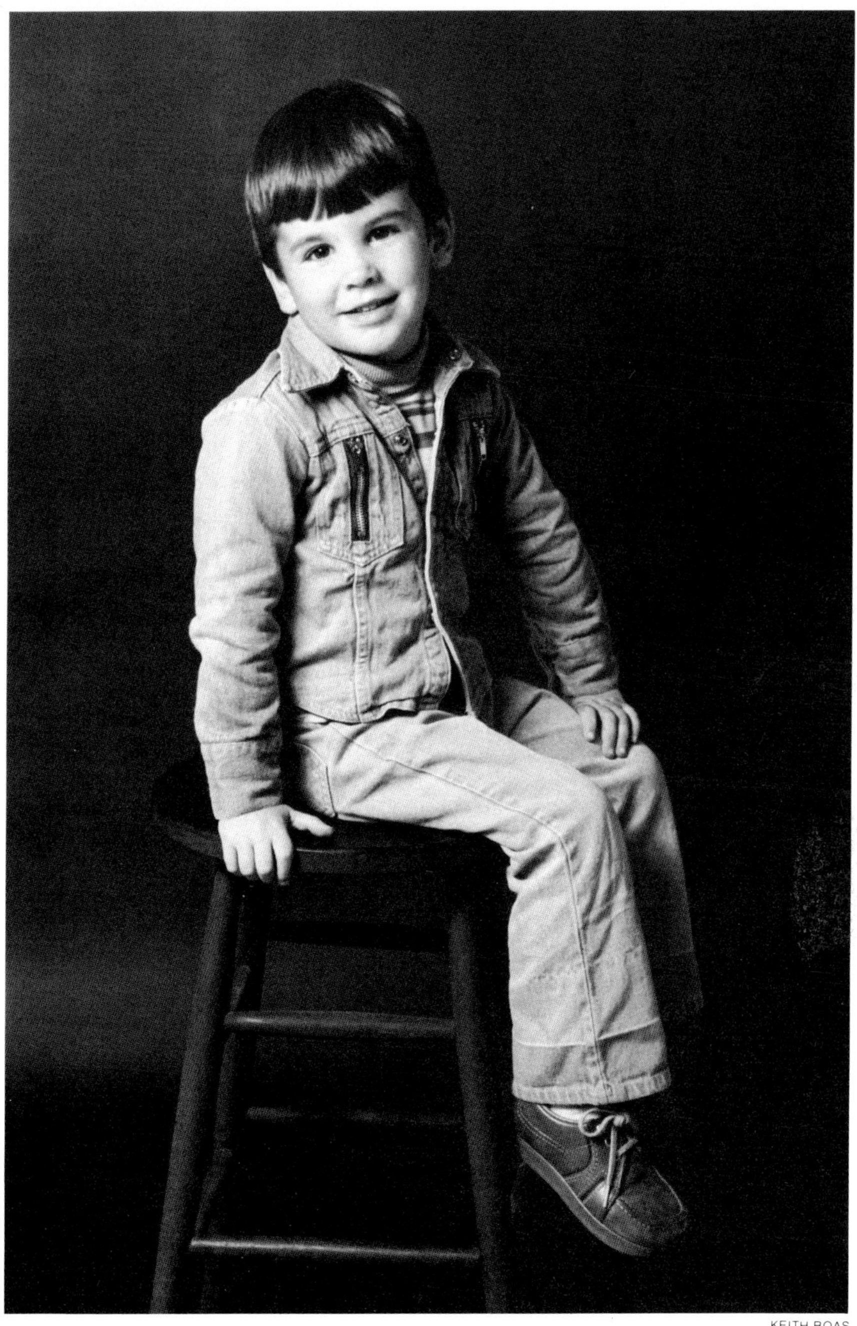

KEITH BOAS

This shot was taken with one electronic flash unit bounced from a reflecting umbrella which gives a soft, natural lighting effect. Since some light is lost when you bounce the flash off an umbrella, you must use about 1 stop more exposure than the exposure required for direct flash. TRI-X Pan Film, 1/60 sec *f*/11.

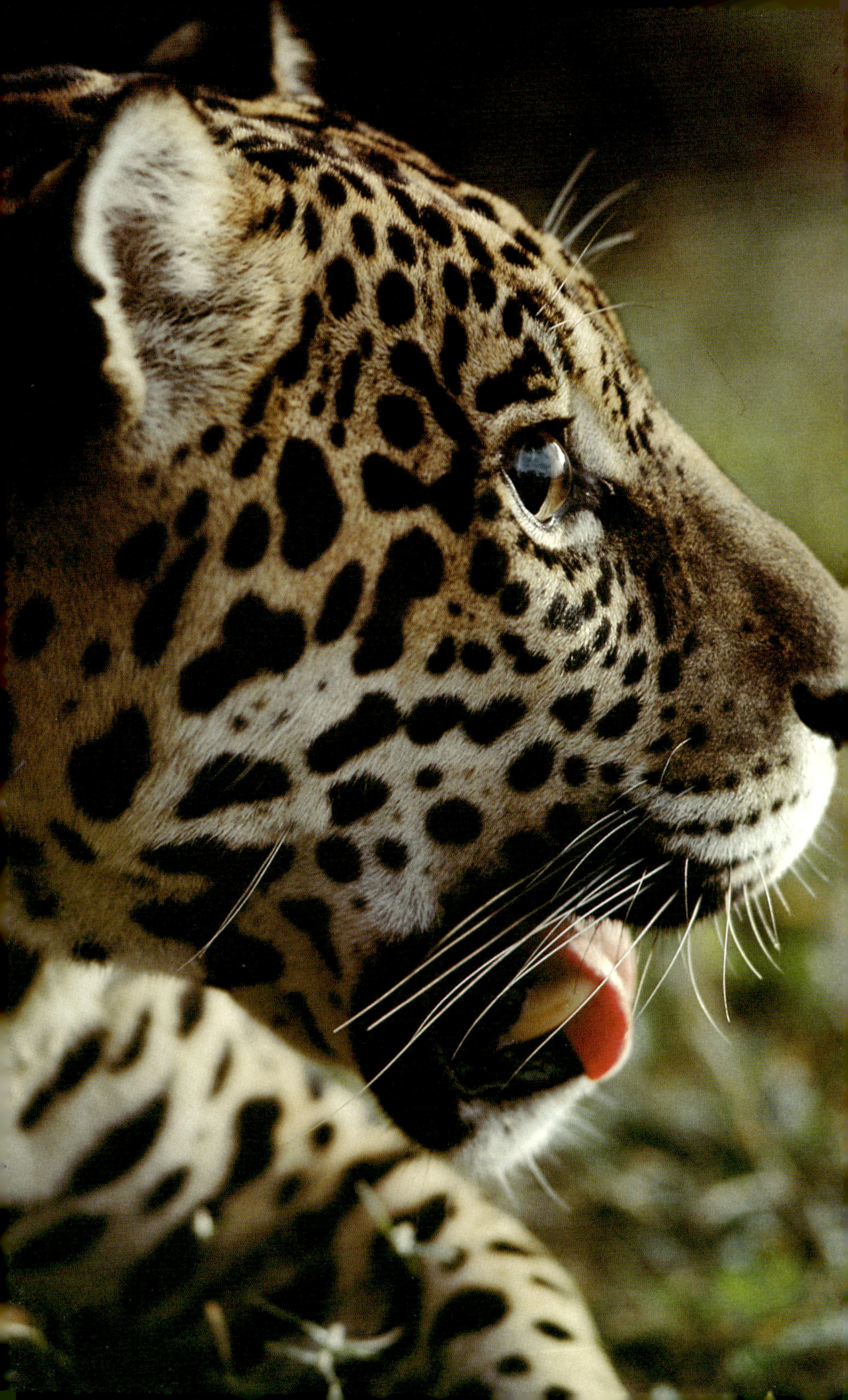

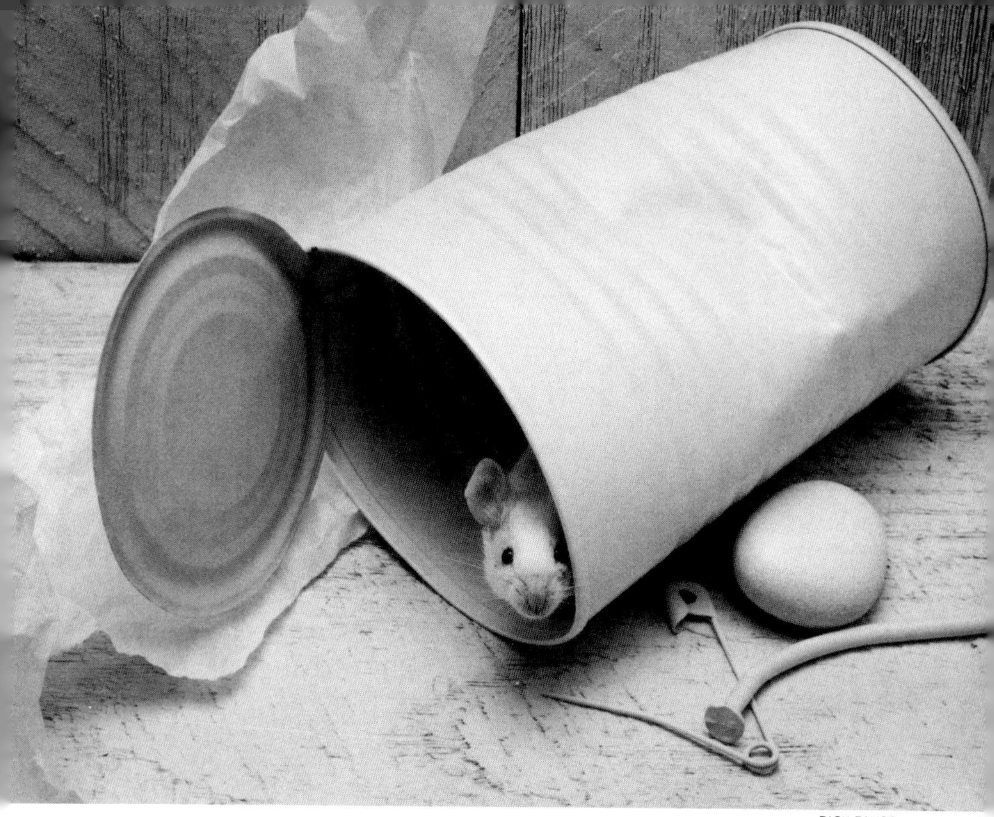

DICK FAUST

Storage and Care of *Kodak* Films

Photographic films are perishable products and are damaged by high temperatures, high relative humidities, and harmful gases. Some photographic characteristics—speed, color balance, and contrast of color films and speed, contrast, and fog level of black-and-white films—change gradually after manufacture. Adverse storage conditions accelerate these changes. Color films are more seriously affected than black-and-white films because adverse conditions usually affect the three emulsion layers of a color film to different degrees. Moisture may also cause various physical defects such as mottle and abrasions.

For best results, handle and store films properly both before and after exposure, with adequate protection against heat, moisture, and harmful gases. Unprocessed films must be protected from x-rays and radioactive substances. When the climate is moderate, storage precautions are few and simple. Greater care is necessary under hot and humid conditions. Processed films also require proper storage and care for maximum permanence.

TACHROME 200 Film (Daylight).
L MONTANUS

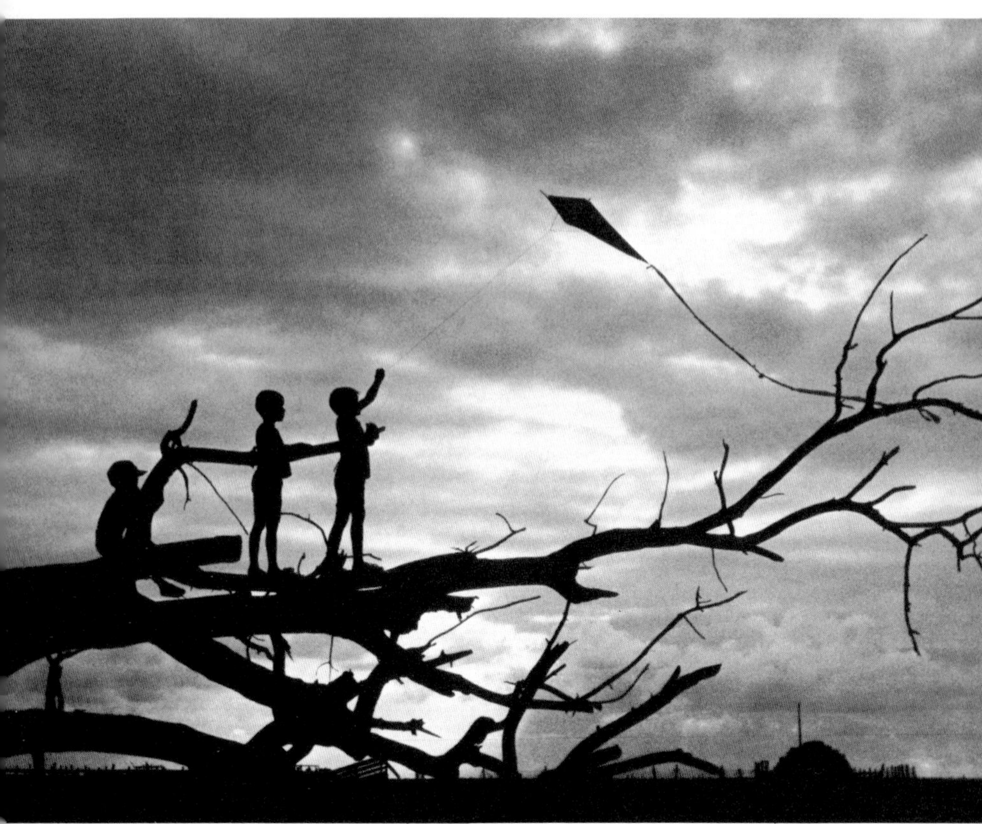

PANATOMIC-X Film.

JERRY MCCUNE, KINSA

STORAGE IN THE ORIGINAL PACKAGE

Kodak supplies 135, 126, 110, roll, and instant print films in water-vaportight packaging. The 135 films are packaged in snap-cover plastic cans; the other films in heat-sealed foil pouches. The vaportight packaging provides protection from humidity in areas such as tropical regions or any other locality where relative humidities of 70 percent or higher prevail. You may encounter such conditions in a number of areas in the United States.

Protection from Humidity. Kodak films supplied in vaportight packaging require no additional protection against high humidities until you open the package. *So don't open the vaportight packaging until you are ready to use the film.* Otherwise the protection originally provided is no longer effective.

It is the *relative humidity*, not the *absolute humidity*, that determines the moisture level of the air affecting the film. Relative humidity is measured best with a sling psychrometer, but in a small storage chamber you can use a humidity indicator such as the type sold for home use.

KODACHROME 64 Film (Daylight), 1/4 sec *f*/5.6, 24 mm lens.
NEIL MONTANUS

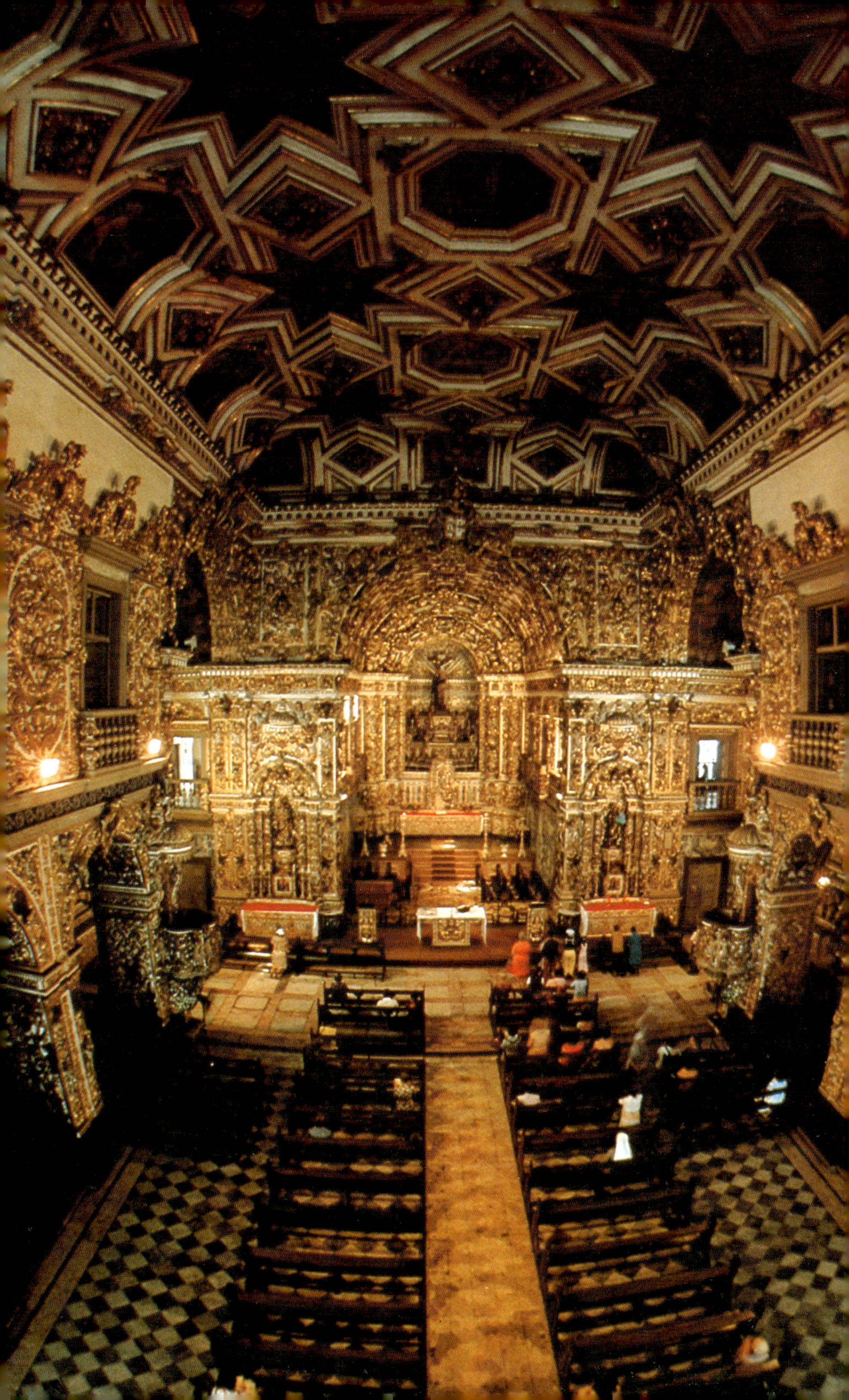

Protection from Heat. *Vaportight packaging is not heatproof.* Regardless of the type of packaging, don't leave your films near heat registers, steam pipes, or other sources of heat. In warm weather, do not leave them in areas on the top floors of uninsulated buildings or in hot places in a car, especially when it's parked in the sun on a warm or hot day.

As we mentioned earlier, Kodak color-negative films and Kodak color-slide films are both available in films designed for general use and in films designed for professional use. The requirements for storing and handling color films for critical photography by professional photographers are more rigid than those for films for general use.

When Kodak color films for general use are made, the changes in speed, color balance, and contrast that will occur from natural aging are anticipated. The film is manufactured to have optimum quality when it is most likely to be used by the photographer.

Kodak color films for general use are designed for storage at normal room temperature before use. These films mature under these conditions. By the time the films are shipped from the factory, they have become and will remain relatively stable when kept at room temperature until the expiration date. The film should be protected from heat.

Kodak professional color films are designed for optimum performance to make the best pictures at the time of manufacture without regard for changes that may occur under general, or nonprofessional, use. To retain the original characteristics for critical photography where small color deviations would be important, professional color films should be stored under refrigeration before exposure.

Both Kodak films for professional use and for general use are equally as stable when they are used under identical conditions.

Under normal temperature conditions, 75°F (24°C) or below, Kodak color films for general use and Kodak black-and-white films do not require refrigeration. The film carton and the instruction sheet packaged with some films tell how to store the film. The storage recommendations for Kodak films for general use say KEEP COOL or PROTECT FROM HEAT; those for Kodak professional black-and-white films say STORE IN A COOL, DRY PLACE; and those for Kodak professional color films that should be refrigerated say STORE AT 55°F (13°C) OR LESS. Some special-purpose films such as KODAK EKTACHROME Infrared Film require storage at 0 to −10°F (−18 to −23°C) and KODAK High Speed Infrared Film and KODAK EKTACHROME Slide Duplicating Film 5071 at 55°F (13°C) or lower.

During summer heat, temperatures over 75°F (24°C), we recommend refrigerated storage for keeping all Kodak films cool, provided they are in vaportight packages or in sealed cans or jars. To avoid condensation of moisture on cold film surfaces, remove unopened film packages from cold storage and allow 1 to 2 hours for them to reach approximate room temperature before you open the package. This recommendation also applies to KODAK Instant Print Film that has been stored under refrigeration at 55°F (13°C) or lower but not at freezing temperatures. If this film has been stored in a freezer at 0 to −10°F (−18 to −23°C), allow 24 hours for the film to reach approximate room temperature before you use it.

When the ambient temperature has returned to normal, 75°F (24°C) or below, remove Kodak color films for general use from refrigerated storage so they can mature as anticipated in manufacture. If after testing some rolls of film, you want to maintain the film at that specific color balance for an extended period, you can store other rolls

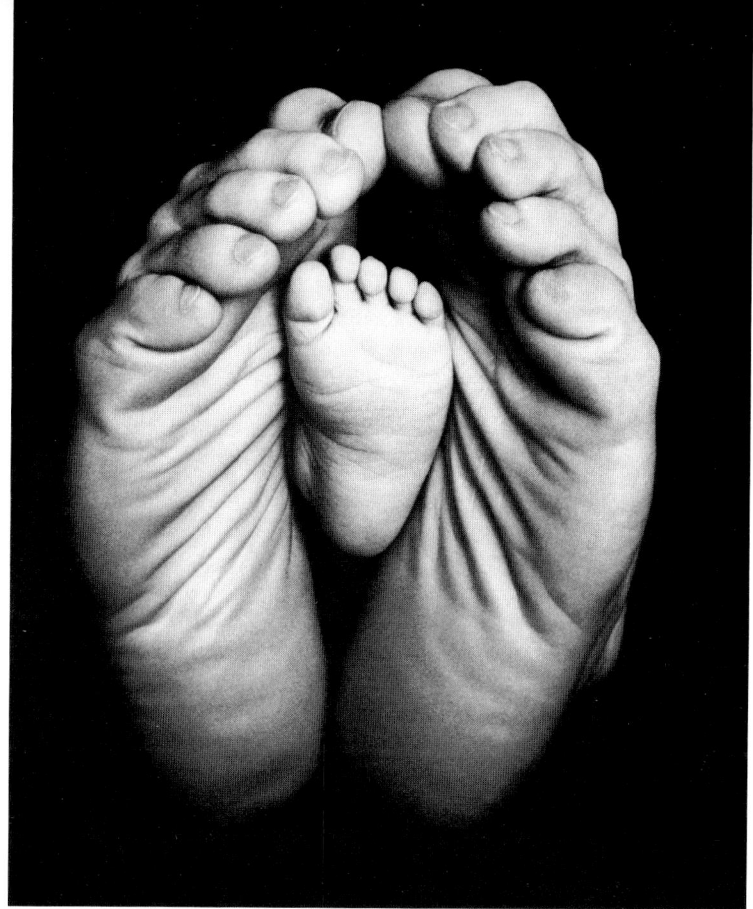

TRI-X Pan Film, electronic flash, 1/60 sec *f*/16.

CRAIG STEWART, SKPA

of the same emulsion in a refrigerator or freezer. The emulsion number is printed on the film carton.

You can store unexposed black-and-white films under normal temperature conditions, temperatures that don't exceed 75°F (24°C), for storage periods up to 2 months. For longer storage periods, when possible, maintain the following storage temperatures for black-and-white films:

For storage periods up to	2 months	6 months	12 months
Keep black-and-white films below	75°F 24°C	60°F 16°C	50°F 10°C

When you're traveling in a car, don't leave your film in a closed car parked in the sun on a warm, sunny day. The temperature can quickly reach 140°F (60°C) or more. If this is unavoidable, keep your film in an ice chest like those used for camping or in an insulated picnic bag. It may be best to place the container in the trunk. Avoid keeping your film in the glove compartment, on the rear window shelf, over hot spots on the car floor, or in areas in direct sunlight inside the car. If ice or cold packs are available, you can use them to help keep your film cool. If you use ice, keep the film packages dry. Also, see "Protection of Films After You Open the Package," page 114.

Expiration Date. You should expose and process each roll of Kodak film before the expiration date printed on the package. Films kept beyond this date may be unsatisfactory due to changes in speed, contrast, fog, stain, and color reproduction. The last two effects, of course, apply only to color films. The magnitude of changes in a film is largely dependent on the conditions of storage. Proper storage conditions decrease the rate of changes inherent in films but won't eliminate changes entirely.

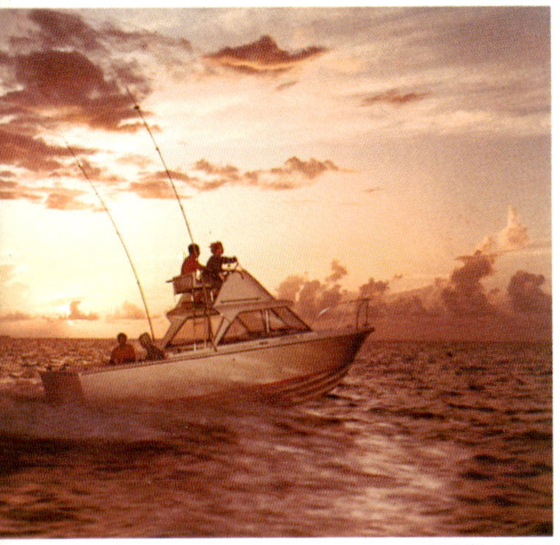

ARDEAN MILLER

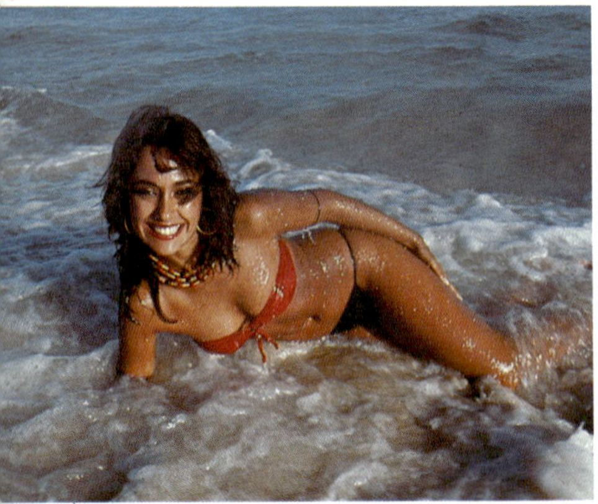

NEIL MONTANUS

KODACHROME 25 Film (Daylight), 1/250 sec $f/5.6$.

Protection from X-rays. X-ray equipment can fog your unprocessed film when the radiation level is high or the film receives several low-level doses. The effect of exposure to x-rays is cumulative. Film which has been processed, however, is not affected.

For the protection of travelers, many airports, airlines, and law-enforcement agencies around the world are using electronic devices to check passengers and x-ray equipment to check their luggage for concealed bombs and weapons. If you travel by commercial airline, your luggage may be subjected to x-ray examination each time you prepare to board the aircraft. All carry-on luggage is x-rayed unless you can obtain a visual inspection instead. Checked luggage may also be x-rayed.

While some x-ray exposure can usually be tolerated, excessive amounts may result in objectionable fog and extraneous shadow images on film contained in the luggage. It is usually possible for passengers to avoid this danger to their unprocessed film by hand-carrying their supply, including loaded cameras, and requesting a *visual* rather than an x-ray inspection of it. The walk-through and handheld electronic devices used at many airports to check passengers separately from their luggage, are not x-ray equipment and have no effect on film.

In the United States, at the airport boarding gates for domestic airline flights, regulations require that x-ray inspection be conducted only with low-output devices. These subject luggage to less than 1 milliroentgen of x-ray exposure per inspection which should not perceptibly fog camera-type films. However, since the effects of x-rays on film are cumulative, it is possible for films to be fogged by repeated exposures of less than 1 milliroentgen each but totaling more than 5 milliroentgens. So for travel within the United States, requests for visual inspections should be

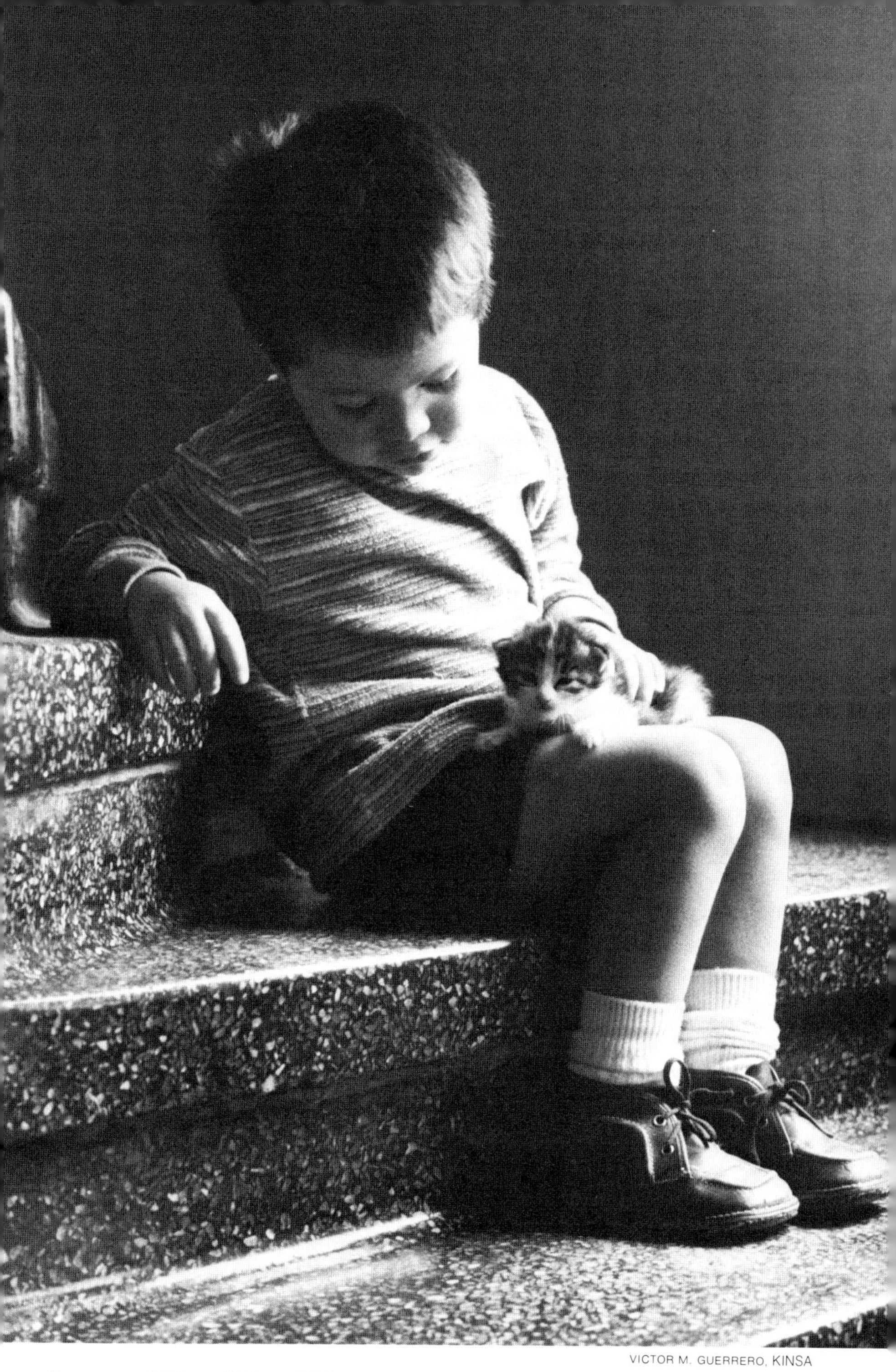

VICTOR M. GUERRERO, KINSA

PANATOMIC-X Film, 1/30 sec *f*/2.8.

unnecessary—unless more than five inspections are encountered with the same film.

Visual inspection of film is particularly important when traveling abroad, including traveling by airline from international air terminals in the United States. A wide variety of luggage-inspection systems may be encountered both for checked and carry-on luggage. Some of these systems are known to operate at relatively high x-ray levels. If you are unable to obtain a visual inspection, we suggest that you ask pertinent questions of airline authorities to determine in doubtful situations whether your film can be damaged.

If you plan to use KODAK Mailers, you can send your exposed film to a Kodak Processing Laboratory instead of carrying it with you and risking exposure to x-rays.

If you're in doubt about the safety of the equipment in use, or if your luggage will be examined more than five times, or when you're traveling to a foreign country, you can minimize the possibility of damage to your film in the following ways:

- Carry your film in hand luggage, arrive early, and ask airport authorities for a visual inspection at each checkpoint, stressing the fact that the sensitive photo material you're carrying might be ruined by x-rays. Not all inspectors will cooperate; however, those who do will help reduce the possibility of film damage.
- Each time you pack your bag, arrange the contents so that the film is not always oriented in the same way. You can achieve a similar effect by orienting your bag differently each time it passes through x-ray inspection.
- Carry KODAK Mailers or other mailers provided by photofinishers on your trip, and mail each roll of film in for processing as soon as it has been exposed. As an added bonus, your processed film may already be waiting for you when you return home.
- If your trip will simply be from one city to another in the United States and back again, there's probably little need for concern. But the 12-countries-in-10-days, whirlwind-tour sort of trip may present a problem to your film.

Sometimes mailed packages are also x-rayed, so if you include unprocessed film in a package, label the package "Undeveloped Photographic Film. Please Do Not X-Ray." Film mailed in processing mailers provided by processors—and clearly marked as film—usually is not subject to x-ray inspection.

PROTECTION OF FILMS AFTER YOU OPEN THE PACKAGE

When the vaportight film package is opened, the film is no longer protected from high humidity and harmful gases. *Expose and process your films promptly after you open the package.* When films for general use are manufactured, an average delay after exposure before the film can be processed is planned for. You get the best results, however, when you have your exposed film processed promptly. Process professional films soon after exposure. If you can't have professional film processed promptly, you should keep it refrigerated until you can have it processed

High relative humidity and high temperature often cause undesirable changes in the latent image—the undeveloped image on the exposed film. Therefore, under these conditions, it's particularly important that you have your exposed films processed as soon as possible.

Under adverse conditions of heat or humidity, don't keep films in your camera any longer than necessary.

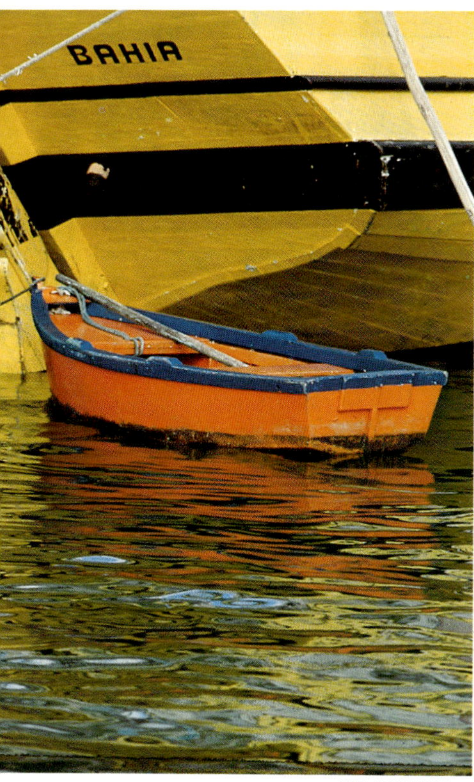

NEIL MONTANUS

EKTACHROME 200 Film (Daylight).

Protect your films by keeping them in a carrying case, and shield the case from direct sunlight; otherwise, the temperature inside the case may become extremely high even in a temperate region. Similarly, don't leave your films in a closed car parked in the sun on a warm, sunny day. Follow the same recommendations for films kept in cars given on page 111 under "Protection from Heat," except that you *should not refrigerate the container* the film is kept in because there is no humidity protection for the film after you open the vaportight packaging.

Don't store opened packages of film in damp basements, iceboxes, refrigerators, or other places where the relative humidity is high. A moderate temperature and moderate relative humidity, such as 60°F (16°C) and 40 percent RH, are better than a low temperature with high relative humidity, such as 40°F (4°C) and 80 percent RH. The ideal relative humidity for storage of such film packages is between 40 and 60 percent, preferably near 40 percent.

When you can't avoid humid storage locations, or when you must store your films in a refrigerator to keep them cool, place opened packages of film in a can or jar which you can seal tightly to provide moisture protection. If the prevailing relative humidity is above 60 percent, dry your films with a suitable desiccating agent, such as activated silica gel, before storing them in cans or jars in humid or cold locations. You can buy silica gel from chemical-supply firms. Small, inexpensive containers of silica gel called Davison Silica Gel Air Dryers are available. Write to W. R. Grace & Company, Davison Chemical Division, 10 East Baltimore Street, Baltimore, Maryland 21202, for the name of a local distributor.

Keep opened packages of film away from industrial gases, motor exhausts, and vapors of mothballs, formaldehyde, paints, solvents, cleaners, and mildew or fungus preventives. Since clothes closets and drawers often contain mothballs or mildew and fungus preventives, check carefully to be sure you don't store films and cameras in compartments containing these chemicals. Do not store films or cameras in drawers of new furniture in which some glues that were used during manufacture may give off fumes harmful to films.

Static. Advancing and rewinding roll film too rapidly or other careless handling can produce discharges of static electricity which cause marks on the processed film. Static discharges occur most often when the relative humidity is low, such as indoors during winter months. Marks produced by static can appear as lightning streaks, small dots, or fogging. High-speed films are more susceptible to the effects of static than are medium- or slow-speed films. When the humidity is low, you can minimize static discharges by slowly advancing the film for each picture, slowly rewinding 135 film in your camera after the last exposure, and handling the film carefully.

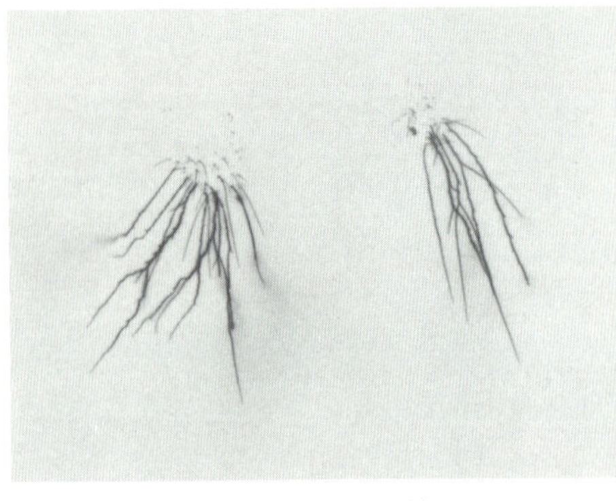

This is one type of static markings on film caused by static discharges. Friction generated while winding the film too rapidly in the camera is the main cause of static charges. As a rule, static is most troublesome when the relative humidity is low.

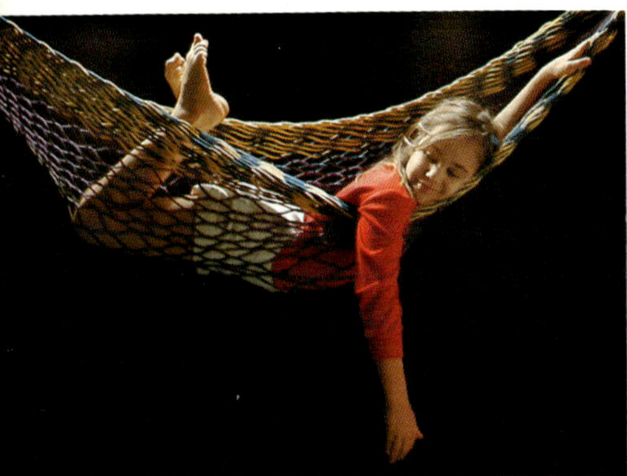

NICHOLAS C. SCOTT, KINSA

STORAGE AND CARE OF PROCESSED FILMS

For maximum life of processed films, follow the processing recommendations very closely. Incorrect processing procedures, such as faulty agitation, excessive times in certain solutions, insufficient fixing, and inadequate or excessive washing, can result in defects after long-term storage that were not apparent shortly after processing.

In time, all dyes may change to some extent. The dyes used in Kodak color films are as stable as they can be, considering all the requirements in making color photographs. The primary factors affecting the life of color films are light, moisture, and heat. For maximum permanence, store processed color films where it's dark, dry, and cool. You can store processed color films successfully in many areas on the main floors of buildings, but never in damp basements or in hot attics. A relative humidity between 15 and 40 percent and a temperature of 70°F (21°C) or less are best. Avoid a relative humidity below 15 percent because excessive brittleness may result. Never humidify color films, except under carefully controlled conditions. High relative humidities are dangerous because they increase the possibility of fungus growth.

Protect color negatives from exposure to light. For information on long-term storage of color negatives (refrigerated storage), see your photo dealer for the KODAK Publication *Storage and Care of KODAK Color Films* (E-30). Or you can obtain single copies from the address given on page 51.

For archival storage of color images, have three-color separation negatives made on black-and-white film. You can have color images made from them at any time in the future. Custom processing laboratories do this type of work.

Storage conditions for black-and-white films are less demanding than those for color films. All Kodak films are now made with a safety base and have been for many years. They are edge-marked "KODAK Safety Film." You can store black-and-white negatives (or black-and-white slides) which are on safety base at normal temperatures, such as 60 to 80°F (16 to 27°C). Store them where it's dry, below 60 percent relative humidity, to avoid the possibility of mold or fungus growth. Since the silver image may be attacked by certain sulfur compounds, protect your negatives from fumes of hydrogen sulfide and coal gas.

Protection from Physical Damage. Keep slides and negatives as clean and dustfree as possible. A good rule is never to touch the film with your fingers, except by the edges. The best way to protect negatives is to store them in envelopes with side seams. The paper and adhesive should meet the requirements of American National Standard PH4.20-1958. You can obtain a free list of AN Standards and their prices by writing to the American National Standards Institute, Inc., 1430 Broadway, New York, New York 10018. Stores that sell photo products usually offer a variety of containers for storing 2 x 2-inch slides.

Don't store color negatives or slides near moth-preventive chemicals, which tend to crystalize on the films and damage the adhesive used in slide mounts. Exposure to nitrous oxide, hydrogen sulfide, or sulfur dioxide gas may cause slow fading of color dyes. The solvents and chemicals used in insecticides and fungicide sprays may be harmful to processed films and slide mounts. Keep films away from chemical dust; alkaline dust particles and hypo particles on the emulsion may cause dye fading after a prolonged storage period. Protect your film from insects, because some species will eat the gelatin emulsion.

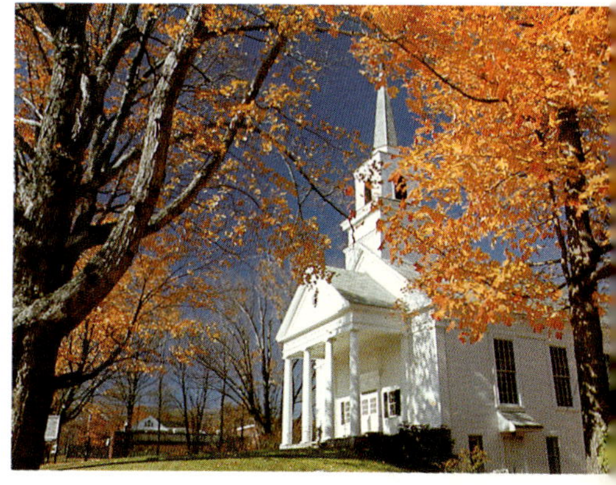

HERB JONES

CARE IN PROJECTION OF SLIDES

Slides that are properly cared for will have a useful life of many years. However, the light and heat that result from prolonged projection with high-wattage lamps will shorten the life and may even distort the slides. Avoid projection times longer than 1 minute. Never remove the heat-absorbing glass or use a lamp of higher wattage than recommended for the projector. Don't obstruct the air intake or outlet for cooling the projector.

Binding slides in glass will not have any significant effect on their useful life other than protecting them from physical damage such as dirt and scratches. When you use glass-mounted slides in high-wattage projectors, moisture may condense on the inside of the glass. You can usually eliminate the moisture by storing slides with activated silica gel.

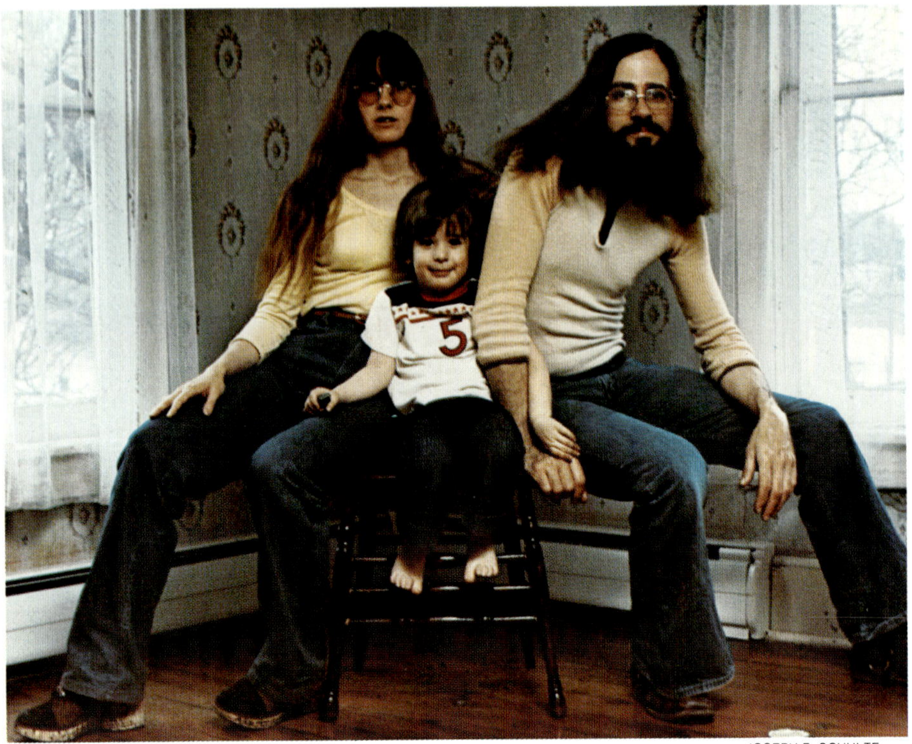

JOSEPH F. SCHULTE

Existing light plus bounce flash.

HOW TO SAVE WATER-SOAKED FILMS

Water from floods, fire-fighting, burst pipes, and leaky roofs can cause serious damage on stored negatives and slides. You can keep the damage to a minimum when you act quickly to salvage the films.

The first thing to remember is to keep the water-soaked films and their enclosures, such as slide mounts, envelopes, and sleeves, wet. Do not allow them to dry. Immerse them completely in plastic containers of cold water below 65°F (18°C), containing about 15 mL of formaldehyde solution per litre of water. The cold water and the formaldehyde will help prevent swelling and softening of the gelatin emulsion which are the major causes of damage and the growth of bacteria. When handling chemicals, be sure to observe and follow the precautionary information printed on the chemical containers.

As soon as possible, carefully separate the films from their enclosures and wash the films for 10 to 15 minutes in water at 65°F (18°C) or lower. If necessary, you can clean the films by swabbing them with a tuft of cotton *underwater*. Use extreme care because the wet emulsion is very susceptible to physical damage. Avoid any sudden temperature changes in the wash water. Rinse negatives and slides for 1 minute in diluted KODAK PHOTO-FLO Solution before drying.

Keep exposed water-soaked film wet and process it as soon as possible.

PLUS-X Pan Film
R. E. BALCH, KINSA

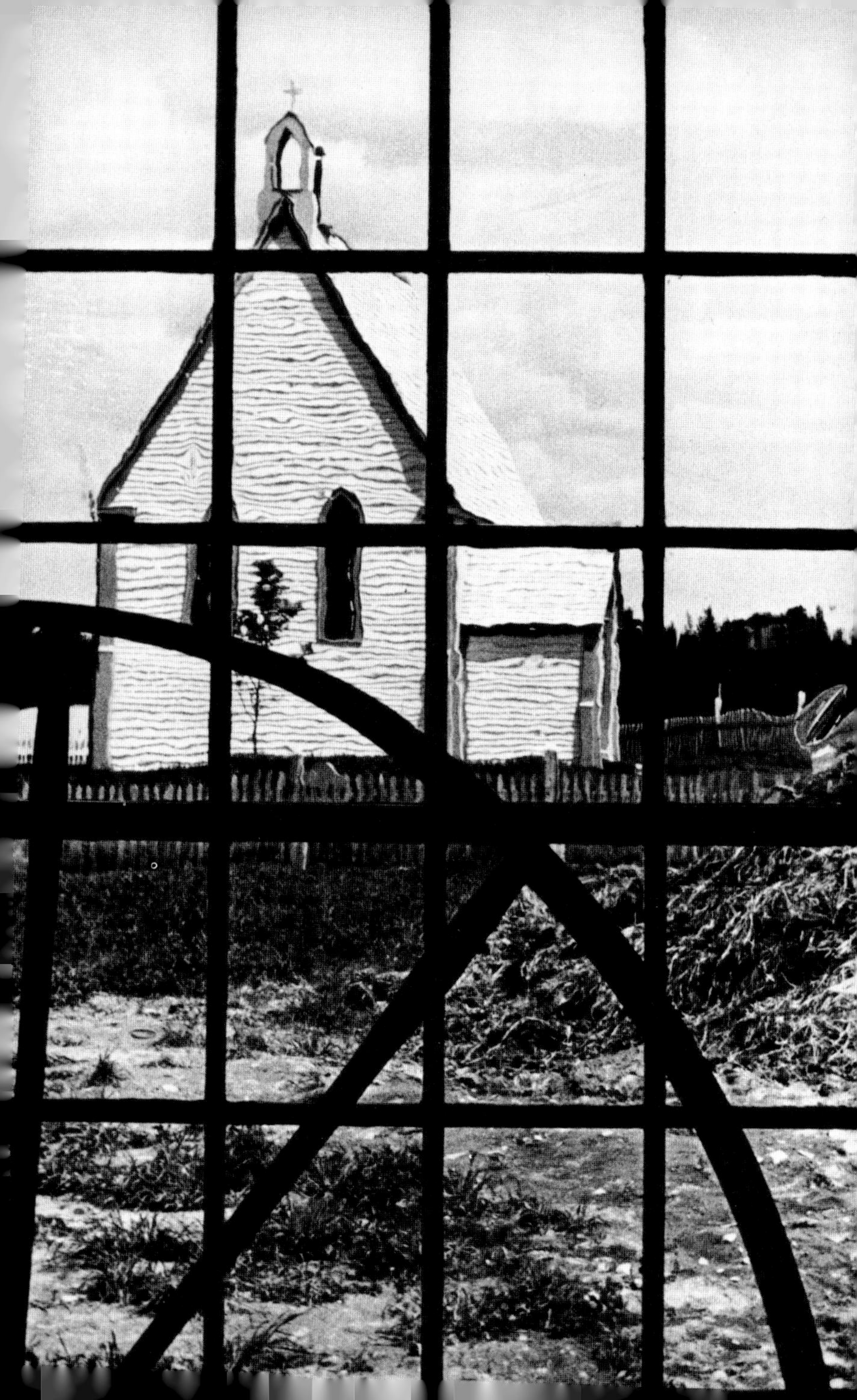

Condensed Information

KODAK COLOR FILMS FOR STILL CAMERAS

KODAK Film	Type of Pictures	For Use with	ASA Film Speed and Filter: Daylight	Photolamps 3400 K	Tungsten 3200 K	Sizes Available	Processed by	Process
KODACOLOR II (C)	Color Prints	Daylight, Electronic Flash, or Blue Flash. Also Existing Light with KODACOLOR Films	**100**	**32** No. 80B	**25** No. 80A	135-24, 135-36 110-12, 110-20 126-12, 126-20 120, 127, 620 828, 616, 116	Kodak, other labs, or users	C-41
KODACOLOR 400 (CG)	Color Prints		**400**	**125** No. 80B	**100** No. 80A	135-24, 135-36 110-12, 110-20, 120	Kodak, other labs, or users	C-41
Instant Print Film (PR)	Instant Color Prints		Exposure Index **150**	—	—	PR10	Users	Instant
KODACHROME 25 (Daylight) (KM)	Color Slides	Daylight, Electronic Flash, or Blue Flash	**25**	**8** No. 80B	**6** No. 80A	135-20, 135-36	Kodak and other labs	Commercial Laboratory K-14
KODACHROME 64 (Daylight) (KR)	Color Slides		**64**	**20** No. 80B	**16** No. 80A	135-20, 135-36 110-20, 126-20	Kodak and other labs	Commercial Laboratory K-14
EKTACHROME 64 (Daylight) (ER)*	Color Slides		**64**	**20** No. 80B	**16** No. 80A	135-20, 135-36 110-20, 126-20, 127	Kodak, other labs, or users	E-6
KODACHROME 40 5070 (Type A) (KPA)	Color Slides	Photolamps 3400 K	**25** No. 85	**40**	**32** No. 82A	135-36	Kodak and other labs	Commercial Laboratory K-14
EKTACHROME 200 (Daylight) (ED)*	Color Slides	Daylight, Electronic Flash, Blue Flash, or Existing Daylight	**200**	**64** No. 80B	**50** No. 80A	135-20, 135-36 126-20	Kodak, other labs, or users	E-6
			400†	**125†** No. 80B	**100†** No. 80A			
EKTACHROME 400 (Daylight) (EL)	Color Slides		**400**	**125** No. 80B	**100** No. 80A	135-20, 135-36 120	Kodak, other labs, or users	E-6
			800†	**250†** No. 80B	**200†** No. 80A			
EKTACHROME 160 (Tungsten) (ET)*	Color Slides	Tungsten Lamps 3200 K or Existing Tungsten Light	**100** No. 85B	**125** No. 81A	**160**	135-20, 135-36	Kodak, other labs, or users	E-6
			200† No. 85B	**250†** No. 81A	**320†**			

For *Kodak* Films

EKTACHROME Infrared (IE)	Color Slides	Daylight, Electronic Flash, or Blue Flash	**100** No. 12 or 15	**50** No. 12 or 15 + CC50C-2	—	135-20	Kodak, other labs, or users	E-4
EKTACHROME Slide Duplicating 5071	Color Slides	Tungsten Lamps 3200 K, Daylight, or Electronic Flash‡	**4‡**	—	**4‡**	135-36	Kodak, other labs, or users	E-6

*Size 120 rolls are available in the professional versions of these KODAK EKTACHROME Films. See page 39.

†With KODAK EKTACHROME 400, 200, and 160 Films, 135 size, and ESP-1 Processing. See page 52. ‡See Data Sheet pages D 24 and D 25 for filter information.

Note: See page D 1 for an explanation of the code letters after each film name.

KODAK BLACK-AND-WHITE FILMS FOR STILL CAMERAS

KODAK Film	Film Speed	Definition				Sizes Available
		Graininess	Resolving Power	Sharpness	Degree of Enlargement Allowed§	
VERICHROME Pan (VP)	ASA 125	Extremely Fine	High	Very High	High	110-12, 126-12 120, 127, 620
PLUS-X Pan (PX)	ASA 125	Extremely Fine	High	Very High	High	135-20, 135-36
PANATOMIC-X (FX)¶ PANATOMIC-X Professional (FXP)	ASA 32	Extremely Fine	Very High	Very High	Very High	135-20, 135-36 / 120
TRI-X Pan (TX)	ASA 400	Fine	High	Very High	Moderate	135-20, 135-36 126-12, 120
ROYAL-X Pan (RX)	ASA 1250	Medium	Medium	Very High	Moderately Low	120
Recording 2475 (ESTAR-AH Base) (RE)	1000	Coarse	Medium	Very High	Low	135-36
High Speed Infrared (HIE)	125** No. 25 Filter	Fine	Medium	Low	Moderately Low	135-20
High Contrast Copy 5069 (HC)	64**	Extremely Fine	Ultra High	Very High	Extremely High	135-36

§For good-quality negatives.

¶With special reversal processing, PANATOMIC-X Film in 135 size will produce black-and-white positive slides. See page D 31 for film speeds.

**Speed for tungsten light.

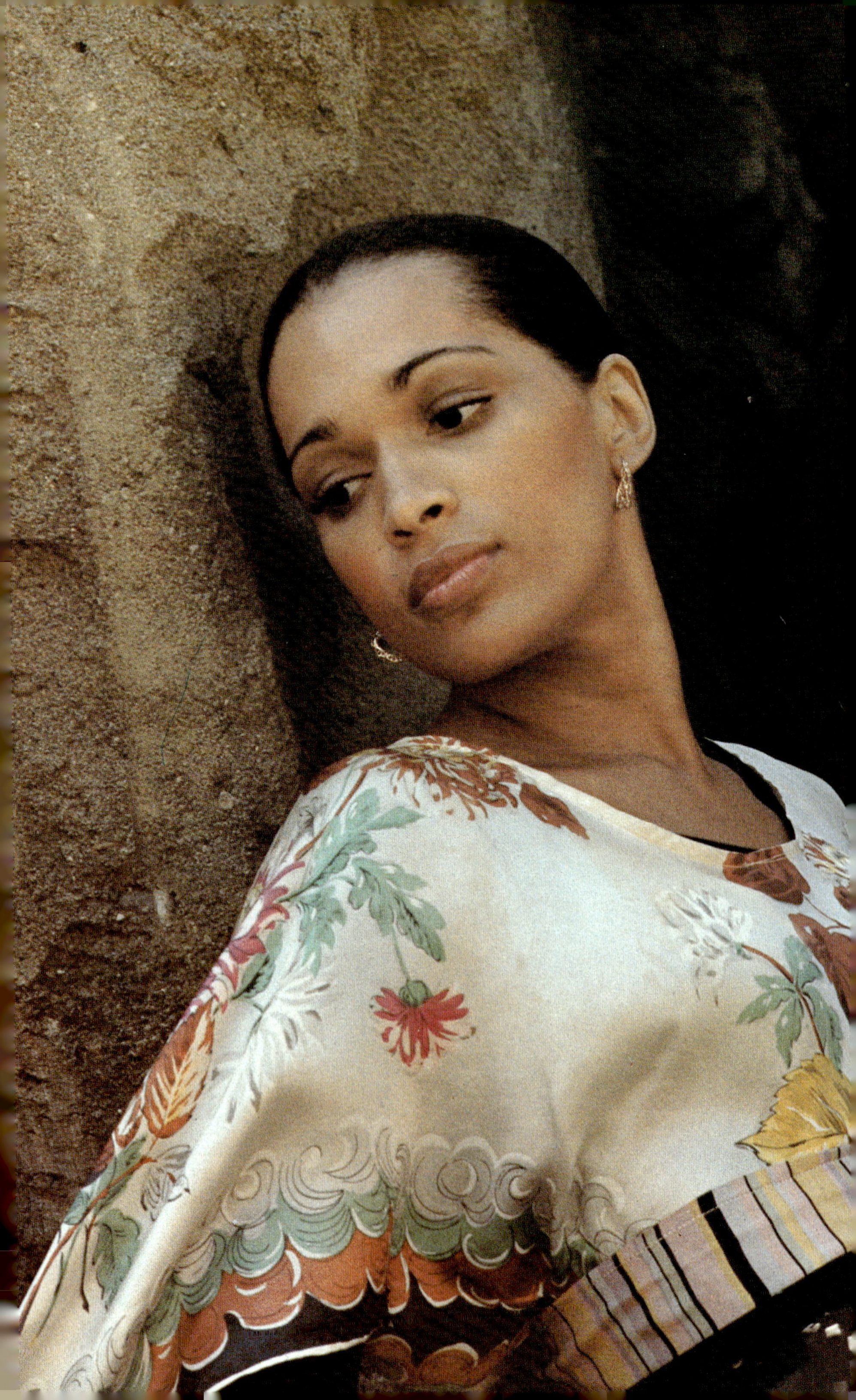

Data Sheets

KODAK Films for General Use

The following Data Sheets provide detailed information to help you obtain the best possible results with each film. Since recommendations may change, whenever these Data Sheets do not agree with the instruction sheet packaged with the film, follow the instruction sheet. Film instruction sheets are updated more frequently.

The film code letter designation and the film code number for each film are given on the Data Sheets. The code letter designation is printed on the film carton, on 135 magazines, 110 and 126 cartridges, and rolls to help identify the kind of film. For example, KODACHROME 64 Film (Daylight) is identified by the letters "KR." This film in 135 size with 20 exposures, is identified as KR135-20.

The film code number is printed on the actual film itself for most sizes so that you can identify the film after it's processed, if necessary. The film code number for KODACHROME 64 Film (Daylight) is 5032, for example.

COLOR FILMS

Page

BLACK-AND-WHITE FILMS

KODACOLOR 400 Film, 1/250 sec *f*/11.
JEANNETTE KLUTE

For Color Prints

A general-purpose, color-negative film with high sharpness and extremely fine grain. The film was modified to raise its speed to ASA 100. Its fast speed is just right for most picture-taking situations. You can take pictures with this film by daylight, electronic flash, or blue flashbulbs. KODACOLOR II Film is noted for its wide exposure latitude, which minimizes the effects of exposure errors. This film is designed for producing color prints, but color slides and black-and-white prints can also be made from the negatives.

Sizes Available: 135-24 exposures, 135-36 exposures; 110-12 exposures, 110-20 exposures; 126-12 exposures, 126-20 exposures; 120; 127; 620; 828; 616; 116.

Film Code Letter Designation: C.

Film Code Numbers: 5035—sizes 135, 110, 126, 828; 6014—sizes 120, 127, 620, 616, 116.

EXPOSURE

Speeds and Filter Recommendations:

Type of Light	Film Speed	Filter
DAYLIGHT	**ASA 100**	**None**
PHOTOLAMPS 3400 K	ASA 32	No. 80B
TUNGSTEN 3200 K	ASA 25	No. 80A

NOTE: If your camera has a built-in exposure meter that makes the reading through a filter used over the lens, see your camera manual for instructions on exposure with filters. Also, see page 97.

Daylight Exposure Table: For average subjects.

Shutter Speed 1/125 Second

Bright or Hazy Sun Distinct Shadows		Weak Hazy Sun Soft Shadows	Cloudy Bright No Shadows	Heavy Overcast	Open Shade†
On Light Sand or Snow	Average Subjects				
f/16	*f*/11*	*f*/8	*f*/5.6	*f*/4	*f*/4

**f*/5.6 at 1/125 second for backlighted close-up subjects.

†Subject shaded from the sun but lighted by a large area of sky.

Electronic Flash Guide Numbers: Use this table as a starting point in determining the correct guide number for electronic flash units rated in beam candlepower seconds (BCPS). Divide the proper guide number by the flash-to-subject distance in feet to determine the *f*-number for average subjects.

Output of Unit—BCPS	350	500	700	1000	1400	2000	2800	4000	5600	8000
Guide Number*	40	50	60	70	85	100	120	140	170	200

*If your prints are consistently too blue, use a No. 81B filter and increase your exposure by ⅓ stop.

Flash Guide Numbers: *Use blue flashbulbs or flashcubes.* Divide the proper guide number by the flash-to-subject distance in feet to determine the *f*-number for average subjects.

Syn-chroni-zation	Shutter Speed	Cube		Shallow Cylin-drical Reflector	Inter-mediate-Shaped Reflector		Polished Bowl-Shaped Reflector		Inter-mediate-Shaped Reflector		Polished Bowl-Shaped Reflector	
		Flash-cube	HI-POWER Flash-Cube	AG-1B	M2B	AG-1B	M2B	AG-1B	M3B 5B 25B	6B* 26B*	M3B 5B 25B	6B* 26B*
X	1/30	90	130	65	85	90	120	130	130	NR	180	NR
M	1/30	60	85	45	NR	65	NR	90	120	130	170	180
	1/60	60	85	45	NR	65	NR	90	110	90	160	130
	1/125	50	70	38	NR	55	NR	75	90	60	130	85
	1/250	38	55	32	NR	45	NR	65	75	42	110	60
	1/500	32	45	24	NR	34	NR	50	55	30	80	44

*Bulbs for focal-plane shutters; use with FP synchronization. NR—Not Recommended.

WARNING: Bulbs may shatter when flashed; use a flashguard over your reflector. Flashcubes have a built-in flashguard. **Do not use flash in an explosive atmosphere.**

Reciprocity Characteristics: The following table gives the exposure and filter compensation for different exposure times. The exposure increase includes the adjustment required when a filter is indicated.

Exposure Time in Seconds						
1/10,000	1/1000	1/100	1/10	1	10	100
None No Filter	None No Filter	None No Filter	None No Filter	+½ stop No Filter	+1½ stops CC10C	+2½ stops CC10C+CC10G

PROCESSING

You can have your film developed and printed by Kodak or another laboratory by returning the film to your photo dealer, or by mailing it directly with the appropriate prepaid processing mailer. Your dealer can also order enlargements or color slides from your negatives.

You can develop KODACOLOR II Film in your own darkroom and print the negatives on KODAK EKTACOLOR 74 RC Paper. Process the film in the KODAK FLEXICOLOR Processing Kit for Process C-41 or equivalent, available from photo dealers. If you want black-and-white prints from your color negatives, you can use KODAK PANALURE Paper. Instructions are included with both types of paper and with the processing kit.

DEFINITION

Graininess	Resolving Power	Sharpness	Degree of Enlargement Allowed*
Extremely Fine	High	High	High

*For good-quality negatives.

For Color Prints

An exceptionally fast color-negative film for photographing dimly lighted subjects, such as those in existing light; fast action; and subjects that require good depth of field and high shutter speeds; and for extending the flash distance range. The film is color-balanced for daylight, electronic flash, or blue flash. It also has special sensitizing characteristics that give you good pictures under other light sources, such as household light bulbs and fluorescent lamps, without using filters on your camera. You can use this film to photograph subjects ranging from bright sunlight to very dim light, depending on your camera. In addition, KODACOLOR 400 Film offers wide exposure latitude.

Sizes Available: 135-24 exposures, 135-36 exposures; 110-12 exposures, 110-20 exposures; 120.

Film Code Letter Designation: CG.

Film Code Numbers: 5075—sizes 135, 110; 6075—size 120.

EXPOSURE

Speeds and Filter Recommendations for Critical Use:

Type of Light	Film Speed	Filter
DAYLIGHT	**ASA 400**	**None**
PHOTOLAMPS 3400 K	ASA 125	No. 80B
TUNGSTEN 3200 K	ASA 100	No. 80A

NOTE: If your camera has a built-in exposure meter that makes the reading through a filter used over the lens, see your camera manual for instructions on exposure with filters. Also, see page 97.

Daylight Exposure Table: For average subjects.

Shutter Speed 1/500 Second	Shutter Speed 1/250 Second				
Bright or Hazy Sun Distinct Shadows	Bright or Hazy Sun Distinct Shadows	Weak Hazy Sun Soft Shadows	Cloudy Bright No Shadows	Heavy Overcast	Open Shade†
On Light Sand or Snow	Average Subjects				
f/16	*f*/16*	*f*/11	*f*/8	*f*/5.6	*f*/5.6

**f*/8 at 1/250 second for backlighted close-up subjects.
†Subject shaded from the sun but lighted by a large area of sky.

Existing-Light Exposure Table: Use an exposure meter or an automatic camera if you have one. For cameras without exposure meters, try the settings suggested in the table. These exposures are *guides;* for more assurance, bracket your exposures 1 stop on each side of the suggested exposure.

Picture Subject	Shutter Speed	Lens Opening
Home Interiors at Night— Areas with bright light	1/30	*f*/2.8
Areas with average light	1/30	*f*/2
Candlelighted Close-ups	1/15*	*f*/2
Interiors with Bright Fluorescent Light	1/60	*f*/4
Indoor, Outdoor Christmas Lighting at Night	1/15*	*f*/2
Brightly Lighted Downtown Street Scenes at Night	1/60	*f*/2.8
Brightly Lighted Theatre Districts—Las Vegas or Times Square	1/60	*f*/4
Neon Signs, Other Lighted Signs	1/125	*f*/4
Store Windows at Night	1/60	*f*/4
Floodlighted Buildings, Fountains, Monuments	1/15*	*f*/2
Distant View of City Skyline at Night	1*	*f*/2.8
Skylines—10 minutes after sunset	1/60	*f*/5.6

*Use a tripod or other firm camera support.

Picture Subject	Shutter Speed	Lens Opening
Fairs, Amusement Parks	1/30	*f*/2.8
Aerial Fireworks Displays— Keep camera shutter open on "BULB" or "TIME" for several bursts	BULB*	*f*/16
Night Football, Baseball, Racetracks	1/125	*f*/2.8
Basketball, Hockey, Bowling	1/125	*f*/2
Boxing, Wrestling	1/250	*f*/2
Stage Shows— Average lighting	1/60	*f*/2.8
Bright lighting	1/125	*f*/4
Circuses—Floodlighted acts	1/60	*f*/2.8
Ice Shows—Floodlighted acts	1/125	*f*/2.8
Ice Shows, Circuses— Spotlighted acts (carbon arc)	1/250	*f*/2.8
School—Stage and auditorium	1/30	*f*/2
Swimming Pool—Indoors, tungsten lights above water	1/60	*f*/2
Church Interiors— Tungsten lights	1/30	*f*/2

Electronic Flash Guide Numbers: Use this table as a starting point in determining the correct guide number for electronic flash units rated in beam candlepower seconds (BCPS). Divide the proper guide number by the flash-to-subject distance in feet to determine the *f*-number for average subjects.

Output of Unit—BCPS	350	500	700	1000	1400	2000	2800	4000	5600	8000
Guide Number	85	100	120	140	170	200	240	280	340	400

Flash Guide Numbers: *Use blue flashbulbs or flashcubes.* Divide the proper guide number by the flash-to-subject distance in feet to determine the *f*-number for average subjects.

Synchronization	Shutter Speed	Cube		Shallow Cylindrical Reflector	Intermediate-Shaped Reflector		Polished Bowl-Shaped Reflector		Intermediate-Shaped Reflector		Polished Bowl-Shaped Reflector	
		Flashcube	HI-POWER Flashcube	AG-1B	M2B	AG-1B	M2B	AG-1B	M3B 5B 25B	6B* 26B*	M3B 5B 25B	6B* 26B*
X	1/30	180	260	130	170	180	240	260	260	NR	360	NR
M	1/30	120	170	90	NR	130	NR	180	240	260	340	360
	1/60	120	170	90	NR	130	NR	180	220	180	320	260
	1/125	100	140	75	NR	110	NR	150	180	120	260	170
	1/250	75	110	65	NR	90	NR	130	150	85	220	120
	1/500	65	90	50	NR	70	NR	100	110	60	160	85

*Bulbs for focal-plane shutters; use with FP synchronization. NR—Not Recommended.

WARNING: Bulbs may shatter when flashed; use a flashguard over your reflector. Flashcubes have a built-in flashguard. **Do not use flash in an explosive atmosphere.**

Reciprocity Characteristics: The following table gives the exposure compensation for different exposure times.

Exposure Time in Seconds						
1/10,000	1/1000	1/100	1/10	1	10	100
None No Filter	None No Filter	None No Filter	None No Filter	+½ stop No Filter	+1 stop No Filter	+2 stops No Filter

PROCESSING

You can have your film developed and printed by Kodak or another laboratory by returning the film to your photo dealer, or by mailing it directly with the appropriate prepaid processing mailer. Your dealer can also order enlargements or color slides from your negatives.

You can develop KODACOLOR 400 Film in your own darkroom and print the negatives on KODAK EKTACOLOR 74 RC Paper. Process the film in the KODAK FLEXICOLOR Processing Kit for Process C-41 or equivalent, available from photo dealers. If you want black-and-white prints from your color negatives, you can use KODAK PANALURE Paper. Instructions are included with both types of paper and with the processing kit.

DEFINITION

Graininess	Resolving Power	Sharpness	Degree of Enlargement Allowed*
Very Fine	Medium	Medium	Moderately Low

*For good-quality negatives.

For Color Prints

KODAK Instant Print Film is designed for use in KODAK Instant Cameras. This film produces color prints directly from the camera which develop in a matter of minutes. You don't have to time development or peel off any components. The film is litter-free except for packaging materials, the empty film pack, and the film cover. KODAK Instant Prints have a KODAK SATINLUXE™ Finish and excellent grain and sharpness characteristics. This surface lets you handle prints without fingerprinting and with a minimum of scratching. The film is color balanced for daylight, blue flash, and electronic flash.

Size Available: PR10, 10 exposures.

Film Code Letter Designation: PR.

Picture Size: The overall print size, including the white borders, is 3¹³⁄₁₆ x 4 inches (9.7 x 10.2 cm). The actual image size within the borders is 2⅝ x 3⁹⁄₁₆ inches (6.8 x 9.1 cm).

Camera Loading: Before loading your camera, check to see that the rollers are clean. If the rollers need cleaning, follow the instructions in your camera manual. Whenever possible, avoid loading the film pack in direct sunlight. Hold the film pack by the edges only. Be careful not to squeeze the pack or apply pressure to the film cover, since this could allow light to spoil your pictures.

EXPOSURE

Speed and Filter Recommendations:

Type of Light	Film Speed	Filter
DAYLIGHT	Exposure Index 150	None

Flash: Use blue flash or electronic flash. See your camera and electronic flash manuals for detailed information on flash.

Lighten/Darken Control: Under most conditions, you should set the Lighten/Darken control on your camera in the normal, center position. However, the lightness or darkness of your prints can be affected by such factors as temperature and type and brightness of the subject. The Lighten/Darken control helps you to compensate for these effects. After taking a picture, if you want to take a lighter or darker picture of the same subject in the same location without changing the lighting or your position, adjust the Lighten/Darken control *before* taking the next picture. To take a lighter picture, move the control toward Lighten; for a darker picture, move the control toward Darken.

If you take flash pictures of subjects outside the recommended flash distance range, subjects closer than the minimum distance will probably be too light and unsharp; subjects farther than the maximum distance will probably be too dark, regardless of the Lighten/Darken control setting. For additional information, see your camera and electronic flash manuals.

DEVELOPMENT

Pictures begin to develop as they are ejected from the camera. Hold the prints by their borders, and don't bend, flex, or attempt to fold them. Never leave prints in direct sunlight or on hot surfaces during development.

An image will begin to appear in approximately 1 minute under room temperature conditions, 72°F (22°C). You can judge exposure after approximately 5 minutes. Development is essentially complete after about 8 minutes at this temperature. Prints will appear lighter when judged in direct sunlight than they will under normal room lighting.

Temperature Effects on Prints: The recommended temperature range during development of prints is 60 to 100°F (16 to 38°C). At temperatures below 60°F (16°C), place your prints in a warm place—an inside pocket, for example—as soon as they are ejected from the camera, and leave them there during development. Otherwise, your prints may appear too light. It may be desirable at the upper end of the temperature range—approaching 100°F (38°C)—to set the Lighten/Darken control toward Lighten to keep prints from becoming too dark.

STORAGE AND CARE OF FILM AND PRINTS

Avoid storing the camera and film in a hot place such as the glove compartment or rear-window shelf of a car in the sun because this may result in reduced picture quality and damaged equipment. If you inadvertently leave the camera and film in a hot place, allow them to cool for at least one hour before taking any pictures. Also, allow them to return to normal temperature if they have been left in a cold place.

Store your prints in a cool, dry place. Color dyes may change over a period of time. Print colors will remain unchanged longer if you protect your pictures from long exposure to bright light.

Each picture is a sealed unit that contains a caustic fluid. Never cut, trim, puncture, tear, or separate the picture unit, since this may allow some of the fluid to escape and come into contact with skin or eyes.

CAUTION: Picture units contain a caustic fluid. Normally fluid will not appear. If it does, alkali burn may result from direct contact. Keep fluid away from eyes, mouth, and skin. Avoid fluid contact with fabrics, carpeting, and furniture to prevent stain.

In case of contact with eyes, immediately flush with plenty of water and get medical attention. In case of any other contact, wash thoroughly at once.

ADDITIONAL PRINTS AND SLIDES

You can have additional color prints and color enlargements made from your original instant color prints. When made by a Kodak Processing Laboratory, the prints are called KODAK Color Copyprints; the enlargements, KODAK Color Copy Enlargements.

You can also have color slides made from your color prints. When Kodak makes these slides, they are called KODAK Color Copy Slides.

For Color Slides

A favorite for color slides because of its excellent color quality, high sharpness, and extremely fine grain. The film retains good detail in both highlights and shadow areas. Its speed is adequate for many picture-taking situations and it has good exposure latitude. It therefore produces acceptable results even with moderate overexposure or underexposure. This film is designed for use in daylight, or with electronic flash or blue flashbulbs.

Size Available: 135-20 exposures, 135-36 exposures.

Film Code Letter Designation: KM.

Film Code Number: 5073.

EXPOSURE

Speeds and Filter Recommendations:

Type of Light	Film Speed	Filter
DAYLIGHT	**ASA 25**	**None**
PHOTOLAMPS 3400 K	ASA 8	No. 80B
TUNGSTEN 3200 K	ASA 6	No. 80A

NOTE: If your camera has a built-in exposure meter that makes the reading through a filter used over the lens, see your camera manual for instructions on exposure with filters. Also, see page 97.

Daylight Exposure Table: For average subjects.

Shutter Speed 1/125 Second				Shutter Speed 1/60 Second	
Bright or Hazy Sun Distinct Shadows		Weak Hazy Sun Soft Shadows	Cloudy Bright No Shadows	Heavy Overcast	Open Shade†
On Light Sand or Snow	Average Subjects				
f/11	*f*/8*	*f*/5.6	*f*/4	*f*/4	*f*/4

*f/4 at 1/125 second for backlighted close-up subjects.

†Subject shaded from the sun but lighted by a large area of sky.

Electronic Flash Guide Numbers: Use this table as a starting point in determining the correct guide number for electronic flash units rated in beam candlepower seconds (BCPS). Divide the proper guide number by the flash-to-subject distance in feet to determine the f-number for average subjects.

Output of Unit—BCPS	350	500	700	1000	1400	2000	2800	4000	5600	8000
Guide Number*	20	24	30	35	40	50	60	70	85	100

*If your slides are consistently too blue, use a No. 81B filter and increase your exposure by ⅓ stop.

Flash Guide Numbers: *Use blue flashbulbs or flashcubes.* Divide the proper guide number by the flash-to-subject distance in feet to determine the *f*-number for average subjects.

Syn-chroni-zation	Shutter Speed	Cube		Shallow Cylin-drical Reflector	Inter-mediate-Shaped Reflector		Polished Bowl-Shaped Reflector		Inter-mediate-Shaped Reflector		Polished Bowl-Shaped Reflector	
		Flash-cube	HI-POWER Flash-Cube	AG-1B	M2B	AG-1B	M2B	AG-1B	M3B 5B 25B	6B* 26B*	M3B 5B 25B	6B* 26B*
X	1/30	45	65	32	42	45	60	65	65	NR	90	NR
M	1/30	30	42	22	NR	32	NR	45	60	65	85	90
	1/60	30	42	22	NR	32	NR	45	55	45	80	65
	1/125	26	36	20	NR	28	NR	38	45	30	65	42
	1/250	20	28	16	NR	22	NR	32	38	22	55	30
	1/500	16	24	12	NR	18	NR	24	28	15	40	22

*Bulbs for focal-plane shutters; use with FP synchronization. NR—Not Recommended.

WARNING: Bulbs may shatter when flashed; use a flashguard over your reflector. Flashcubes have a built-in flashguard. **Do not use flash in an explosive atmosphere.**

Reciprocity Characteristics: The following table gives the exposure and filter compensation for different exposure times. The exposure increase includes the adjustment required when a filter is indicated.

Exposure Time in Seconds

1/10,000	1/1000	1/100	1/10	1	10	100
None No Filter	None No Filter	None No Filter	None No Filter	+1 stop CC10M	+1½ stops CC10M	+2½ stops CC10M

PROCESSING

You can have your film processed by Kodak or another laboratory by returning the film to your photo dealer, or by mailing it directly with the appropriate prepaid processing mailer. Your dealer can also order duplicate slides, color prints, or enlargements from your slides.

You can't process KODACHROME Films successfully in your own darkroom because the process is highly complex and requires commercial photofinishing equipment.

DEFINITION

Graininess	Resolving Power	Sharpness
Extremely Fine	High	High

KODACHROME 64 Film (Daylight)

For Color Slides

A medium-speed, color-slide film for general picture-taking. The ASA 64 speed makes the film a good choice for making color slides when lighting conditions are less than ideal. Under normal lighting conditions, you can use high shutter speeds or small lens openings. KODACHROME 64 Film exhibits remarkable sharpness and freedom from graininess. Color rendition is excellent. The film is for use with daylight, electronic flash, or blue flashbulbs.

Sizes Available: 135-20 exposures, 135-36 exposures; 110-20 exposures; 126-20 exposures.

Film Code Letter Designation: KR.

Film Code Number: 5032.

EXPOSURE

Speeds and Filter Recommendations:

Type of Light	Film Speed	Filter
DAYLIGHT	**ASA 64**	**None**
PHOTOLAMPS 3400 K	ASA 20	No. 80B
TUNGSTEN 3200 K	ASA 16	No. 80A

NOTE: If your camera has a built-in exposure meter that makes the reading through a filter used over the lens, see your camera manual for instructions on exposure with filters. Also, see page 97.

Daylight Exposure Table: For average subjects.

Shutter Speed 1/125 Second

Bright or Hazy Sun Distinct Shadows		Weak Hazy Sun Soft Shadows	Cloudy Bright No Shadows	Heavy Overcast	Open Shade†
On Light Sand or Snow	Average Subjects				
f/16	*f*/11*	*f*/8	*f*/5.6	*f*/4	*f*/4

**f*/5.6 at 1/125 second for backlighted close-up subjects.

†Subject shaded from the sun but lighted by a large area of sky.

Electronic Flash Guide Numbers: Use this table as a starting point in determining the correct guide number for electronic flash units rated in beam candlepower seconds (BCPS). Divide the proper guide number by the flash-to-subject distance in feet to determine the *f*-number for average subjects.

Output of Unit—BCPS	350	500	700	1000	1400	2000	2800	4000	5600	8000
Guide Number*	32	40	45	55	65	80	95	110	130	160

*If your slides are consistently too blue, use a No. 81B filter and increase your exposure by ⅓ stop.

Flash Guide Numbers: *Use blue flashbulbs or flashcubes.* Divide the proper guide number by the flash-to-subject distance in feet to determine the *f*-number for average subjects.

Syn-chroni-zation	Shutter Speed	Cube		Shallow Cylin-drical Reflector	Inter-mediate-Shaped Reflector		Polished Bowl-Shaped Reflector		Inter-mediate-Shaped Reflector		Polished Bowl-Shaped Reflector	
		Flash-cube	HI-POWER Flash-Cube	AG-1B	M 2 B	AG-1B	M 2 B	AG-1B	M3B 5B 25B	6B* 26B*	M3B 5B 25B	6B* 26B*
X	1/30	70	100	50	70	75	100	100	100	NR	150	NR
M	1/30	50	70	36	NR	50	NR	75	90	100	130	140
	1/60	50	65	36	NR	50	NR	70	90	75	130	100
	1/125	40	55	30	NR	45	NR	60	75	50	110	70
	1/250	30	45	26	NR	36	NR	50	60	34	85	50
	1/500	26	36	20	NR	28	NR	40	45	24	65	34

*Bulbs for focal-plane shutters; use with FP synchronization. NR—Not Recommended.

WARNING: Bulbs may shatter when flashed; use a flashguard over your reflector. Flashcubes have a built-in flashguard. **Do not use flash in an explosive atmosphere.**

Reciprocity Characteristics: The following table gives the exposure and filter compensation for different exposure times. The exposure increase includes the adjustment required when a filter is indicated.

Exposure Time in Seconds						
1/10,000	1/1000	1/100	1/10	1	10	100
None No Filter	None No Filter	None No Filter	None No Filter	+1 stop CC10R	NR	NR

NR—Not Recommended.

PROCESSING

You can have your film processed by Kodak or another laboratory by returning the film to your photo dealer, or by mailing it directly with the appropriate prepaid processing mailer. Your dealer can also order duplicate slides, color prints, or enlargements from your slides.

You can't process KODACHROME Films successfully in your own darkroom because the process is highly complex and requires commercial photofinishing equipment.

DEFINITION

Graininess	Resolving Power	Sharpness
Extremely Fine	High	High

For Color Slides

An excellent film for general picture-taking when you want color slides. This film replaced KODAK EKTACHROME-X Film. Color reproduction has been improved. EKTACHROME 64 Film produces vivid colors, clean highlights, and good shadow detail. It has improved sharpness and low graininess which gives very good image quality. The medium speed of the film helps you to take good pictures in the shade or on overcast days. It's balanced for daylight; for flash pictures, use electronic flash or blue flashbulbs. A feature of this film, as with all KODAK EKTACHROME Films, is that you can process it in your own darkroom if you want to.

Sizes Available: 135-20 exposures, 135-36 exposures; 110-20 exposures; 126-20 exposures; 127.

Film Code Letter Designation: ER.

Film Code Numbers: 5031—sizes 135, 110, 126; 6031—size 127.

EXPOSURE

Speeds and Filter Recommendations:

Type of Light	Film Speed	Filter
DAYLIGHT	**ASA 64**	**None**
PHOTOLAMPS 3400 K	ASA 20	No. 80B
TUNGSTEN 3200 K	ASA 16	No. 80A

NOTE: If your camera has a built-in exposure meter that makes the reading through a filter used over the lens, see your camera manual for instructions on exposure with filters. Also, see page 97.

Daylight Exposure Table: For average subjects.

Shutter Speed 1/125 Second					
Bright or Hazy Sun Distinct Shadows		Weak Hazy Sun Soft Shadows	Cloudy Bright No Shadows	Heavy Overcast	Open Shade†
On Light Sand or Snow	Average Subjects				
f/16	*f*/11*	*f*/8	*f*/5.6	*f*/4	*f*/4

**f*/5.6 at 1/125 second for backlighted close-up subjects.

†Subject shaded from the sun but lighted by a large area of sky.

Electronic Flash Guide Numbers: Use this table as a starting point in determining the correct guide number for electronic flash units rated in beam candlepower seconds (BCPS). Divide the proper guide number by the flash-to-subject distance in feet to determine the *f*-number for average subjects.

Output of Unit—BCPS	350	500	700	1000	1400	2000	2800	4000	5600	8000
Guide Number*	32	40	45	55	65	80	95	110	130	160

*If your slides are consistently too blue, use a No. 81B filter and increase your exposure by ⅓ stop.

Flash Guide Numbers: *Use blue flashbulbs or flashcubes.* Divide the proper guide number by the flash-to-subject distance in feet to determine the *f*-number for average subjects.

Synchronization	Shutter Speed	Cube		Shallow Cylindrical Reflector	Intermediate-Shaped Reflector		Polished Bowl-Shaped Reflector		Intermediate-Shaped Reflector		Polished Bowl-Shaped Reflector	
		Flashcube	HI-POWER Flash-Cube	AG-1B	M2B	AG-1B	M2B	AG-1B	M3B 5B 25B	6B* 26B*	M3B 5B 25B	6B* 26B*
X	1/30	70	100	50	70	75	100	100	100	NR	150	NR
M	1/30	50	70	36	NR	50	NR	75	90	100	130	140
	1/60	50	65	36	NR	50	NR	70	90	75	130	100
	1/125	40	55	30	NR	45	NR	60	75	50	110	70
	1/250	30	45	26	NR	36	NR	50	60	34	85	50
	1/500	26	36	20	NR	28	NR	40	45	24	65	34

*Bulbs for focal-plane shutters; use with FP synchronization. NR—Not Recommended.

WARNING: Bulbs may shatter when flashed; use a flashguard over your reflector. Flashcubes have a built-in flashguard. **Do not use flash in an explosive atmosphere.**

Reciprocity Characteristics: The following table gives the exposure and filter compensation for different exposure times. The exposure increase includes the adjustment required when a filter is indicated.

Exposure Time in Seconds

1/10,000	1/1000	1/100	1/10	1	10	100
+½ stop No Filter	None No Filter	None No Filter	None No Filter	+½ stop CC10B	+1 stop CC15B	NR

NR—Not Recommended.

PROCESSING

You can have your film processed by Kodak or another laboratory by returning the film to your photo dealer, or by mailing it directly with the appropriate prepaid processing mailer. Your dealer can also order duplicate slides, color prints, or enlargements from your slides.

To process the film yourself, use the KODAK EKTACHROME Film Processing Kit, Process E-6 or equivalent, sold by photo dealers.

DEFINITION

Graininess	Resolving Power	Sharpness
Very Fine	High	High

For Color Slides

An improved film for use with 3400 K photolamps. It replaced KODACHROME II Professional Film (Type A). KODACHROME 40 Film has finer grain, high sharpness, and improved color quality. It has exceptional definition for which KODACHROME Films are noted. Its speed is sufficient for photolamp illumination. KODACHROME 40 Film is excellent for informal portraits, close-ups, title slides, and for copying color originals. You can also take pictures in daylight with this film by using a No. 85 filter over your camera lens. This film is designed for the same commercial process as KODACHROME 25 and 64 Films (Daylight).

Size Available: 135-36 exposures.

Film Code Letter Designation: KPA.

Film Code Number: 5070.

EXPOSURE

Speeds and Filter Recommendations:

Type of Light	Film Speed	Filter
PHOTOLAMPS 3400 K	**ASA 40**	**None**
TUNGSTEN 3200 K	ASA 32	No. 82A
DAYLIGHT	ASA 25	No. 85

NOTE: If your camera has a built-in exposure meter that makes the reading through a filter used over the lens, see your camera manual for instructions on exposure with filters. Also, see page 97.

Photolamps—3400 K: The following table is based on the use of two 500-watt reflector-type photolamps 3400 K, such as General Electric DXC and Sylvania DXC reflector floodlamps. Use one as a fill-in light close to the camera at lens level; the other as the main light on the opposite side of the camera, 2 to 4 feet higher, and at a 45-degree angle from the camera-subject axis. Position both lights the same distance from the subject.

EXPOSURE TABLE FOR 500-WATT REFLECTOR-TYPE PHOTOLAMPS 3400 K			
Set Shutter Speed at 1/60 Second			
Lamp-to-Subject Distance	4½ ft	6 ft	9 ft
Lens Opening	*f*/4	*f*/2.8	*f*/2

NOTE: Use these camera settings as guides only. The lamp-to-subject distances give a lighting ratio of 2:1. For a 3:1 ratio, place the fill-in light at a distance from the subject 1.4 times the distance for the main light and use a lens opening ½ stop larger.

This table is based on the use of new lamps. After the lamps have burned for 1 hour, use a lens opening ½ stop larger; after 2 hours, use a lens opening 1 stop larger.

Daylight Exposure Table: For average subjects. *Use a No. 85 filter.*

Shutter Speed 1/125 Second				Shutter Speed 1/60 Second	
Bright or Hazy Sun Distinct Shadows		Weak Hazy Sun Soft Shadows	Cloudy Bright No Shadows	Heavy Overcast	Open Shade†
On Light Sand or Snow	Average Subjects				
f/11	*f*/8*	*f*/5.6	*f*/4	*f*/4	*f*/4

**f*/4 at 1/125 second for backlighted close-up subjects.

†Subject shaded from the sun but lighted by a large area of sky.

Electronic Flash Guide Numbers: *Use a No. 85 filter.* This table is intended as a starting point in determining the correct guide number for electronic flash units rated in beam candlepower seconds (BCPS). Divide the proper guide number by the flash-to-subject distance in feet to determine the *f*-number for average subjects.

Output of Unit—BCPS	350	500	700	1000	1400	2000	2800	4000	5600	8000
Guide Number	20	24	30	35	40	50	60	70	85	100

Flash Guide Numbers: *Use blue flashbulbs or flashcubes and a No. 85 filter.** Divide the proper guide number by the flash-to-subject distance in feet to determine the *f*-number for average subjects.

Synchronization	Shutter Speed	Cube		Shallow Cylindrical Reflector	Intermediate-Shaped Reflector		Polished Bowl-Shaped Reflector		Intermediate-Shaped Reflector		Polished Bowl-Shaped Reflector	
		Flashcube	HI-POWER Flash-Cube	AG-1B	M2B	AG-1B	M2B	AG-1B	M3B 5B 25B	6B† 26B†	M3B 5B 25B	6B† 26B†
X	1/30	45	65	32	42	45	60	65	65	NR	90	NR
M	1/30	30	42	22	NR	32	NR	45	60	65	85	90
	1/60	30	42	22	NR	32	NR	45	55	45	80	65
	1/125	26	36	20	NR	28	NR	38	45	30	65	42
	1/250	20	28	16	NR	22	NR	32	38	22	55	30
	1/500	16	24	12	NR	18	NR	24	28	15	40	22

*If you prefer, you can use clear flashbulbs. Multiply the guide numbers in the table by 1.4, and use a No. 81EF filter with AG-1 and M3 flashbulbs or a No. 81C filter with other clear flashbulbs.

†Bulbs for focal-plane shutters; use with FP synchronization. NR—Not Recommended.

WARNING: Bulbs may shatter when flashed; use a flashguard over your reflector. Flashcubes have a built-in flashguard. **Do not use flash in an explosive atmosphere.**

Reciprocity Characteristics: The following table gives the exposure compensation for different exposure times.

Exposure Time in Seconds

1/10,000	1/1000	1/100	1/10	1	5	10	100
None No Filter	None No Filter	None No Filter	None No Filter	+½ stop No Filter	+1 stop No Filter	NR	NR

NR—Not Recommended.

PROCESSING

You can have your film processed by Kodak or another laboratory by returning the film to your photo dealer, or by mailing it directly with the appropriate prepaid processing mailer. Your dealer can also order duplicate slides, color prints, or enlargements from your slides.

You can't process KODACHROME Films successfully in your own darkroom because the process is highly complex and requires commercial photofinishing equipment.

DEFINITION

Graininess	Resolving Power	Sharpness
Extremely Fine	High	High

For Color Slides

A high-speed color-slide film for photographing dimly lighted subjects, fast action, subjects that require good depth of field and high shutter speeds, and for extending the distance range for flash pictures. This film replaced KODAK High Speed EKTACHROME Film (Daylight). EKTACHROME 200 Film has higher speed, improved color rendition, and improved sharpness and graininess. It is designed for use with daylight, electronic flash, or blue flashbulbs. You can use this film for existing-light subjects, such as performers illuminated by carbon-arc spotlights or indoor scenes illuminated by existing daylight. An exceptional feature is that with special processing, you can expose the film at speeds higher than its normal speed.

Sizes Available: 135-20 exposures, 135-36 exposures; 126-20 exposures.

Film Code Letter Designation: ED. **Film Code Number:** 5076.

EXPOSURE

Speeds and Filter Recommendations:

Type of Light	Film Speed	Filter
DAYLIGHT	**ASA 200***	**None**
PHOTOLAMPS 3400 K	ASA 64	No. 80B
TUNGSTEN 3200 K	ASA 50	No. 80A

*See footnote in Daylight Exposure Table below.

NOTE: If your camera has a built-in exposure meter that makes the reading through a filter used over the lens, see your camera manual for instructions on exposure with filters. Also, see page 97.

Daylight Exposure Table (ASA 200): For average subjects. Exposure recommendations are for cameras with focal-plane shutters. For leaf-type shutters, see explanation under table.

Shutter Speed 1/500 Second*	Shutter Speed 1/250 Second*				
Bright or Hazy Sun Distinct Shadows	Bright or Hazy Sun Distinct Shadows	Weak Hazy Sun Soft Shadows	Cloudy Bright No Shadows	Heavy Overcast	Open Shade‡
On Light Sand or Snow	Average Subjects				
f/16	*f*/16†	*f*/11	*f*/8	*f*/5.6	*f*/5.6

*When using a camera with a leaf-type shutter under lighting conditions that require high shutter speeds and medium or small lens openings (lens openings beginning about midway on your camera lens-opening scale), reduce exposure as follows: at 1/250 second, use a lens opening ½ stop smaller than indicated; at 1/500 second, use a lens opening 1 stop smaller than indicated.

†*f*/8 at 1/250 second for backlighted close-up subjects.

‡Subject shaded from the sun but lighted by a large area of sky.

Existing-Light Exposure Table (ASA 200): Use an exposure meter or an automatic camera if you have one. For cameras without exposure meters, try the settings suggested in the table. These exposures are *guides;* for more assurance, bracket your exposures 1 stop on each side of the suggested exposure.

Picture Subject	Shutter Speed	Lens Opening
Skylines—10 minutes after sunset	1/60	*f*/4
Interiors with Bright Fluorescent Light*	1/30	*f*/4
Ice Shows, Circuses—Spotlighted acts (carbon arc)	1/125	*f*/2.8
Brightly Lighted Downtown Street Scenes at Night	1/30	*f*/2.8
Brightly Lighted Nightclub or Theatre Districts at Night—Las Vegas or Times Square Store Window Displays at Night	1/30	*f*/4

*May require correction filters for optimum results. See page 46.

Picture Subject	Shutter Speed	Lens Opening
Neon and Other Lighted Signs at Night	1/60	*f*/4
Floodlighted Buildings, Fountains, Monuments	1/2†	*f*/4
Christmas Lighting, Trees—Indoor and Outdoor	1†	*f*/5.6
Fairs, Amusement Parks at Night	1/30	*f*/2
Night Football, Baseball, Racetracks	1/60	*f*/2.8

†Use a camera support for exposure times longer than 1/30 second.

▭ Tungsten light produces yellow-red color rendition.

Electronic Flash Guide Numbers: Use this table as a starting point in determining the correct guide number for electronic flash units rated in beam candlepower seconds (BCPS). Divide the proper guide number by the flash-to-subject distance in feet to determine the *f*-number for average subjects.

Output of Unit—BCPS	350	500	700	1000	1400	2000	2800	4000	5600	8000
Guide Number*	60	70	85	100	120	140	170	200	240	280

*If your slides are consistently too blue, use a No. 81B filter and increase your exposure by ⅓ stop.

Flash Guide Numbers: *Use blue flashbulbs or flashcubes.* Divide the proper guide number by the flash-to-subject distance in feet to determine the *f*-number for average subjects.

Syn-chroni-zation	Shutter Speed	Cube		Shallow Cylin-drical Reflector	Inter-mediate-Shaped Reflector		Polished Bowl-Shaped Reflector		Inter-mediate-Shaped Reflector		Polished Bowl-Shaped Reflector	
		Flash-cube	HI-POWER Flash-Cube	AG-1B	M2B	AG-1B	M2B	AG-1B	M3B 5B 25B	6B* 26B*	M3B 5B 25B	6B* 26B*
X	1/30	130	180	90	120	130	170	180	180	NR	260	NR
M	1/30	85	120	65	NR	90	NR	130	170	180	240	260
	1/60	85	120	65	NR	90	NR	130	160	130	220	180
	1/125	70	100	55	NR	75	NR	110	130	85	180	120
	1/250	55	80	45	NR	65	NR	90	110	60	150	85
	1/500	45	65	34	NR	50	NR	70	80	44	110	60

*Bulbs for focal-plane shutters; use with FP synchronization. NR—Not Recommended.

WARNING: Bulbs may shatter when flashed; use a flashguard over your reflector. Flashcubes have a built-in flashguard. **Do not use flash in an explosive atmosphere.**

Reciprocity Characteristics: The following table gives the exposure and filter compensation for different exposure times.

Exposure Time in Seconds						
1/10,000	1/1000	1/100	1/10	1	10	100
+½ stop No Filter	None No Filter	None No Filter	None No Filter	+½ stop CC10R	NR	NR

NR—Not Recommended.

PROCESSING

You can have your film processed by Kodak or another laboratory by returning the film to your photo dealer, or by mailing it directly with the appropriate prepaid processing mailer. Your dealer can also order duplicate slides, color prints, or enlargements from your slides.

Special Processing for Increased Film Speed: You can increase the effective speed of this film 2 times to ASA 400 when you order special processing by Kodak. Use the KODAK Special Processing Envelope, ESP-1, sold by photo dealers. The cost of the ESP-1 Envelope is in addition to the regular charge for KODAK EKTACHROME Film processing. Follow the instructions and exposure recommendations included with the envelope. Other laboratories may process this film to various film speeds.

You Can Process the Film Yourself: Use the KODAK EKTACHROME Film Processing Kit, Process E-6 or equivalent, sold by photo dealers. By changing the first development time, you can change the speed of the film to any of a variety of film speeds. See page 53.

DEFINITION

Graininess	Resolving Power	Sharpness
Very Fine	High	High

KODAK EKTACHROME 400 Film (Daylight)

For Color Slides

A very high-speed color-slide film for photographing dimly lighted subjects, such as those in existing light; fast action; and subjects that require both good depth of field and high shutter speeds. It lets you take flash pictures at greater distances than other Kodak color-slide films. The film is color-balanced for daylight, electronic flash, or blue flashbulbs. You can also use this film for photographing performers illuminated by carbon-arc spotlights. The film is excellent for indoor scenes illuminated by existing daylight. EKTACHROME 400 Film has fine grain in addition to its high speed of ASA 400. An exceptional feature of this film is the excellent results you can obtain with special processing to achieve a film speed of ASA 800. The film can also be processed to various other speeds. See page 53.

Sizes Available: 135-20 exposures, 135-36 exposures; 120.

Film Code Letter Designation: EL.

Film Code Numbers: 5074—size 135; 6074—size 120.

EXPOSURE

Speeds and Filter Recommendations:

Type of Light	Film Speed	Filter
DAYLIGHT	**ASA 400***	**None**
PHOTOLAMPS 3400 K	ASA 125	No. 80B
TUNGSTEN 3200 K	ASA 100	No. 80A

*See footnote in Daylight Exposure Table below.

NOTE: If your camera has a built-in exposure meter that makes the reading through a filter used over the lens, see your camera manual for instructions on exposure with filters. Also, see page 97.

Daylight Exposure Table (ASA 400): For average subjects. Exposure recommendations are for cameras with focal-plane shutters. For leaf-type shutters, see explanation under table.

Shutter Speed 1/1000 Second	Shutter Speed 1/500 Second*				
Bright or Hazy Sun Distinct Shadows	Bright or Hazy Sun Distinct Shadows	Weak Hazy Sun Soft Shadows	Cloudy Bright No Shadows	Heavy Overcast	Open Shade‡
On Light Sand or Snow	Average Subjects				
f/16	f/16†	f/11	f/8	f/5.6	f/5.6

*When using a camera with a leaf-type shutter under lighting conditions that require high shutter speeds and medium or small lens openings (lens openings beginning about midway on your camera lens-opening scale), reduce exposure as follows. At 1/500 second, use a lens opening 1 stop smaller than indicated. If you set your shutter at 1/250 second, use a lens opening ½ stop smaller than your exposure meter indicates.

†f/8 at 1/500 second for backlighted close-up subjects.

‡Subject shaded from the sun but lighted by a large area of sky.

Existing-Light Exposure Table (ASA 400): Use an exposure meter or an automatic camera if you have one. For cameras without exposure meters, try the settings suggested in the table. These exposures are *guides;* for more assurance, bracket your exposures 1 stop on each side of the suggested exposure.

Picture Subject	Shutter Speed	Lens Opening
Skylines—10 minutes after sunset	1/60	f/5.6
Distant View of City Skyline at Night	1†	f/2.8
Interiors with Bright Fluorescent Light*	1/60	f/4
Ice Shows, Circuses—Spotlighted acts (carbon arc)	1/250	f/2.8
Brightly Lighted Downtown Street Scenes at Night	1/60	f/2.8
Brightly Lighted Nightclub or Theatre Districts at Night—Las Vegas or Times Square Store Window Displays at Night	1/60	f/4

*May require correction filters for optimum results.

Picture Subject	Shutter Speed	Lens Opening
Neon and Other Lighted Signs at Night	1/125	f/4
Floodlighted Buildings, Fountains, Monuments	1/15†	f/2
Christmas Lighting, Trees—Indoor and Outdoor	1/15†	f/2
Fairs, Amusement Parks at Night	1/30	f/2.8
Night Football, Baseball, Racetracks	1/125	f/2.8
Stage Shows—Average lighting Bright lighting	1/60 1/125	f/2.8 f/4

†Use camera support for 1/30 second or slower.

▭ Tungsten light produces yellow-red color rendition.

Electronic Flash Guide Numbers: Use this table as a starting point in determining the correct guide number for electronic flash units rated in beam candlepower seconds (BCPS). Divide the proper guide number by the flash-to-subject distance in feet to determine the *f*-number for average subjects.

Output of Unit—BCPS	350	500	700	1000	1400	2000	2800	4000	5600	8000
Guide Number*	85	100	120	140	170	200	240	280	340	400

*If your slides are consistently too blue, use a No. 81B filter and increase your exposure by ⅓ stop.

Flash Guide Numbers: *Use blue flashbulbs or flashcubes.* Divide the proper guide number by the flash-to-subject distance in feet to determine the *f*-number for average subjects.

Synchronization	Shutter Speed	Cube		Shallow Cylindrical Reflector	Intermediate-Shaped Reflector		Polished Bowl-Shaped Reflector		Intermediate-Shaped Reflector		Polished Bowl-Shaped Reflector	
		Flashcube	HI-POWER Flash-Cube	AG-1B	M2B	AG-1B	M2B	AG-1B	M3B 5B 25B	6B* 26B*	M3B 5B 25B	6B* 26B*
X	1/30	180	260	130	170	180	240	260	260	NR	360	NR
M	1/30	120	170	90	NR	130	NR	180	240	260	340	360
	1/60	120	170	90	NR	130	NR	180	220	180	320	260
	1/125	100	140	75	NR	110	NR	150	180	120	260	170
	1/250	75	110	65	NR	90	NR	130	150	85	220	120
	1/500	65	90	50	NR	70	NR	100	110	60	160	85

*Bulbs for focal-plane shutters; use with FP synchronization. NR—Not Recommended.

WARNING: Bulbs may shatter when flashed; use a flashguard over your reflector. Flashcubes have a built-in flashguard. **Do not use flash in an explosive atmosphere.**

Reciprocity Characteristics: The following table gives the exposure and filter compensation for different exposure times. The exposure increase includes the adjustment for the filter indicated.

Exposure Time in Seconds						
1/10,000	1/1000	1/100	1/10	1	10	100
None No Filter	None No Filter	None No Filter	None No Filter	+½ stop No Filter	+1½ stops CC10C	+2½ stops CC10C

NR—Not Recommended.

PROCESSING

You can have your film processed by Kodak or another laboratory by returning the film to your photo dealer, or by mailing it directly with the appropriate prepaid processing mailer. Your dealer can also order duplicate slides, color prints, or enlargements from your slides.

Special Processing for Increased Film Speed: You can increase the effective speed of this film 2 times to ASA 800 when you order special processing by Kodak. Use the KODAK Special Processing Envelope, ESP-1, sold by photo dealers. The cost of the ESP-1 Envelope is in addition to the regular charge for KODAK EKTACHROME Film processing. Follow the instructions and exposure recommendations included with the envelope. Other laboratories may process this film to various film speeds.

You Can Process the Film Yourself: Use the KODAK EKTACHROME Film Processing Kit, Process E-6 or equivalent, sold by photo dealers. By changing the first development time, you can change the speed of the film to any of a variety of film speeds up to ASA 1600. See page 53.

DEFINITION

Graininess	Resolving Power	Sharpness
Fine	Medium	Medium

For Color Slides

A high-speed color-slide film for photographing subjects lighted by tungsten light. This film replaced KODAK High Speed EKTACHROME Film (Tungsten). EKTACHROME 160 Film has higher speed, improved color rendition, and improved sharpness. It's designed for use with 3200 K tungsten lamps, but it's excellent for existing tungsten light, such as the light from household lamps and other general-purpose lamps. Outdoors at night you can use this film for pictures of illuminated buildings, fountains, statues, signs, street scenes, and similar subjects. You can take pictures in daylight or with blue flash when you use a No. 85B filter over your camera lens. An exceptional feature is that with special processing, you can expose the film at speeds higher than its normal speed.

Sizes Available: 135-20 exposures, 135-36 exposures.

Film Code Letter Designation: ET. **Film Code Number:** 5077.

EXPOSURE

Speeds and Filter Recommendations:

Type of Light	Film Speed	Filter
TUNGSTEN 3200 K	**ASA 160**	**None**
PHOTOLAMPS 3400 K	ASA 125	No. 81A
DAYLIGHT	ASA 100	No. 85B

NOTE: If your camera has a built-in exposure meter that makes the reading through a filter used over the lens, see your camera manual for instructions on exposure with filters. Also, see page 97.

Tungsten Lamps—3200 K (ASA 160): The following table is based on the use of two 500-watt reflector-type tungsten lamps 3200 K. Use one as a fill-in light close to the camera at lens level; the other as the main light on the opposite side of the camera, 2 to 4 feet higher, and at a 45-degree angle from the camera-subject axis.

EXPOSURE TABLE FOR TUNGSTEN LAMPS 3200 K

Lamp-to-Subject Distance in Feet • Set Shutter Speed at 1/60 Second

Lamp	Lens Opening ▶	*f*/8	*f*/5.6	*f*/4	*f*/2.8
General Electric EAL (reflector type)	Main Light	4	5½	8	11
	Fill-in Light	5½	8	11	15½
Sylvania DXH, Type R-32 (reflector type)	Main Light	5	7	10	13½
	Fill-in Light	7	10	13½	20

NOTE: Use these camera settings as guides only. The lamp-to-subject distances give a lighting ratio of about 3:1. For a 2:1 ratio, place the fill-in light at the same distance from the subject as the main light and use a lens opening ½ stop smaller.

Existing-Light Exposure Table (ASA 160): If you don't have an exposure meter or a camera with a built-in meter, try the settings suggested in the table. These exposures are *guides;* for more assurance, bracket your exposures 1 stop on each side of the suggested exposure.

Picture Subject	Shutter Speed	Lens Opening
Home Interiors at Night— Areas with bright light	1/30	*f*/2
Areas with average light	1/15*	*f*/2
Candlelighted Close-Ups	1/8*	*f*/2
Indoor, Outdoor Christmas Lighting at Night	1*	*f*/5.6
Brightly Lighted Downtown Street Scenes at Night	1/30	*f*/2.8
Brightly Lighted Theatre Districts—Las Vegas or Times Square	1/30	*f*/4
Neon Signs, Other Lighted Signs	1/60	*f*/4
Store Windows at Night	1/30	*f*/4
Floodlighted Buildings, Fountains, Monuments	1/2*	*f*/4
Distant View of City Skyline at Night	1*	*f*/2
Fairs, Amusement Parks	1/30	*f*/2

*Use a tripod or other firm camera support.

Picture Subject	Shutter Speed	Lens Openin
Aerial Fireworks Displays— Keep camera shutter open on "BULB" or "TIME" for several bursts	BULB*	*f*/11
Night Football, Baseball, Racetracks†	1/60	*f*/2.8
Basketball, Hockey, Bowling	1/60	*f*/2
Boxing, Wrestling	1/125	*f*/2
Stage Shows— Average lighting	1/30	*f*/2.8
Bright lighting	1/60	*f*/4
Circuses—Floodlighted acts	1/30	*f*/2.8
Ice Shows—Floodlighted acts	1/60	*f*/2.8
School—Stage and auditorium	1/15*	*f*/2
Swimming Pool—Indoors, tungsten lights above water	1/30	*f*/2
Church Interiors— Tungsten lights	1/15*	*f*/2

†When lighting at these events is provided by mercu[ry] vapor lamps, you'll get better results by using Daylight film.

Daylight Exposure Table (ASA 100): For average subjects. *Use a No. 85B filter.*

Shutter Speed 1/250 Second	Shutter Speed 1/125 Second				
Bright or Hazy Sun Distinct Shadows	Bright or Hazy Sun Distinct Shadows	Weak Hazy Sun Soft Shadows	Cloudy Bright No Shadows	Heavy Overcast	Open Shade†
On Light Sand or Snow	Average Subjects				
f/16	*f*/16*	*f*/11	*f*/8	*f*/5.6	*f*/5.6

**f*/8 at 1/125 second for backlighted close-up subjects.

†Subject shaded from the sun but lighted by a large area of sky.

Electronic Flash Guide Numbers: *Use a No. 85B filter.* This table is for use with electronic flash units rated in beam candlepower seconds (BCPS). To determine the *f*-number for average subjects, divide the proper guide number by the flash-to-subject distance in feet.

Output of Unit—BCPS	350	500	700	1000	1400	2000	2800	4000	5600	8000
Guide Number	40	50	60	70	85	100	120	140	170	200

Flash Guide Numbers: *Use blue flashbulbs or flashcubes and a No. 85B filter.** Divide the guide number by the flash-to-subject distance in feet to find the *f*-number for average subjects.

Synchronization	Shutter Speed	Cube		Shallow Cylindrical Reflector	Intermediate Shaped Reflector		Polished Bowl-Shaped Reflector		Intermediate Shaped Reflector		Polished Bowl-Shaped Reflector	
		Flashcube	HI-POWER Flash-Cube	AG-1B	M2B	AG-1B	M2B	AG-1B	M3B 5B 25B	6B† 26B†	M3B 5B 25B	6B† 26B†
X	1/30	90	130	65	85	90	120	130	130	NR	180	NR
M	1/30	60	85	45	NR	65	NR	90	120	130	170	180
	1/60	60	85	45	NR	65	NR	90	110	90	160	130
	1/125	50	70	38	NR	55	NR	75	90	60	130	85
	1/250	38	55	32	NR	45	NR	65	75	42	110	60
	1/500	32	45	24	NR	34	NR	50	55	30	80	44

*If you prefer, you can use clear flashbulbs. Multiply the guide numbers in the table by 1.4, and use a No. 85C filter with AG-1 and M3 flashbulbs or a No. 81EF filter with other clear flashbulbs.

†Bulbs for focal-plane shutters; use with FP synchronization. NR—Not Recommended.

WARNING: Bulbs may shatter when flashed; use a flashguard over your reflector. Flashcubes have a built-in flashguard. **Do not use flash in an explosive atmosphere.**

Reciprocity Characteristics: This table gives the exposure and filter compensation for different exposure times. The exposure increase includes the adjustment for the filter indicated.

Exposure Time in Seconds

1/10,000	1/1000	1/100	1/10	1	10	100
+½ stop No Filter	None No Filter	None No Filter	None No Filter	+½ stop CC10R	+1 stop CC15R	NR

NR—Not Recommended.

PROCESSING

You can have your film processed by Kodak or another laboratory by returning the film to your photo dealer, or by mailing it directly with the appropriate prepaid processing mailer.

Special Processing for Increased Film Speed: You can increase the speed of this film 2 times to ASA 320 when you order special processing by Kodak. Use the KODAK Special Processing Envelope, ESP-1, sold by photo dealers. The cost of the ESP-1 Envelope is in addition to the regular charge for KODAK EKTACHROME Film processing. Follow the instructions and exposure recommendations included with the envelope. Other laboratories may process this film to various film speeds.

You Can Process the Film Yourself: Use the KODAK EKTACHROME Film Processing Kit, Process E-6 or equivalent, sold by photo dealers. By changing the first development time, you can change the speed of the film to any of a variety of film speeds. See page 53.

DEFINITION

Graininess	Resolving Power	Sharpness
Very Fine	High	High

For Color Slides

KODAK EKTACHROME Infrared Film is a fast "false-color" film for experimental pictorial photography when you want unusual and abstract results. This film is sensitive to both visible and infrared radiation. The film records colors differently from what we normally see. For example, green grass and trees become red, a red rose records as yellow, and black cloth may turn out red, but a blue sky photographs as blue. Flesh tones will have a greenish cast. EKTACHROME Infrared Film is designed for daylight-quality illumination with a No. 12 or No. 15 yellow filter over the camera lens. This film is primarily intended for aerial photography and some scientific applications.

Film Storage and Camera Loading: Store unexposed film in a freezer at −10 to 0°F (−23 to −18°C) in the original sealed container. Load and unload your camera in subdued light. Have the film processed promptly after exposure.

Size Available: 135-20 exposures.

Film Code Letter Designation: IE.

Film Code Number: 2236.

EXPOSURE

Speeds and Filter Recommendations: Exposure meter readings serve only as rough guides for daylight exposures with this film since the ratio of visible to infrared radiation varies, and exposure meters respond to visible light only. For more assurance of properly exposed pictures, bracket your exposures. See page 96. For pictorial slides taken by daylight, electronic flash, or blue flash, you can use a No. 12 or No. 15 filter or other filters for different color effects. For scientific and other critical applications, you should use the No. 12 filter. For critical use with photolamp 3400 K illumination, you should use a No. 12 filter with a KODAK Color Compensating Filter CC20C (cyan) plus a Corning Glass Filter CS No. 3966 (1-59) and a meter setting of 50. No focus correction is required with EKTACHROME Infrared Film.

Type of Light	Film Speed	Filter
DAYLIGHT	**100**	**No. 12 or 15**
PHOTOLAMPS 3400 K	50	No. 12 or 15 plus CC50C-2*

*See section on "Photolamps" on the next page.

NOTE: If your camera has a built-in exposure meter that makes the reading through a filter used over the lens, see your camera manual for instructions on exposure with filters. Also, see page 97.

Daylight Exposure: For frontlighted, average subjects in bright sunlight, use 1/125 second *f*/16 as the basis for trial exposures. Use a No. 12 or No. 15 filter.

Electronic Flash Guide Numbers: *Use a No. 12 or No. 15 filter.* This table is intended as a starting point in determining the correct guide number for electronic flash units rated in beam candlepower seconds (BCPS). Divide the proper guide number by the flash-to-subject distance in feet to determine the *f*-number for average subjects.

Output of Unit—BCPS	350	500	700	1000	1400	2000	2800	4000	5600	8000
Guide Number	40	50	60	70	85	100	120	140	170	200

Flash Guide Numbers: *Use blue flashbulbs or flashcubes and a No. 12 or No. 15 filter.* Divide the proper guide number by the flash-to-subject distance in feet to determine the *f*-number for average subjects. Flashbulbs and flashcubes are not recommended for critical use.

Syn-chroni-zation	Shutter Speed	Cube		Shallow Cylin-drical Reflector	Inter-mediate-Shaped Reflector		Polished Bowl-Shaped Reflector		Inter-mediate-Shaped Reflector		Polished Bowl-Shaped Reflector	
		Flash-cube	HI-POWER Flash-Cube	AG-1B	M2B	AG-1B	M2B	AG-1B	M3B 5B 25B	6B* 26B*	M3B 5B 25B	6B* 26B*
X	1/30	90	130	65	85	90	120	130	130	NR	180	NR
M	1/30	60	85	45	NR	65	NR	90	120	130	170	180
	1/60	60	85	45	NR	65	NR	90	110	90	160	130
	1/125	50	70	38	NR	55	NR	75	90	60	130	85
	1/250	38	55	32	NR	45	NR	65	75	42	110	60
	1/500	32	45	24	NR	34	NR	50	55	30	80	44

*Bulbs for focal-plane shutters; use with FP synchronization. NR—Not Recommended.

WARNING: Bulbs may shatter when flashed; use a flashguard over your reflector. Flashcubes have a built-in flashguard. **Do not use flash in an explosive atmosphere.**

Photolamps—3400 K: The following table is based on the use of two 500-watt reflector-type photolamps 3400 K or two No. 2 photoflood lamps 3400 K in 12-inch reflectors. Place one lamp on each side of the camera at an angle of 45 degrees to the camera-subject axis. Use a No. 12 or No. 15 filter plus a KODAK Color Compensating Filter CC50C-2 over your camera lens. These exposure settings are suggested starting points, so it's a good idea to bracket your exposure.

EXPOSURE TABLE FOR 500-WATT PHOTOLAMPS 3400 K			
Set Shutter Speed at 1/30 Second			
Lamp-to-Subject Distance	3 ft	4½ ft	6½ ft
Lens Opening	*f*/5.6 ↓ 8	*f*/4 ↓ 5.6	*f*/2.8 ↓ 4

Reciprocity Characteristics: The following table gives the exposure and filter compensation for different exposure times. The exposure increase includes the adjustment required when a filter is indicated.

Exposure Time in Seconds		
1/1000	1/100	1/10
None No Filter	None No Filter	+1 stop CC20B

PROCESSING

You can have your film processed by Kodak or another laboratory by returning the film to your photo dealer, or by mailing it directly with the appropriate prepaid processing mailer. Your dealer can also order duplicate slides, color prints, or enlargements from your slides.

To process the film yourself, use the KODAK EKTACHROME Film Processing Kit, Process E-4 or equivalent, sold by photo dealers.

DEFINITION

Graininess	Resolving Power
Fine	Medium

KODAK EKTACHROME Slide Duplicating Film 5071 (Process E-6)

For Color Slides

This film is for making duplicate color slides from original slides made on color-slide films, such as KODACHROME or KODAK EKTACHROME Films. EKTACHROME Slide Duplicating Film is primarily intended for tungsten illumination 3200 K, but you can also use the film with sunlight and electronic flash with the appropriate filters. This film produces excellent color-slide duplicates. It's often difficult to distinguish between the duplicate and the original. Since a duplicate slide, however, is a photograph of another photograph, there is a slight reduction in photographic quality when critical quality standards are applied.

Film Storage: Store unexposed film in a refrigerator at 55°F (13°C) or lower in the original sealed container. Have the films processed promptly after exposure.

Size Available: 135-36 exposures. **Film Code Number:** 5071.

EXPOSURE

You can make duplicate slides by using a single-lens reflex camera with a through-the-lens exposure meter and a slide-duplicating attachment or slide-duplicating equipment. You can also use a contact printer. Using a diffused light source and a lens to transmit the image of the original onto the duplicating film offers the least difficulty with dust and scratches.

This film is intended primarily for use with 3200 K tungsten illumination, such as tungsten photo enlarger lamps or tungsten halogen lamps. You can also use the film with daylight and electronic flash. Results with electronic flash used with the appropriate filters, while less than optimum, are generally satisfactory. Exposure with fluorescent lamps is not recommended.

Camera Exposure: For exposure meters marked for ASA speeds or Exposure Indexes. Use these speeds as starting points for determining proper exposure.

Type of Light	Film Speed*
TUNGSTEN 3200 K	**4**
DAYLIGHT†	4

*Based on an exposure time of 1 second. If the ASA speed dial on your camera does not have a speed of 4 on it, set the dial on 32 and increase the exposure by 3 stops.

†Set a piece of white paper on the ground in sunlight and point the camera with a slide-copying attachment at the paper.

With electronic flash, make an exposure series to determine the best lens opening.

Filter Recommendations: Use these filter packs as starting points.

KODAK Film Original to be Duplicated	Light Source		
	Tungsten 3200 K	Daylight	Electronic Flash‡
EKTACHROME 64, 160, 200, 400*	50G + 35Y	30G+ 60Y	No. 2B + 110Y + 20C
EKTACHROME-X, High Speed EKTACHROME† EKTACHROME Infrared	40G + 45Y	20G + 70Y	No. 2B + 110Y + 10C
KODACHROME 25, 40, 64 KODACHROME II, KODACHROME-X†	50G + 35Y	30G + 60Y	No. 2B + 110Y + 20C

*Also KODAK EKTACHROME Professional Films, Process E-6. †Discontinued Kodak films.

‡If you use an automatic electronic flash unit, set it on manual.

Note: Except for the No. 2B filter, the filters in the table are KODAK Color Compensating Filters, CC, or KODAK Color Printing Filters, CP, sold by photo dealers. CC filters are for use in the image-forming light, such as between the camera lens and the original slide, and CP filters are for use only in nonimage-forming light, such as between the light source and the original slide.

It's best to place the filters between the slide and the light source. Since the filter and exposure recommendations for this film are starting points, take test pictures with the filters listed and with filters of all six colors that vary at least plus and minus CC10 from the starting point filters. Bracket your exposures by taking pictures at the indicated exposure and at −½ and −1 stop less, and at +½ and +1 stop more exposure than indicated.

DEFINITION*

Graininess	Resolving Power	Sharpness
Extremely Fine	High	High

*These definition classifications apply to EKTACHROME Slide Duplicating Film only. The quality of the duplicate slides will be a function of the original slides being duplicated and the quality of the equipment you use for duplicating.

Adjusting the Filter Pack: To evaluate color balance, project the duplicate slides in a darkened room or compare them with the original slides on an illuminator. If corrections are necessary, determine what color is in excess. You can do this by viewing the duplicates through various CC or CP filters. When judging the color, look at the middletones instead of the highlights or shadows. To adjust the filter pack, you can either remove a filter of the color of the overall hue that's in excess or add a filter that's complementary to the overall hue.

Overall color balance of original	Subtract these filters or—	Add these filters
Yellow	Yellow	Magenta + Cyan (or Blue)
Magenta	Magenta	Yellow + Cyan (or Green)
Cyan	Cyan	Yellow + Magenta (or Red)
Blue	Magenta + Cyan (or Blue)	Yellow
Green	Yellow + Cyan (or Green)	Magenta
Red	Yellow + Magenta (or Red)	Cyan

Keep the number of filters in the filter pack to a minimum by removing filters from the pack whenever possible. If all three subtractive colors—cyan, magenta, and yellow—are in the filter pack, they form neutral density which increases exposure time without making any correction in color rendition. You should eliminate neutral density by removing the color that has the lowest value and reducing the other two colors by the same amount. For example, if the pack contains 40C + 40M + 20Y, remove 20 filtration from all three filters.

Filter Pack	40C + 40M + 20Y	
Subtract	20C + 20M + 20Y	Remove .20 neutral density.
Minimum Filter Pack	20C + 20M	

You can reduce the 20C + 20M filters further to a 20B filter which is the equivalent. When you change the filter pack, you'll have to adjust the camera exposure settings due to the difference in light absorption of the filters and the number of filter surfaces. If a primary color—red, green, or blue—is in the filter pack with other filters and you want to determine if neutral density would be present when you change the filter pack, for the calculation, convert the primary color to its equivalents in the subtractive colors. For example, 40G = 40C + 40Y.

Adjustment for Emulsion Number Changes: Each quantity of this film is assigned an emulsion number. To help you properly expose a new roll of film with a different emulsion number, filter and exposure data are given on the film carton. The filter data are expressed in cyan and yellow filtration from average and exposure data are given in half-stop variations from average.

When you change to a new emulsion number, subtract the data on the old film carton from the data on the new film carton. Apply the difference to the filter pack and exposure you were using. The number in the last column is the change in exposure in *f*-stops. For example:

Exposure data on new film carton.	−05C +10Y +0.5	
Exposure data on old film carton.	+10C −05Y −0.5	Subtract
Change in filter pack and exposure.	−15C +15Y +1.0	

The difference in exposure data from the old emulsion to the new one applies regardless of the filter pack you were using for the old emulsion. Assume with the old emulsion that you used a filter pack of CC30C plus CC50Y and 1-second exposure at *f*/11. Change the filter pack by subtracting CC15C (or by adding CC15R) and adding CC15Y (or subtracting CC15B). Change the exposure by increasing it 1 stop. For example:

Used for old emulsion.	CC30C + CC50Y	1 second *f*/11
Change for new emulsion.	−CC15C + CC15Y	+ 1 stop
Use for new emulsion.	CC15C + CC65Y	1 second *f*/8

When there is not enough cyan or yellow filtration in the filter pack to remove, add the complementary filter. Instead of changing the lens opening, you can change the exposure time, although you may have to make an additional adjustment in the filter pack.

PROCESSING

Your film can be processed by Kodak or another laboratory by returning the film to your photo dealer, or by mailing it directly with the appropriate prepaid processing mailer. Your dealer can also order duplicate slides, color prints, or enlargements from your slides. To process the film yourself, use the KODAK EKTACHROME Film Processing Kit, Process E-6 or equivalent.

For Black-and-White Prints

A fast panchromatic film with extremely fine grain. Its excellent gradation and wide exposure latitude make it ideally suited to most picture-taking situations. It is the first choice among black-and-white films for general use in most types of roll-film and cartridge cameras—from simple cameras to the most advanced models.

Sizes Available: 110-12 exposures; 126-12 exposures; 120; 127; 620.

Film Code Letter Designation: VP.

Film Code Numbers: 7042—size 110; 8041—size 126; 6041—sizes 120, 127, 620.

EXPOSURE

Speed: ASA 125

Daylight Exposure Table: For average subjects.

Shutter Speed 1/250 Second			Shutter Speed 1/125 Second		
Bright or Hazy Sun Distinct Shadows		Weak Hazy Sun Soft Shadows	Cloudy Bright No Shadows	Heavy Overcast	Open Shade†
On Light Sand or Snow	Average Subjects				
f/16	*f*/11*	*f*/8	*f*/8	*f*/5.6	*f*/5.6

**f*/8 at 1/125 second for backlighted close-up subjects.

†Subject shaded from the sun but lighted by a large area of sky.

Filter Factors: Increase the normal exposure by the filter factor in the table. However, if your camera has a built-in exposure meter that makes the reading through a filter used over the lens, see your camera manual for instructions on exposure with filters. Also, see page 97.

Filter	No. 6	No. 8	No. 15	No. 11	No. 25	No. 58	No. 47	Polarizing Screen
Daylight	1.5	2*	2.5	4	8	6	6	2.5
Tungsten	1.5	1.5	1.5	4*	5	6	12	2.5

*For correct gray-tone rendering of colored objects.

Electronic Flash Guide Numbers: Use this table as a starting point in determining the correct guide number for electronic flash units rated in beam candlepower seconds (BCPS). Divide the proper guide number by the flash-to-subject distance in feet to determine the *f*-number for average subjects.

Output of Unit—BCPS	350	500	700	1000	1400	2000	2800	4000	5600	8000
Guide Number	45	55	65	80	95	110	130	160	190	220

Flash Guide Numbers: Divide the proper guide number by the flash-to-subject distance in feet to determine the *f*-number for average subjects. These guide numbers are for blue flashbulbs. If you use clear flashbulbs, reduce the lens opening by ⅔ stop.

Synchronization	Shutter Speed	Cube		Shallow Cylindrical Reflector	Intermediate-Shaped Reflector		Polished Bowl-Shaped Reflector		Intermediate-Shaped Reflector		Polished Bowl-Shaped Reflector	
		Flashcube	HI-POWER Flashcube	AG-1B	M2B	AG-1B	M2B	AG-1B	M3B 5B 25B	6B* 26B*	M3B 5B 25B	6B* 26B*
X	1/30	100	140	75	100	100	130	150	140	NR	200	NR
M	1/30	70	90	50	NR	70	NR	100	130	140	180	200
	1/60	65	90	50	NR	70	NR	100	120	100	180	140
	1/125	55	80	42	NR	60	NR	85	100	70	150	100
	1/250	44	65	36	NR	50	NR	70	85	50	120	70
	1/500	36	50	28	NR	38	NR	55	65	34	90	50

*Bulbs for focal-plane shutters; use with FP synchronization. NR—Not Recommended.

WARNING: Bulbs may shatter when flashed; use a flashguard over your reflector. Flashcubes have a built-in flashguard. **Do not use flash in an explosive atmosphere.**

DEVELOPMENT

Safelight: *Total darkness required.* However, when development is half completed, you can use a safelight at 4 feet (1.2 metres) for a *few* seconds. Equip the safelight with a KODAK Safelight Filter No. 3 (dark green), or equivalent, and a 15-watt bulb.

Developing Times are for small roll-film tanks with agitation for 5 seconds at 30-second intervals throughout development. The most widely used times and temperature are in heavy type. If your negatives are consistently too low in contrast, increase development time; if too high in contrast, decrease development time.

KODAK Packaged Developers	Developing Times in Minutes*				
	65°F (18°C)	**68°F (20°C)**	70°F (21°C)	72°F (22°C)	75°F (24°C)
D-76	8	**7**	5½	5	4½
D-76 (1:1)	11	**9**	8	7	6
MICRODOL-X	10	**9**	8	7	6
MICRODOL-X (1:3)†	15	14	13	12	**11**
POLYDOL	8	**6**	5	4½	4
HC-110 (Dilution B)	6	**5**	4½	4	2

*Unsatisfactory uniformity may result with development times shorter than 5 minutes.
†For greater sharpness.

Rinse, fix, wash, and dry in the usual manner. Use fixing times of 5 to 10 minutes with KODAK Fixer or KODAK Fixing Bath F-5, or 2 to 4 minutes with KODAK Rapid Fixer or KODAFIX Solution, at 65 to 75°F (18 to 24°C) with agitation.

DEFINITION

Graininess	Resolving Power	Sharpness	Degree of Enlargement Allowed*
Extremely Fine	High	Very High	High

*For good-quality negatives.

For Black-and-White Prints

A general-purpose panchromatic film for 35 mm cameras that offers the optimum combination of a fast speed, extremely fine grain, and excellent picture sharpness even at high degrees of enlargement. It's ideally suited to most picture-taking situations.

Size Available: 135-20 exposures, 135-36 exposures.

Film Code Letter Designation: PX.

Film Code Number: 5062.

EXPOSURE

Speed: ASA 125

Daylight Exposure Table: For average subjects.

Shutter Speed 1/250 Second			Shutter Speed 1/125 Second		
Bright or Hazy Sun Distinct Shadows		Weak Hazy Sun Soft Shadows	Cloudy Bright No Shadows	Heavy Overcast	Open Shade†
On Light Sand or Snow	Average Subjects				
f/16	*f*/11*	*f*/8	*f*/8	*f*/5.6	*f*/5.6

**f*/8 at 1/125 second for backlighted close-up subjects.

†Subject shaded from the sun but lighted by a large area of sky.

Filter Factors: Increase the normal exposure by the filter factor in the table. However, if your camera has a built-in exposure meter that makes the reading through a filter used over the lens, see your camera manual for instructions on exposure with filters. Also, see page 97.

Filter	No. 6	No. 8	No. 15	No. 11	No. 25	No. 58	No. 47	Polarizing Screen
Daylight	1.5	2*	2.5	4	6	8	6	2.5
Tungsten	1.2	1.5	1.5	4*	4	8	12	2.5

*For correct gray-tone rendering of colored objects.

Electronic Flash Guide Numbers: Use this table as a starting point in determining the correct guide number for electronic flash units rated in beam candlepower seconds (BCPS). Divide the proper guide number by the flash-to-subject distance in feet to determine the *f*-number for average subjects.

Output of Unit—BCPS	350	500	700	1000	1400	2000	2800	4000	5600	8000
Guide Number	45	55	65	80	95	110	130	160	190	220

Flash Guide Numbers: Divide the proper guide number by the flash-to-subject distance in feet to determine the *f*-number for average subjects. These guide numbers are for blue flashbulbs. If you use clear flashbulbs, reduce the lens opening by ⅔ stop.

Syn-chroni-zation	Shutter Speed	Cube		Shallow Cylin-drical Reflector	Inter-mediate-Shaped Reflector		Polished Bowl-Shaped Reflector		Inter-mediate-Shaped Reflector		Polished Bowl-Shaped Reflector	
		Flash-cube	HI-POWER Flash-Cube	AG-1B	M2B	AG-1B	M2B	AG-1B	M3B 5B 25B	6B* 26B*	M3B 5B 25B	6B* 26B*
X	1/30	100	140	75	100	100	130	150	140	NR	200	NR
M	1/30	70	90	50	NR	70	NR	100	130	140	180	200
	1/60	65	90	50	NR	70	NR	100	120	100	180	140
	1/125	55	80	42	NR	60	NR	85	100	70	150	100
	1/250	44	65	36	NR	50	NR	70	85	50	120	70
	1/500	36	50	28	NR	38	NR	55	65	34	90	50

*Bulbs for focal-plane shutters; use with FP synchronization. NR—Not Recommended.

WARNING: Bulbs may shatter when flashed; use a flashguard over your reflector. Flashcubes have a built-in flashguard. **Do not use flash in an explosive atmosphere.**

DEVELOPMENT

Safelight: *Total darkness required.* However, when development is half completed, you can use a safelight at 4 feet (1.2 metres) for a *few* seconds. Equip the safelight with a KODAK Safelight Filter No. 3 (dark green), or equivalent, and a 15-watt bulb.

Developing Times are for small roll-film tanks with agitation for 5 seconds at 30-second intervals throughout development. The most widely used times and temperature are in heavy type. If your negatives are consistently too low in contrast, increase development time; if too high in contrast, decrease development time.

KODAK Packaged Developers	Developing Times in Minutes*				
	65°F (18°C)	**68°F (20°C)**	70°F (21°C)	72°F (22°C)	75°F (24°C)
D-76	6½	**5½**	5	4½	3¾
D-76 (1:1)	8	**7**	6½	6	5
MICRODOL-X	8	**7**	6½	6	5½
MICRODOL-X (1:3)†	—	—	11	10	**9½**
POLYDOL	6½	**5½**	4¾	4¼	3¼
HC-110 (Dilution B)	6	**5**	4½	4	3½

*Unsatisfactory uniformity may result with development times shorter than 5 minutes.
†For greater sharpness.

Rinse, fix, wash, and dry in the usual manner. Use fixing times of 5 to 10 minutes with KODAK Fixer or KODAK Fixing Bath F-5, or 2 to 4 minutes with KODAK Rapid Fixer or KODAFIX Solution, at 65 to 75°F (18 to 24°C) with agitation.

DEFINITION

Graininess	Resolving Power	Sharpness	Degree of Enlargement Allowed*
Extremely Fine	High	Very High	High

*For good-quality negatives.

For Black-and-White Prints

An extremely fine grain panchromatic film with very high sharpness. It has adequate speed for many picture-taking situations. This is an excellent film to use when you want prints made with a very high degree of enlargement. With special processing, the 135-size film will produce positive black-and-white slides.

Sizes Available: PANATOMIC-X Film, 135-20 exposures, 135-36 exposures; PANATOMIC-X Professional Film, 120.

Film Code Letter Designation: FX; FXP (Professional).

Film Code Numbers: 5060—size 135; 6040—size 120.

EXPOSURE

Speed: ASA 32

Daylight Exposure Table: For average subjects.

Shutter Speed 1/125 Second				Shutter Speed 1/60 Second	
Bright or Hazy Sun Distinct Shadows		Weak Hazy Sun Soft Shadows	Cloudy Bright No Shadows	Heavy Overcast	Open Shade†
On Light Sand or Snow	Average Subjects				
f/11	*f*/8*	*f*/5.6	*f*/4	*f*/4	*f*/4

**f*/4 at 1/125 second for backlighted close-up subjects.

†Subject shaded from the sun but lighted by a large area of sky.

Filter Factors: Increase exposure by the filter factor in the table. However, if your camera has a built-in exposure meter that makes the reading through a filter used over the lens, see your camera manual for instructions on exposure with filters. Also, see page 97.

Filter	No. 6	No. 8	No. 15	No. 11	No. 25	No. 58	No. 47	Polarizing Screen
Daylight	1.5	2*	2.5	4	8	6	8	2.5
Tungsten	1.5	1.5	1.5	4*	5	6	16	2.5

*For correct gray-tone rendering of colored objects.

Flash Guide Numbers: Divide the proper guide number by the flash-to-subject distance in feet to determine the *f*-number for average subjects. These guide numbers are for blue flashbulbs. If you use clear flashbulbs, reduce the lens opening by ⅔ stop.

Synchronization	Shutter Speed	Cube		Shallow Cylindrical Reflector	Intermediate-Shaped Reflector		Polished Bowl-Shaped Reflector		Intermediate-Shaped Reflector		Polished Bowl-Shaped Reflector	
		Flashcube	HI-POWER Flash-Cube	AG-1B	M2B	AG-1B	M2B	AG-1B	M3B 5B 25B	6B* 26B*	M3B 5B 25B	6B* 26B*
X	1/30	50	70	36	50	50	70	75	75	NR	100	NR
M	1/30	34	50	26	NR	36	NR	50	65	70	90	100
	1/60	34	45	26	NR	36	NR	50	65	50	90	75
	1/125	28	40	22	NR	30	NR	45	55	34	75	50
	1/250	22	32	18	NR	26	NR	36	42	24	60	34
	1/500	18	26	14	NR	20	NR	28	32	17	45	24

*Bulbs for focal-plane shutters; use with FP synchronization. NR—Not Recommended.

WARNING: Bulbs may shatter when flashed; use a flashguard over your reflector. Flashcubes have a built-in flashguard. **Do not use flash in an explosive atmosphere.**

Electronic Flash Guide Numbers: Use this table as a starting point in determining the correct guide number for electronic flash units rated in beam candlepower seconds (BCPS). Divide the proper guide number by the flash-to-subject distance in feet to determine the *f*-number for average subjects.

Output of Unit—BCPS	350	500	700	1000	1400	2000	2800	4000	5600	8000
Guide Number	24	28	32	40	50	55	65	80	95	110

DEVELOPMENT

Safelight: *Total darkness required.* However, when development is half completed, you can use a safelight at 4 feet (1.2 metres) for a *few* seconds. Equip the safelight with a KODAK Safelight Filter No. 3 (dark green), or equivalent, and a 15-watt bulb.

Developing Times are for small roll-film tanks with agitation for 5 seconds at 30-second intervals throughout development. The most widely used times and temperature are in heavy type. If your negatives are consistently too low in contrast, increase development time; if too high in contrast, decrease development time.

KODAK Packaged Developers	Developing Times in Minutes*				
	65°F (18°C)	**68°F (20°C)**	70°F (21°C)	72°F (22°C)	75°F (24°C)
D-76	6	**5**	4½	4¼	3¾
D-76 (1:1)	8	**7**	6½	6	5
MICRODOL-X	8	**7**	6½	6	5
MICRODOL-X (1:3)†	13	12	11	10	**8½**
POLYDOL	6½	**5½**	5	4½	3½
HC-110 (Dilution B)	4¾	**4¼**	4	3¾	3¼

*Unsatisfactory uniformity may result with development times shorter than 5 minutes.
†For greater sharpness.

Rinse, fix, wash, and dry in the usual manner. Use fixing times of 2 to 4 minutes with KODAK Fixer or KODAK Fixing Bath F-5, or 1 to 2 minutes with KODAK Rapid Fixer or KODAFIX Solution, at 65 to 75°F (18 to 24°C) with agitation.

DEFINITION

Graininess	Resolving Power	Sharpness	Degree of Enlargement Allowed*
Extremely Fine	Very High	Very High	Very High

*For good-quality negatives.

SPECIAL PROCESSING FOR SLIDES

Exposing and Processing: When you use PANATOMIC-X Film, 135 size, as a positive slide film, expose it at a speed of **80** for daylight and **64** for tungsten. Process your film in the KODAK Direct Positive Film Developing Outfit. With the temperature of all the solutions at 68°F (20°C), follow the processing steps below. Agitate continuously during the first 30 seconds in each solution, and for 5 seconds every minute thereafter.

1. First Developer . . . . .8 minutes
2. Water Rinse . . . . .2 to 5 minutes*
3. Bleach . . . . .1 minute
4. Clearing Bath . . . . .2 minutes
5. Redeveloper . . . . .8 minutes
6. Water Rinse . . . . .1 minute
7. Fixing Bath . . . . .5 minutes
8. Wash . . . . .20 minutes

*A 2-minute rinse is sufficient with a running-water wash and good agitation.

Safelight: *Total darkness is required* until you have completed the bleaching step. For the rest of the process you can use a safelight equipped with a KODAK Safelight Filter OA (greenish yellow), or equivalent, and a 15-watt bulb. Keep the safelight at least 4 feet (1.2 metres) from the film. Do not turn on the normal room lights until the film has been fixed, or the highlights may appear gray.

For Black-and-White Prints

A high-speed panchromatic film with fine grain and excellent sharpness. Its high speed makes it especially useful for photographing dimly lighted subjects, such as those in existing light; fast action; subjects requiring good depth of field and high shutter speeds; and for extending the distance range for flash pictures.

Sizes Available: 135-20 exposures, 135-36 exposures; 126-12 exposures; 120.
Film Code Letter Designation: TX.
Film Code Numbers: 5063—sizes 135, 126; 6043—size 120.

EXPOSURE

Speed: ASA 400

Daylight Exposure Table: For average subjects.

Shutter Speed 1/1000 Second	Shutter Speed 1/500 Second	Shutter Speed 1/250 Second			
Bright or Hazy Sun Distinct Shadows	Bright or Hazy Sun Distinct Shadows	Weak Hazy Sun Soft Shadows	Cloudy Bright No Shadows	Heavy Overcast	Open Shade†
On Light Sand or Snow	Average Subjects				
f/16	*f*/16*	*f*/16	*f*/11	*f*/8	*f*/8

**f*/11 at 1/250 second for backlighted close-up subjects.
†Subject shaded from the sun but lighted by a large area of sky.

Filter Factors: Increase exposure by the filter factor in the table. However, if your camera has a built-in exposure meter that makes the reading through a filter used over the lens, see your camera manual for instructions on exposure with filters. Also, see page 97.

Filter	No. 6	No. 8	No. 15	No. 11	No. 25	No. 58	No. 47	Polarizing Screen
Daylight	1.5	2*	2.5	4	8	6	6	2.5
Tungsten	1.5	1.5	1.5	3*	5	6	12	2.5

*For correct gray-tone rendering of colored objects.

Existing-Light Exposure Table: Use an exposure meter or an automatic camera if you have one. For cameras without exposure meters, try the settings suggested in the table. These exposures are *guides;* for more assurance, bracket your exposures 1 or 2 stops on each side of the suggested exposure.

Picture Subject	Shutter Speed	Lens Opening
Home Interiors at Night—Areas with bright light	1/30	*f*/2.8
Home Interiors at Night—Areas with average light	1/30	*f*/2
Candlelighted Close-Ups	1/15*	*f*/2
Interiors with Bright Fluorescent Light	1/60	*f*/4
Indoor, Outdoor Christmas Lighting at Night	1/15*	*f*/2
Brightly Lighted Downtown Street Scenes at Night	1/60	*f*/2.8
Brightly Lighted Theatre Districts—Las Vegas or Times Square	1/60	*f*/4
Neon Signs, Other Lighted Signs at Night	1/125	*f*/4
Store Windows at Night	1/60	*f*/4
Floodlighted Buildings, Fountains, Monuments	1/15*	*f*/2
Distant View of City Skyline at Night	1*	*f*/2.8
Skylines—10 minutes after sunset	1/60	*f*/5.6
Fairs, Amusement Parks at Night	1/30	*f*/2.8

Picture Subject	Shutter Speed	Lens Opening
Aerial Fireworks Displays—Keep camera shutter open on "BULB" or "TIME" for several bursts	BULB*	*f*/16
Night Football, Baseball, Racetracks	1/125	*f*/2.8
Basketball, Hockey, Bowling	1/125	*f*/2
Boxing, Wrestling	1/250	*f*/2
Stage Shows—Average lighting	1/60	*f*/2.8
Stage Shows—Bright lighting	1/125	*f*/4
Circuses—Floodlighted acts	1/60	*f*/2.8
Ice Shows—Floodlighted acts	1/125	*f*/2.8
Ice Shows, Circuses—Spotlighted acts (carbon arc)	1/250	*f*/2.8
School—Stage and auditorium	1/30	*f*/2
Swimming Pool—Indoors, tungsten lights above water	1/60	*f*/2
Church Interiors—Artificial light	1/30	*f*/2

*Use a camera support for exposure times longer than 1/30 second.

Electronic Flash Guide Numbers: Use this table as a starting point in determining the correct guide number for electronic flash units rated in beam candlepower seconds (BCPS). Divide the proper guide number by the flash-to-subject distance in feet to determine the *f*-number for average subjects.

Output of Unit—BCPS	350	500	700	1000	1400	2000	2800	4000	5600	8000
Guide Number	85	100	120	140	170	200	240	280	340	400

Flash Guide Numbers: Divide the proper guide number by the flash-to-subject distance in feet to determine the *f*-number for average subjects. These guide numbers are for blue flashbulbs. If you use clear flashbulbs, reduce the lens opening by ⅔ stop.

Syn-chroni-zation	Shutter Speed	Cube		Shallow Cylin-drical Reflector	Inter-mediate-Shaped Reflector		Polished Bowl-Shaped Reflector		Inter-mediate-Shaped Reflector		Polished Bowl-Shaped Reflector	
		Flash-cube	HI-POWER Flash-Cube	AG-1B	M2B	AG-1B	M2B	AG-1B	M3B 5B 25B	6B* 26B*	M3B 5B 25B	6B* 26B*
X	1/30	180	260	130	170	180	240	260	260	NR	360	NR
M	1/30	120	170	90	NR	130	NR	180	240	260	340	360
	1/60	120	170	90	NR	130	NR	180	220	180	320	260
	1/125	100	140	75	NR	110	NR	150	180	120	260	170
	1/250	75	110	65	NR	90	NR	130	150	85	220	120
	1/500	65	90	50	NR	70	NR	100	110	60	160	85

*Bulbs for focal-plane shutters; use with FP synchronization. NR—Not Recommended.

WARNING: Bulbs may shatter when flashed; use a flashguard over your reflector. Flashcubes have a built-in flashguard. **Do not use flash in an explosive atmosphere.**

DEVELOPMENT

Safelight: *Total darkness required.* However, when development is half completed, you can use a safelight at 4 feet (1.2 metres) for a *few* seconds. Equip the safelight with a KODAK Safelight Filter No. 3 (dark green), or equivalent, and a 15-watt bulb.

Developing Times are for small roll-film tanks with agitation for 5 seconds at 30-second intervals throughout development. The most widely used times and temperature are in heavy type. If your negatives are consistently too low in contrast, increase development time; if too high in contrast, decrease development time.

KODAK Packaged Developers	Developing Times in Minutes*				
	65°F (18°C)	**68°F (20°C)**	70°F (21°C)	72°F (22°C)	75°F (24°C)
D-76	9	**8**	7½	6½	5½
D-76 (1:1)	11	**10**	9½	9	8
MICRODOL-X	11	**10**	9½	9	8
MICRODOL-X (1:3)†	—	—	15	14	**13**
DK-50 (1:1)	7	**6**	5½	5	4½
POLYDOL	8	**7**	6½	6	5
HC-110 (Dilution A)	4¼	**3¾**	3¼	3	2½
HC-110 (Dilution B)	8½	**7½**	6½	6	5

*Unsatisfactory uniformity may result with development times shorter than 5 minutes.
†For greater sharpness.

Rinse, fix, wash, and dry in the usual manner. Use fixing times of 5 to 10 minutes with KODAK Fixer, KODAK Fixing Bath F-5, or KODAFIX Solution, or 2 to 4 minutes with KODAK Rapid Fixer, at 65 to 75°F (18 to 24°C) with agitation.

DEFINITION

Graininess	Resolving Power	Sharpness	Degree of Enlargement Allowed*
Fine	High	Very High	Moderate

*For good-quality negatives.

For Black-and-White Prints

A panchromatic film for 120-size cameras that has extremely high speed and medium grain. Use ROYAL-X Pan Film for situations where the highest film speed is essential, such as for taking action photographs by existing light, for taking pictures in interiors of buildings when you need the shortest possible exposure times, or for obtaining adequate depth of field under poor lighting conditions.

Size Available: 120.

Film Code Letter Designation: RX. **Film Code Number:** 6046.

Camera Loading: Because of the extremely high speed of this film, always load and unload your camera in subdued light.

EXPOSURE

Speed: ASA 1250. For low-contrast scenes, you can obtain good negatives by setting your exposure meter for film-speed numbers up to 2000 with normal development, and up to 4000 if you increase development 50 percent by using the extended times given in the development table.

Suggested Exposure Settings:

Lighting Conditions	Average Subject—Normal Development	Low-Contrast Subject—Extended Development
Existing Light Home Interiors at Night— Areas with bright light Areas with average light	 1/60 sec *f*/4 1/30 sec *f*/4	 1/60 sec *f*/5.6 1/60 sec *f*/4
Night Football, Baseball, Racetracks, Boxing, Wrestling	1/250 sec *f*/4	1/500 sec *f*/4
Basketball, Hockey, Bowling	1/250 sec *f*/2.8	1/250 sec *f*/4
Interiors with Bright Fluorescent Light	1/125 sec *f*/5.6	1/250 sec *f*/5.6
School—Stage and auditorium	1/30 sec *f*/4	1/60 sec *f*/4
Church Interiors—Artificial light	1/30 sec *f*/4	1/60 sec *f*/4
Daylight Heavy Overcast or Open Shade—Subject shaded from the sun but lighted by a large area of sky	1/250 sec *f*/16	1/250 sec *f*/22
Cloudy Bright—No shadows	1/250 sec *f*/22	1/500 sec *f*/22
Weak Hazy Sun—Soft shadows	1/500 sec *f*/22	1/500 sec *f*/32
Bright or Hazy Sun—Distinct shadows	1/500 sec *f*/32	—
Flashbulbs M3B, 5B, or 25B Flashbulbs at 1/500 Second, M Synchronization	*f*/5.6 at 50 feet	*f*/8 at 50 feet

Electronic Flash Guide Numbers: Use this table as a starting point in determining the correct guide number for electronic flash units rated in beam candlepower seconds (BCPS). Divide the proper guide number by the flash-to-subject distance in feet to determine the *f*-number for average subjects.

Output of Unit—BCPS	350	500	700	1000	1400	2000	2800	4000	5600	8000
Guide Number	150	180	210	250	300	350	420	500	600	700

Filter Factors: Increase the normal exposure by the filter factor in the table. However, if your camera has a built-in exposure meter that makes the reading through a filter used over the lens, see your camera manual for instructions on exposure with filters. Also, see page 97.

Filter	No. 6	No. 8	No. 15	No. 11	No. 25	No. 58	No. 47	Polarizing Screen
Daylight	1.5	2*	2.5	4	8	8	6	2.5
Tungsten	1.5	2	2	4*	5	8	12	2.5

*For correct gray-tone rendering of colored objects.

DEVELOPMENT

This film must be processed by using the following procedure. Only the developers listed are recommended. If a photofinisher processes this film, make sure that he can provide the special processing service required.

Safelight: *Total darkness required.*

Developing Times are for small roll-film tanks with agitation for 5 seconds at 30-second intervals throughout development. The most widely used times and temperature are in heavy type. Note: A slight fog density is normal. If your negatives are consistently too low in contrast, increase development time; if too high in contrast, decrease development time.

KODAK Packaged Developers	Developing Times in Minutes*									
	Average Subjects					Low-Contrast Subjects				
	65°F (18°C)	**68°F (20°C)**	70°F (21°C)	72°F (22°C)	75°F (24°C)	65°F (18°C)	**68°F (20°C)**	70°F (21°C)	72°F (22°C)	75°F (24°C)
POLYDOL	8	**7**	6½	6	5	12	11	10	9	7½
DK-50	5½	**5**	4¾	4¾	4½	8	7½	7	—	6½
HC-110 (Dilution A)	6	**5**	4¾	4½	4¼	9	7½	7	6½	6
HC-110 (Dilution B)	10	**9**	8	7½	6½	15	14	12	11	10

*Unsatisfactory uniformity may result with development times shorter than 5 minutes.

Note: Use fresh developers, because exhausted developers may produce a deposit of dichroic fog. You can usually swab this off while the film is still wet.

Use an Acid Stop Bath. Rinse in KODAK Indicator Stop Bath or KODAK Stop Bath SB-5 at 65 to 75°F (18 to 24°C) for 30 seconds to 1 minute *with constant agitation.* Drain the film for 2 to 5 seconds before immersing it in the fixing bath.

Note: This step is important. The use of an acid stop bath minimizes the tendency for dichroic stain deposits to form on the film surface.

Fix for 5 to 10 minutes at 65 to 75°F (18 to 24°C) with KODAK Fixer or KODAK Fixing Bath F-5, or 3 to 5 minutes with KODAK Rapid Fixer. *Agitate films frequently during fixing.*

Wash and dry in the usual manner. See page 79.

DEFINITION

Graininess	Resolving Power	Sharpness	Degree of Enlargement Allowed*
Medium	Medium	Very High	Moderately Low

*For good-quality negatives.

KODAK Recording Film 2475 (ESTAR-AH) Base

For Black-and-White Prints

An extremely high-speed panchromatic film for 35 mm cameras that has extended red sensitivity and coarse grain. Use this film in situations where the highest film speed is essential and fine grain is not important to you, such as for taking action photographs when the light is extremely poor, for taking pictures in interiors of buildings when you need the shortest possible exposure times, or for obtaining adequate depth of field under poor lighting conditions.

Size Available: 135-36 exposures.

Film Code Letter Designation: RE. **Film Code Number:** 2475.

Camera Loading: Because of the extremely high speed of this film, always load and unload your camera in subdued light.

EXPOSURE

Speed: 1000. For exposure meters marked for ASA speeds or Exposure Indexes. For low-contrast scenes, you can obtain good negatives by setting your exposure meter for film-speed numbers up to 1600 with normal development, and up to 4000 if you increase development 50 percent by using the extended times given in the development table.

Suggested Exposure Settings:

Lighting Conditions	Average Subject—Normal Development	Low-Contrast Subject—Extended Development
Existing Light		
Home Interiors at Night—		
Areas with bright light	1/60 sec *f*/4	1/60 sec *f*/5.6
Areas with average light	1/30 sec *f*/4	1/60 sec *f*/4
Night Football, Baseball, Racetracks, Boxing, Wrestling	1/250 sec *f*/4	1/500 sec *f*/4
Basketball, Hockey, Bowling	1/250 sec *f*/2.8	1/250 sec *f*/4
Interiors with Bright Fluorescent Light	1/125 sec *f*/5.6	1/250 sec *f*/5.6
School—Stage and auditorium	1/30 sec *f*/4	1/60 sec *f*/4
Church Interiors—Artificial light	1/30 sec *f*/4	1/60 sec *f*/4
Daylight		
Heavy Overcast or Open Shade—Subject shaded from the sun but lighted by a large area of sky	1/250 sec *f*/16	1/250 sec *f*/22
Cloudy Bright—No shadows	1/250 sec *f*/22	1/500 sec *f*/22
Weak Hazy Sun—Soft shadows	1/500 sec *f*/22	1/500 sec *f*/32
Bright or Hazy Sun—Distinct shadows	1/500 sec *f*/32	—
Flashbulbs		
M3B, 5B, or 25B Flashbulbs at 1/500 Second, M Synchronization	*f*/5.6 at 50 feet	*f*/8 at 50 feet

Electronic Flash Guide Numbers: Use this table as a starting point in determining the correct guide number for electronic flash units rated in beam candlepower seconds (BCPS). Divide the proper guide number by the flash-to-subject distance in feet to determine the *f*-number for average subjects.

Output of Unit—BCPS	350	500	700	1000	1400	2000	2800	4000	5600	8000
Guide Number	130	160	190	220	260	320	380	450	530	630

Filter Factors: Increase the normal exposure by the filter factor in the table. However, if your camera has a built-in exposure meter that makes the reading through a filter used over the lens, see your camera manual for instructions on exposure with filters. Also, see page 97.

Filter	No. 6	No. 8	No. 15	No. 11	No. 25	No. 58	No. 47	Polarizing Screen
Daylight	1.5	2*	2	6	3	10	6	2.5
Tungsten	1.2	1.2	1.5	6*	2	12	16	3

*For correct gray-tone rendering of colored objects.

DEVELOPMENT

Safelight: *Total darkness required.*

Developing Times are for small roll-film tanks with agitation for 5 seconds at 30-second intervals throughout development. The most widely used times and temperature are in heavy type. If your negatives are consistently too low in contrast, increase development time; if too high in contrast, decrease development time.

KODAK Packaged Developers	Developing Times in Minutes*				
	65°F (18°C)	**68°F (20°C)**	70°F (21°C)	72°F (22°C)	75°F (24°C)
Average Subjects—					
DK-50	7	**6**	5	4¾	4
HC-110 (Dilution A)	5½	**4½**	4	3½	3
HC-110 (Dilution B)	11	**9**	8	7	6
Low-Contrast Subjects—					
DK-50	10½	**9**	8½	7½	6½
HC-110 (Dilution A)	9½	**8**	7½	6½	5
HC-110 (Dilution B)	17	**15**	12	11	10

*Unsatisfactory uniformity may result with development times shorter than 5 minutes.

Note: Use fresh developers, because exhausted developers may produce a deposit of dichroic fog. You can usually swab this off while the film is still wet.

Use an Acid Stop Bath. Rinse in KODAK Stop Bath SB-1a at 65 to 75°F (18 to 24°C) for 30 seconds to 1 minute *with constant agitation.*

Note: This step is important. The use of an acid stop bath minimizes the tendency for dichroic stain deposits to form on the film surface.

Fix for 8 to 12 minutes at 65 to 75°F (18 to 24°C) with KODAK Fixer or KODAK Fixing Bath F-5, or 3 to 5 minutes with KODAK Rapid Fixer. *Agitate films frequently during fixing.*

Wash and dry in the usual manner. See page 79.

DEFINITION

Graininess	Resolving Power	Sharpness	Degree of Enlargement Allowed*
Coarse	Medium	Very High	Low

*For good-quality negatives.

KODAK High Speed Infrared Film

For Black-and-White Prints

A moderately high-contrast, infrared-sensitive film that has high speed and fine grain. With a red filter, it gives striking and unusual effects. This film is commonly used for distant landscape photography to show detail ordinarily obscured by atmospheric haze. It is also useful in aerial, scientific, industrial, legal, and documentary photography, and in photomicrography.

Size Available: 135-20 exposures.

Camera Loading: Film magazines must be handled in total darkness when the magazines are outside the film cans. Load and unload your camera only in total darkness. Store 135 magazines of this film in the tightly closed film cans or in total darkness at 55°F (13°C) or lower.

Film Code Letter Designation: HIE. **Film Code Number:** 2481.

EXPOSURE

Focusing: Camera lenses do not focus infrared rays in the same plane as visible light rays. Some cameras have index marks on their focusing scales for taking infrared pictures. If your camera has one, use it. Otherwise, set your lens at the smallest opening that conditions permit. If you have to use large lens openings, and your camera has no infrared focusing mark, try to focus on the near side of the main subject. Or you can focus normally and then move the entire camera away from the subject by 0.25 percent of the subject-to-lens distance.

Filters: To obtain infrared rendition in your pictures, you must use a filter over the lens (or light source) to absorb the blue and green light to which the film is sensitive. For general photography, a No. 25 filter is recommended; or you can use a No. 29 or No. 70 filter. When you want to record only the infrared radiation, use a No. 89B, No. 88A, No. 87, or No. 87C filter.

Speeds: It's not possible to give exact speeds for KODAK High Speed Infrared Film, because the ratio of infrared to visible light is variable, and exposure meters do not respond to infrared radiation. Similar levels of visible light may be vastly different in the amounts of infrared radiation they contain. Make trial exposures to determine the proper exposure for the conditions under which you take your pictures.

You can use the following speeds as a basis for determining exposures under average conditions with meters marked for ASA speeds or Exposure Indexes. With cameras that have a built-in exposure meter that makes the reading through a filter used over the lens, use these film speeds and make the meter reading before you put the filter on the camera. Or, use a hand-held meter.

Filter	Film Speed*	
	Daylight	Tungsten
No. 25, 29, 70, or 89B	50	125
No. 87, 88A	25	64
No. 87C	10	25
No Filter	80	200

*Recommended development in KODAK Developer D-76.

Daylight Exposures: Subjects in bright or hazy sunlight, distinct shadows. Use these recommendations as the basis for trial exposures.

Exposed Through a No. 25 Filter	
Distant Scenes	Nearby Scenes
1/125 second *f*/11	1/30 second *f*/11

Photolamps: For use with a No. 25 filter over the camera lens. The following table is based on the use of two 500-watt reflector-type photolamps. Place one lamp on each side of the camera at an angle of 45 degrees to the camera-subject axis.

EXPOSURE TABLE FOR 500-WATT REFLECTOR-TYPE PHOTOLAMPS			
Set Shutter Speed at 1/30 Second			
Lamp-to-Subject Distance	3 ft	4½ ft	6½ ft
Lens Opening	*f*/11	*f*/8	*f*/5.6

Electronic Flash Guide Numbers: For use with a No. 87 filter. This table is intended as a starting point in determining the correct guide number for electronic flash units rated in beam candlepower seconds (BCPS). Divide the proper guide number by the flash-to-subject distance in feet to determine the *f*-number for trial exposures.

Output of Unit—BCPS	350	500	700	1000	1400	2000	2800	4000	5600	8000
Guide Number for Trial	20	24	30	35	40	50	60	70	85	100

Flash Guide Numbers: Use a filter such as a No. 25, No. 29, No. 70, or No. 89B with clear flashbulbs. Divide the proper guide number by the flash-to-subject distance in feet to determine the *f*-number. If you use a No. 87 or No. 88A filter, increase exposure by 1 stop. If you use a No. 87C filter, increase exposure by 2 stops.

Synchronization	Shutter Speed	Shallow Cylindrical Reflector	Intermediate-Shaped Reflector	Polished Bowl-Shaped Reflector	Intermediate-Shaped Reflector		Polished Bowl-Shaped Reflector	
		AG-1	AG-1	AG-1	M3 5 25	6* 26*	M3 5 25	6* 26*
X	1/30	90	120	180	200	NR	280	NR
M	1/30	60	85	120	170	200	240	280
	1/60	60	85	120	170	130	240	180
	1/125	50	70	100	140	90	200	130
	1/250	40	60	80	110	65	160	90
	1/500	32	45	65	85	50	120	65

*Bulbs for focal-plane shutters; use with FP synchronization. NR—Not Recommended.

WARNING: Bulbs may shatter when flashed; use a flashguard over your reflector. **Do not use flash in an explosive atmosphere.**

DEVELOPMENT

Safelight: *Total darkness required.*

Developing Times are for small roll-film tanks with agitation for 5 seconds at 30-second intervals throughout development. The most widely used times and temperature are in heavy type. If your negatives are consistently too low in contrast, increase development time; if too high in contrast, decrease development time.

KODAK Packaged Developers	**Developing Times in Minutes***				
	65°F (18°C)	**68°F (20°C)**	70°F (21°C)	72°F (22°C)	75°F (24°C)
D-76	13	**11**	10	9½	8
HC-110 (Dilution B)	7	**6**	6	5½	5
D-19†	7	**6**	5½	5	4

*Unsatisfactory uniformity may result with development times shorter than 5 minutes.

†For maximum contrast.

Rinse, fix, wash, and dry in the usual manner. Use fixing times of 5 to 10 minutes with KODAK Fixer or KODAK Fixing Bath F-5, or 2 to 4 minutes with KODAK Rapid Fixer, at 65 to 75°F (18 to 24°C) with agitation.

DEFINITION

Graininess	Resolving Power	Sharpness	Degree of Enlargement Allowed*
Fine	Medium	Low	Moderately Low

*For good-quality negatives.

For Black-and-White Prints

This is a high-contrast panchromatic film designed for making reduced (35 mm or smaller) copy negatives of printed matter, such as books, newspapers, maps, engineering drawings, documents, and similar originals. The film has extremely fine grain, ultra-high resolving power, and very high sharpness. High Contrast Copy Film produces good quality in copies of originals that contain both line and halftone material, such as magazine pages.

Size Available: 135-36 exposures.

Film Code Letter Designation: HC.

Film Code Number: 5069.

EXPOSURE

Speed: *Tungsten*—64

This film speed is for exposure meters marked for ASA speeds or Exposure Indexes and is based on recommended development. Set this speed on your exposure meter for determining trial exposures in copying. You can use this meter setting with incident-light meters directly and with reflected-light meters when you make a meter reading of a KODAK Neutral Test Card, 18 percent gray side, at the copyboard. Or you can make a meter reading of a matte white card, then set 12 on the meter dial for calculating the exposure.

Illumination: The recommended lighting setup for copying consists of two light sources, one on either side of the copy material, with the lights placed so that they are at an angle of 45 degrees to the material. Use a sheet of clean plate glass to hold the original flat.

Exposure Examples: With two No. 2 photoflood lamps in matte-surfaced reflectors 24 inches from the copy, use an exposure of about 1/15 second at *f*/11. With No. 1 photoflood lamps the same distance from the copy, use about 1/8 second at *f*/11. To obtain an image of sufficient size with some cameras, it may be necessary to use a supplementary close-up lens on the camera. Center the copy and focus the camera carefully.

Filter Factors: Usually, a filter will not be required to achieve the desired contrast between background and subject matter. In special cases, such as in copying old newspapers or books with yellowed paper, use a No. 8 yellow filter or a No. 15 deep-yellow filter. For copying blueprints, use a No. 25 red filter. Increase the normal exposure by the filter factor given in the table. However, if your camera has a built-in exposure meter that makes the reading through a filter used over the lens, see your camera manual for instructions on exposure with filters. Also, see page 97.

Filter	No. 8	No. 15	No. 25
Tungsten	1.2	1.5	8

DEVELOPMENT

Safelight: *Total darkness required.* However, when development is half completed, you can use a safelight at 4 feet (1.2 metres) for a *few* seconds. Equip the safelight with a KODAK Safelight Filter No. 3 (dark green), or equivalent, and a 15-watt bulb.

Developing Times are for small roll-film tanks with agitation for 5 seconds at 30-second intervals throughout development. The most widely used time and temperature are in heavy type. If your negatives are consistently too low in contrast, increase development time; if too high in contrast, decrease development time.

KODAK Packaged Developer	Developing Times in Minutes*				
	65°F (18°C)	**68°F (20°C)**	70°F (21°C)	72°F (22°C)	75°F (24°C)
D-19	7	**6**	5	4½	4

*Unsatisfactory uniformity may result with development times shorter than 5 minutes.

Rinse in KODAK Stop Bath SB-5a at 65 to 75°F (18 to 24°C) for about 30 seconds with agitation.

Fix for 2 to 4 minutes with KODAK Fixer or KODAK Fixing Bath F-5, or 1 to 2 minutes with KODAK Rapid Fixer, at 65 to 75°F (18 to 24°C). Agitate films frequently during fixing.

Wash and dry in the usual manner. For more rapid and complete washing, use KODAK Hypo Clearing Agent after fixing. See page 79.

Processing for Long-Term Keeping: Follow the special procedures described in the section "Processing for Long-Term Keeping" in the KODAK Data Book *Processing Chemicals and Formulas* (J-1), $1.95.

DEFINITION

Graininess	Resolving Power	Sharpness	Degree of Enlargement Allowed*
Extremely Fine	Ultra High	Very High	Extremely High

*The degree of enlargement allowed usually will be limited by camera and subject conditions rather than by film characteristics.

Reciprocity Characteristics for KODAK Black-and-White Films for General Use*

Exposure Time in Seconds	Either: Increase Lens Opening by	Or Use Corrected Exposure Time in Seconds	Change Developing Time by
1/100,000	+1 stop	Use lens opening correction	+20 percent
1/10,000	+½ stop	Use lens opening correction	+15 percent
1/1,000	None	No change	+10 percent
1/100	None	No change	None
1/10	None	No change	None
1	+1 stop	2	−10 percent
10	+2 stops	50	−20 percent
100	+3 stops	1200	−30 percent

*This table does not apply to KODAK High Speed Infrared Film and KODAK High Contrast Copy Film 5069. For these films, determine exposure and developing corrections by experiment when you use very short or long exposure times.

Selecting a KODAK Developer for Black-and-White Film—Key Properties

KODAK Developer

D-76 Long a favorite of pictorialists, it is well known for superior performance. This developer produces full emulsion speed and maximum shadow detail, with normal contrast, and gives moderately fine grain. It produces a long density scale, and its excellent development latitude permits forced development with relatively low fog. If you want to use one developer for all types of roll film, we highly recommend KODAK Developer D-76. For greater sharpness, but with a slight sacrifice in graininess, you can dilute the developer 1:1.

HC-110 A highly active developer for rapid processing of most black-and-white films. Photographic properties—such as sharpness, graininess, and shadow detail—are similar to those produced by KODAK Developer D-76. Both developer and replenisher are conveniently supplied in highly concentrated liquid form in plastic bottles. Dilution A gives short development times; Dilution B is for longer development times which yield better development uniformity.

MICRODOL-X An excellent fine-grain developer which is designed to produce low graininess and high sharpness with minimum speed loss. This developer is particularly suited for developing small negatives intended for making big enlargements. It is clean-working and has a long life. You can obtain even greater image sharpness by using MICRODOL-X Developer diluted 1:3, but with a slight increase in graininess.

POLYDOL A high-capacity developer designed for long life. You can use KODAK POLYDOL Developer as a general-purpose developer for both roll film and sheet film. It features good speed with medium grain, superior tonal-reproduction characteristics, and stable replenishment properties for consistent negative quality throughout its use.

DK-50 A popular general-purpose developer which works well with or without dilution. Moderately fast acting, it produces crisp, clean negatives with good highlight detail and medium grain.

D-19 A high-capacity, rapid-working developer yielding high-contrast negatives. It is especially suited to copying and technical applications where higher-than-normal contrast is required.

DOROTHY TSE

SNOW AND SHADOW

DOROTHY TSE

SNOW AND SHADOW

Translated by
Nicky Harman

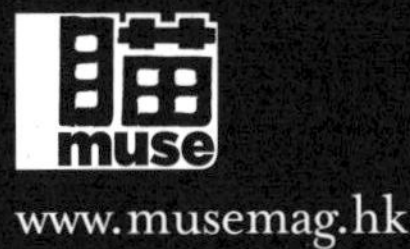

www.musemag.hk

SNOW AND **SHADOW**

Published by
East Slope Publishing Limited 東坡出版有限公司
PO Box 33744, Sheung Wan, Hong Kong
March 2014

"The Love Between Leaf and Knife," "The Traveling Family,"
"Head," "Blessed Bodies," "A Street in the Wind," "Black Cat City," and
"The Apartment Block" appeared originally in Chinese in *So Black* (《好黑》).
"The Mute Door" and "Bitter Melon" appeared originally in Chinese in *A Dictionary of Two Cities* (《雙城辭典》).
"March: Quiet," "April: Pregnant," and "May: Bird" appeared originally in Chinese in *Monthly Matters* (《月事》).
"Woman Fish" appeared originally in English in *The Guardian* as part of the series "Water Stories."

Book Design: Ringo Hui at BWDC / info@bwdc.com.hk
Cover Art by Firenze Lai
Printer: Green Production (Overseas) Group
Edition: 1st edition, March 2014
2014年3月初版
ISBN: 978-988-16046-0-6
Retail Price 定價: HK$140

Muse is a registered trademark of:
East Slope Publishing Limited, Post Office Box 33744, Sheung Wan, Hong Kong
Tel: +852 9170 5484 | Fax: +852 2541 1527
Website: www.musemag.hk | Email: muse@musemag.hk

We would like to acknowledge the generous support of the following partners:

香港藝術發展局
Hong Kong Arts Development Council

Hong Kong Arts Development Council
and the Hong Kong Literature Translation Project

The SOMA Project's HKAtlas series, initiated at the City University of Hong Kong my thanks to JS

CONTENTS

INTRODUCTION:

Dorothy Tse's Short Stories

What will readers expect to find when they open this book? A realistic depiction of life in Hong Kong? A sort of equivalent to the neo-realism found in Chinese mainland literature? Adventure, or romance, or personal and introspective musings? They'll find none of the above. Instead, we have surreal tales—fantastic in parts—but made the more effective for being grounded firmly in reality at the same time.

Dorothy's stories often start in a vein of apparently innocent realism. Then we find ourselves brought up short by an unexpected twist: the boy narrator in "The Traveling Family," recalling his father, says, "I'd always assumed he enjoyed the chore of catching the mice in my hair." Then the plot itself begins to take us in very odd directions. In "Head," the story of an overprotective father seems entirely normal, except that the son inexplicably wakes up minus his head and, when the father decides to donate his own, "[his] decision did not surprise anyone." In "The Love Between Leaf and Knife," the lovers squabble, in the way couples do. It is only as tensions rise, and each tries to outdo the other in proving their love, that events take an alarming turn. "The Traveling Family" describes how a poverty-stricken family leaves home in search of a better future elsewhere. So far, so normal...but the pages gradually become populated with ever-weirder characters: the members of a political party that hijack their bus; "the amazing Babaqi weeping actors," a theatre troupe with a strange specialty; and so on. What happens at each stage of this disorienting journey turns all our expectations on their heads, until finally only the boy remains to conclude the tale.

Dorothy's stories are carefully crafted and her writing is notably taut and spare. No superfluous repetition, none of the strings of adjectival phrases that can challenge translators of some mainland authors, and a total absence of sentimentality. It all gives us, as readers, a distinct sense of detachment, yet we keep turning the pages—intrigued, shocked, amused, sometimes moved.

Dorothy deliberately uses names to create an effect. As a distancing device, some characters are called only by initials instead of names: for instance, the emperors K and J in "Snow and Shadow," the story that has given its name to the book, and the characters in "The Apartment Block." In other instances, the names she has chosen add to the pervasive sense of surrealism. In some extremely interesting email conversations she and I had about the translation of the book, Dorothy asked me to give the names of some characters a clear semantic meaning. So *Jik Nin* (憶年) and *Gei Yuht* (紀月), the couple in "Black Cat City," became Memoria and Recall. She was also insistent that all of the place and product names should be invented in the translation, as they are in the original Chinese, to distance them from real Hong Kong life; so we get the delightfully named "Loch Ness Monster Pizza," the Tuesday special in "The Mute Door."

Snow and Shadow is not for the faint-hearted—limbs, and even heads, are lopped off with alarming regularity—although the cool tone of the writing somewhat mitigates the horror. Cool should not be taken to mean humdrum. In "The Mute Door," the opening paragraph about doors in mime is frankly poetic: "No groundwork is necessary for a house like that, no foundation on rock—this house is built from the poetry of the body and the mystery of bones and flesh in motion." And the story continues in a similarly dreamlike vein. Other stories, such as "Bed," a personal favorite of mine, stir our emotions in a disquieting way: a girl, driven from home when her sister and father begin an incestuous relationship in the only bed in their home, dreams obsessively of finding another bed and accepts sexual exploitation as the only way to get what she wants. This does not, however, convey the complexity of the story, which has a pervasive sense of menace that is reinforced by the helplessness of the girl. Dreamscapes interlock with a narrative which, though superficially realistic, itself feels quite unreal. Reading "Bed" is rather like moving through layers of hanging veils.

Surrealism occupies a special place in Hong Kong writing. In a recent essay for the University of Iowa, Dorothy Tse describes the inhabitants of Hong Kong as "hovering among languages" (Cantonese, Mandarin, other Chinese dialects, English), and goes on to say, "[for Hong Kong writers, written Chinese] is a language of distance and requires meditation... Contrary to the mainland literature that tried to borrow languages from the working class as well as the farmers in the '50s as a way to reach the public, Hong Kong's literature has a tradition of resistance to the language of daily life. Its highly experimental language is a strategy to distinguish a literary work from an entertaining and commercial one. In Hong Kong, writing itself is an active rejection of utilitarian society and mundane everyday life."

Dorothy Tse is a truly original writer whose stories experiment with theme and narrative alike. In this book, not only do weird things happen, but they are juxtaposed in ways that confound all logical expectations. The results are alternately beguiling and deeply disturbing.

Nicky Harman
February 2014

WOMAN FISH

He knows his wife will never be able to tell lies again.

All night long, the weary sound of water dripped from the air conditioner, slowly eroding into coral dreams. He awoke from the sleep that had borne him like an ocean, and saw the buildings outside, packed cheek to cheek. People squeezed breathlessly through the cracks in the city, eager to find a Christmas tree in the shopping mall, though it was only August. One of the bulbs on its plastic branches had a burnt-out filament, a blind eye amid brilliant illuminations.

Outside the mall, the stagnant air had lain beached too long—it felt as if all things had come to an end. People looked up and the tight-shut, overcast sky opened its toothless mouth, spattering their faces with rain. He opened his umbrella and the raindrops pelted down on it like deafening bullets. He sealed himself inside his house, the thrumming of the downpour extending to every pane of glass.

"It doesn't matter how much I wash my eyes, things still get twisted out of shape until I can't tell what they are." "I can feel my brain shrinking like a dried-out sponge." "Faraway things are too small to make out."

His wife's complaints had been fragments of countless lies floating around in his head—fragments he hadn't been able to reassemble into a complete picture.

One morning, he realized that his wife's sleek, pale head was completely without hair. Her mouth was huge, protruding like a ship cleaving the still waters of the sea. Her eyes had slipped to the sides of her face. Her breasts were two melting glaciers, slowly sinking into her body. When she walked naked towards him, all that was left of the woman were her smooth, muscular legs. Apart from that, she had transformed completely into a fish.

He used to wake from watery dreams to the whitish, otherworldly light from the computer screen. She would be there—sitting at the keyboard, joyfully making collages of photographs for some popular magazine to publish with the news stories she concocted from his strange, early-morning reveries. He knew then why he could always smell the odor of dreams in the grave faces of the television newscasters, in the front-page banner headlines.

Every morning, as she gulped down a can of viscous green fluid, a slimming shake, his wife used to say with a shrug, "It's just a pack of lies." But he kept searching her photographs for the river of his dreams: a river of surreal blue that enveloped all that had disappeared on land. He was looking for his dead mother, her white hair spread across her shoulders, walking with the dog that had died when he was thirteen years old. The dog's pale-gold eyes narrowed to slits, then opened again, round as walnuts. A popsicle in red, green, and blue was wedged in the coral reef, and a shoal of fish swam over a floor tiled in a diamond pattern. The broken clock tower, which once stood on the jetty, floated in the river, shattering the water into innumerable wavelets as it rocked and swayed.

But the rivers in his wife's collages were often murky: a figure squatting at the water's edge, looking around, eyes bulging like a frog, pulling a fishing net—a mesh of eyes—from the unfathomable depths and shaking out discarded tires, dead phones, dirty needles, lumpy unraveling sweaters, the maimed limbs of some animal with four fingers (possibly human)...all ready for recycling into a rainstorm to drench the earth with a fantastic whispering, re-entering the world's flesh through the trees, the beasts, and human skin.

Some sounds are lost forever. He will never hear his wife tapping at the computer again. She never sits on the sofa, looking down at her fingernails as she slowly paints on layer after layer of scarlet varnish, looking up to tell him some invented story about a helicopter or a cat. Now his wife's rounded shadow rarely slants across the windowpane; outside the city is gradually getting colder. Her ice-cold hands have shrunk to little fins that, it seems, will never again touch things on dry land.

Sometimes she soaks herself in the bathtub, lying back to reveal her pasty fish's belly. He sees long, slender legs stretching from her belly, muscles running up her thighs towards spiraling genitalia. Sometimes they make love. His wife's huge mouth opens and shuts, sending out bubbles with a fishy smell that fills the room. He shuts his eyes—he can no longer distinguish ecstasy from anguish in his wife's shrill gasps.

Hidden eyes in the corridor open slowly to reveal a razor-sharp gaze. One narrow evening he notices them on a dried-out city street, making ripples on his wife's skin. They walk into their usual Japanese restaurant and the chef takes a quick look at his wife, then silently takes a slab of dark red flesh from a glass shelf covered with gutted fish. The chef throws the chunk down onto the white counter. His eyes fix on the gleaming silver knife in his hand, then flick towards her. He presses the blade down into flesh. There is an odd, sharp hiss as he slits it open. Her lips part, but no sound comes out from between her sharply pointed teeth. Her round eyes pop wide, revealing black centers buried in the silver surround.

He imagines waking from a nightmare to find his wife has gone out through the unlocked door alone, losing herself in the city's lawless back streets, ending up auctioned off in an underground seafood restaurant. Or maybe she'll be spotted by pimps and installed as a diversion in a brothel. He sees his wife flattened out, studded with glinting light bulbs on an enormous poster. But one bulb has blown and the filament sticks in his head, the scene before him gradually fading into darkness.

His wife has stopped eating. He fills a huge fish tank for her and sets it up in the middle of the sitting room. When she puts her head into it, he hears a gurgling sound and a stream of bubbles rises to the surface. But most of the time she sits motionless on a chair in front of the picture of a river that hangs on the wall. In her eyes, a torrent of ambiguous color surges past, gradually narrowing until it vanishes into transparency.

All night long he can hear the waters pulling back. He tries making another map of the city in his head and tracing the course of the river. Driving around the outskirts they can't find where it starts. A river flows in blue paint on the wooden hoardings that enclose the city's waterways. Behind the boards he can hear machines dumping silt.

Their car shoots across a collapsing bridge. Distant factory chimneys belch thick smoke like fiery, inverted rockets. The ground splits and cracks into fissures as enigmatic as oracle bones. His lungs swell silently until they almost burst. He does not know if they have arrived at the river, but he can smell an appalling stench. The humidity keeps rising and his wife, overcome with excitement, beats her body against the car door, making a slapping sound on the glass.

THE LOVE BETWEEN LEAF AND KNIFE

Neither of them remembered exactly where things went wrong. But at some point Knife started to cough.

Though it was only a grain of rice lodged in his throat, to him it felt like a walnut. It was much too big to pass down his dark, narrow esophagus and its rough surface grated on the soft, slippery flesh. His face puffed up and suffused with red, while his lips began to turn blue. He bent over, his legs splayed wide, and coughed and retched until tears came to his eyes. He really thought he was going to die.

He imagined Leaf putting down her bowl and chopsticks, coming up behind him, and gently rubbing his back with her bony fingers. As she rubbed the left shoulder blade, he could feel the hard warmth of bone against bone. It was like once when he had a slight cold and lay on his side in bed, joking about it, but she had cried and run her fingers down his back like the trickle of a breeze. It had gone on till the next morning and his coughing had finally eased.

But Leaf just carried on sitting opposite him, ignoring his coughing and retching. She gazed at the flickering candle flame in the center of the table, arm raised, thumping herself on the back.

This morning when she woke up with a backache, it had occurred to Leaf that a mung bean under the mattress must have caused it. Not surprising, she thought. The pain was spreading and she felt as if a rib had caved in. She gave her back a hard thump, but the more she thumped the more it hurt, and now it seemed as if all the other ribs were shifting. Why didn't Knife come over and rub her back for her? Like once when she had pretended to be asleep on his lap, and he had used his thumb and forefinger to trace gentle circles that rippled outwards over her back. Just a gentle massage like that and the pain would get better.

Knife looked at Leaf and realized it was no good coughing. He just had to force down the thick broth of butter, strawberries, vinegar, fish sauce, and peanuts in his bowl. (Those were the only flavors he could distinguish in its murky depths.) Leaf's soups became denser every day, not like the cream of tomato or cream of mushroom soups she used to prepare when they first met, which he could gulp down by the bowlful. Leaf always smiled with satisfaction at that, showing a row of innocent-looking teeth.

"You love me," she would say firmly.

Now, though, Leaf secretly hoped that he would not be able to finish the soup. Then she could walk coldly past him without even a backward glance, and say the words:

"You don't love me."

Knife seemed to know what was going through her mind and forced down the soup with a pained expression, as if he was struggling through the last stage of a marathon. His thoughts were, of course, more on the baggy, black polo neck sweater that lay in the suitcase, a present he had once given to Leaf.

It had been a hot summer's day—thirty-two degrees Celsius! Leaf sat on the beach at Pak Sha Wan, wiping the drops of sweat from her forehead, her face burnt red by the sun.

It had nothing to do with the weather. Knife took a swig of ice-cold Coca-Cola, looked at Leaf dressed in that sweater, and thought contentedly that she looked like a docile, tropical black bear. He wasn't going to let Leaf plead: "This has nothing to do with whether or not I love you."

Knife quickly drank the last mouthful of soup and picked up his bowl and chopsticks. As far as eating went, he'd always had the upper hand. He cleared everything off the table and carried it into the kitchen.

He wouldn't be getting any bouquets, however, for as little dishwashing as this. So he bent down, peered into the kitchen cupboard, and got out some cups that had not been washed for a very long time—in fact, they were mildewed and smelled as if they might still contain the dregs of Leaf's milky instant tea. Then he ran into the bedroom and pulled out a pair of pink underpants wedged down behind the wardrobe. They were Leaf's too; there was no denying it. Knife kept turning up item after item of Leaf's, every one of them dirty, and heaping them into the sink until the water overflowed.

In the kitchen, the grimy ventilation fan revolved slowly, giving off a whiff of grease. Knife rolled up his sleeves and thrust his arms into the soap suds, then looked back almost exultantly at Leaf, who was standing in the kitchen doorway.

Leaf took in the scene. She flushed slightly but remained calm. Then she shrugged, went into the bedroom, and slowly pulled a case out from under the bed. She wiped the dining table clean and spread a red plush cloth on it. Then she opened the case and took out one knife after another and placed them on the tablecloth. The knives came in all shapes and sizes: some with wooden or PVC handles or hollow handles, steak knives, kitchen knives... There were piles of them, all glinting in the light, looking like an ice-cold knife mountain.

Every birthday, Christmas, Easter, and Valentine's Day,

Leaf had given him a different knife, but this was the most she had ever given him at one time, and she felt elated at her achievement.

There were one hundred and thirty-one altogether.

"Happy Valentine's Day," she said to Knife with deliberate casualness, as he emerged from the kitchen.

But to her surprise, Knife did not betray any excitement. He just shook the water from his hands and wiped them on his jogging pants.

"Happy Valentine's Day," he responded coldly, and took a case out of a drawer in the wall cabinet.

He opened it, and Leaf saw that it was full of leaves pierced and strung together on cords. She recognized fan-shaped gingko leaves, needle-shaped pine leaves, and maples. Knife climbed on the table and hung the strings from the ceiling like Christmas decorations. A few leaves she did not recognize dropped into Leaf's palms. Knife looked down, expecting to see excitement on Leaf's face, but there was nothing. She just stood there, not even looking at him.

Leaf was busy counting the leaves:...one thousand and twenty-five, one thousand and twenty-six... He had obviously beaten her in terms of pure numbers. But knives were harder to collect, and she could not help feeling aggrieved.

She turned away and chose a CD from the rack and put it on. She could never remember if the name of the band was The Ants or The Geckos. She had bought it three years ago at a music trade fair. In fact, she could have bought the CD anywhere. She had only gone to the trade fair so she could queue up for five hours—asphyxiating in other people's BO and feeling put upon—and then come home and go on about it to Knife.

"I stood in line for five hours just to buy this CD for you," she kept saying to him.

Leaf expected Knife to react, but all he said was:

"Do you want to dance?"

It was not what Leaf was expecting.

That evening, Leaf and Knife danced in their tiny, cramped apartment on the Lower Ngau Tau Kok Estate, but neither seemed to be paying much attention to the music and they were constantly out of step.

Knife's gaze slipped past Leaf, falling on the cabinet, the floor, and the lattice window, all of which he had polished to a high shine, and the bedsheet, washed just this afternoon and hung out of the window to dry.

But Leaf was looking at something over Knife's shoulder. Everything seemed to be whizzing around the room: from the monster phone that she had drunk seventy-six cans of Happy Milko to get, to the toy basketball frame she had won in ring toss after forty-three tries, and...

At that moment, Knife accidentally stepped on the hem of Leaf's long skirt and Leaf slumped to the floor—deliberately, he was sure.

"Sorry!..." Knife looked dazed, then peered at the wall behind Leaf as if deep in thought. Leaf thought he was about to reach out and help her up, but he suddenly raised one hand and slapped himself hard on the cheek.

Leaf stared at him from where she sat on the floor. "Why are you hitting yourself?" Knife thought Leaf would jump to her feet and sympathetically rub his jaw for him. But Leaf only gave her own face a fierce, hard slap.

Knife bit his lip and took a step back. "If you hit yourself again, I'll... I'll knock my head against the wall." Then he walked to the wall and banged and banged until his forehead went red.

Leaf did not go to look at Knife's injured forehead. Instead she jumped up and said, "If you're going to knock your head against the wall, then so will I, against another bit of wall." She thought Knife might try and stop her, but he didn't.

Knife, who was feeling dizzy from the knocks, straightened up and turned his attention to the knives on the dining table. He picked up a kitchen knife and yelled at Leaf: "If you keep on knocking your head against the wall, I'll cut my arm off!"

Leaf turned to look at him, her forehead red from the pounding she had given it. "Fine!" She picked up a meat cleaver. "Then I'll cut mine off too!"

Knife raised the knife and took a swipe—a piece of arm as long as a lotus root fell to the floor with a thud, and rolled against the wall.

Leaf was no less valiant, but she was not as strong as Knife. When she slashed, her arm hung from the elbow joint, swinging to and fro, before finally falling to the floor with a dull thump, and rolling over to the wall next to Knife's arm.

"You really cut your arm off," Leaf said, gazing at the two forearms.

Knife looked down at them and nodded.

"And you really cut yours off too," he added.

"Shouldn't we go to the hospital?"

"Yes," Leaf nodded.

They were heading for the door, still dazed, when Knife

gently stopped Leaf.

He turned to pick up his forearm and handed it to her, then took Leaf's arm himself.

Leaf looked blankly at him.

"We can go now," Knife said.

On Valentine's Day evening, the streets were full of boys and girls carrying bouquets of flowers, or cuddly toys, or heart-shaped balloons... There were not many like Knife and Leaf, carrying each other's arm.

"Shouldn't we walk a bit faster?"

"Yes, definitely."

However, they showed no signs of hurrying as they strolled along side by side.

"Can you rub my back?" Knife asked suddenly.

Leaf was taken aback. Then she held up Knife's arm and used it to scratch his back gently.

"Now can you rub me here?" Leaf asked, glancing over her shoulder.

So Knife held up Leaf's forearm and used it to trace circles on her back.

Leaf felt the ripples spreading outwards and, although something was not exactly the same, it reminded her of that first taste of love.

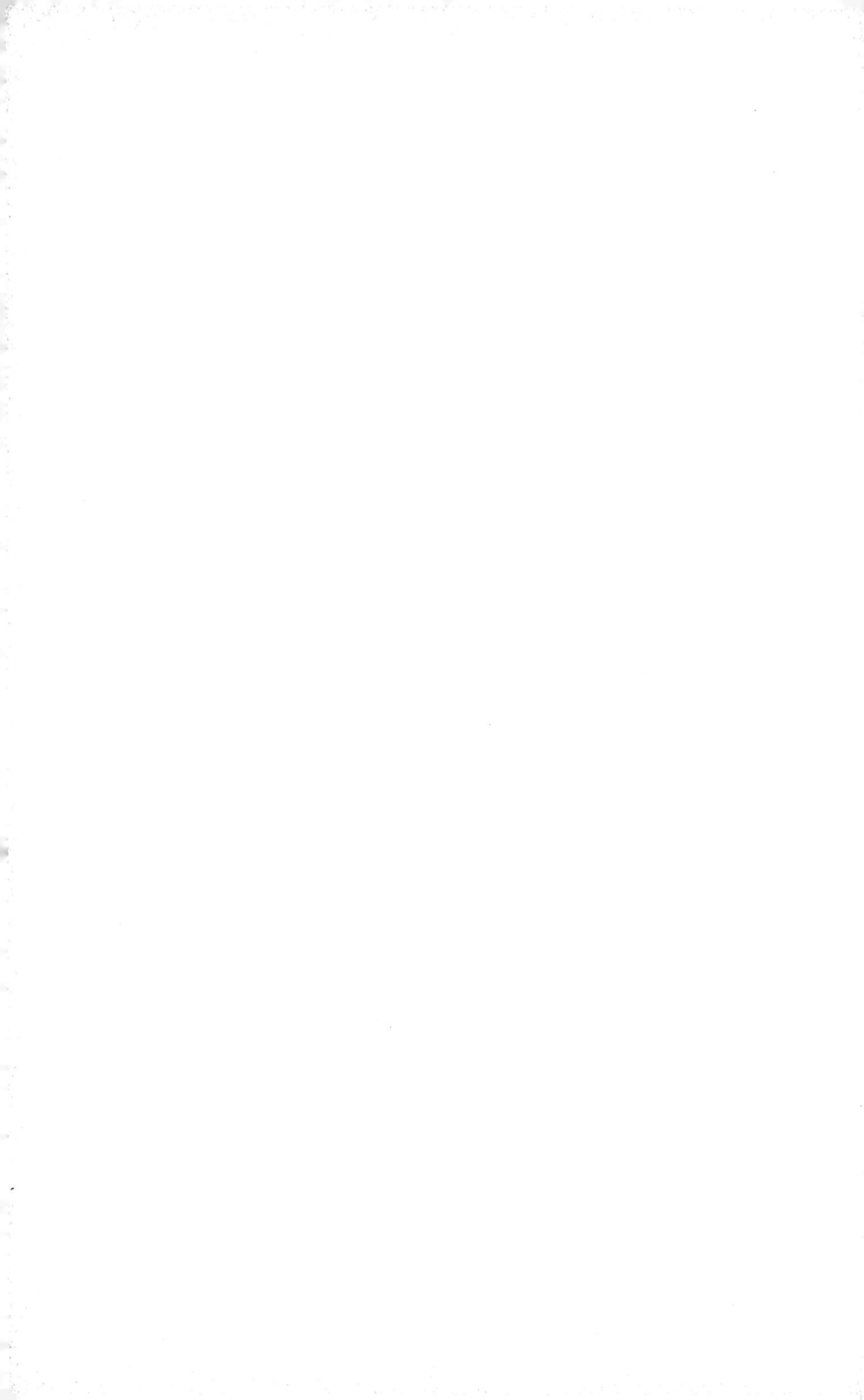

THE TRAVELING FAMILY

As I whizzed down the winding streets of Babaqi on my bike, bumping over the gutters, I couldn't help remembering the Grandma, Dad, Mom, and Sis I had once had.

I was passing the building whose top floor I used to call "home." This was my last "home" in Babaqi. The top floor windows were now covered in cobwebs. A gaudy spider rested there, as if guarding the myth of my past life. Back then, sounds of clattering and banging often floated from the windows as we knocked over Grandma's tins of fish, jars of pickled plums, or her vat of fermenting wine; or as the eggs Mom was boiling rolled onto someone's foot and they yelled in protest, "Ai-ya!" I could still hear myself kicking the toilet door so my elder sister, snoozing inside, would hurry up. But after we decided to pull up stakes and go traveling in 1987, those sounds all ceased.

We were dirt poor and hardly set foot outside the house from one year to the next, so going traveling was a big deal for us. But I was young and that wasn't the way I saw it then. I was just curious. In my memory of our departure, I was the only one in the mood for the trip as I dashed off towards the Khaki Street bus station. I was wearing the family bamboo sieve on my head to keep the sun off. I can still see myself turning to look back, laughing at my family for being so slow, speckles of sunlight falling on my face.

We got to the bus station and prepared to board the bus going south. Just then, a tour group came by. "The signboards have been here for decades and each board bears a different number; some of them are in English as well, which is quite unusual," said the tour leader. He was short, and spittle gathered at the corners of his mouth as he talked, a detail I remember to this very day.

The tour guide led his group onto a double-decker bus. They sat down inside, chatting and munching on snake-meat kebabs, which made me very envious. However, my dad decided that, to save money, the five of us would sit on the bus roof, though it would be more accurate to say we lay on our bellies.

I soon discovered it was fun being on the roof. If we gripped the aluminum window frames of the upper deck, we could see the passengers inside or we could look up and watch the scenery go by. I was in a relaxed mood and began to bawl out songs, which my father, who was sitting beside me, joined in. His breath, as he opened his mouth, smelled fishy, reminding me of the ink-black lulu fish soup he'd eaten the evening before. I had watched resentfully as he helped himself to the last bowlful.

The swirling dust along Babaqi Road was an impressive sight, and looked like a cloud of moths fluttering towards me. This was the first time I had gone on a trip, which made seeing the moths even more exhilarating. As the wind picked up, I looked to see where they had flown off to, but just then the bus went under a footbridge and Dad yelled at us to keep our heads down. I looked through one of the upper deck windows and saw a girl eating vanilla ice cream, a layer of white cream sticking to her lips. When I looked up again, the bus had been hijacked.

Being robbed the first time you leave home could be regarded as really bad luck, but actually I found it exciting. What I did not foresee was that Dad's excitement would be far greater than mine.

The five thieves were clad in the leather uniform worn by members of the Pipi Party. One, armed with a long-handled *guandao*, pushed my head down and sat on top of me. It was only later that I realized how influential the Pipi Party was in Babaqi; in fact, it eclipsed every other group. At the time, I thought it was funny. With my head forced down, I looked at the girl on the upper deck again and saw that one of the Pipi had taken her ice cream. I could not help grinning and pulled a face at her. The way she stared mutely back put me in a very good mood. The bus stopped and two of the Pipi transferred passengers' luggage from the compartment under the bus to a truck. As they passed the bags across, they seemed as awkward as scuttling crabs, and I felt a young man's contempt for them. When I saw them making off with the bottles and jars that Grandma had packed away, I was overcome by a sudden sense of self-righteousness, and I hawked and spat a thick gob of phlegm at them. Although my gob missed its target, it lay thick and green on the ground and I felt hugely proud.

One of the Pipi looked up, pulled a boomerang from his belt, and slung it at me. I felt a chill on my scalp and a tuft of hair floated down and landed on my phlegm. The boomerang looped and returned to its owner's hand. The man's smug expression infuriated me. Then I saw how apathetic Grandma looked and was even more indignant. I was aware that Dad, beside me, was staring hard at the Pipi Party man. Fondly imagining that he was planning to avenge me, I gloated.

If I had paid more attention, I would have noticed that Dad's expression was full of admiration. For the first time, his face glowed. That glow made me realize just how utterly gloomy he normally looked as he paced back and forth at home every day, stepping over Grandma's pickled plum jars as he went.

After the Pipi Party people had cleaned out all the passengers' luggage from the bus, the one beside me jumped down onto the truck and they got ready to drive off. Dad suddenly stood up and yelled at them to stop. I was still under the illusion that he wanted to teach them a lesson for the way they had treated me. I saw them look up at him in surprise and felt an enormous sense of superiority.

Now that I think back on it, my conviction that he was going to avenge me was no different from the way I'd always assumed he enjoyed the chore of catching the mice in my hair. Actually, when I laid my head proudly in his lap, Dad's attention was anywhere but on the job. I would hear my mother's voice from the kitchen, "Don't let the mice nibble our things!"

In my memory I can see Dad that day, floating through the air like a translucent snowflake. I had never seen him like that in our cramped home. I feel now that when he finally landed on the truck, it really was just like a snowflake landing in snow.

He was not going to challenge the Pipi Party people, still less was he about to start a fight with them. I saw them exchange a few words and then they gave him one of their leather outfits to put on. Dad ostentatiously sat down on Grandma's jars and waved at us with a smile. I had never seen him smile so contentedly before. As the truck slowly pulled away, I still did not understand quite what had happened. I was even more surprised when they all started singing a song I had once taught Dad. I saw the dark O's of their mouths opening and shutting and it was like they were one big family. Eventually, I could not even tell which one was my father.

As the truck vanished into the distance, I suddenly pulled

myself together and started denouncing my father's shameful behavior at the top of my lungs. No one paid any attention. It was as if it had never happened. Grandma was still lying apathetically on the bus roof. Even Mom seemed to have forgotten all about Dad and was joking with my sister about their first periods. The bus soon set off again and some of the passengers began to sing; others clapped along and danced. I certainly didn't feel like singing, and carried on complaining bitterly. It never occurred to me then that not only would Dad never come back, but Mom would soon be leaving us in the same manner.

The bus, with its happy passengers, stopped on a deserted street and the driver ordered us off. Then, without a word, he drove away. We had no idea where we were. As the driver looked back at us, I saw him chewing on a toothpick and smiling oddly. I tugged at the hem of Mom's jacket so she would look at the driver, but it was obvious that she was quite uninterested.

She took my sister and me by the hand and we went on with our journey, with the stooped figure of Grandma trailing along behind us.

I soon stopped denouncing Dad; the scenery made me forget all about him. In fact, by the time we came upon a troupe of actors erecting a stage, I was as excited as I had been when we left home.

I pushed my way through the crowd and saw a large group of sad-faced performers on the stage. Every one of them was weeping. At first, they merely wept tears and sniveled, but gradually their tears turned into bees and centipedes, flowers and grass. The bees buzzed past my ears; the flowers filled the street. The actors' weeping had transformed the street into a brilliantly colored and bustling scene.

I learned later that these were Babaqi's famous weeping actors. The residents of Babaqi found tears extremely funny, so weeping actors were always popular. I thought their faces looked as wrinkled as the pickled plums in Grandma's jars. I got as close as I could and tried to imitate their expressions, but I couldn't help bursting into laughter.

Not that anyone heard me because another loud laugh drowned me out. The troupe manager, a cleaning rag draped over his shoulder, was slapping his buxom wife's bottom and whooping with laughter. His laugh sounded false to me, as if he was just trying to attract attention. His wife turned to glare at him, then came over to greet us. My family sat down around one of the tables set out in the street. She asked if I wanted anything to eat, but I had no time to answer; I was secretly trying to out-laugh the troupe manager. I was also eager to give my sister's buttocks a slap for good measure, but they remained obstinately glued to her stool.

By this time, I had laughed myself hoarse, but to no avail. Of course, I was unwilling to admit defeat, but the manager suddenly stopped laughing and stared coldly at me. As I stuck out my tongue at him, I discovered a meal in front of us—a bowl of his wife's special fried frogs and four bottles of Mosquito Soda.

I brushed away the insects hovering around the bottle tops and sipped the drink with its violet-colored bubbles. I have forgotten what flavor it was, but I do remember a frog that was not quite dead pulling out Grandma's false teeth. I watched it chomping on them as it hopped away like a green rubber ball. Grandma grabbed another frog and threw it at the thief, but missed.

If I think back on what happened that day, I realize I completely ignored my mother, who was engrossed with the actors. I don't know if I could have stopped her from leaving us if I had noticed her brimming, reddened eyes sooner. The manager and his wife had fastened onto her right from the start. There were fewer and fewer people who knew how to weep in Babaqi, and they saw that she was a superb weeping performer.

Finally Mom burst into a flood of tears and I saw that she was crying fireworks and waterfalls, an elephant and a lion. I had never seen her weep such glittering tears. When she was slicing onions at home, the tears she shed had been nothing special. Yet now the elephant and the lion paced before me, and the lion's yawning maw gave me quite a fright.

When the manager caught hold of Mom, I was just spitting out the eyeballs of the last frog. One rolled under Mom's feet and the manager kicked it away. I rushed over to Mom and grabbed the man's leg so she could pull free of his grasp. But then, to my amazement, Mom bent down and pried my fingers from his leg. I expected her to explain her behavior, but she simply dried her eyes and struck up a conversation with the manager and his wife. I felt she wasn't seeing me at all.

Ignoring my anger, Mom began to help them put the stools away. I thought that if I sat on the ground with my arms akimbo as I usually did, she would look down and beg me in a low voice to stand up again. But I had forgotten that I was not at home sitting in the kitchen doorway. There was no need for me to get out of the way; she could just leave. I watched as she walked away with the weeping performers. I did not stand up—it was beneath my dignity. When Mom was quite far away, she looked back at us, but it was too far to see her expression.

Grandma and my sister pulled me to my feet. Grandma pointed to the sky. "The weather's really good." Sis nodded. "It looks like rain's on the way." I looked up too, but I couldn't see a thing.

I began to lose my taste for travel after Mom and Dad left. Transferring my anger at them to the plants and insects, I scissored off beetles' wings, trampled new grass shoots, and cut centipedes up into sections. In Babaqi, only the butterflies escaped my murderous attentions. I liked watching butterflies, and squatted by the roadside with Sis to watch these brilliant creatures resting on the crab-flowers. When they took off, we pursued them down the road until we got to the Babaqi Butterfly House.

Babaqi butterflies must be the biggest, most colorful, and most varied in the world. The Butterfly House, according to official propaganda, would turn any young girl into a beautiful butterfly—she just had to dress up in one of their outfits. I was pretty skeptical, but for most Babaqi girls, becoming a butterfly was the dream of a lifetime. A famous author even wrote a book called *Butterfly Dreams*, analyzing the psychological reasons why Babaqi girls longed to become butterflies.

That day, as Sis and I pressed our noses to the window of the Babaqi Butterfly House and watched the butterflies dancing in the air, I had no idea that Sis would soon be leaving too.

There was always a long line of girls at the Butterfly House door. From a distance, the line looked like an enormously long, gaudily colored, wriggling caterpillar as the girls patiently waited to turn into butterflies. I was enthralled at the sight. Sis pulled me over to the line. "Don't you want to have a look?" she asked. I remember that the sound of her voice wafted to me like a scented breeze. I looked up at her: the flickering lights outside the Butterfly House shone on her so that she looked like a butterfly too. The glare from the striplights was getting in my eyes and I could only squint and nod my head.

For the first time, I saw that Sis could be beautiful. Before that, I thought all she could do was sit at the washbasin, her hair hanging loose, and swat at the cloud of mosquitoes that hung around her head.

We stood together at the Butterfly House doors and watched the butterflies emerge, one by one, gorgeously colored and extraordinarily graceful. Then something dusty-black flashed past—just specks of dust blown by the wind, said Sis.

There was a lot of pushing and shoving in the line. Sis held my head in her hands. I felt their warmth. But I was a bit fed up by now. I tugged at her hand and said, "Let's go."

She shook her head. "Don't worry, it will soon be our turn." She was not looking at me. Her eyes were full of butterflies. I remembered how she used to stand on tiptoe on Grandma's pickled plum jars and gaze out the window. I don't know what she had in her eyes back then.

Not every girl could get into the Butterfly House. First, they had to get past the man in the black coat at the door. I don't know what special charms Sis used but she seemed to have no trouble getting in. I wanted to shout for her to stop, but suddenly someone clamped a hand over my mouth. I bit it hard, but then I discovered it was Grandma. By the time I looked around again, Sis had disappeared.

Even if Grandma had not restrained me, I could never have stopped Sis. She was deaf to the world by then and had eyes only for the butterflies. As they flew upwards, she saw herself flying up into the air too, and looking back at that tiny window...

Grandma and I waited outside the Butterfly House doors. I wanted to see Sis fly out, transformed into a fabulous butterfly. We stood there for a very long time, but we saw no butterflies, only one dull gray moth, which floated by in the dust.

Eventually, Grandma took my hand and we left the Butterfly House. I must have cut a forlorn figure, not at all like my normal self. I had long since forgotten my annoyance with Grandma, and could only hope that she would take pity on me.

I can't remember how far we had walked when Grandma suddenly came to a halt. It was there, in Babaqi's old-fashioned streets, that she said she was leaving too. That was also the moment when she told me the real aim of our trip: we had to get away from a home that would soon disappear, and each of us had to find our own individual space, one that belonged just to us. I noticed for the first time that she was terribly stooped and I could only see her face by crouching down. Tears dripped from her eyes, some collecting in her wrinkles, others falling to the ground.

When I reached out to wipe her face, she said she had to go though she didn't want to. Actually...no. She said nothing more, nor did she shed a tear. She left, her lips curved downwards in a smile. She was walking with such a stoop that she seemed to be walking into her own back, still with a smile on her face.

"Where will you go, Grandma?" She took a jar of pickled plums from an inside pocket—it must have been the last one she had left. I don't know if she was planning to sell it or if she was going to scoop out the plums and make the bottle her home.

I remained crouched on the ground until Grandma had shrunk as small as a speck of dust, which was blown away by the wind and vanished. Until the black night, and the white dawn that followed it, I stayed, crouched there on the ground, daydreaming. My dreams were often of riding a bicycle along Babaqi's winding streets, looking for a place that belonged to me. Now, when I look up at the home that was once mine, I don't know whether I've left my dream or am still in it.

Sometimes, I wish I could give up this unending search. Or am I really looking for another home? I must be the only one from Babaqi still to have this fantasy. Anyway, it's only occasionally that I feel this way and I really don't know if it would make things any better than they are now.

HEAD

When Flower got up that morning, Tree's head had vanished.

She got a bamboo clothes pole and poked around under the bed and in the cracks in the walls, opened every drawer one by one, and searched through the cans of KK chocolate creams and cream twists. (Her son had once said he liked the brand.) But there was no sign of Tree's head.

The morning sun was so warm that its rays leapt down into people's collars like lively fleas. People were having their usual breakfast drinks—the ones with indeterminate ingredients that came in cartons—and stuffing their mouths with snacks or noodles (dehydrated, preserved, or "ever-fresh") in preparation for rushing around, or lazing around, just as they had done the day before. Then someone twitched the corner of the curtains to take a look outside, and was greeted by the sight of young Tree, headless, being escorted to an ambulance by his parents. Watching the vehicle jounce out onto the dusty highway, the onlooker yawned.

"You'd better take him home."

The doctor, who was suffering badly from insomnia, did not even glance at Tree. He just shook his head mournfully and looked at Tree's parents through sunken eyes. "You'll just have to wait until the police find his head. There's nothing more we can do."

The puffiness of the doctor's eyes seemed to add weight to his words. He stuck his hands in his pockets and slouched out of the room. Hospital beds and wheelchairs whizzed back and forth, many of them occupied by patients who had lost noses, limbs, hearts, and other organs. They too were puffy-eyed and pale and, except for the lack of uniforms, looked much the same as the doctors. Polyester coats rustled to and fro and the scene was riotous with the smell of medicine—there was something curiously festive in the atmosphere. It agitated Flower, who looked at her headless son and burst into tears. Tree's father, Wood, said nothing. But before the white-coated doctor had vanished down the long corridor, he came to a decision: he would donate his own head to his twenty-five-year-old only son.

The doctor raised his eyebrows slightly at Wood, but gave a tired smile. "The law states that you can agree to donate any organ to a close family member."

Wood's decision did not surprise anyone. According to some, his relationship with his son had long hinted at such an outcome, though others disagreed.

◦ ◦ ◦

Tree had been born on November 13, 1977, at 11:05 p.m.

The first time Wood set eyes on his son, he seemed to have been waiting so long for this moment that he had no idea how to react.

He spent a very long time in the deserted hospital corridor, squinting through the glass at his son and sucking his index finger. "He looks exactly like me," he said finally.

No one could fathom how Wood could see his own image in this furiously bawling baby. Tree was a crybaby. One old neighbor recalled how, not long after Tree's birth, the scrawny figure of his father could be seen running along the riverbank at night with the bawling baby bouncing on his shoulder and then running back again. He would come back, out of breath, puffing and panting. As the riverbank emptied of visitors, the sight of Wood's lanky figure speeding up and down was reminiscent of a planet in relentless orbit.

When a neighbor, kept awake by the bawling, rang Wood's doorbell, he said, "My son's caught a cold. He's got a stuffed up nose."

Looking worried, he bent over the cot and sucked a long, shiny trail of snot from Tree's tiny nostrils.

Watching this tender scene, the neighbor forgot about not being able to sleep and remembered the soft and tasty malt candy the street hawkers sold on weekends.

"Want some malt candy, Tree?"

The little old man selling malt candy at the underpass entrance was a familiar face who sometimes appeared on TV variety shows.

Tree gave a shriek of excitement as he was handed the stick of candy. Whenever he got excited, he would clutch at his father's nose, which was soon covered in bloody scratches. "That kid just loves my nose, much more than my eyes or mouth," said Wood to Flower.

◦ ◦ ◦

The head transplant operation was successful and, on an auspicious day for housework, woodcutting, and so on, Flower brought father and son home. Before that, however, she put up new curtains and hung beef bones, juniper leaves, and chicken feathers at the front door and windows. She was not sure what their purpose was. Perhaps she was hoping that, even as she fantasized about creating a new life, things would actually go on just the same as before.

Wood's body carried on doing its morning exercises on the balcony, so the figure seen dressed in shirt and trousers, running for the bus and then arriving home carrying cakes and beers in the evening, could only have been Tree, couldn't it? It was the idle neighbors who figured this out. They gathered each morning in the shady pavilion, and engaged in long, meaningless debates, only to forget everything by sunset. On several occasions, Flower made a point of walking past them, but they would hurriedly pretend nothing was up. Flower knew very well what they were talking about, and was slightly put out at being excluded.

Actually, Flower would have been happy to tell them all about Wood and Tree. This community was bound together by whisperings among the neighbors and Flower had always been an active participant in such gossip.

Flower and Wood were now thrown together more than they had ever been. Without a head, Wood could not go to the bookshop that had been his business for years. He occasionally stumbled around the apartment, knocking over a flower vase or a fish bowl and depositing a gasping, half-dead fish on the floor. But most of the time he lazed in the swing seat on the balcony, scratching an itchy spot on his body with long, slender fingers.

Tree kept the bookshop going for his dad. And before he left for work in the morning, he always remembered to crouch down and inject Wood with the daily nutrients that had been prescribed by the doctor.

The sun shed its usual generous warmth on Wood's body. Flower did not know whether it was latent memory or physical energy that was controlling that body—but then, there are far more significant things that we don't know, aren't there? thought Flower. It was such a sunny day, why not wash the quilts and hang them out to dry on the flat rooftop?

◦ ◦ ◦

The rattan swing seat Wood was sitting on was the one they had bought when Tree was fourteen months old. Tree was unperturbed when he saw it for the first time, taking it as just another toy car or bleeping play phone.

But when his dad went to put him on it and his bottom landed on the rattan seat, he reacted the way he always did to anything new: he gave shriek after shriek, then stuck his thumb in his mouth as a dazed look came over him. He was taken by surprise, however, when Wood gave the swing a hefty shove and the seat soared high into the air, so high it seemed as if it was going to catapult him into the river. Tree clutched the side ropes in terror, shrunk back into the seat and looked down helplessly. Wood just laughed cheerfully, got out a completed painting, and showed it to Tree. The boy looked uneasily at his father, wary in case the seat should propel him into the air again.

The swing seat was, you could say, where Tree's first home schooling took place. As the seat creaked to and fro, Wood told Tree all about the fifty-four works of art he had painted between the ages of seven and fifteen. Wood repeatedly stressed the differences in composition, colors, and concept between the paintings. He encouraged Tree to look closely at them and to touch them. But before Wood had time to tell his son about his later paintings—those he called his "Rat Period" works—these activities were abruptly brought to an end.

This happy time in Wood's life lasted only until Tree could stand firmly on his two feet, jump down from the swing seat, and run away.

Hiding in the kitchen cupboard, Tree could see Wood searching for him through a crack in the door. Looking disappointed, Wood stood on the balcony, one hand on the swing seat, casting a dark shadow over the bright floor.

Now the swing seat was creaking again. Tree finished giving his father the injection and got to his feet. As he turned towards her, Flower had the feeling that the old days were coming back again.

° ° °

Today, Tree had on a yellow shirt and a mustard-colored tie. Even his trousers were canary yellow. Flower remembered Wood's words: "Yellow is a lucky color."

Tree had a date with Bean. He had met up with her several times since the operation.

To Bean, Tree's change of head was no different from any other irreversible life change, and she took it in stride. Admittedly, the sagging skin and plethora of liver spots on what had been Wood's old face got her down a bit, but she was by nature an open-minded girl and soon came to accept it as

Tree's face.

It was intriguing to find that a body one knew well was thinking in new ways, so it was quite natural that Bean and Tree should start a new way of dating, talking, and having physical contact. But in the process, Bean made a major discovery: Tree had a dull gaze now, was taciturn, and could sometimes be heard reciting lines of poetry to himself.

"It's summer. Should we die in the tree together...?" the hero on the cinema screen was saying, his eyes fixed on a cicada. Bean had eaten all the popcorn, and gave another yawn. It was just then that Tree proposed to her. Bean accepted a portrait of Wood as an engagement present.

With the portrait in her arms, she sat sleepily in the empty subway car, watching the metal hanging rings swaying from the ceiling. The long summer school holiday had just begun and Bean had lost her interest in travel, reading, and collecting glass bottles. Soon, she was tired of everything in her room as well, and was especially fed up with the unchanging shape of her bed. However, getting rid of everything and starting afresh was too much of a bother. Cultivating an interest in marriage might not be a bad idea, Bean thought. But before marriage, she thought of something else to do.

She took a sharp pair of scissors and cut out Tree's original head from the old photos of them together. Before that, she had taken a pile of pictures of Wood from Flower's house. Plenty of them had heads, and these she cut out and stuck in place of Tree's.

Sometimes Bean really missed the paper dolls she had played with as a child. She used to love to separate the bodies, clad only in underwear, from the heads, and then reassemble them, pasting them together with glue. Looking at Tree now often made her think of that game. The fun, both then and now, lay in the sense of unfamiliarity after she had made new combinations.

◦ ◦ ◦

As Tree learned to use his legs and took delight in showing off his walking and running, Wood began to dream that his son was leaving him, in various ways. At first, the dream was just that Tree sat in a boat or a balloon and floated off, with Wood in hot pursuit. Then he would dream that Tree had entered a crowd of people who suddenly became faceless, so that Wood had no way of picking him out. Finally, Wood dreamed he was holding a dish brimming with water. In it, he held Tree's upside-down reflection—that was all. Then, inevitably, the reflection would evaporate, drop by drop, in the deadly heat of the sun.

Wood did not ignore the symbolism of these dreams and began to make up all sorts of lies to tell Tree: "Flower pots and TV sets are being dropped from buildings all over the city." Or, "The number of street murders is going up every day." Or, "Every day, 8,723 people die violent deaths and ninety percent of them are children under seven." Wood produced piles of photographs of corpses as proof. At night, Wood would stand behind Tree and whisper in his ear, "You see that lamp post? And that mailbox? Well, behind all those sorts of things, there are ghosts." Tree shut his eyes tight and crouched on the floor, refusing to get up. Wood gently stroked his head. By now, Wood had even convinced himself that the world was full of perils.

Tree gradually began to imagine that he was seeing and hearing things. At night, he had nightmares, and by day he was even frightened by his own shadow. Then Wood thought of another idea: he would put lead in Tree's shoes. It made walking very hard work. Tree would pour with sweat and look beseechingly at his parents, until Wood gently picked him up and carried him, even though by now Tree was as heavy as a submarine.

◦ ◦ ◦

In 1974, Wood opened a bookshop in the most crime-ridden area of the city.

The bookshop was on the second floor of a shopping center and, like the other shops there, sold a great variety of pornography.

The shop had a color photocopier that Wood used every day to make copies of his own artwork. These he folded inside the erotic magazines. Practically all the customers chucked the photocopies away before they were even out of the shopping center, although some used them to put under wobbly table legs, or for jotting down the phone numbers of takeaways, or as bookmarks for the best pages in the magazines.

Wood's bookshop was the only store in the shopping center that never turned its lights on. A few dim rays of sunshine moved slowly across the bookshop floor during the day. Wood used to do his painting in a dark corner of the shop, which startled the customers coming hesitantly through the door. Now it was Tree they saw, but he looked pretty much the same, apart from the fact that he was much taller.

The walls, ceilings, and floors of this musty-smelling bookshop were covered in brightly colored pictures of deformed bodies. These meticulously drawn figures, Wood's masterpieces, included basketball players with limbs in place of torsos and torsos in place of limbs; and a body on which two heads had blossomed, sitting in a bathtub. One person's face appeared repeatedly with different bodies: Wood's—or Tree's—it was hard to tell them apart now.

Punctually at a quarter past one in the afternoon, Flower would arrive, carrying lunch. By now she was used to seeing her son there. At twenty-five, his face had more wrinkles than hers, but she realized she had forgotten what he used to look like.

"You must find it a comfort that Tree has taken over the family business," said Flower to the body of her husband lying silently at her side.

◦ ◦ ◦

Wood felt that in some unexpected way Tree was drawing further away from him.

One day, Wood put up the easel and, grabbing Tree's hand, showed him how to spread watercolor paints on the art paper. But Tree flung his father's hand away and disappeared in the direction of the soccer field.

Wood stood at the edge of the grassy field, and did not take another step forward. To Wood, that green grass should have been a picture made up of multiple shades of green; it amazed him that Tree could enter this world.

Once Tree was there, he gradually stopped believing what his father said. That was after he started school. The lead weights in his shoes were confiscated during a school uniform inspection, and he regularly played soccer with other children in the sunshine.

One day, Wood came to the school and peered through the wire mesh fence. Inside, he saw a crowd of children running around, chasing something white. As he tried to see what it was, he felt as if his own head was wobbling too, and had come loose from his neck.

Wood rattled the mesh and beckoned to the big man standing in the sun. He asked him to bring his son over, but the man shook his head. "I'm sorry. We're having a P.E. lesson."

Distressed, Wood crouched down outside and watched his son trapped inside. He was there for a very long time until he began to melt in the sun, getting smaller and smaller.

◦ ◦ ◦

Now, without his head, Wood's body seemed to grow thinner and weaker. He lay silent on the bed like a dark-colored tea tray.

Flower lay beside him, bored, eating melon seeds and flicking the husks onto Wood's sunken belly. She began to talk about the new cleaner that their neighbor, Mrs. Ma, had acquired. Mrs. Ma had a husband with no eyebrows who sold fake designer handbags in the city center.

"You can only tell the fakes from the genuine bags by the sound they make when you flick your finger against the leather.

Only experienced customers know how to do the test."

Flower glanced at Wood, happy that he could no longer frown and leave the room before she got going on her topic of conversation.

There was a big pile of melon husks on his belly and Flower, who by now had talked herself hoarse, brushed them off into the palm of her hand. Then, with her fingertips, she gently scraped up the russet-colored bits that had stuck in the folds of his flesh—Flower wanted Wood as clean as any other piece of family furniture. But, on this stifling afternoon, her movements stimulated Wood in a way she had not foreseen.

Before she could leave the room, she felt a skinny hand embracing her from behind and fingers sliding over her body until they stopped at her most secret place.

Flower was astonished that, although Wood had lost his head, he still had sexual urges—in fact, he was bolder in his movements than ever before. It was easy for her to push him to the floor, but he struggled to get up again. In the sunshine, his body looked innocent but stubborn, and something made Flower change her mind. She put her arms around Wood's body and gently lifted him onto the clean sheets...

On this clammy afternoon, Flower felt that Wood's body was reminding her how things used to be long ago. Back then, the curtains were dark green and she often dreamed that she had given birth to a willow tree. That was before Tree was born.

When Flower first got pregnant, Wood often made her undress, sit on a chair, and model nude for him. Flower thought he was in love with her naked, pregnant body and was happy to pose for him in all sorts of positions. But later she discovered she had been mistaken.

On Wood's art paper, Flower found, not herself, but a swollen belly with the shape of a fetus clearly visible inside it. Wood did sketches every week, each one showing the minute changes in the fetus. As Flower looked at the pictures, she could almost believe that Tree really was taking shape this way.

But gradually Flower lost interest in being a model. She would sit on the chair, relaying tidbits about their neighbors' affairs. She actually wondered if that was the real reason she had married Wood. She needed someone to listen to her rambling stories to affirm her own existence. Once she found that Wood could not stand it, she turned to the neighbors and actively cultivated relationships with them. The intimate details of her marriage became the currency with which she consolidated these friendships.

Wood allowed Flower to leave the chair, and he sat alone drawing the baby instead.

"The child's not born yet. Who are you drawing?" Flower could not help asking, as she nibbled on some pickled vegetables.

Wood smiled and pulled out a photograph of himself. "I'm using this. That kid's going to be the spitting image of me."

◦ ◦ ◦

People commented on how tall Tree was, quite unlike his father, especially as Wood grew skinnier with each passing day, until his cheek bones protruded and his complexion turned a sickly sallow color. The surprising thing was that Wood not only concurred, but even began to deny that Tree was his son. He could not produce any evidence for this; he just kept stubbornly insisting, "You're not my son, so don't go impersonating him."

As he spoke, he stared fixedly at one particular painting. The two figures in it both resembled Wood, and looked like twin brothers, though Wood swore it was a picture of himself and his son, Tree. He hung it over the bed and gazed at it all day long. Occasionally he would smile, or his eyes would glisten with tears.

"Stop looking at it," said Flower. "It won't get you another son!"

Wood felt a little embarrassed. But then he thought…could he have another son? Perhaps he could. His gaze skirted Flower, who was too old, and settled on Bean.

"Hello, Tree's Dad," Bean greeted him.

He had only begun to notice Bean after Tree had brought her home to meet his parents several times. One day, Wood brought out a big bowl of grapes for her and watched as she took the large round grapes off the stems, peeled each one, and put the fruit in her mouth. It seemed to Wood that each grape was a seed and he seemed to see Bean's belly begin to swell with what was going to turn into a baby boy.

"It'll be the image of me," smiled Wood, unconsciously sucking his forefinger.

Bean left, and Wood, elated, asked Tree innocently, "When's the baby due?"

"What baby?" said Tree. "I've never wanted babies, not even one."

° ° °

A week before the wedding, Tree gave Bean a big box of porn magazines. Then he took her to all sorts of porn films. In the morning, they would go to the adult cinema and then eat lunch at the restaurant opposite. As they silently made their way from one side of the street to the other, their days seemed to acquire a physical rhythm—watch a film, eat, watch another film...

Apart from the details of the plot (and you could take them or leave them) and the clothes of the actors, which scarcely varied, Bean felt that what she saw on the screen was no more than a series of sounds and movements repeated over and over. Tree's expression as he watched was earnest and stern, but Bean kept yawning before nodding off into a deep sleep.

"I thought it might get you interested in sex," said Tree disconsolately when Bean finally woke up.

"Why are you trying to force me to be interested?" asked Bean, rubbing her eyes.

"Because I have to do it with my wife to have a son, and soon you're going to be my wife."

Bean was a bit surprised by how goal-oriented Tree was about all this stuff. She had been doing it for a long time but had never imagined it meant anything or would lead to anything. If she thought about pregnancy at all, it seemed to her something that needed no planning, something that made the body undergo a series of changes according to a specific rhythm. She suddenly had a sense of calm resignation at the thought of it.

The day before the wedding, Bean and Tree were in a good mood and had sex.

Bean told Tree afterwards that his movements had been

simple and to the point; he had avoided introducing any extraneous details. Tree thanked her for the compliment and asked if she would like to pose for him. Bean shrugged, and lay back on the bed. She realized, in disappointment, that the shape of Tree's bed was as boring as the one in her own room.

In her state of extreme boredom, she became aware of a creaking sound coming from the veranda. It was the swing seat, which held Flower and a headless body, sending them soaring time after time into a cloudless blue sky.

◦ ◦ ◦

Apparently, the evening before Tree lost his head, Wood and Tree had been seen in the riverside park. The onlookers were reminded of Tree's early years with his father, and they could not help imagining the scene as one brimming with tenderness.

"It's late. What are we doing here?"

Wood took a saw out of his backpack. "City folk have lost the spirit of adventure. I suggest we play a brand new game."

Tree was always ready to try out new and stimulating forms of entertainment, and immediately perked up. "Sounds like a great plan! What are we playing?"

"Let's take turns cutting our heads off, and play hide-and-seek with them. See who can find one quickest."

Tree took his watch off and tossed it to his father. "I'll go first. You watch the time, and no cheating!"

Wood, who was quite tired, nodded vigorously.

Tree sawed his own head off with no trouble at all. After all, he was young. As his son's head hit the ground with a thud,

Wood grabbed it and took off at top speed.

"Wood ran and ran that evening, and when he woke up the next morning, his arms and legs felt like jelly," went the gossip. But the people who heard this story did not believe it.

◦ ◦ ◦

When Bean and Flower both became pregnant, the family decided to move house.

Early in the morning, Tree and the movers together heaved the last cardboard box into the moving van. Tree had taken off his shirt and you could see his sturdy, muscular body. What no one noticed was that the head donated by Wood had undergone distinct changes. The wrinkles and liver spots of old had faded, and were replaced by supple, glowing flesh, as if some particularly creative grafting technique had been employed. In the sunshine, Tree's slightly flushed face—or was it Wood's?—seemed to glow with health.

Flower's and Bean's freshly swelling bellies also seemed to be thriving. Flower had been waiting in the truck for some time. She had no particular attachment to the community in which she had been living, but had few expectations for the future either. Her life would be reestablished in exactly the same way as before, she thought.

Bean was dozing, her head resting in Flower's lap. She had no interest in the move. Her only wish was to get a new, round bed, the kind you saw in the bedrooms of love hotels.

The movers carelessly loaded Wood into the back of the truck with other odds and ends, having assumed he was a unique piece of upholstered furniture. What did seem odd to passersby behind the truck, however, was the sight of a headless body jolting along, scratching itself with long, slender fingers.

◦ ◦ ◦

Wood had been born on August 14, 1952, at 3:40 p.m. People did not begin to say he was autistic right away; that was only much later, when he started crouching on the balcony, yelling at anyone whose shadow fell across his paintings to clear off.

No one knew why, all of a sudden, Wood got this frenzied desire for a son. But they did see him trying out sex with different women, showing the same fervor he had devoted to his painting. His actions had unexpected consequences. In the school's empty music room, he was slapped and bitten by a brawny schoolgirl. Then he was beaten up by the husband of another woman on the way to school. But he was not deterred. He pursued his plan and, realizing that getting married and moving into his own apartment was the surest way to achieve sex in this city, he dedicated all his efforts in that direction.

Later, as his son gradually took shape in Flower's belly, he would cautiously press his ear against it and, with Flower's encouragement, touch it gently with his fingers. This was the first time he had experienced the truth through sound and touch, and it was even more real than seeing himself in the mirror.

BLESSED BODIES

Y-land had no marriage system but was famous for its prosperous sex industry. Even bartering was allowed: when the male clients could not afford to pay, they could obtain sexual services by trading their body parts. At the moment of sexual arousal, a man would stand in the doorway, peeping into a dim room where a woman reclined on the bed. Once she adopted the desired position, he no longer cared about his arms or legs. But with the ebbing of arousal, the man would open his eyes to see what had once been his limb—first amputated, then frozen, bottled, and removed. Only then would he be astonished at the impulsive decision he had made.

Amputees could be seen all over Y-land, hobbling heroically along the city streets. The limbs that had once belonged to them were stored in special depots. There, glass bottles of all sizes were arrayed on rusty iron shelves in packed rows. The refracted light made the limbs, floating in preserving fluid, appear grossly deformed. Soon they would be loaded onto ships and sold to the developed countries that bordered Y-land.

At times of peak arousal, the impoverished men of Y-land milled around in the streets, gazing up at the dead leaves that floated from the trees or down at their own big feet. In the sunshine, they were accompanied by anxious shadows that crept along behind them, looming over the bodies to which they were attached.

◦ ◦ ◦

In October, the girl and her brother arrived in Y-land by boat. The streets were full of people selling creamlettes. They ladled golden batter onto sizzling hot-plates, where it spread out and set in perfect disks that seemed to hint at a blessed life.

"You'll lose your body here," said her brother as he bought her a creamlette.

The cream oozed out, over the thin greaseproof paper and onto her brother's hand—like happiness brimming over. But the fragrant smell of the creamlette just made her want to vomit.

A doctor, sitting across the rectangular white table from them, reassured her, "Being sick has nothing to do with pregnancy. You're only feeling seasick because you've imagined your room as a boat."

They took the girl and her brother up to the top floor of an old building. It was just as she had imagined it, so dark green it seemed to have moldered to the point of disintegrating.

In this gloomy apartment there were two rooms, each with gray walls and an over-sized bed. It took the girl some time to locate the tiny window, high up on the wall and pasted shut with newspaper that had yellowed with age. She stood on tiptoe on the bed, pushed the window open, and saw the mist from the street rippling towards her.

The girl really did believe from the start that this building was a boat. The first time she stepped on the floor, it felt insubstantial. The sound of waves reached her from outside the window, and the floor seeped water, so that the girl, alone with the few sticks of furniture, became frantic at the thought of going moldy.

In the middle of the night, the girl always felt terrified that the boat was spinning on the crest of a wave. The floor seemed to be bucking and rearing, and she would stagger into the other room, crawl into her brother's bed, and sleep with him. When she woke up the next morning, she would rush to the window and look out, to reassure herself that she had not been carried off to another unknown place.

The girl liked the narrow street outside the building. Sometimes, the street was enlivened by men passing by, brandishing knives or glass jars, especially when their rich red blood dyed the asphalt and the trash heaped on it. Her eye was often caught by a bloodstained plastic bag fluttering in the breeze.

It did not take her brother long to discover that she had brought in sacks filled with stones. These she placed individually in each corner. But nothing stopped her feeling queasy, and she was forced to take the seasick pills the doctor had prescribed.

In November, the girl placed her feet side by side, joining her big toes together. It was cold, as cold as the yellow glass on the opposite side of the street. Behind the glass, she could see the face of a young man, tilted slightly upwards. The young man's gaze was climbing right into her window. The face appeared so often that she came to regard it as part of the street scene.

◦ ◦ ◦

Her brother was surprised when she said she wanted to go outside and put up leaflets to sell herself.

She had head lice. He made her sit on a stool and he carefully separated the strands of her hair, combing out the gray-black eggs with a fine-toothed comb so that they plopped onto a metal tray. He had to crack the really stubborn ones between his fingernails before he could pull them out.

"They said you could wait six months," said her brother, dousing her head with kerosene and wrapping it in a towel. There was a powerful stink in the air.

The girl paid no attention. She just smiled. Her face was covered in dimples, so that when she smiled, it always looked as if she was crying.

The girl told them she wanted a huge mirror so that she could see her whole body. It should be smooth and shimmering and reflect her in the minutest detail. When she washed her hair, she would sit in front of the mirror and coil it up. Then she would strip naked and look at her budding figure. She was so skinny that her bone structure was clearly visible under the skin. Under her right breast, there was one abnormally sunken rib.

"What do you think?"

Her brother was standing by her bed, looking out the window at the scenery. "Too pale, too thin."

"How about these?" asked the girl, indicating the slight protuberances of her breasts.

"Them too."

But the girl realized her brother was not looking at her properly so, paying no attention to what he thought, she dressed again, grabbed a sheaf of leaflets, and ran downstairs. All down the stairwell, the walls were completely covered with black leaflets, and there were more in the noodle shop at the bottom of the stairs. The people slurping their noodles and looking through the window, at a world made dark by the leaflets, thought it was the end of the world. No matter, the sorrow they felt sharpened their appetites and the hot noodles made them a little tipsy. The steam from their bowls obscured their coarse features and, in their excitement, men and women began to play footsie under the tables.

The young man came over to the girl. He was dressed in a baggy black sweater, and his hair was cropped short. The girl had not realized until then just how pallid he was, almost like someone in a black-and-white photograph. He tore down one of her leaflets, and a single patch of red appeared on each pale cheek. It was, thought the girl, as rich a color as the bloodied plastic bags that she had seen in the street.

◦ ◦ ◦

The mother, seeing her one-armed son standing in the doorway, was not surprised. It was as she had foreseen. The night sky was not very dark. There was a row of four streetlamps, but only one of them emitted a flickering light, and her son stood under it in his black sweater. His empty left sleeve dangled limply, showing that now he was a man. He had grown tall and slender, and looked as desolate as an empty road.

His amputation did not worry his mother. All the men in Y-land learned to do everything one-handed from boyhood, even buttoning their coats with both feet, as well as all sorts of other minor tasks. What did worry her was the way he lay in bed biting his fingernails and smiling a little smile. He just looked too blessed. It seemed that he didn't regret the loss of an arm at all.

Silently, in a funereal mood, his mother got his dinner ready. Her son carried on lying on the bed: his head to one side, his eyes shut, day after day, in the same position. His mother was mostly puzzled by this, although sometimes the scene filled her with an almost religious fervor.

Hordes of ants began to gather at his bedside, as if on a pilgrimage. His mother took a broom and, as she swept, heaps of Coca-Cola cans clattered out from under the bed. She remembered how, years before, he used to lie in bed, obsessed by books on witchcraft. He ate nothing as he read; he just drank Coke. He kept this up for four years. After his mother washed the old Coke cans, she covered the walls of the house with them, and used them to erect a fence outside the house too. The dazzling red of the cans filled her with a near certainty that he would risk his life for his obsession.

Once when she was sure that her son was asleep, she located the ten cans in the Coke wall that she had marked and stuffed with twenty-dollar bills, and skillfully extracted them. After she checked to make sure that none of the money was missing, she hesitated for a very long time, thinking about whether to use the money to fulfill her son's desires, but finally decided against it. Before putting the cans back in place, she took a roll of bills from one of them and put it under the seventh floorboard from the door, the one right next to the wall.

The money would be enough to give her son a decent funeral, she thought to herself.

° ° °

The young man was dreaming of a vast ocean.

At first it was not an ocean, but a huge bed. The naked girl was at one end of the bed, sitting cross-legged. Above her knees, he could see a pair of flat breasts that looked like oversized eyes. But the eyes were not looking at him. They gazed at a boat far, far in the distance.

The girl told him that before he came along, she often felt she was being bowled over and over in the sea, all alone, being blown by the wind to a place she did not recognize. So every time she got out of bed, she thought she had landed on a strange, new shore.

"After you came along, I felt that we were trying madly to reach the shore together, but just as we were almost there, you would turn and leave me."

The girl's words hurt the young man. He began to weep, his tears salty like seawater. His sorrow turned blue and shrouded the whole dream. This persuaded him that the ocean was huge.

When the young man woke up, he told his dream to a man in a black jacket who happened to be passing by outside the front door. "This must be what they call love, mustn't it?" the man responded in a low voice.

He did not know the man, but he ended up inviting him into the house. As a result, the man became his mother's client, and so lost an eye.

◦ ◦ ◦

The girl had few visitors, and those that did come hardly ever came back for another visit. The girl had nothing to do. She stood on the bed with her brother, looking out the tiny window into the narrow alley outside. Occasionally there were passersby, and the girl made her brother guess whether they would come upstairs.

By now the weather was getting warmer; people were wearing clothes that were too tight and made them puff and pant. Two men stood down below, looking up at the girl's window. They stood there a long time.

"They won't come," her brother said, as he always did.

The girl was indignant. She stuck her head out of the window and waved energetically, but the men below lowered their heads and hurried away.

Her brother could not help smiling.

He had not told the girl how he detested her shutting the apartment door and making him wait outside. When that happened, he fidgeted anxiously, then got out his pen and wrote random hieroglyphics all over the gray wall. On and on he wrote, until his hand and arm ached.

When the visitor finally left, the girl liked to go up to the wall, connect the hieroglyphics, and make them into a song. She would sing out hoarsely: *hua-hua-you-dad-tu-tu...la-la... sha-bu-dong-me-he-ya...*

She made the tune sound quite festive, and could keep it up until evening. Her brother particularly disliked having visitors in the evening because, if no one came, the girl would put her arms around his neck, bury her head in his armpit, and fall fast asleep. When she woke up again, she would tell him all the dreams she'd had.

Just at that moment, someone else came into view down in the street. It was the young man, now one-eyed, walking with the aid of a stick, tapping his way along with a cheerful rhythm.

Of all the visitors, her brother disliked the young man most, because when he and the girl shut the door on him it always felt like a century before they opened it up again.

Y-land folk all knew that the young man had already lost an arm and a leg and an eye for the girl. "You should hang onto your hand," the girl told him, "to stroke my face, my thigh, and my ribs... What else can you give them?"

"It's my liver this time," said the young man, with a slight smile, his pale face flushing once more.

The girl was reassured and smiled. Everyone said that when the girl smiled, it always looked as if she was crying.

◦ ◦ ◦

The girl dreamed she was sitting in a boat, sailing to a small island. But it was too dark on the island, and the girl could not be sure that was what it was.

Then she saw a light, perhaps from a streetlamp in the center of the island. She felt her way towards the source of the light, only to find that it was not a streetlamp but the young man standing there. By now he had lost both arms, and was left with just one leg to hold his body upright. It was his right eye that was emitting the light. She had not realized it was so bright. It was a pity that the eye was so high up; she could not reach it, even on tiptoe. Otherwise, she could have dug it out and patrolled the island, holding it in her cupped hands. The young man's remaining leg had sunk deep in the ground by now and the girl sat down, leaning against his leg, until the light disappeared.

When she woke up, she told the dream to her brother. He

said nothing, just gently wiped the sweat from her body. His hand slid from her flat chest, down over the sunken rib. Then it stopped, and he kissed her.

° ° °

A light spread out in all directions, and it was possible to make out things that were represented by a variety of colors. The pink seemed to be dust, the green was mold, the violet was a puff of hypnotic powder, and the yellow was aged light. Finally, everything faded from view.

Such was the scene the young man saw before he lost his second eye. When everything had gone pitch-black, and the blackness had no trace of color left in it, he discovered he was in terrible pain. He begged to be taken home. After all, he was an old customer.

They told him they were putting him into a wooden cart, but it felt to him like he was being tossed head over heels like a fish in a huge frying pan, until every one of his still-unhealed wounds burst open. He could not tell whether what he was feeling was scorching heat or pain.

They laughed at him. "That's because Y-land's roads are full of potholes," they said, "and have wrecked cars, dead fish, and bottles of lubricating oil piled up on them."

As they went along, they took turns describing the scenery to the young man so he could tell them the way. There was an abortion clinic on the corner, they said, the one run by the woman doctor, Dr. Tang, with the gleaming white skin and great fat fingers. There was a stall selling placenta next door to the clinic, but most of the placenta was fake, just something made from gelatin. He said he did not remember the clinic or the shop. He probably had not come this way before.

"Then you can't have been inside Y-land's first cinema, right? They show all sorts of porn films there."

This made them all feel sorry for the newly blind young man. By this time, they had given up asking him how to get back to his home, and were just taking him wherever they felt like, singing at the top of their voices: *hua-hua-you-dad-tu-tu...la-la...sha-bu-dong-me-he-ya...*

Meanwhile, the young man's mother had gotten his dinner ready and had been sitting waiting for him for a long time. Her eyelids felt so heavy, and even though she heard the distant sound of singing, her head dropped on the table and she fell fast asleep.

The young man did not know what time it was—probably morning, to judge by the slight warmth of the sun that fell on his face. Now he had a new way to experience the sun.

"It's so dark," he said.

◦ ◦ ◦

The girl did not know if the young man ever visited again, because soon afterwards, she left Y-land.

On her brother's bed, she discovered a wad of cash. "They want you to get rid of the child," said her brother.

But his mouth was full of toothpaste and the girl could not understand what he was saying.

When he finished brushing his teeth and went back into the

room to find her, the girl was gone, wandering aimlessly and alone through the dawn streets. On the pavement, there was a one-eyed old man making stuffed creamlettes with golden-yellow cream, too much of it. The girl bought one. It was the first time she had tasted one of these golden creamlettes. Its sweetness startled her, as did the fact that she liked it very much.

The street cleaner was washing down the pavement with detergent. The girl sat on a bench, nibbling carefully at the creamlette until it was all gone. By the time she had finished, bubbles were rising up from the street into the air, sailing towards some nearby railings in the morning sunlight, and then bursting, perhaps because the sun was too bright. Beyond the railings, countless silent boats were moored.

The girl finally bought herself a boat ticket to an unknown destination. When she stepped on deck, it felt curiously stable. She would not have known they were moving but for the ship's horn. After she got pregnant, she did not vomit anymore. Her body felt heavier and heavier, and even standing on deck she did not feel like she was floating.

It was night and the boat passengers had gone to sleep. The girl discovered the cabin was full of doors, all with bolts. She tried to open them and realized they were not real bolts at all. There was nothing behind most of the doors, just an enormous hold which seemed bigger even than the entire boat. Behind one, however, was a room filled with bottles of yellow liquid. Each bottle was marked with a time and date. The largest bottles were filled with very long legs; the smallest held eyeballs. The girl crouched down and found a bottle labeled "2002-7-28 19:30," with a small, bright eyeball in it. She picked it up and put it in her pocket. Once, she remembered, this eye had been firmly embedded in the young man's face.

She realized that there was one woman on the boat who was not asleep. The woman's son had died a week before. The woman had sold as many of her son's body parts as she could, so she did not have to pay a cent for the funeral. The mother, old and faded-looking, had decided to leave Y-land after it was over. Before she left, she strung together some of the Coke cans she had stored in her son's room and attached them to her only long skirt. Now she was on the boat, and the clanking of the cans, with their glittering red color, was her way of grieving for her son.

A STREET IN THE WIND

A dark red insect with a long, pointy body covered in fine hairs thudded against the windowpane in a frenzy. The shutter was open and the insect fluttered up and down both sides of the glass. It was hard to tell if it was really trying to break into—then break out of—the room, or was simply possessed by madness.

Mr. Lam, his tie still knotted around his neck, looked blankly out the window, then found his attention drawn back to the flickering TV screen. Every day when he got home from work, it was his habit to fling himself down on the sofa and watch the dramas on TV. This was the seventh episode of a cop series in which, on one particular street, several people had been mysteriously murdered. The police had not figured out who the killer was. Engrossed in the intricacies of the case, Mr. Lam did not notice that his pile of beloved car magazines had been diminishing, day by day, until now there were none left. In their place was a dust-free rectangle, which revealed the original color of the bookshelf.

From the bathroom came the sound of pop music. Lam Yan was standing in front of the mirror using the red hair-dryer. She had treated herself to a fashionable perm now that her university entrance exams were over. Emerging from the hair salon, she felt as if her girlhood years had been clipped off, bit by bit, and left behind on the shiny tiled floor of the salon. Outside, men's glittering eyes homed in on her from all sides. Bathed in the light of their gazes, she felt she was growing up fast. Lam Yan hummed a pop song, and her curls danced on her head as lively as freshly hatched bugs in the summer sunshine.

On this summer evening, Lam Tun could tell that no one

at home was bothered about him. As his exams drew near, he had become obsessed with origami. It was, he felt, the most fun thing he had ever done. He hid away in his room all day, on the pretext that he was studying, cutting up page after colored page of his father's car magazines, and folding them into all sorts of strange animals. He had just finished one and held it up in his cupped hands to inspect it. A ray of evening sunlight fell on it and this made him decide that it was a headless blue rabbit. He put it, and the other origami creatures that sat on the table, into a cardboard box.

He had asked Ah Fan in the stationery shop downstairs for the cardboard box. When he had used up all the magazines at home, he begged her for a stack of colored paper, too.

"I'll swap it for that," Ah Fan said, looking at the Twins CD in Lam Tun's hand.

Lam Tun shrugged. It was his elder sister's CD, not his.

For the last few days, the weather had been very muggy. Lam Tun got up onto the desk and pushed the window open a bit more. He poked his head out but there was no cooling breeze. The stuffy heat seemed to turn people's brains to sludge. In the street, people strode past, their heads bobbing, imbecilic expressions on their faces. Dirty water had collected in a pothole in the road, refusing to go down the drain even though it was only a short distance away.

Lam Tun watched Ah Fan sitting behind the counter of the stationery shop across the street, the CD player he had lent her in her hand, apparently intoxicated by the music. When Ah Fan put the earphones in, it gave her a strange, new feeling: her chunky body seemed to float skyward, like a pink balloon held in a girl's hand. Ah Fan looked up at Lam Tun, and had the sudden impression that the hand holding the balloon string had slackened its grip, and she was floating away. Up, up into the twilight sky, with its fluffy dull red clouds.

"What are you doing in there?" His sister's voice made Lam Tun jump.

"What's up?" he said.

"Dinnertime. Come on down."

Lam Tun jumped off the desk and kicked the cardboard box under the bunk bed.

"Fish again." Lam Tun glanced at the stir-fried cabbage and steamed mandarin fish and grimaced. But then he saw his sister's face fall and said nothing more.

With his chopsticks, he pulled some fish off the bones and was about to put a morsel in his mouth when, unaccountably, Mr. Lam shouted, "DO—NOT—EAT—THAT—FISH!" He must have come into the room unnoticed. Then he picked up a bowl of rice, helped himself to some of the cabbage and, holding his bowl in both hands, sat back down on the sofa.

The TV ads had just finished and Detective Lau Yung's handsome face reappeared on the screen.

The detective was inspecting a murder scene. It was an ordinary apartment on a housing estate. Two corpses lay in the sitting room: one was a girl of about seventeen or eighteen, and the other a boy of primary school age. Their faces were blue from cyanosis and their eyes stared. The girl's hair was spread out on the floor, some strands lying, insect-like, over the boy's face. The boy's lips seemed to move, perhaps because the hairs tickled.

Seated in front of the TV, Mr. Lam could not control his agitation. It looked to him like his own son and daughter lying there.

The preliminary diagnosis for cause of death was poisoning, and the time about eight o'clock the previous evening. Suddenly the police pathologist, who was crouching on the floor, got to his feet. As he did so, he blocked out the sunlight coming in through the window.

"Why isn't their father there?" In the dim room, the detective's face looked unutterably gloomy.

"Because he didn't eat the fish," Mr. Lam muttered.

"The fishmonger poisoned the fish. Everyone on the street who died had eaten it."

Mr. Lam had had his eye on the fishmonger since the previous evening. He had caught sight of him through the window: the old man was sitting at the window of an apartment in the opposite block, half of him hidden behind the white curtains, turned violet in the twilight. He was staring out.

The preview for the next episode had finished. Mr. Lam rushed over to the window—and there was the fishmonger again. Looking through his binoculars, Mr. Lam saw that he was sitting in a rattan armchair. His sagging flesh made it hard to discern the expression on his face. The eyes embedded in it were milky and unfocused, making him look even more treacherous and inscrutable.

In fact, there was only a hazy light in the fishmonger's eyes. Leaning back in his chair on this summer evening, he was just waiting for time to pass. He had lived many years on this street. Since the death of his wife, it seemed as if the only things left which gave him a sense of security were the potholed asphalt road, the iron railings—by now twisted completely out of shape—and the streetlamps that were erected every dozen or so paces along the sidewalk.

But this familiar street became quite unreal at night. A silver electric bike flashed by when he was not expecting it, or there was a sudden shrill sound, and the fishmonger felt that he was rapidly losing his grip on reality. He felt overwhelmed by monstrous apparitions. He began to wonder if he was still capable of separating real life from the fantasies that threatened to swallow his whole world. For instance, looking to the left of the balcony where there was an old gray wall, he sometimes saw a strange shadow like that of a body falling headlong—one arm outstretched, its thin fingers splayed, as if grasping at something. Was Death giving him a heavy hint? wondered the fishmonger. He thought of his late wife, who used to take a low stool to the corner and sit there with her nose in a novel. Before she died, she would raise her sallow, wizened face, and say through cracked, dried lips, "I see the shadow of Death coming closer every day."

Mr. Lam put down the binoculars. He had no way of guessing what was going through the fishmonger's mind. When he turned back to the room, he saw that Lam Yan and Lam Tun had disappeared off somewhere, leaving the remnants of dinner on the table. Some nameless early summer insects whined and hurled themselves at the lampshade and the table surface.

Recently, Lam Yan would gulp down her dinner, instruct her brother to clear away the bowls and chopsticks, and then leave the house with a preoccupied air. But Lam Tun did not clear the table right away tonight. He snuck off to their bedroom, as if he had suddenly remembered something, and took some comics, *Girl Stories*, from his sister's drawer. He was going to swap them with Ah Fan for more colored paper.

◦ ◦ ◦

Everyone on the street felt Ah Fan was somehow different from the rest of them. She sat behind the counter, resting her round chin on her hand, one plump white finger twisting strands of her jet-black hair. A woman customer, walking out of the shop with too much change in her hand, would think to herself, she's over forty, but she behaves like a sixteen-year-old.

Ah Fan closed her copy of *Girl Stories #6*, and laid it on the counter. She had an odd feeling, one she could not put a name to, as if she had tipped over a bowl of wheat porridge, spilling its sweet mushiness on the table. The feeling impelled her to amble out into the road.

Ah Fan normally sat in the shop from morning till night, and she realized she had never paid any attention to the gray-blue pavement. The horseshoe-shaped bricks were arranged in a herringbone pattern and seemed to continue almost as far as the mountains, hazy in the distance. Above her, there was a tangle of electric cables. A pigeon suddenly flew up and away.

In summer it was common for insects to whiz past the ear, emitting a disorienting whine. Ah Fan turned and saw a silver beetle land on the dark-gray lamppost. The post was as tall as a tree and stretched up into the sky, blossoming into a white cloud. Ah Fan felt a warm breeze lift her floral-patterned dress, making it ripple, she felt, like the water on a pond.

Ah Fan and Lam Yan brushed past each other, both of them looking to the side of the street, so that neither realized they were both wearing the same floral-patterned dress.

Lam Yan went into the fishmonger's. The pungent smell rushed up her nostrils. The old man put his black-gloved hand into the tank where the fish blew listless bubbles. Unable to get away, they made futile, terrified splashes. He neatly caught one and slapped it down on the counter. Lam Yan watched as, with practiced ease, he scraped off the gorgeous fins and scales, slit it open and removed the yellowish-gray entrails, then chucked the fish, like a piece of garbage, into a black plastic bag. Lam Yan covered her nose with her hand and took the bag from him. She remembered what her father had said several times over the last few days, "There's nothing people won't do when they handle knives every day at work."

Lam Yan could not be bothered to find out what he had meant by that. She just sniffed in disgust at the fishy smell on her hands.

From the rooftop, Lam Tun saw Lam Yan approaching. He jumped down from a gas pipe, and launched a three-winged origami bird in graceful, curving flight through the gray sky and into the cardboard box full of his origami. With some reluctance, Lam Tun taped the box up and threw it into the shed.

Someone—he did not know whom—had erected this shed from three sheets of corrugated iron, leaving the fourth side open to the elements. The iron was heavily rusted and covered in crude graffiti. When Lam Tun looked up, he could see that the shed roof was punctured all over with small holes. The afternoon sunshine projected fantastically fragmented shafts of light through the holes and onto squashed fizzy drink cans, used condoms—and a brand new porn mag. Lam Tun picked it up and leafed through it. All the pages were in color and instantly Lam Tun thought of scores of new origami techniques. He slapped his neck where a mosquito had just bitten him, and could not help laughing.

When Lam Yan got back, she was in time to see her brother slipping into the bedroom. She suddenly remembered that his final exams were approaching. In the past, she used to flip through his homework and nag him about school, but recently she had begun to ignore him. She dumped the food she had bought onto the dining table and then slipped away to her father's room.

It was after he finished dinner that Mr. Lam discovered someone had been rummaging through his wardrobe. He stood in front of its open door and looked at the mess, but it seemed to him to have no connection with the real world. His head was full of the TV program he had just been watching.

A dark shadow filled the room. The children's father had arrived at the crime scene. Their corpses, and much else that would serve as evidence, had been taken away; the space was transformed, and this solitary, puny figure looked quite out of place.

The father went into his room and opened his wardrobe. A long, thin shadow was the only thing that inhabited the empty space. Mr. Lam remembered that the police had taken nothing from the wardrobe as evidence, so someone must have broken in and stolen things.

What was missing? Standing in front of the wardrobe, Mr. Lam could not think of anything. He seemed to smell a faint fishy odor, however, and the fishmonger's inscrutable expression floated into his mind. He was sure that the father of the two dead children had also detected a fishy smell.

The camera lens followed the father's gaze and moved around the living room. A number of magazines and books had disappeared from the bookshelves, leaving dust-free shapes behind on the brightly colored surfaces.

Mr. Lam looked at the empty spaces on the bookshelves in his sitting room and had the feeling that something was missing, though he could not for the life of him think what. There was nothing on the table except the dinner leftovers, and his son and daughter were nowhere to be seen. He looked out the window, where the nighttime streets were hushed and quiet. He suddenly felt as lonely as one of those tall, thin lampposts.

After dinner, Lam Yan had gone out, just as she had done for the past few evenings. Lam Tun watched her retreating figure and thought longingly of his cardboard box. He shot a quick glance at the half-open door of his father's room, then snuck out on the heels of his sister.

The sky was a murky gray color mixed with dark red. Lam Tun walked along the gas pipe that snaked over the flat roof and went into the shed. He bent down to his right and saw that the cardboard box was still sitting where he had put it.

The summer night was drearily quiet, with only a few dragonflies skimming the ground. Lam Tun walked around the edge of the roof terrace. Below him, on a neighboring building, he could see a girl with fluffed-up hair leaning over the railings.

Half her body was leaning out and she held a fishing rod, as if she was fishing for something in the air. Then he realized that this crazy-looking girl was his sister.

◦ ◦ ◦

Ah Fan hung a clumsily made rag doll in front of the shop. It flopped over to one side, probably because its head was too heavy. A careful observer would have seen that there was a note attached to one foot, with the scribbled words:

Send rain.

The night before, Ah Fan had cut up a silk vest. As she hastily tacked the pieces of material together, she thought of the magazine, *Your Life in the Stars*, that Lam Tun had given her. Under Pisces was written:

On the day it rains, you will find true love.

Ah Fan looked up at the red-tinged, gray sky. It looked to her as warm as the hot water bottle she used to cuddle when she was a little girl. You just had to pull out the stopper, and the water would gurgle and gush out of it.

What did such a gloomy sky mean to old folk, who were approaching the end of life? The fishmonger looked up and felt an involuntary shiver of foreboding. He remembered the shadow he had seen the night before, dangling a fishing rod in the air. In fear, he smelled for the first time the fishy stink that impregnated his hands. Perhaps this was an appropriate hint from Death to an old fishmonger.

After he had sold the fish to Lam Yam that day, he seemed to lack the strength to pick up the knife again. The fish he had netted and put in the bucket, he now tipped back into the tank. As he watched the little shoal, suddenly lively again, he felt older and older. He rinsed out the fish bucket and sloshed the dirty water outside where it spattered the ground and made little puddles in the potholes. A host of brown, freshly hatched insects immediately gathered over them.

Mr. Lam, in his leather shoes, skirted the puddles. He was on his way home from work, and it seemed to him that the fishmonger had pulled down his rusty old shop shutters early today. There was a note stuck there, fluttering in the wind. The writing was a scrawl and hardly legible. From a distance, it looked like a death notice.

Mr. Lam's heart skipped a beat. Maybe something was about to happen.

Maybe it already had happened.

On the TV screen, the father had arrived at a corner store. In the background, there was an untidy jumble of plastic dishes, toilet brushes, and rice baskets. The sales assistant, a plump woman, sat behind the counter. The father asked her for a knife.

"What kind of knife would you like?"

"Any kind. But it must be sharp enough to kill someone."

The woman gave a girlish laugh. She was forty-something but behaved like a sixteen-year-old.

Carrying the knife, wrapped in newspaper, the father made his way back over the gray-blue paving stones. The horseshoe-shaped bricks were arranged in repeating rows that stretched away into the distance. In the darkness, a tangle of electric cables hung down, and a startled pigeon suddenly flew up and away.

There followed an advertisement for Hua Hua shower gel.

Mr. Lam hurried into the kitchen. The fish soup in the ceramic pot boiled furiously. Bubbles hissed and popped from under the lid and moisture dripped down the side of the pot onto the stovetop. Mr. Lam took down the biggest Japanese steel knife hanging on the wall and quietly stashed it away under his bed.

By the time Lam Yan turned off the stove, most of the soup had boiled over. She gave the stovetop a quick wipe and went into the bathroom.

She peered at herself in the mirror, then stepped back. Her black dress with its pattern of red fan-shaped petals was stretched over her plump curves. She gave herself an appreciative look and reached behind to pull up the zipper. She remembered the blue-eye-shadowed sales assistant in the fashion boutique saying, with shrill emphasis, "Only one left. You'll never get another one like it... Ever... Anywhere."

But Lam Yan had seen the exact same floral-patterned dress fluttering from the roof terrace of the apartment block opposite at night. So every time she put it on, she felt the shadow of that other dress floating behind her in the gloom. She must tear that shadow to shreds or she would never rest easy.

She finished her shower and knocked at the bedroom door. To her surprise, it was unlocked and, even though it was not dinnertime yet, Lam Tun was fast asleep on the bed. She was even more surprised when she saw, lying on the table, a pair of scissors and a shredded porn mag.

She may have been his elder sister but she did not know that the awful truth had finally dawned on him—his exams were tomorrow. He had concluded, with distress, that his origami work on the table was just a heap of rubbish. Then he leafed through a few pages of his textbook, before he finally decided to take refuge in sleep. Things must be better when he woke up again.

◦ ◦ ◦

During the night, the heavens opened and the clouds burst like a piñata. The capricious wind strummed the driving lines of rain like a mad guitar player. It howled overhead. The fishmonger closed his shutters, but an icy draft still slipped through the cracks. The trees in the street bent under the force of the wind, then sprang back, silhouetted against the sky like some demonic forest. The fishmonger looked again at that shadow and trembled.

From the rooftop, Lam Yan leaned out and looked up at the sky. The raindrops splattered into her eyes. She blinked and looked again. Above her head a cluster of lights shook violently. She was soaked. She looked anxiously at her fishing line, which touched the flowery dress once more, then blew away.

The fishmonger watched the fishing line being blown about. The whole street seemed to be shaking in the storm. He felt a surge of anxiety. In a cold sweat, he recalled his wife's face, and something seemed to block his chest, making him gasp.

Mr. Lam did not know he was dreaming—that was why it was so quiet.

He sat in front of a glinting blue mirror, but a middle-aged stranger looked back at him. The man's profile seemed blurred.

"So it's you," Mr. Lam said to the mirror. "Why are you hiding? The police might think you're the killer."

"I'm going to kill that fishmonger," replied the man in the mirror.

"It was always going to be him, wasn't it? I've been watching him for a while too."

"That's why I've come looking for you. Haven't you got a knife hidden under the bed? Get a good grip on it. I think he'll be here tonight."

Mr. Lam nodded and got out the Japanese steel knife. He perched on the edge of the bed and, in the darkness, felt himself fighting sleep. At the moment when he felt he was in danger of dropping off, he found that, in fact, he had just woken up. In the street outside he could hear the siren of an ambulance. So there's been an accident! he thought.

Mr. Lam rushed out into the street, knife in hand, terrifying a handful of bystanders, who dodged out of the way. Two apathetic-looking ambulance workers carried a stretcher out of the apartment block opposite. He went closer and saw the fishmonger being shoved into the back of the ambulance. A startled look flashed across the fishmonger's ashen face. Mr. Lam relaxed. This is a safe street again now, he reassured himself.

The shed on the roof terrace clattered in the wind and the bystanders looked up. The lid of the cardboard box that sat in the corner of the shed blew off and a sudden gust of wind whirled the strange origami objects into the air. They tumbled around on the roof and were blown away.

It's raining, Ah Fan thought to herself as she stood, sleepy-eyed, on the roof terrace.

"On the day it rains, you will find true love," Ah Fan muttered.

It really was coming down in torrents. She reached out and the rain trickled through her fingers. But she seemed to have caught something. When she opened her hand to examine it, she decided almost immediately that the sodden scrap of paper was a headless blue paper rabbit.

Lam Yan put on a dry T-shirt and emerged from the bathroom. As she approached the window, she was surprised to see a flowery dress billowing up into the sky. It fluttered like a brightly colored bird before being beaten down by the raindrops and landing on the ambulance roof.

Lam Yan opened the window and a blast of wind made her curls dance up and down again like lively bugs. She watched happily as the ambulance, its red light flashing through the murky gray rain, puttered forlornly out of the narrow street.

° ° °

Lam Tun had just woken up when he heard a familiar woman's voice on the radio say, "The Education Department has cancelled classes in all schools."

He suddenly remembered the stack of notebooks he had hidden away long ago. He fished under the bed and with some difficulty extracted a dusty notebook. He opened it to a clean white page and wrote:

This is the first storm of summer.

BLACK CAT CITY

1

According to Puryatevich Loosai, when their memories start to fade, people get a subconscious urge to kill a cat.

K City teemed with cats, all of them black, like mislaid shadows. When people pushed their windows open at night, still bleary-eyed with sleep, they often caught sight of cats leaping across roofs, from one apartment block to another, so fast that in the feeble glow of the streetlights all that could be seen was a stream of black silhouettes.

If Loosai is right, then those cats fleeing down dark alleys must surely fall into the clutches of amnesiacs lying in wait for them. Even barehanded, the cat hunters would normally be quite nimble enough to capture cats. The cat, of course, would fight to the death, clawing wildly in the air, but then there would be a crack as its neck snapped. Alternatively, cat hunters might arm themselves with brooms and mop handles to whack the cats over the head and shatter their skulls, spilling blood and pink-tinged brain matter all over the ground and releasing a splendidly pungent odor into the air. The cat hunters never forgot to wash the dead cats carefully and toss their corpses or limbs into black trash bags and tie the tops, before going home, climbing into bed, and falling soundly asleep. Every back alley and side street saw the slaughter of countless cats every night, but when morning came and the city was bathed in sunshine, the happenings of the nighttime vanished, along with people's memories.

Where Memoria lived, there was a depot where the trash bags that had been heaped in the alleys were taken every morning, to await the truck that came jouncing along to take them all away. Memoria had been told that they would all end up being dumped into the river. She imagined the bags floating downstream past other cities until, eventually, they got to the ocean far, far away from here; then they floated away on the surface of the seawater, until mere dots remained, like the dark night dispersed by the sunshine, a forlorn sight that would soon disappear.

Memoria was recovering from amnesia. She stood at her window looking out at the black bags left on the ground outside. The tops of the bags rustled and trembled in the wind, looking from a distance like a field filled with black blossoms. Then suddenly, one bag-blossom seemed to burst open. Memoria thought she could see an old cat with a shiny black coat and two beady yellow eyes scrabbling its way out of the bag, then rapidly leaping the nearby fence and disappearing. In the street outside the trash depot, people bustled past as usual. It must have been her imagination—of course it was. That was not surprising. People were always imagining things in this city.

2

A woman in a long black raincoat was walking past the depot. She suddenly realized that she had seen this scene of blackness many times before. She looked up at the towering apartment blocks around her, their dark windows like so many muted mouths. She had obviously forgotten where she was heading. She looked around with the panicky suspicion of an incipient amnesiac. Then she fumbled in her coat pocket, took out a black notebook, and seemed to calm down.

2.15 Take black bag to Red Light Hill.

She realized with disappointment that she had no black bag with her. Then she saw the wire fence that enclosed a mound of black bags. She pressed herself against the unyielding wire but was unable to figure out what the bags had to do with her.

And where was Red Light Hill?

A man in a white shirt clattered past behind her and the woman turned to watch him stride off and disappear into a distant side street. Time passed—she was not sure how long—and another man in white passed behind her, but again the woman did not ask for directions. She walked quietly on, into the dark underpass at the end of the street.

3

The doctor on his way to Memoria's home caught a glimpse of the woman pressed to the wire fence. He thought she had been one of his patients once, and turned to look back, only to find the street was now deserted.

Since he began treating Memoria, the doctor always seemed to be in a bit of a trance. He was coming to believe that, as the biologist Loosai had said, amnesia was contagious.

About a month previously, Recall had come to him, convinced that his wife was suffering from amnesia. They had been married for many years, but recently, every time he and his wife made love, she burst into tears. Her long hair spread over her shoulders, she would recoil from Recall and curl up in a corner, peering at him with intense hostility and accusing him of rape.

4

On the first visit the doctor paid to Recall's home, he saw Memoria curled up next to the window. Her skin was so thin that the veins showed through, giving it an unreal bluish cast. Her slender hands and feet were bound with rope and she was tethered to the window frame, but she still gave the impression of being about to disappear at any moment. All the windows were shut and Memoria was gazing outside.

Recall had tied her up because he was worried she might run away and not be able to find her way home, he explained. Then he whispered to the doctor, "Of course, the old folk say that shutting the windows is enough to stop memories from making a run for it."

The doctor paid no attention to Recall. He bent down and spoke gently to Memoria. "What can you remember?"

Memoria turned and looked carefully at the doctor, as if watching an ant crawl up his face. Finally, she said, "Like many people, I can only remember a part of reality."

The doctor avoided her eyes—her pupils were glassy and he had the sensation that looking at them might shatter him to pieces. He turned to Recall and said, "Excellent. It doesn't seem as if your wife's problem is too serious."

He told Recall to sit down and pulled up another chair for himself. Then he asked Recall to tell him everything that had happened between him and his wife.

Recall glanced at Memoria warily, then back at the doctor. He did not speak for a long time. When he did, it was to ask hesitantly, "What do you want me to tell you?"

"Whatever you like. For instance, what were you wearing the

first time you met?"

Recall exhaled, and looked again at his wife. "I do remember that," he said. "She was wearing a pink tunic with a stand-up collar, the sort that nurses wear. And jeans... I first thought she had pink studs in her ears, but when I brushed her hair back, I discovered that they were her earlobes. They were a bit puffy and inflamed."

"Very good. Go on... What did you do then?"

"I took her to the park." Recall hesitated. Then he smiled. "Actually, we just kissed and held each other... What else would we do?"

"There was a stall selling baked sweet potatoes," Memoria suddenly put in.

"But it was summer! There couldn't possibly have been," said Recall, frowning.

The doctor ignored Recall and asked Memoria casually, "Were they purple inside?"

"Yes, I saw one cut open. The flesh of a purple sweet potato has concentric ripples that radiate outwards."

The doctor looked up at the ceiling and continued, "It was drizzling that day, wasn't it? The kind of rain we don't often get in winter..."

"...So the hawker's voice sounded a bit moist."

"In fact, the street was deserted. Only one old woman, holding a biscuit tin and buying a baked sweet potato..."

Recall listened to the doctor and his wife talking about past events that seemed to have nothing to do with him. There was nothing he could say. He was anxious, and wanted to interrupt them until he saw how unusually calm and gentle Memoria had become. He found himself resting his hand on the closed window. He was surprised that he could not push it all the way through the cold glass to make contact with the world outside.

The therapy went on all afternoon. At dusk, as the doctor was leaving, he untied Memoria. "Believe me," he said, "your wife won't forget her way home."

And Memoria did seem to get better. She prepared their meals deftly and, at dinnertime, chatted cheerfully to Recall about the old days, sometimes even giving a little laugh, while modestly covering her mouth with her hand. But Recall was distressed to find that he could remember very little of what she was talking about.

For several days after that, the doctor sat with Memoria by the window, questioning her about her courtship with Recall and even, later on, about how they made love—every slight physical sensation. Her descriptions were so true to life that Recall could not bear to listen. He had to turn away and look out the window. On the rooftop of the building opposite he seemed to see shadowy cats constantly flitting past. Every time one disappeared, he had the impression it was carrying away his memories in its mouth.

Memoria, on the other hand, smiled ever more brilliantly. She looked so young and healthy that now Recall began to tell people that he was the one who was sick, not Memoria.

He felt melancholy, but did not ask the doctor for help. Instead, he started seeing an old lover again.

5

In order to reassemble his memories, Recall went along to a high school reunion. But while his fellow students regaled each other with stories of the old days, he simply gazed abstractedly at an empty space at the neighboring table. Was that his place? he wondered.

As the partygoers dispersed into the darkness of the night, a smiling Prolongia came up to him in the dimly lit street. Recall had no memory of her. But from the warm greeting she gave him, Recall could only conclude that they must have been lovers once.

Prolongia took Recall on a tour of all their old haunts. Although the city had changed so much it was impossible to be sure exactly where those once-familiar places had been, Prolongia took out an old map and then pointed straight ahead. There, she told Recall happily—that was where they had hung out all those years ago. But when they got there, she was disappointed to discover that the park of her memories had disappeared. Instead, there was a bleached-out plaza, and an old woman clutching a biscuit tin who peered at them suspiciously.

A hawker was selling baked sweet potatoes at the entrance to the plaza and the old woman stood nearby. She had apparently been staring at the steaming yams for some time. Finally, hesitantly, she took a few coins out of her biscuit tin, bought one, and wandered away muttering, "I don't think it's going to be very sweet..."

There was a tall bronze statue in the center of the plaza and Prolongia and Recall went up to it.

"Who's this?" asked Recall.

It was Loosai, the city's fourth mayor. He had pushed through a successful cleanup program, read Prolongia from the inscription. She and Recall gazed up at his glistening bronze face for a long time.

The city was covered with such commemorative statues and plaques these days. It was as if, that way, memories could be preserved in time. But when Recall glanced up at the large TV screen above the plaza, and found himself looking at images of the dead cats that had floated up onto the sandbars of C City, he felt as if so many memories had died.

The municipal authorities of C City were currently investigating where this shoal of dead cats had come from and why. They could not exclude the possibility that it was connected with recent terrorist activity...

Recall and Prolongia, sitting on the bed in her apartment, were bewildered by what was happening in the world around them. They held each other tight—it was the only way to stop the uncontrollable trembling.

The winter wind whistled through a window that had been left ajar, making the blinds shiver and the frame rattle. Recall and Prolongia felt that the world had somehow become lighter, and disintegrated into a sea strewn with floating cat corpses. Terrified, they fumbled in the darkness for each other's bodies as if clutching desperately for a floating log that continued to roll perilously, however tightly they gripped it.

6

After her assignation with Recall, Prolongia's old illness returned with a vengeance.

The mementos from Recall—hair, fingernails, photographs of them together—unaccountably disappeared once she returned home. She thought she had opened the fridge, and was surprised when pairs of red and green shoes fell out. She started to see strangers sitting on her sofa: there was a pizza delivery man, munching on a pepperoni pizza; a fat woman—her foot on the sofa, trimming her toenails—turned and gave her a friendly smile, whereupon Prolongia felt the slipper she had in her hand, ready to swat cockroaches, suddenly float up in the air like a kite.

She shut herself in her room, but woke up in the middle of the night and discovered a strange man sitting naked on top of her. Prolongia leaped out of bed with a scream, pushed open a door to somewhere that felt like an unknown street, then searched for her bathroom. She took refuge there and spent the rest of the night listening to the dripping tap, the water droplets spattering loudly into the washbasin.

Her home felt so strange to her that Prolongia was overcome with a frantic longing to see Recall again. He seemed to be her only link to reality. Carefully, she wrote down the next day's meeting in her notebook:

2.15 Take black bag to Red Light Hill.

When Recall had mentioned Red Light Hill to her that day, Prolongia felt a spark of enthusiasm. She remembered their furtive meetings in the apartment block there when they were sixth graders. She had once snuck a black condom from her father's drawer, but it had gone unused.

7

Recall waited a long time for Prolongia at the building site. He was beginning to worry that she might have gotten lost.

He was in a fever of anticipation. He had invited Prolongia here because he had found a notebook at home from his high school days:

2.15 Take black bag to Red Light Hill.

He could no longer remember what "black bag" meant, whether 2.15 had been February 15 or 2:15 p.m., or what he wanted to do at Red Light Hill, but he did remember that it was a place where he used to hang out as a schoolboy. Its name came from the beacon tower on top of the hill that could be seen flashing at night. Probably only the locals still knew its name.

When Recall asked Prolongia if she remembered Red Light Hill, she blushed and smiled, then said firmly, "I'll never forget it."

Returning after many years, Recall found that the road up the hill had been marked off with red-and-white checkered tape. The word was that it was being developed as a tourist attraction. The wall flanking the road had once been covered by students in a mess of graffiti but now that had all been cleaned off. The tower was gone too. Recall went up to the wall at the foot of the hill. Looking at the silent shadow cast before him, he wondered if this really was the Red Light Hill he had frequented in his youth.

At that moment, there was a shrill squeal from the hill. On

the other side of the orange mesh barrier, Recall saw a black cat balancing on a glittering steel bar. As he moved closer, the cat leapt into the air and disappeared behind a pile of earth.

8

The undercover investigator who had been sent from C City to K City decided to drop in on his old high school friend Recall on the way. Unfortunately, Recall had just gone out. His wife, Memoria, showed the investigator into the sitting room, but he noticed that she seemed nervous. She was fiddling with the hem of her dress and he got the impression that she wanted him out of there as soon as possible.

After a long hesitation, Memoria finally went into the kitchen to make the investigator a cup of coffee, leaving him seated on the sofa. On the coffee table, a black notebook caught his eye, and inquisitively he flipped it open. The only words in it read:

2.15 Take black bag to Red Light Hill.

The investigator was dumbstruck when he saw "Red Light Hill," because he recognized it as the name of a C City terrorist cell. He had suspected that the dead cats were a secret signal meant to mobilize the terrorists, and this seemed to confirm his suspicion.

The investigator questioned Memoria about what was written in her diary. Memoria was evasive: it was just something she had scribbled when she was suffering from amnesia. This further convinced him that she was hiding a secret. Without waiting for Recall to return, he spirited her away.

9

When the doctor arrived at Memoria's home, he discovered the door wide open and the apartment empty. The evening sunshine shed narrow rungs of light on the sitting room floor. The rope was still attached to the window frame, where it dangled limply.

He stood in the doorway, suddenly realizing he had forgotten why he was here. It must be because he'd been under pressure at work recently, he thought.

The nurse did not know why the doctor, on his return to the clinic, hung a "Do Not Disturb" sign on his office door. When she had a moment, she snuck a look in. He was sitting in his office chair with his feet on the desk, absorbed in a novel.

The title was *Black Cat City* by Puryatevich Loosai.

THE APARTMENT BLOCK

Corridor, 13th Floor

"The shoes at home have all burst into flower," said A.

As A was speaking, a ray of sunshine slanted in through the corridor window, falling between him and K. K saw dust motes drift over A's face, making him look exhausted. The sunbeam finally landed on a shoe rack under the number plate of Apt. 2. The stems of insanely colored sunflowers entwined wearily together and the shoe openings vomited floral foam that spread in clumps all over the floor.

Five minutes before, A had phoned the management office, and K knew that it must be something to do with J's Third Auntie. He put down his half-finished bowl of fried noodles and the book, *Enemy*, that he was on the point of finishing, and realized he had a strand of noodle stuck between his teeth.

In the elevator, K tried every which way, but he could not get the noodle out. With his tongue, he explored his teeth to find where exactly it was, before giving it up as hopeless and ringing the doorbell of Apt. 1.

It was no surprise that J wasn't home. K sat in front of the iron security gate all morning, but there was no sign of J. Where could she have got to?

K was just about to shrug and suggest to A that they give up, when the door to Apt. 1 slowly opened. A bright red mouth gaped at K, showing a row of rugged, yellowing teeth. The teeth reminded him of a country trail with the wind whistling along it, wafting the scent of greenery.

In the doorway stood a woman. Her slim body looked insubstantial in her billowing nightgown; only a pair of shriveled legs gripped the floor like old tree roots. K saw that her feet were soaking wet, and the water trickled over the floor towards his own feet in a fantastical way. It was only then that he heard the sound of water slopping out from behind her and saw the watering can in her hand. She was still smiling, faint crow's feet radiating outwards like another kind of sunshine.

Apt. 4, 13th Floor

O peered through the peephole into the thirteenth floor corridor, certain that the footsteps belonged to the caretaker. He was standing at J's door but O was not about to tell J.

"No one's here yet," said O.

The bedroom door banged shut and there was the sound of sobbing inside. O imagined J curled up on the other side of the door, her legs tucked under her and her long hair falling over her chest, licking herself as a cat does.

If O had gently pushed the door open, he would have seen J at his feet, like a discarded bundle. Then O might have bent down and picked her up in his arms like a package, laid her on the bed and untied the string. There would be the sound of brown wrapping paper tearing, as J's limbs unfolded and sprawled across the bed.

O lit a cigarette.

Sitting on the sofa, O reflected that the sky this afternoon had depths all its own, and was more evocative even than a girl's naked body. The sounds in the bedroom gradually faded to silence. No doubt J had taken the scissors out of the bedside cupboard and, climbing onto the bed, had stabbed them into her chest...

O imagined her blood soaking the bed sheet on which he

and his wife had slept the night before, and then dripping onto the floor. Some hours later, when he mopped J's floor, he discovered the bloodstain looked just like a flower.

But he could not see his own expression, so he retraced his feelings to another sunny, cloudless afternoon. Drably dressed pallbearers had stepped out of the funeral parlor carrying a heavy coffin. Mourners followed silently behind, heads bowed. He was the only one who slowly raised his head. A black kite fluttered in the sky above the funeral parlor. He had observed the kite the way he now observed these elegant musings.

At a moment like that, would Third Auntie have been standing in the crowd watching him?

O remembered how J had nestled against his legs just an hour ago, and told him about her Third Auntie.

Her head in her hands, J said earnestly, "One day I might kill her."

At that moment, O was only wondering what pattern she had on her bra today, and did not know what to say in response. But there was probably no need to say anything because J was soon absorbed in a gossip magazine. On the front cover was a color picture of a man and a woman seen from behind. The caption identified them as two famous actors. They were walking along a dun-colored trail and their figures were so blurred that it looked like they might soon disappear. O felt like he recognized the couple—they looked like his wife and a good friend of his.

O was just about to take a closer look when J suddenly closed the magazine and dropped a kiss on O's calf. O felt deeply touched, until he remembered that his feet always stank.

Fortunately, J quickly moved her mouth up his calf and, as she did so, O carefully pressed himself back on the sofa, watching as J rose up to him like the sun.

O remembered having this feeling when J first moved in. She had suffused him with a warmth that made him break out in a sweat. J gave him her card, and he thought it was a paper handkerchief. She was a reporter for *Sun Magazine*. She could work as she pleased and did not need to spend long hours in the office, she added.

"That's perfect!" O burst out.

"Why? Are you a reporter too?"

"No, no," O felt himself flush, "I do cartoons for people. What I mean is...we'll have lots of time to relax at home during the daytime."

And what he had imagined came true. O shut his eyes and felt as if he was in an ancient pagoda with dark red flowers growing up the walls. He climbed up their branches and, one after another, the flowers burst into bloom. He looked up at a window at the top of the tower, longing to learn more about the exhilarating light that shone from it. It seemed as if J's whole body was going to become transparent.

Just then J suddenly pulled away and asked, inconsequentially, "How come it's not here yet?"

O opened his eyes and saw that J was frowning. He was nonplussed, until he realized she was referring to the take-out they had just ordered. "It'll be here soon," he said vaguely.

But J was very agitated. She yanked open the drawers of the wardrobe and rifled through a pile of leaflets from take-out food joints. She extracted one and tossed it at O. "That's really annoying! You give them a ring," she urged him. "Tell them to get a move on."

"How can I ask that?" said O unwillingly.

J refused to look at O. She seemed pissed off with him and went off to the other end of the sitting room.

As O watched, she paused and then, cat-like, lifted a fingernail and scratched his Michael Jordan poster. Then she bent her head a little and a tear rolled down her cheek. She made a sound that O found unbearably shrill.

Footsteps suddenly sounded in the corridor.

"That's it, isn't it?" O said, and went to the door.

Apt. 2, 13th Floor

A pea rolled across the dining table and stopped by D's finger.

D looked up to see a pallid-looking man sitting down beside her. She remembered that this was her new husband, A. There were four lunch boxes in front of A. He was just selecting a pea from one of the boxes with a toothpick, so focused on the task that his eyes glared like a fighting cock.

"One day I might stuff those flowers up her ass." It might have been something like this that A said when he came in a few moments before, or maybe not. He was carrying a shoe rack and went into the bathroom. D watched his slender figure disappear through the bathroom door, leaving behind a patch of sunlight that changed shape as the curtains fluttered. The scene made her feel like their marriage was both make-believe and, at the same time, very real.

D remembered when she first came here with A, six months back. The white muslin curtains were not yet in place and the walls were glaringly white. The building manager had been babbling about something; it sounded like the pattering of rainfall inside her. She saw her shadow retreating under her feet and felt she was about to go moldy and rot.

Nowadays, she often saw her husband deftly arranging her underwear on the clothes rack, then leaning out of the window and using his long arms to hang the rack in the sunshine. When the sun shone on her multi-colored panties, D felt as if its rays were shining all over her own body.

Just as she always did, D had woken up today and stood at the window watching the sunshine move along the street. When the sun was at its fiercest, she often saw a young man delivering take-out food in a plastic basket, sauntering across the street. The basket swayed on his arm until it looked as if the food would tip out onto the ground. The young man was soon out of view, leaving only the sun traveling down the street. After a little while, she would hear the doorbell ring. When she opened the door, she saw a man standing there, holding two lunch boxes. That man was her husband.

However, when she opened the door today, she failed to notice that it was not A standing there. She took the boxes from the delivery man and shut the door. Then it occurred to her that her husband had not come back.

Now, the four lunch boxes sat on the table, and A was still focused on picking out peas and putting them on the sheets of old newspaper spread out underneath.

"What are you doing?" asked D, watching her husband with some impatience.

A said nothing. But after a while, he looked up. "You don't

like orangutans, do you?"

D could not remember whether she did or not. She looked away and used the remote to turn on the TV. On the screen, a woman with long, flowing hair holding a butcher's knife in one hand and a crying baby in the other, sat on the ground.

"You don't like orangutans, do you?" D heard her husband ask again.

On TV, the woman brandished the knife as if she was going to stab the baby, but then the knife halted in midair. D could not tell whether this was a film or a news clip.

"I don't understand why you don't like orangutans." At that, D turned to look at her husband. He was pressing on a pea with his forefinger. Its skin had split and the pulpy flesh was stuck to the tabletop. He looked exasperated.

A banged the table with his hand. It seemed like a hard blow, although it only made a faint sound. The peas on the sheet of newspaper remained intact and did not move. Then he took a glass vase from the table and rushed into the kitchen.

D wondered what he was going to do with it. It was such good weather today—perhaps her husband was going to smash the vase against his head. The fragments of glass would rain down, landing on the tiled floor with a tinkle. The blood would trickle down her husband's bony face onto his shirt collar, staining the white fabric bright red. D sighed faintly at the thought. She seemed to see her husband sitting that evening in the bathroom, wearily bent over his shirt as he washed it. The blood stains from the shirt mixed with the water in the dark blue washbasin, their crimson spreading senselessly outwards and eventually staining a pair of her panties that were also in the basin.

On the Stairs (1)

L, the cleaning woman, dragged a heavy rubbish bag down the stairs, heedless of the sound of broken glass, or that she was walking over a scattering of sunflowers and treading one of them to pulp. On this warm afternoon, she seemed lost in thought, unaware that one of her hands was roving across her chest...

On the Stairs (2)

When H met L on the stairs, his face wore an odd smile. He pretended to be going up to the fourteenth floor until he could no longer hear the cleaner's footsteps, then he doubled back down the stairs to the thirteenth floor.

H went up to the window on the stairs and looked out. He could see a woman in an apartment one floor below practicing aerobics, her voluptuous flesh wobbling as she did so. H unzipped himself...

Apt. 3, 12th Floor

The mahjong tiles on the table had not moved for nearly an hour.

M watched as P's chunky arm jerked up and down in front of her, her belly rolls jiggling in time with the swaying of her body. It annoyed her intensely. No wonder P's husband wanted to...thought M, with a smile.

To P, M's smile seemed malicious, though she did not make the connection with her husband. She knew he was working hard to finish *Paragons of Youth*, which was due for publication. Yesterday evening, P had had an argument with her husband about the plot of the comic. She did not understand why, in a book written for wholesome young people, her husband insisted that the girl he called Sunflower should strip naked in front of those paragons of youth. P's husband had put an end to the argument with the words, "You're soon going to weigh more than two hundred pounds!"

What really interested P now was the bowl of beef noodles in M's hands. P was on a diet and the slurping M made as she ate her noodles made her belly rumble with hunger.

But M's gaze had shifted to a dark corner of the sitting room. On a side table, a few sunflowers drooped in a Japanese-style vase. To one side of it, H sat on the floor, his face flushed and one leg crooked, snipping half moons off his toenails and sending them flying across the room. H had been pacing restlessly up and down the room when he suddenly grabbed his keys and said, "I'm off to buy something." M had been deeply suspicious, wondering why this seventy-year-old was rushing off to buy a few wilting sunflowers. It reminded her of the sunflower at home, whose stem was soon to be snapped off.

Yesterday evening, M's husband came home crooning a pop song and gave her a sunflower, which was unusual for him. After dinner, when M was washing up, her husband suddenly reached out stealthily, grabbed the saucepan lid from her hand, and pulled her into the bedroom.

This morning, M had sauntered out of the apartment and, on an impulse, slapped the cleaning woman, L, on the chest. M remembered the woman's astonished expression and could not help laughing.

H looked up bleary-eyed at M's laugh, as if he had been in a drunken sleep. He glanced at the jumble of mahjong tiles on the table and looked down again.

An hour before, C had sat down at the mahjong table, tiles in her hand, hesitating a long time before playing any of them. Her eyes flickered. Then finally she sighed and flipped over all the tiles and rushed off to the bathroom. She was in such a hurry that one of her leather slippers fell off, and lay upside down on the floor, its sole stained with age-old dirt.

H had no way of guessing what his daughter-in-law, C, was doing in the bathroom, nor was he interested.

Behind the silent bathroom door, C sat on the toilet, her eyes closed. Her head was tilted to one side and she looked as if she might topple over at any moment. Her pink panties were down to her knees, her left arm hung down and she held something in her hand. In the dimness, it was hard to tell if it was a book, a hairbrush, or a knife. And there was a continuous dribble from the corner of her mouth, which might have been saliva, or perhaps blood.

Downstairs

It was dusk when K cycled away from the apartment building and, compared with daytime, the contours of the street were softer, as if it might change direction at any moment and take passersby to a different, unknown place.

The shouts and cries of children at play came from the park opposite. K saw a child in red hurtling past the park gate. A girl standing at the top of the slide suddenly shot down. From where K stood, she seemed to vanish from sight.

Something—he was not sure what—made K stop and look back at the apartment block. Sunflowers tumbled down from one of the windows but, with the last rays of sun in his eyes, he could not tell which one. Dust and bits of litter bowled gently along the street, blown by the evening breeze. The scene filled K with a rush of sweetness.

By the time the sunflowers landed on the street, K had already hurried past. He was thinking that the first thing he would do when he got home was to clean his teeth, and extract that bit of noodle stuck between them.

MONTHLY MATTERS

March: Quiet

March is immersed in a gray drizzle, but the city streets are like rigid, dried-up riverbeds. Crowds of people with souls like fish walk listlessly past shops with drawn-down shutters. We get off the bus and walk along, each as silent as the other. Once we happen to look up and find that Mui Mui, my younger sister, has morphed into a trancelike play of light and shadow. The city's silence is not surprising. What is surprising is that we grit our teeth and endure it.

We emerge from a back street hemmed in by apartment blocks, and see the sea. But the opposite shore is as murky as this one. I remember that at night Mui Mui always settles on the billboard on the opposite shore, like a black spider. But I must be mistaken because most of the time I can see her two hands gripping the steel clothes rack outside, only the upper half of her face, and her eyes, visible from my window.

I look at the clock on the shelf. It is dawn. I go out of my room. In the sitting room, the sofa has a warm dip in it that still holds the hint of a human form. The measly drops of water collecting in the tap suddenly gush out. I look around. Outside, the gray rain is still falling, carrying with it a faint whiff of rust.

As I patrol our apartment armed with a flashlight, I come across my father standing stiffly between the bookshelf and the CD rack. The flashlight beam, like a blunt knife, hesitantly pares off a piece of my father's face the size of my hand; then it becomes entangled in the pent-up frustrations at his throat. I pull a small knife from my pocket and, crouching on the floor, play at pricking balloons again. They pop like faint flares in the dark room and settle at my father's feet like a heap of rubber corpses.

The whole afternoon is still—apart from Mui Mui lying on the dining table with her dress tucked up under her breasts. The bulb hanging from the ceiling gives a false glow to her belly, which has only a very slight bulge. But it swells gradually until it resembles a huge, plump egg. I climb on the table, lie down beside her, and tuck my own clothes up. I shut my eyes and feel a warmth descend on my belly. I open my eyes again, and there is not a prick of light anywhere.

When we go down to the street together again, Mui Mui's belly is as swollen as a woman about to give birth. We pass a lamppost we must have passed dozens of times before, and Mui Mui suddenly hoists her dress up, revealing her smooth round abdomen, and indicates that I should stab her. I stand watching, waiting for my father to take the knife from his trouser pocket and rush at her.

The eyes of passersby fall on us like leaves shaken from a forest full of trees. My father pulls the knife from Mui Mui's belly and retreats a couple of paces. We all wait for something to happen but Mui Mui just falls to the ground, without even a moan, like a much-weathered statue crumbling to dust. Then there is just air, like in a silent movie, with everything coalescing into a monochrome painting. The rain seems to float in midair, emitting the pattering sound of static on the TV screen.

April: Pregnancy

In April, there is another rush of pregnant women into the city. At this point, we are still living with the wolf.

A wolf draped in a woman's overcoat has slunk into the city

by night. When the pregnant women rush into other people's houses, the wolf rushes into ours.

"They occupy our biggest rooms, and they've eaten up all the pickled vegetables we've been storing for years," say the neighbors.

It is hard to tell the difference between the wolf and the women, but when the neighbors complain, we cannot help gloating. The most the wolf will do is prowl around the apartment, licking up the dust particles in the air.

The pregnant women vomit noisily all day, but the wolf sneaks silently into our bathroom. There it curls up in the dark, damp corner under the sink, and shuts its eyes. Every day, we strip in front of the wolf and show it our nakedness. The wolf opens its eyes and fixes us with a measuring stare.

I do not remember when the wolf finally agrees to share a bed with Mui Mui and sit at the dinner table with us. By now, the city hospitals are packed with big-bellied pregnant women. Once they have aborted their fetuses, they will go back home. Only the wolf remains—awaiting the birth of its infant, its departure date uncertain.

We secretly bring the fetuses discarded behind the hospital back home and feed them, bowlful by bowlful, to the wolf. But the wolf eats little, and sometimes in the middle of dinner starts to pace back and forth in front of the window. We know that it is staring out at the hospital building.

"If we don't kill the next generation, our own generation may become extinct..." I try to explain this to the wolf but it looks at me uncomprehendingly. It seems to find the city more and more intolerable. However, as a mother, it has tacitly consented to giving birth in the hospital.

We take the wolf to the hospital early one morning. Finally, its belly has begun to swell. As we watch, the doctor slits the wolf's belly open and takes out a bloody lump of matter. As we expect, it is not the wolf's infant—it is Mui Mui, sound asleep.

"The wolf's belly is very warm," Mui Mui tells us. She has never had such a sound sleep.

"This is the right place to nurture an infant, but the wolf isn't pregnant," said the doctor. "Maybe the wolves that could have impregnated it have gone extinct."

There is still a constant stream of pregnant women arriving in town, but I know that the last wolf has died in our hospital; even though, for a while, Mui Mui insists she is the wolf's progeny.

May: Birds

Nothing noteworthy happens in May, except that Dad buys a huge fridge.

"It's as big as an elephant," I say to Mui Mui, after the fridge has been moved into the apartment. We watch as Dad reaches into its deepest recesses. "We have to empty it completely, and then we can fill it with all the dead birds."

The meteorologist suggests that we regard the stink from our bodies as part of the city's destruction. "There are always omens before any business is wrapped up. It's like the changing of the seasons."

"I reckon the time's not far off," I say to Mui Mui. When the temperature rises at midday, I can't bear the smell and have to leave the apartment. Dad pretends to call some government department on the phone to find out what is going on, then gives us a casual lie. "It's all because of the birds," he tells us. "They fly low around the apartment blocks, and hurl themselves at the closed windows. They're the source of all this evil. They carry disease from one city to another."

I strain my ears and I think maybe the sound I hear is the wind whistling through my body. It is only later that I see them in the bathtub. The birds all have their eyes closed and their heads droop on their breasts in exhaustion. I pick the birds up one by one, and drop them in the trash can, but it becomes pungent with the odor of blood and there is a flurry of feathers in the air.

I look around. Mui Mui is standing in the entrance hall, her white hands hanging at her side. In the end she killed all the birds in the recommended way, she says.

Dad fills the fridge with the bird corpses, and they become the basis of our dinner each day. He carries bowl after bowl, brimming with bird meat, to the table. The quantities are astounding. Mui Mui munches away at a little bird's head and then quickly sucks the rest of its body into her mouth like a snake, with an expression of indifference on her face. I see her cheeks pooch out like a frog's, and avert my eyes.

I shut the door and lie on the bed, feeling like a blob of soft mud. I hear a faint noise, like wings flapping, as if some task remains incomplete. Outside, the rain is falling, and something sprouts from my body.

According to Mui Mui, the birds are still flying over our city. I can only see the mold that covers every corner of the house after the rain. Fine green hairs grow from every part of my face and body and I cannot scrub them off no matter how hard I try. I ask Dad why this has happened, but he just points to the suitcase and tells us that the time has come. Everyone has to get as far away as possible from where the birds are gathered, and look for fresh air.

After Dad leaves, Mui Mui and I avoid each other, but continue to share meals of dead birds. Then, one day, I open the fridge to find her curled up among the birds. My sister lies there deathly pale—apparently still warm, but her body is as hard as iron. Apart from the frost gathering on her face, she looks unchanged. I shut the fridge door, but the stench is still in the air. There is no sound, but the flying birds are an intangible presence. I don't believe that anyone, even my father, will ever be able to figure out where this smell is coming from.

BED

"But how did this happen?"

"I just remember the shape of those beds: some as broad as a plaza so it seemed you could dance on them; others as narrow as a steel cable, so that you'd fall off them if you didn't watch out. I longed for the lights to go out quickly, and the bed to settle into a whirlpool as thick and black as tar, so I could sink into a bottomless sleep."

And then they would stop asking questions. Even though the spotlights hurt the girl's eyes and she could see the people in masks with strangers' eyes, she knew that sleep was not far away when the nurse began to inject the anesthetic. So she shut her eyes, and allowed them to come in with their ice-cold instruments, draw marks with indelible pen on her belly, peel it open like the skin of a grapefruit, and pull out the dead fetus curled up, beanlike, inside.

She felt extraordinarily calm, knowing no one could push her off the bed. The drugs began to take effect and she felt her muscles and her skeleton suddenly fall apart like when a bundle of firewood is untied. She fell onto the surface of the water and gradually lost shape, as if she were a translucent jellyfish, even her memory softening. That was the moment when she fell in love with the hospital bed, all deathly whiteness, and the dizzying, soporific smell of the hospital.

The beige hospital curtains were thick and heavy. Occasionally, the breeze stirred them and rays of light slipped in and played on the faces of those who might have been sound asleep, or dead.

The nurses discovered the girl in the last bed when they made their rounds. "There are no records for her." "She doesn't look like a patient, or a relative." "But how did she get in?" The hospital walls were high and topped with shards of glass. Nothing like this had ever happened before. The nurses argued back and forth but came to no conclusion. "Well, she can't stay here." The doctor nodded. "Let's try and wake her."

So they all bent over, like a flock of ducks converging on the food trough. A nurse put her mouth to the girl's soft ear and called to her, raising her voice when it had no effect. One by one, the slumbering patients were startled awake, returning as if from a long journey to the other side of the world with the look of alien lands in their eyes. They stared at the girl with curiosity, then stumbled out of bed and surrounded her. They called as loudly as the nurses, as if afraid she was stuck in dreams that were sucking her deeper and deeper into a muddy swamp.

In the girl's home, there had only been one bed, hibernating in the very center of the house.

Every night, the girl, her elder sister, and her father lay down on the bed and went to sleep together. They might even meet in their dreams, like cars speeding past on the highway, but they never spoke a word. They were used to sharing the house, and appeared to have forgotten one another's existence. For them, there was nothing surprising in it at all.

To start with, the girl found the bed enormous, until her and her sister's bodies began inexorably to grow bigger and the bed grew smaller and smaller. By night, they lay with their arms and legs entangled like flayed pig carcasses littering the slaughterhouse, and their dreams thickened and darkened, becoming as heavy as lead. Sometimes, jerking awake, they smelled the stink of each other's sweat and grumbled and yanked at each other's hair before eventually falling asleep, exhausted. The sky outside was often starless and the city lights glared in, illuminating the expressions, by turns distressed and vengeful, on their faces. From between their lips a brittle stream of sleep mutterings burbled forth. They knew that they shouldn't sleep too deeply in case they got a vicious kick that threw them from the bed. Then they would wake up the next morning to find themselves curled up on the floor, every bone in their bodies aching.

The bed was so fragile it seemed to have shrunk to a floating log. But none of them had given up. They clung fiercely to it because they longed for sleep, like one longs for another country even after the world has gone by.

When, against all expectations, the girl came to, she found herself in the doctor's clinic lying on an examination couch. She had been stripped naked and, without even a sheet to cover her, goose pimples as delicate as grains of rice had spread over her body. The doctor had a stethoscope hanging around his neck, and in his hands were some X-rays that he was holding up to the light. The girl did not know if the bleached white skeleton on the X-rays was hers, but she felt the doctor did not need to look at her; he had already seen into her bones. Just now she was transparent, and everyone could see her heart tiredly beating.

The doctor smiled elegantly, showing teeth so white as to be scarcely believable.

The girl stared up at him from the couch.

"Where do you live?" asked the doctor. "Far from here?"

The girl shook her head. "Even if the place still exists, I've forgotten the way back."

"You can stay here," said the doctor, after a moment's thought.

"But can I have my own bed?"

"Only patients need a bed," said the doctor, annoyed. "As far as I can tell, there's absolutely nothing wrong with you physically."

"Do you never need a bed then, doctor?" the girl asked in disbelief. She noticed how quiet the hospital was. It was as if everyone was sound asleep except the doctor, who showed no signs of fatigue.

The doctor did not answer. It occurred to him that he had not slept for a very long time. Outside the hospital in the gray, misty dawn, a cobbled road wound past the deep green lawn and away. Pigeons were startled into flight and vanished into the sunlight. It all felt far away from him.

The girl had walked a long way to get here. At midnight, she had pushed open the door of her home and gone down the grimy steps, weeping and mumbling about how her father had died. "He fell, his head was twisted to the left, blood kept trickling out of his mouth." She crossed the square and stood in front of a row of food kiosks, all closed, their shutters hanging heavily. It was only when a street cleaner slapped her on the face and told her, "Your father isn't dead," that she woke up from her dream.

By the time the girl had wiped away these mysterious tears and taken the familiar route back home, it was all too late. The house was in darkness and there seemed to be a huge beast lying in wait on the bed. She pulled back the mound of bedding and discovered her father and big sister had taken up the whole bed. But they seemed not to need those brightly colored pajamas anymore. They were completely naked and tightly embraced, their fingernails dug deeply into the skin of each other's back. They seemed fast asleep, curled tightly together like a pair of fetuses. No matter how hard the girl tried, she could not pull them apart, and they were too heavy to push out of bed.

The girl just had to sit on the floor, listening all night long to her father and sister emitting low groans like an insect makes just before it pupates and the sound is cut off midstream. The air seemed full of butter about to precipitate, stiflingly hot.

This went on night after night, with father and daughter painstakingly re-enacting the same monotonous movements, till the girl was convinced that she would never get to lie in the bed again. If only I could control the urge to sleepwalk, it wouldn't be me who lost my place in the bed, she thought to herself. She had not shut her eyes in a long time; she just looked down and fiddled with her toes, knowing that she would have to leave to find herself a place for a proper sleep.

The nurses felt that if the girl wanted to stay in the hospital, she would have to work like them. Every day, she had to help paralyzed patients into bed and plug tubes in all over their bodies until all they could do was pant in desperation.

"It's very simple. You can learn how to do injections too. And with the annoying ones you just pull their trousers down and make them stick their bottoms in the air and jab the needle in, and they'll fall asleep, as quiet as floppy puppets. In fact, it won't be long before you get rid of them all—you wrap them up when they look like they've snuffed it, and once they atrophy and turn livid, you send them to the mortuary, and that's that."

So the girl put on a nurse's white overalls and, just as if she was delivering a baby, took from them someone who had just died. The body was so light that the organs seemed to have been scooped out, leaving just the shell. The face looked shrunken and wizened, like a bruised raisin, and its features were now indistinguishable.

The nurses took the girl to a door so narrow it was easy to forget it was there. Behind it, a spiral staircase snaked downwards, past other, sealed-up rooms until it reached the lowest level of the hospital basement.

They pushed open the heavy metal door and the girl saw two rows of drawers in the wall, all with labels on them. She opened one at random and found a corpse. Its eyes were half open and its lips slightly parted, as if it had died in the act of singing. She opened more drawers, one after the other—all were occupied.

"These are all corpses that haven't been claimed by their families. We've sent letters and phoned to tell them their relatives have died, but they just pretend they've forgotten all about it, and there's absolutely nothing we can do." As the nurse talked, she pressed one of the occupants flat as if it were a sponge, took the corpse from the girl, and squeezed it in on top of the first one. The drawers were tiny and they were all full, so the girl knew there was no space for her to sleep here. Then, she noticed a glass door leading outside.

"That's where the corpses are buried," said the nurse, "but actually we only get rid of the rotten corpses that way." The nurse continued with a mysterious air, "Every night, the doctor comes down here. It's said that he talks to the corpses all night long, but he also plants poisonous roses here. Think about it: for people who never sleep, the nighttime must be very, very lonely."

The girl pushed open the door. A flock of brightly colored butterflies fluttered in. There was an aroma of rotten corpses and roses in the air.

The smell was a mixture of sleep and bacteria. The girl passed a row of people lying by the roadside, their faces concealed by their long hair, cardboard boxes with their belongings and plastic bottles scattered around them. They lay motionless as if asleep, though some suddenly sat up and yelled at her to go away.

She retreated into a corner and opened the only notebook she had. It was packed full of people's names and the names of streets she had never been to. She quickly picked out a friend and checked where she lived on the map.

She had settled on that particular friend, not because they were close but because, when they played together at her friend's house, she had discovered a huge pink bed. A bed like that could sleep half a dozen people, she thought.

She rang the doorbell and a man with a facial twitch answered it. The left side of his mouth jerked randomly, and he gave a crooked smile. The girl remembered visiting her friend and playing in a desultory way with plastic dolls as the man sat on the enormous bed, smoking impatiently. Cigarette ends lay on the floor like dispirited bugs that had just expired around his feet. Occasionally the man glanced at the girls as if he would like to drive them out of the house.

The girl looked at the notebook again to check her friend's name before she said it.

"She's dead!" was the man's response. Then he turned and went inside.

"It doesn't matter," said the girl, still standing in the doorway.

"I only need a little bit of..."

The man stopped as if he was waiting for the girl to go on.

"I only need a little bit of space in your bed."

The man turned his head slightly and looked the girl up and down, from her youthful face to her slippered feet. His mouth twitched more violently than ever, as if something might leap out of it and attack someone, but then he went back inside, drew back the grille with a screech, and let the girl in.

In the great, gloomy house, there was a light on in only one room. The bed was in there, and the girl was pleased to see it was as enormous as she remembered it. She could also see it was made of carved wood, with a soft mattress in which she could feel some lingering warmth. The man's shadow silently came nearer and she saw his face, twitching in the half-light, but she had already thrown herself on the bed. It was like wallowing in a warm bath. She began to find it hard to breathe. It had to happen, was the thought that came to her before she lost consciousness.

The beds did not remain empty for long after the dead had been taken away. Very soon another old person would be clumsily carried in on a stretcher. Their features were veiled by an assortment of spots and wrinkles like the outspread, veined wings of a butterfly, but it did not take the girl long to recognize her father. His head was bent, his neck drooped, and his weary flesh spilled out in folds. His sallow cheeks were curiously flushed as if he had just woken up from a deep sleep.

The girl took off her father's clothes and dressed him in one of those white hospital gowns and trousers that are easy to get on and off. Her father's body had begun to shrink and become lighter, she noticed, his hands and feet like hollow lotus roots that yielded when she played with them. As she put him on the bed, she thought he looked like a prematurely aged child. She sat at his bedside into the night, waiting to yell at him and wake him up. But before long she pillowed her head on his soft belly, her long hair spread out like a fan, and, with no warning at all, was asleep.

Night, like an intricate, indigo veil, crept over the high wall of the hospital, gradually enveloping the building and grounds. At dusk, the doctor busied himself by the wall, pruning the roses, scrambling up their creeping tendrils until he got halfway up the building. A long-drawn-out snoring reverberated through the silence of the hospital. The corpses that were not completely decomposed conversed quietly with the dreamers, a sound the doctor was well used to. Now, however, to his surprise, he found himself yawning drowsily at the sky. The lonely eye of the moon glared down at him.

They brought in a very large screen, and from morning until noon every day broadcast gory images. They pointed to all the pictures of dead fetuses and streams of bloody water, describing the process of abortion in meticulous detail, until some of the students leaned against the wall and threw up. Spreading shoals of filth soon covered the floor like lotus leaves and attracted lively hordes of bluebottles.

"Those girls have thrown up all last night's dinner," a teacher reported to the director of studies, who stood on the platform surveying the vomit. The male teachers led the girls in reciting the Bible aloud. "Thou shalt not commit adultery!" On the rainy sports ground, the female students huddled close together, soaked in sweat. The girl was among them. She saw the director of studies coming over to them carrying a long ruler. He was very strict but, for the last few nights, his bed had magnanimously taken the girl in. As the sun came up in the

morning, he even embraced her feet and begged her not to go.

The girl gradually understood it had always been like this: when one door shut, another door opened to her. Often night fell too soon, and then the girl would scuttle up and down the city streets, going in at different doors. Once she discovered she was in a wilderness surrounded by skinny, feral dogs vomiting their guts out. A sandstorm scratched her face. She was in pain and blood trickled down her thighs, splattering on the ground like a sunburst. The girl began to wonder if she had ever been asleep.

Her father often jerked awake at night to find his fellow patients lying as still as corpses. Terrified, he would grip a corner of the bedsheet and whimper, hoping that someone would notice him. As his eyes grew accustomed to the darkness, he seemed to see dancing shadows, perhaps the souls of the patients staggering blindly around the room. Quietly, he dragged himself into the corridor, keeping away from the shadows. There, he shouted and shouted until the nurses appeared and turned the lights on. In the ward, all was as quiet as before.

"What's happened?" Before her father had time to scramble back into bed and hide under the sheets, the nurses had surrounded him. He was silent, though his lips trembled slightly, as if he wanted to explain himself but could not get the words out. He stood by the bed, looking aggrieved, his feet splayed and his legs shaking. The nurses looked down and saw a flood of hot, yellow liquid that pooled on the floor like a tardy twilight.

"Did you know there are thousands of beds here?" said the girl as she put her father into a wooden tub and scrubbed him clean. "But that doesn't mean it's easy to get to sleep. Just like you, I've started meeting all sorts of sick people in my dreams. That means they're just pretending to be asleep. They're really wandering around like sleepless ghosts. Some of them hover around me, some ask me the way out of the hospital. They have no idea that this place will soon be enveloped in climbing roses. And what's the good of leaving here, anyway? From what I've heard, all the bed spaces everywhere are occupied and anyone without one will soon be arriving here." The girl remembered the doctor saying, "That's why the best thing sick patients can do is die quickly. Otherwise, they'll have to learn how to do without sleep." The doctor was leaning over the bed as he spoke, yawning his head off and looking so desperate for sleep that the girl almost took him for just another patient.

Her father's eyelids were so heavy that he heard nothing the girl was saying. At some point—he did not know when—he had been stripped naked and had fallen asleep in the bathtub. The water had crept up to his lips and he breathed warm air into it, making bubbles that floated away one by one. The girl wanted to wake him up but was almost overcome by somnolence herself. She could not help drifting off, a piece of soap still clutched in her hand, a soaking wet towel hanging over the edge of the tub, dripping water quietly onto the floor.

As her body became heavier and heavier, the girl sank deeper into the bed until she melded completely into it.

She told the men that she felt her belly growing. Even if she beat it or drank glasses of cold water, there was no sign of it shrinking. She reckoned that the skin of her belly would soon be stretched so thin it would be translucent and you could peek inside and see the network of veins and squirming intestines.

At first they didn't believe her, until finally the girl, giddy and bloated, started to vomit violently. They made suggestions. "You'll feel better tomorrow." "Go and have a walk outside." "Look up at the sun and take a deep breath." The next day, when the girl left, they quickly shut the door. It would not be opened again. The girl stood alone in the middle of the chilly street, still longing to sleep. It seemed to her that she kept walking until at some point she found herself falling to the ground in a deep sleep. In her dream, she was lying on a vast bed and, even though her stomach had swelled until she could no longer recognize it, she still felt that she was very, very fortunate.

Her body felt immensely heavy. When she woke up, her father was leaning against her back. There were so many hospital beds, the girl did not know how her father had found out where she was sleeping. He had clambered onto the bed, clamping his hands around her neck. He was so frail she felt she could push him to the ground with the slightest shove. However, now that he was deeply asleep, his hands gripping her so tightly, it was as if she was carrying an infant on her back. She went to the window. When she looked down, she saw the roses in full bloom, just as if they had grown out of the doctor's dreams. They grew so quickly they would soon be up to the windows.

"Let's buy...a double bed," the doctor finally suggested one evening. He had realized quite some time ago that, incurable insomniac though he was, his desire to go to sleep with the girl kept growing. She felt unusually tired that day. After she had helped her father squeeze out a few drops of urine into a small bottle, she kept remembering its bright yellow color and the smell still stung her nostrils. Like his body, her father's penis had shrunk to almost nothing. The girl thought he would probably soon be so small that he could fit into a mortuary drawer. The doctor's body, on the other hand, was somehow as tall and sturdy as a tree. He kept urging the girl, "How about this bed?"

It was the first time in a long while that the doctor had left the hospital. He drove the girl to a furniture shop where they hurriedly picked out a double bed. No one cared how similar the bed's design was to a hospital bed. The doctor, although astonished by this turn of events, pulled money out of his pocket and went to the cashier to pay. The bed still had its label "Display Only," but the girl in her white overalls just had to lie down on it. She curled up and sank into a sleep as soft as the earth, from which it was impossible to extricate herself.

People passing the showroom window and seeing the girl lying asleep just like an overripe apple fallen from the tree swarmed up like bluebottles drawn by the fruity nectar of her dreams. The doctor approached her resolutely, but still she refused to wake up. She must have known that this was her last chance for a sound sleep. Every night from then on, the doctor would clamber into the bed and wake her up.

THE
MUTE DOOR

The door is constructed in such a way as to conceal the fact that it does not exist. Precisely because entering and departing leaves no trace, it becomes necessary to suggest it by means of this pantomime. Thus all doors are symbolic, and we can only grope our way blindly. Nothing limits us, nothing protects us. Decisions are impossible.

Among all the doors that I have come across, it is only the invisible doors of mime artists that capture the essence of a door. Whether in streets occupied by the language of colonizers or in a red square in the month of June, mime artists can always silently create a house that is theirs alone. All that is needed is a pair of hands and a posture that implies the actor is walking close to a wall, and an enclosure instantaneously appears and disappears, in accordance with the actor's abrupt footsteps and sudden spins. No groundwork is necessary for a house like that, no foundation on rock—this house is built from the poetry of the body and the mystery of bones and flesh in motion. The room has no boundaries, nor does it have cracks to let anyone in. It dawns on the audience that a door is no more than a fish slipping constantly out of their grasp. One of the sayings of mime artists is, "A door is not outside of you."

Imagine a stranger dressed in the uniform of AA Pizzeria responding to a phoned-in order at 14:21 hours on April 11. He passes through a short tunnel, then down a deserted alleyway, and pushes open a smoked glass door; then into the elevator where he checks the order again and confirms that the delivery address is apartment 3.14. At that point, he is near the moment when he will have fulfilled his task.

However, after exiting onto the third floor and finding doors marked VIII and θ and *Yin* and *Yang* and ↙, he goes downstairs again having seen no sign of apartment 3.14. The stranger then has no choice but to go back into the elevator. There is no thirty-first floor in the building, so he decides to look on the fourth floor. Here too there is no doorplate with 3.14 to be found in the brightly lit corridor.

Unable to make any sense of the doorplates, the stranger tries his luck on another floor, but running around this strange, sealed-in apartment building is soon making him feel dizzy. The elevator ceiling fan clanks away. Stepping out of the elevator again, he sees the number "13" on the wall—the thirteenth floor.

A little to the right, he sees a young woman wearing a bathrobe, lounging on a two-seater ochre leather sofa that could easily sap one's willpower. She extends snow-white legs, resting her crossed feet on an enormous suitcase, and her body forms an L-shape slightly greater than ninety degrees.

There is a fire door at each end of the corridor and, in order to find apartment 3.14, the stranger has to choose between the two. Upon stepping out of the elevator, he changes his mind. He approaches the girl and firmly occupies the empty seat on the sofa, placing his enormous insulated box on its arm. Then, imitating the girl's posture, he takes off his shoes and rests both feet on the suitcase.

The stranger looks at the shadows they cast on the pale gray walls. Occasionally there is a gleam, or a shape appears. And in front of that are placed his and her bare feet.

In a very low voice, the stranger says, "I've no reason to hurry any more. This is my first day at work and my first pizza delivery. The fifty-minute deadline between order and delivery has passed and the customer has probably called to complain.

Even if I do find apartment 3.14, they're sure to give me the worst rating on the customer satisfaction questionnaire and I'll probably lose my job."

Then he turns his shoulder slightly towards the girl. He sees that her eyes are shut, but under the thin lids, her eyeballs whirl around like a windmill spinning rapidly in a gale.

"You don't need to go on looking for apartment 3.14, or lose your job," says the girl, suddenly opening her eyes. Those orbs are so close that the stranger cannot help being pulled into their depths. They look to him like a ceiling fan at rest.

"Let's imagine I'm the owner of apartment 3.14."

The stranger looks down and pulls a thin piece of paper from his pocket—the food order. He sits up and conceals both sides of the order carefully with his hands.

"So, tell me what you ordered," he says.

"Huh?"

"Which pizza?"

The girl puts one hand on her forehead, as if she is making an effort to remember. "Loch Ness Monster Pizza—the Tuesday special."

The stranger's expression reveals nothing. He takes one hand away and, with an air of mystery, looks again at the order. After a long pause, he gives a smile so seamless that it would strike anyone as strange no matter how long they looked at it.

◦ ◦ ◦

People have forgotten that the Displacement Apartments were an experiment, now abandoned, in the history of housing development in City 24. From the outside, it is simply a basic, unadorned sixteen-floor block in the shape of a horizontal H, with the elevator at its center and eight apartments of identical size running along each of the letter's sides. However, for the residents, the apartments are like face-down playing cards on a table top, moving around, taking their doors with them, in a completely random way. That is to say, when the residents leave their apartments, they have to go through the process of finding them once more, with no rules to follow.

Inside the Displacement Apartments, one is always coming across anxious people who have lost their way. When the residents leave their apartments they're in the habit of taking an enormous suitcase with them so that they can easily set up a temporary home in the corridor: there, they open up a folding chair, finish the novel they've been reading, turn on their brand new laptop, or do twenty pushups on the floor. Nevertheless, choosing a floor, and deciding whether to turn left or right in the corridor, is always a gamble. There you stand waiting, watching the doors change, until your apartment arrives. The order has no logic to it. As people wait, they might recall where their apartment stopped last time and wonder anxiously if it will stop this time in some distant, unpredictable place. Eventually they may gather their belongings and decide to go back into the elevator, casting an uneasy glance outside again before they leave. Their apartment is as unreachable as the motherland. Some will find themselves pressing a stranger's doorbell as if longing in this strange land for a chance encounter with a substitute lover, or seeking to make temporary use of a warm bath, soft bedding, and comfort.

The lost probably hope to find someone else who is lost—someone coming back home, or an unlucky visitor, a postman delivering a registered letter, or a complete stranger. Only they can properly understand that feeling of not being quite sure which direction to turn.

◦ ◦ ◦

Imagine she has a dream that she is going to the top floor of the apartment block and that she stands completely naked, except for a pair of high-heeled shoes, on the bottom step of the stairs between floors that are indistinguishable from one another. She is holding a huge suitcase and feels dismayed at the prospect of carrying it up. When she looks up, she sees a strange man at the top of the stairs looking as if he is about to come down, and she decides not to walk up, but to wait until the stranger arrives.

The staircase is short and the stranger is moving fast, yet the distance between them remains the same. She feels that time is standing still. She tries calling out to him but as soon as the sound leaves her lips, it seems to vanish like a burst bubble. So she makes up her mind to drag the suitcase upstairs on her own. She knows her naked body is sturdy as well as voluptuous, even though the suitcase is heavier than she could have imagined. Her arms and shoulders ache, but she gradually gets nearer to him. He seems to be almost entirely bundled up in a black overcoat, white gloves, and a black hat with a brim. All one can see is his silhouette; he has no features. He looks as though he has walked out of a Magritte painting.

"A March Lion."

The stranger has no mouth, so she cannot tell if it is him speaking or not.

"The April 11 order has written on it, 'March Lion.' That's the AA Pizzeria special for March and April. So there's no way you live at apartment 3.14."

"The elevator's out of order, and my suitcase is really heavy," she pants. The stranger's face is completely unmemorable; there is nothing to focus on.

"The apartment block is just your dream," the voice continues. "No one is closer to the core of the building than you are. Only you have a key that can open any apartment in the building. Other people are looking for that familiar sofa, smell, space, rhythm of words—while you're always looking for an unfamiliar door, hoping that you will be mistaken for someone else so you can adjust your expression, posture, tone of voice when the other person stops speaking for a moment. You want to be another you..."

The stairs are completely deserted, although a crack has just appeared in the ceiling and is radiating outwards. In this sealed-in space, the stranger's voice has a shattering strength. She feels weary and spent, and has to rest her suitcase against the wall and crouch down. The sweat on her body feels oddly viscous.

Then she blurts out, "Sometimes I thought I'd already moved to a different building. But I only had to shut my eyes and I had the feeling he was still there. He used to grind his teeth together like an animal. I had no idea what that meant. I'd feel him tremble and twitch. But when I opened my eyes, I could only see part of him. Sometimes late at night, I saw just a hand, without a face, floating in midair as if smoking a cigarette. One afternoon, a disembodied laugh formed in front of me; it was a deep laugh, bubbling out from the lungs in a chest that rose and fell. I inspected the color and decor of the room where the sofa and the dining table had been set down, and I could tell that the whole apartment was just a replica of the original one. Even though I had moved to a new place, everything in it was revolving in the same sequence as before, just like the planets orbiting around the sun."

She looks up again and is amazed to find that the stranger is right in front of her. She stretches out her hand and his blank face vaporizes as rapidly as dry ice meeting heat. He sloughs off his clothes and they fall to the floor, and his black hat floats in the air, then slowly descends.

◦ ◦ ◦

When he wakes up, he discovers he is lying in the fetal position on a suitcase he has never seen before, and his body is unidentifiable. Above his head is the glass box that houses the ninth floor fire extinguisher. He cannot remember if he has fallen asleep waiting for his apartment; in fact, just now he cannot remember anything. The elevator door opens, inviting him to enter. Without hesitation, he does so. Down on the ground floor, in the row of mailboxes that covers the wall, only the one marked "3.14" catches his attention. It looks as if no one has opened the box for a long time and mail spews out of the opening like white vomit foaming from the mouth of a dying patient.

He imagines a door, desolate and cobwebbed, like an old man's back.

◦ ◦ ◦

Imagine that our apartment has more than one door.

Towards the end of dinner, the air is still transparent but then it abruptly congeals. We sink down and down, in an atmosphere where conversation is impossible, our bodies involuntarily falling into pressurized depths. We are forced to turn our faces away from everyone else's, to enable us to breathe normally.

A mother-of-pearl lampshade sways in the air. You look down and cautiously pick up a cup and a plate from the table. Even so, you cannot prevent them from clinking against each other. The sound is like cracks created by expanding air. You flee through the door.

You do not really leave—you just crouch behind the door and wait for me to rush out the same door so we can come back in again together. However, a very long time later, there is still only your curled-up shadow in the corridor, and tears with a salt content of 15cc are dripping onto it. You crane your neck and peer inside the room, finding that I have moved the wooden stool, the one normally used only as a footstool, and am sitting up close to the wall that faces north, the tip of my nose just five centimeters away from it, staring hard in front of me.

You come into the room and stand behind me, thinking I haven't noticed. You focus on a door I have just penciled on the wall in front of me. It is about the size of the door you fled through. It is crudely drawn, and there is no anti-burglar peephole, or lock to turn a key in, but my shadow has already plunged deep into it.

You cannot get me to say a word, so all you can do is take my temperature and inspect my eyes and tongue, although you can make nothing of the results. I am unresisting—just quiet, cold, and hard, gradually solidifying into a stranger, even though you try bending down and putting your head on my knee.

Or perhaps it has already dawned on you that I am just waiting for you to pull out from under the sofa the one suitcase I brought when I moved into this new apartment. It is a toolbox, full of tools for creating and destroying. And you finally take the hammer and nails out of it and chisel out the door for me. You split the wall with the pointed beak of the electric drill, and say that it feels like piercing skin. The sound of the drill makes your head spin, but you do not stop until you have made a big hole in the wall, letting in light from the outside that plays tricks with the shadows on my face.

When you have finished drilling the door, I do not stand up immediately, but wait as you slowly turn your back to me. You hear nothing so you cannot tell whether I have gone until the smell of me in the air has completely dissipated and you look around again. Why has a hole been made in the wall like that? You are scared, but still you walk through. You lean against the wall and try to experience the feeling of having one foot suspended in midair. The wind blows in your face and you are disappointed that a transparent piece of ground does not grow beneath your feet. Instead, all you see are the water tanks on the roofs of some of the lower blocks and flocks of birds flying back and forth over the rooftops in a chaotic dance.

When you turn around, you feel as if you are squeezed between two doors.

You used to believe that our apartment has only one door. It is made of cellulose and wood and is painted with Belle brand #299352 white latex paint.

I suggest you abandon the place where you live now, and move into the apartment building opposite.

Choose an afternoon when the weather's nice and order a take-away pizza that you can eat all on your own. Find an easy chair, and sit by the window and take your time in admiring the empty, rectangular hole—90cm by 210cm—that you personally drilled. You will look through it, searching for the door into the interior of the building where you lived for so long but, from a distance and lacking perspective, it will look like a surreal painting hanging on the wall or could even, from a certain angle, be a shadow falling through the gaping hole.

The wall can be rebuilt, but once the hole is filled in, it will be impossible to find any sign of where it was. You should make a careful observation of its present shape and form, as if it were a mouth slowly opening to swallow you up.

BITTER MELON

In a city where all the trees have disappeared, we still retain a green shadow in our memories.

The torrid heat prowled our part of town like a wild beast. The postman pressed our bell furiously again and again. Father, who was watering the tropical plants on the balcony with a hose, gave no more than an apathetic glance in response to the continual ringing. Mother, her face streaked with tears, stayed in the kitchen. The chopping motions she made with her hands had acquired a mechanical rhythm, which allowed her some peace of mind. A portion of the chopped onions, whose juice was making her cry, had gone into the boiling soup to nourish us, but most of them had fallen under the cooker and the rooster hopped around between mother's legs, pecking at them and growing fatter by the day.

I was not surprised that my parents did not understand my fear of strangers and thus turned a deaf ear to the doorbell. I warned them that the postman's anger would soon seep through the door. Then I shut my laptop and crossed the room, stepping over the bottles strewn all over the floor, so that I could have a look at the postman through the peephole. But all I could see was the winding, dimly lit corridor outside. I wondered if it was all just my foolish imagination, as they reckoned. The postman's hurrying footsteps had faded into the distance. I strained my ears in an attempt to make out the slight turbulence the sounds had left in the air, but like everything that came and went in our lives, it slipped away from me.

The only thing I could be sure of was the package with the name "K" written on it. On the balcony, my father gave something close to a roar of rage; the kitchen knife fell heavily to the floor as my mother was reduced to uncontrollable sobs; and the rooster opened its wings in the confined space of the kitchen and uttered a shrill crow that could have meant anything. "It is unwise to judge by appearances," I silently mouthed the words that Aphasia had written to me, as I tore the layers from the package. Behind me, I could feel my parents creeping closer until we all could finally see what lay tucked deep inside—a bitter melon of a really sinister shape. A thick, poisonous green substance spewed out of it and created clusters of fruit warts on the surface of the skin so densely packed that they looked like they might burst open at any moment.

I heard a voice, submerged in rage, that was almost inaudible. My parents swallowed pills at regular intervals, and they believed that K had disappeared from our lives forever. Yet every evening, as the fierce heat eased slightly, I could hear K's voice from a nearby construction site, coming and going like a tiny, bright green firefly hovering around us.

° ° °

"They told us K had gradually evaporated one boiling hot afternoon, like the girls who used to gather around the construction site..."

The girls had started to appear inside the corrugated iron fence that hid the site from view in springtime. They were bareheaded and silent, and came empty-handed. No one knew how they had avoided the security guards' patrols and gotten inside. At some point, the construction workers, who had just finished pouring concrete, simply looked up and saw the girls quietly dispersing, or lying spread-eagle on the rippling concrete surface, or clutching bulky water pipes, or standing on one leg like cranes at the water's edge beside steel posts sunk deep into the ground. Their eyes, fringed with long lashes, were shut. In their silence, they might have been fast asleep or deep in thought. It was hard to make out their features. TV viewers had to wait for the camera operator's lens to zoom in to see the gradually expanding tattoos of bitter melons, complete with green warty growths that twitched in a most lifelike way on their delicate white arms.

No one had seen a tattoo of such lurid green before. The logo apparently did not belong to any new political party, and it was a while before a few people remembered that the construction site had once been farmland planted with bitter melons. Men like my father who had relinquished the plow years back and worked hard to adapt themselves to city life, had long since transformed into slack-muscled caretakers or roadside pancake sellers constantly scared of being picked up by the police, or had retired to idle their days away on park benches. The girls reminded them of that long-forgotten feeling of sunburned, mud-encrusted hands and the smell of earth and grass roots early in the morning.

However, none of them, my father included, would reveal anything to me of a life that was gone forever. He had brought nothing more from his home village than a handful of seeds, which, once established in our cheap rented home, had gradually become domesticated tropical plants. These could survive in the cramped apartment provided they were watered every day with growth-suppressing chemicals. My mother had brought nothing with her to I City. But after the move, the sight of roosters in cages in the new-style markets brought back memories of her childhood, and she decided to raise some even though she could no longer understand what their crowing meant.

I don't believe my parents ever forgot the land they had once lived on—just as, even though they avoided talking about K, they still hoped for news of her. But sometimes they hoped fervently that a sandstorm would bury all memories. Like so many of our neighbors, my parents preferred to plant their passions in a time before the bitter melon girls appeared. Back then, more and more strangers were moving into the area where we lived, and buses shuttled back and forth past our house constantly, dropping people off at the construction site.

I warned my parents over and over again not to be tempted by these outsiders. They should be on their guard particularly against the trained sales agents, who wore resolute expressions that had taken the place of their real convictions. They had adopted the most superficial features of ancient Greek rhetoric, and would launch blithely into explanations about things they had no understanding of.

My parents got on the bus along with all the other dream-chasers. Just like the others, they received gaudy construction blueprints, crisscrossed with swirling lines, and allowed the agents, with their velvety-toned sales pitches, to shape their vision of the future. After a lifetime of toil, their appetite for these guided tours to the land of illusion took them by surprise. They were taken to an overgrown construction site where they obeyed the directions given to them. Here, determined fingers pointed out to them an ocean they had never seen before.

After my mother came back from the construction site, she began to long for life after death. She spent a great deal of time lying in bed, and would sometimes tell me elatedly about the feeling of death growing within her body.

"At least it's a fresh new feeling," she explained. "There's going to be a huge skyscraper on the site, big enough to shelter all our souls and they've promised that my soul will get preferential treatment, the rooster's too. We'll be closer to heaven than anyone else."

I was comforted when Dad gave her a good telling-off for being ignorant. But on another evening, he brought home some chemical fertilizer. He told us there was no need to worry now about the plants growing too big for the apartment, because the construction site was going to house a shopping mall that would attract hundreds of thousands of people and they had promised him an excellent position on the access road.

"Everyone will have to go past my shop to get in," he said. "And the plants can grow and spread differently from the way they usually do in the city."

My parents may have poked fun at each other's ignorance, but one afternoon I discovered them, for the first time in many years, lying side by side in bed holding hands. Even the broiling sun flooding through the window could not wipe the almost blissful expression from their faces. I said nothing; I just lay on the floor among the bottles, alone with my fear of strangers who gesticulated enthusiastically.

When I left the apartment block, I had to avoid being run

over by the buses and the deluded visitors they carried. Only by getting away completely could I keep my keenness of hearing, and follow the faint, wavering sounds made by K.

◦ ◦ ◦

At noon, a sheet of glass suddenly exploded out from the center of the construction site. A few passersby looked up and were blinded by an unusually fierce downpour. TV news anchors warned that the soaring temperatures concealed a great deal of latent anger and this might cause people who had reached the limits of endurance to turn into unpredictable bombs.

It was probably the obstinate silence of the bitter melon girls that was pushing people to the limits. In fact, almost everyone wanted to drive the increasingly sunburned girls off the site so that work could continue. Someone had to drag the girls out of the way, whether it was citizen volunteers or some burly construction workers.

"They're as heavy as lead."

After the girls had appeared on TV a few times, public opinion gradually polarized. Some saw the drops of sweat that gleamed on the girls' necks as a mark of their determination; others saw it as a sign of lubricity, pointing out that they were exposing their adolescent bodies on the construction site and seducing passersby, although they were unable to explain just who could possibly be attracted to these girls with their peeling, sunburned skin.

When it was all over, there was much praise for the decisiveness of the action taken by the developers. At a crucial moment, a group of young doctors who had been sent to train overseas were recalled, and they issued a stern warning after giving their diagnosis.

"Do not listen to idle speculation," they said. "The girls have just ingested lead over a long period, which is why they're so heavy."

The day after the doctors were stationed on the site, the reporters and some construction workers fainted from sunstroke. "Luckily, we were there in time to provide emergency treatment."

The doctors smiled, revealing gleaming white teeth. They spoke in tones even more forceful than the sales agents, and their words were persuasively backed up by the use of an incomprehensible foreign language. Thus they were able to override all other observers when they announced that the girls had gradually evaporated in the fierce sunshine.

The arrival of the doctors reassured everyone, so that the girls' actions, like their bodies, soon faded from people's memory. However, K's voice in my ears grew increasingly urgent. I could hear it coming from the site, though it was as faint as the bright green fireflies that were also gradually disappearing from the city, and was regarded by the young doctors as some frightful figment of my imagination.

The doctors had issued people living nearby a new type of pill, *gratis*, that they said would temporarily dispel heat-induced hallucinations. My parents were very grateful for the free pills. They were not only calmed by the doctors' clean hands, but they would also advise me—every day after dinner and with terrifying persistence—to believe that K no longer existed.

"The truth is that the girls never left the site. They were chopped up, twisted, and folded into construction materials. The workers carried on building the walls on top of their bodies, squeezing their faces between iron bars, planting their legs in the concrete, as nail after nail was hammered into their foreheads and their soft, heavy bodies became the firmest part of the edifice."

I kept searching the web for a message from Aphasia, hoping she would tell me the whereabouts of K and the bitter melon girls. I had begun to suspect long ago that Aphasia was just a pseudonym for K. K did not know that I was always spying on what she wrote online, just as she did not know that I hid behind the door and spied on her naked body before she left home.

I had seen her snow-white arms and her freshly done bitter melon tattoo. I copied the design and hid it in an orange juice bottle that K had emptied and bequeathed to me. After she disappeared from our lives, I started to collect that brand of orange juice bottle and copied down Aphasia's writings on scraps of paper, using them to fill the empty bottles back up again. It was only with these bottles that I could fill the huge wardrobe that K had left for me.

Even after they had been washed, a smell lingered in the bottles and attracted swarms of nameless insects. They ate their way into the wardrobe until it weakened to the point of collapse. We seemed not to have a lot more space at home, even though K was gone, and at some point, we couldn't find anywhere to put the wardrobe except in the center of the living room. My father complained that it obstructed his view of the TV and my mother's knees were black and blue with bruises from colliding with the wardrobe on her way back and forth to the kitchen, so she wanted to get rid of it. However, my father carried on sprinkling its inner recesses with insect repellent and my mother still brandished her feather duster (the feathers were from the rooster) and carefully dusted inside.

On some afternoons, if my parents had forgotten to take their lunchtime medicine, they would sleep, their heads lolling on the back of the sofa; while I, crouching in front of the TV, found their dreams projected on the screen, dreams not of the tower or the shopping mall of their fantasies, but of K, who would gently push open the door behind me and walk in. At that, they would both wake up with a start, and would tell K that a package from some far-off place had arrived in the mail for her.

◦ ◦ ◦

According to Aphasia, blind spots in memory were like the great fire that once broke out on the construction site: the ashes that lingered in the air clouded people's understanding of the site's history. Apart from farmland, a temporary car park, and a flea market, the site had once held a secret arms factory. No one knew whether the factory belonged to the government, opposition rebels, or the local mafia. They only knew that a group of sturdy young men who had been expelled from X School lived in it.

"Evidence of the young men could not be completely destroyed by the fire, although it was started with care. So, beginning with the springtime change in wind direction, the girls, who had fallen in love with the young men, heard their shouts coming from the site. They had to return to that ghost-ridden place and listen. The bitter melon tattoos on their arms had nothing to do with memories of farming; they were the marks of callow young girls who had at last found happiness in love."

Everything Aphasia said made me feel jealous. I imagined that the girls allowed themselves to be buried in the building so that they could be reunited with the dead young men and build happier lives within the confines of those walls. In fact, after K fell in love with the K from the secret arms factory, she lost her own name. When I pressed my ear to the mouth of the glass bottle and tried to hear K inside, the sounds seemed all mixed up, or were just an empty echo. But then I heard the doorbell ring again and K suddenly appeared, telling us she had brought someone we had never met before.

"This is J," she said.

I was astonished at the warm welcome she and the stranger got from my parents. They smiled politely, talked about changes in the weather, and offered Mr. J some tea and some of the chocolate cake we were just about to dig into.

K told me that she had moved in with J and had allowed him to take over her whole life. He chose her outfits for her, and inspected her nails and teeth. He would stand beside her, checking the speed with which she read, or ate. But she also whispered in my ear, looking confused, that as soon as she shut her eyes, K took over her dreams. One night, she slipped away from J's familiar body and found K sleeping soundly in the shoe cupboard, a sports shoe hanging on each ear so that he could not hear her cry.

"There's no doubt that K's the jealous type," said K. "He doesn't approve of my relationship with J so he keeps coming back at night. I want to wake K up, but every time I open my eyes, there's just me and J."

As I listened to K, I suddenly became aware that my mother's rough hand, which held the fruit knife, was shaking uncontrollably. As she turned the apple in her hand, she was paring away her finger along with the spiral of red peel, causing the rooster to crow monstrously at the smell of blood. My mother put everything down, stood up, and silently left the room. Then my father put down his empty teacup and went out onto the balcony. We heard the lonely snip-snip sounds as he pruned the shoots and leaves of the tropical plants one by one.

By then, only K and I were left sitting quietly at each end of the sofa. She was probably unaware that none of us apart from her could see J, just as I was the only one in the apartment who could still hear K.

◦ ◦ ◦

K did not disturb anyone, just slipped into the house in the dead of night, went into the kitchen, and picked out the bitter melons our mother had left soaking in salt water. The door was slightly ajar and I stood behind it and watched as she took a long watermelon knife and sliced the melons in half longitudinally, revealing the soft flesh inside.

"This all has to be scooped out," said K, turning to look

at me. I came out from behind the door and saw her put the melons gently back into the brimming basin. They no longer looked so sinister, just bobbed around like boats in a lake. K took the melon pieces and put them into the food processor. The whirling blades started up and made a ferocious noise that pounded in my head, tormenting me.

I put up with this painful tinnitus and asked K where the bitter melons had come from. She told me that she and K used to sneak into the secret arms factory and hide behind the engine of one of the machines and make mad, passionate love. K was often weak with hunger and K would then bring out his fierce-looking sex organ. "Eat it!" he suggested. K laughed and said he tried to push it into K's mouth.

"The bitter melon is a substitute sex organ," said K. "It's also a gift, mailed from alien lands."

"I can't remember any fire," said K. "But ever since he became a worker, K's fate had been bound up with that of the factory. He had to keep following the factory as it moved to new areas awaiting development, like the city's other factories. The temperature was as high as forty degrees Celsius in there, and the factory was desolate and completely empty, except for a row of girls dressed in carcinogenic bikinis, lying in the road, waiting hopelessly for men to come and adopt them. But the only creature that was adopted was a homeless frog who, one searing, hot midday, tried to crawl in through K's window before dying of heat stroke."

She finished speaking and brought me a glass of the vivid green juice. I opened my mouth and could see in the glass that the inside of my mouth was full of bubbling blisters caused by the heat of my body. I gulped the juice down and imagined a silent, green river flowing gracefully through me. And before that, the river would have made its way through some unknown place with a solitary factory on it.

A few nights later, I woke up and could not stop pressing the phone number that suddenly popped into my mind, in the hope that K would answer. I wanted to tell her that for a whole week my piss had been a vivid green color. I filled a bottle with it and was going to put it in the wardrobe.

"But when I touched the flimsy door, my eyes were suddenly filled with the image of flames."

The wardrobe had burned up. The fire had been impossible to put out and everything disintegrated. I then discovered that I was standing on the construction site, holding a phone receiver attached to an abandoned phone booth. There was complete silence. On the site there was just a huge gray skeleton, the remains perhaps of some weird animal, and the stench of burning flesh.

SNOW AND SHADOW

The empress hemorrhaged and died at noon. She fell in the snow and was transformed into a shoal of thick blood.

Beforehand, the pregnant empress had spent her time curled up at the window, sewing baby clothes. But she was no seamstress and the shapeless garments she made looked more like a strange sort of human skin. The needle refused to obey her and constantly jabbed her, causing her eyes to fill with tears. And when the blood spurted from her forefinger, she trembled all over like a rabbit.

"It just keeps on snowing," said the sallow-faced serving woman behind her as she fed the fire with sticks, making the tongues of flame leap madly. The empress felt that the infant in her belly was swelling like a wild beast, and a wolf-like howl escaped her.

The serving woman did not look at the empress until she heard the door open with a loud creak. In the nine months that the empress had been pregnant, this was the first time she had stepped out of her room. In the winding passageway stood the guards, hands hanging at their sides, looking as if they hadn't seen her. The empress realized that they were no different now than when she had first arrived in the palace: still ramrod straight, with cold air emanating from them as if they had been turned to ice. The empress, on the other hand, burned with heat, and sweat ran down her young backbone before slowly congealing. The snow was settling outside, and icy pearls of sweat beaded on her forehead.

The serving woman poked her head out of the room just as the empress was taking off her heavy shoes, exposing her youthful feet and ankles. A desolate tolling was heard from the nearby bell tower. She saw the empress run frantically down the spiral staircase, her figure getting smaller and smaller in the gloom, like a rapidly sinking stone.

"A future awaits J and K, but it is inevitable that Q will be destroyed."

When the empress fell outside in the snow, the small group of ministers who held the future of the country in their hands were seated around a table in a room hung with a crystal chandelier, flipping poker cards to determine the country's fate. Messengers and bodyguards buzzed around like blind flies, in search of the emperor. The latter's whereabouts were always a secret: he had a total of sixty-four known bedrooms in which to hide, and many more that no one knew about. The windows of the rooms were kept locked and barred, and the doors were hidden in the shadowy corridors. The messengers stomped up the winding staircase banging on doors, but apart from the wooden-faced guards, hardly anyone was to be seen in the palace.

No one was aware that Emperor J had left the palace over a month before, dressed as a beggar, with a staff in his hand. The roads of the country were littered with the purpling, bloated corpses of his subjects who had starved to death, and passersby could not help treading them underfoot. But the dead were not silent—they glared with indignant eyes, eyeballs bulging as if about to shoot out of their sockets. As a poet, J had written many moving poems about the dead but now he was gripped with fear and had the urge to vomit. He stopped in front of an abandoned restaurant and turned his face to the snowy horizon.

"If this snow is an omen, then it has been snowing much

too long."

"Snow represents nothing. It is the palace that is a metaphor for the future of the country."

In the palace basement, two serving women held oil lamps near a dark hole in the wall, but still they could see nothing. Although the whole of the somber black palace wall was pitted with ant holes, no one had ever seen an ant. The serving women racked their brains to no avail. When the knell sounded, they had to put on their veils and make their way up the staircase to ground level.

It was not clear when Emperor J arrived back at the palace, but he appeared at some point after the funeral musicians had departed. Against the snow, the emperor in his black cloak was the perfect symbol of death.

"The empress's body has dissolved into a bloody foam," said two serving women, as they brought the glass bottle full of blood-red liquid to the emperor for his inspection. J, however, looked at the silent infant in their arms. Her pursed lips seemed like the country's as-yet-undivined future. This was the emperor's daughter, they said, and the ministers named her "Snow" after the snow that was a persistent feature of the country's climate.

The emperor shut his eyes. His black cloak, blown aloft in the snowstorm, made him feel like a great, black bird. A flock of birds flew backwards towards him, turning the sky dark. Their calls made both the living and the dead uneasy.

° ° °

The far end of the road on the snow-blanketed horizon seemed to point upwards like a funeral stele. Along this road, Shadow would come.

"Hasn't it finished yet?" Shadow asked the girl in the mirror. "So when does the game begin?"

The features of the girl in the mirror were similar to Shadow's, but her naked body seemed as perishable as air. The girl appeared to be sleepwalking, just as she always had. When she shut her eyes, even her soft, drooping breasts seemed to be fast asleep.

In her bridal gown, Shadow had stood like a flagstaff since early morning in the center of the lozenge-shaped square behind the palace. She was fourteen years old and looked on her departure from home and impending marriage as a brand new game. She just could not understand why the troops accompanying her were dragging their feet. And she couldn't make up her mind which annoyed her more: the gorgeous outfit that made her look like a butterfly specimen or the jewelry that crawled over her head like maggots. The only thing that gave her satisfaction was the enormous mirror that went with her faithfully wherever she went. When Emperor K had asked her to choose her wedding gift, she had pointed without hesitation at the mirror in the emperor's room. She could not help remembering the expression on K's face—a comical mixture of irritation and embarrassment.

No one attending the ceremony could have failed to see the mirror at the princess's side and the sprig-like body reflected in it. When the heralds began to blow their trumpets, the girl in the mirror opened her eyes and glanced curiously at the players on either side of her. The crowd of onlookers noticed then that she held a fine ox-bone comb in her hand. They watched, enchanted, as she began to comb her hair.

It seemed incomprehensible that Emperor K should give this stunningly beautiful girl away in marriage to a country on its knees. Shadow's beauty was said by some to be so extraordinary as to make opposing armies forget all loyalty to their commander and tear their own comrades limb from limb; others, however, held that the real magic came from the dark arts the princess had studied since she was small.

Emperor K stood at the window of his room, watching the national flag fluttering before his troops. The soldiers accompanying the princess to her new home looked impressive, but K knew quite well that they were just decrepit old men whose bones were brittle and easily broken. K watched them with some unease, seeing in his mind's eye that they were rushing towards death. He seemed to have forgotten that he had arranged this. Now all he could think about was that when his elderly ministers and troops were exiled to the snow-bound outer regions, the whole company would collapse like a house of cards even before reaching the country where the girl was to be married. Between here and the distant road to the other land, he imagined there would be sudden snowstorms so violent that any secret troops sent by rival kingdoms to kidnap the bridal party would end up as bizarre skeletons along the roadside.

The emperor's gaze passed over the heads of those going into exile and fixed on the lone girl visible against the vast expanse of whiteness. He felt compelled to reach out one crooked finger and, although no one saw, felt acutely embarrassed at this sudden, futile gesture.

K recalled the evening before, when he and his daughter were sitting, as they used to, at either end of a table so long that they could not see each other clearly. As was the custom when sending a daughter on her way, K and Shadow each had a delicious-smelling sheep's head in front of them. A feeble candle flickered in the center of the table. K had scarcely any appetite and just allowed the sour wine to stain his teeth red. Shadow, on the other hand, feasted on her sheep's head, devouring it until all that was left on her plate was a bare skull.

After drinking all his wine, K, his face flushed, finally left the table and went into the sorcerer's room. "Let's draw another card!" he said, showing a row of teeth stained blood-red.

"The future is foretold very clearly." The sorcerer, standing at the altar, turned to look at the emperor. It was hard to see by the light of the candle in the emperor's hand, and the weak-sighted sorcerer found himself squinting. As if he had long anticipated the emperor's arrival, he already had his finger on a card, ready to reveal it.

"Q and J keep reappearing but K is nowhere to be seen."

The emperor seemed mesmerized by the shadow that the candle cast in his eye, and did not take in the sorcerer's words. He wandered disconsolately back to his room. It was pitch-black outside his window and there was complete silence.

K had been standing at the window all night and dawn had still not come, he thought. He was waiting for the sun to appear, and bring with it some clearer sign of the future. Finally, at twelve noon, when the sun's rays struck his eyes painfully and the deserted plaza assumed the shape of a collapsed lozenge, K realized that his daughter and her bridal guards had long since departed. A shadow, cast by the high fluttering flag, pointed in the direction they had taken.

◦ ◦ ◦

Before Shadow's arrival, Snow often stood alone at the palace's cave-like windows, gazing out at the road that snaked away towards the forest.

The forest in this country was a cruel place, to which dwarves (who were regarded as demons) were banished. The walls of their mud-built homes, which were hidden among the trees, were full of cracks, and at night the wind howled mercilessly through them into the dwarves' dark eardrums, as they dreamed dreams that made them tremble with fear. It was a bitterly cold place, inhabited by numerous wild beasts. When Snow patrolled it, she often saw the dismembered carcasses of animals under the trees or beside the path. Snow would squat down, and carefully examine the bones and energy channels amid the bloody flesh. The blood would spread slowly over the snowy ground, then quickly congeal into a bright red patch.

Dwarves armed with hunting weapons sometimes lurked behind tussocks, watching the girl. In snowstorms, they screwed up their eyes into slits and seemed unaware of the passing of time. However, in the body of Snow, the dwarves (who had long since forgotten how old they were) rediscovered a magical vitality. Every time she entered the forest, they noticed that her body was increasingly voluptuous. When Snow was fourteen years old, she was able to hoist the legs of a deer over her shoulder and struggle back to the palace with it.

A serving woman went into Snow's room one morning with her broom. Snow's room was even shabbier than the serving woman's own: knives, hooks, and rags hung on the walls, and the floor was littered with lifeless bodies. Snow held the corpse of a young girl in her arms, and a pair of scissors in her hand. She had sliced open the skin from the corner of the girl's eye to her neck, revealing the tissue—scarlet like raw beef—that lay underneath.

"It's wounded," said Snow, lifting her blood-smeared face and indicating an animal behind her. It took the serving woman a few moments to make out what it was: a deer with half the skin of its face removed. The woman watched as the princess, with astonishing skill, grafted onto the deer's neck the resected skin she had just cut from the girl. In no time at all, the animal's round brown eyes danced with life behind the warped human face. The only drawback appeared to be that the human skin graft had lost some of its elasticity; until the day it died, the deer would never be able to shut its eyes. Snow went to the window and watched the deer skitter frantically out of the palace and plunge into the forest.

"There's no one more goodhearted than the princess. You'll be remembered in the people's prayers, even when they're down to their last bone to chew."

Snow looked around and discovered it was the serving woman, lying prostrate on the floor, who was speaking. She was nothing but skin and bones. Her swarthy face looked up at Snow with bloodshot eyes.

"But I don't need to be remembered in their prayers," said

the princess, wiping the scissors clean. "No one can achieve real happiness unless they liberate themselves from the castle of destiny."

The serving woman did not know that the princess was quoting from a moldy old book she had found in the palace. Most of the books in the palace library had been bought from the populace by Emperor J because the ministers viewed all the theories in them as potentially subversive and had banned their publication. But no one could keep the princess from reading the books, from cover to cover, in the palace.

In the days when no one knew Emperor J's whereabouts, the ministers had tried to cajole the princess into taking over his position. Much time passed before they noticed the emperor's shadow concealed behind her body and the despairing expression in her eyes.

It was said that, for an entire year, behind the locked doors of the chandeliered room, the ministers debated how to save the country. Finally, on one morning of blistering sunshine, when anyone who opened their window was almost blinded by the light reflected from the snow, the people received news from the palace: the ministers had received an augury from Spade Q—the country needed a new empress.

◦ ◦ ◦

The departure of the bridal guards did not, as Emperor K had hoped, remove the shadow from his eye. Quite the opposite: from that brilliantly sunny morning onwards, the shadow engulfed his world like the waters of a lake. K often asked the chef to make dinner for him in the early morning when the sun was just up, and got angry when he was not brought his breakfast in the dead of night. Everyone said that the emperor could no longer tell day from night, forcing him to put off his military campaigns and stay in the palace all day. But, as the sorcerer had predicted, he was not turning into a blind man—it was the black shadow of memory that overwhelmed him.

◦ ◦ ◦

K began to see the apparition of his wife again, roaming the palace corridors stark naked, bumping into walls as if she was lost. She had been a frail sixteen when she died, he remembered, soon after giving birth to Shadow. The nation was now becoming stronger day by day, and any minister who heard of the emperor's visions, fearful of bad omens, advised the emperor to have the sorcerer drive the ghost away. However, the emperor was obdurate. He was not afraid of the *yin* airs the ghost gave off. In fact, he secretly opened his bedroom door and prepared to invite his wife back in again from time to time.

One night, the empress's ghost did come into the emperor's room. But she did not climb silently into his bed, as she once used to. Instead, she walked past her husband, pretending not to see him, and made straight for her favorite mirror. Without hesitation, she took the ox-bone comb from the dressing table and, just as she had once done every morning, began slowly to comb out her long hair. The empress's hair still gleamed like a river under the full moon and, as he watched her, the emperor forgave her rudeness. Suppressing his desire for her, he sat all night on the bed, silently gazing at her back and patiently waiting for her to turn around. But the empress stared obsessively at her reflection in the mirror. When the morning sun broke through, dappling his face with light, the emperor awoke and the ghost of the empress had vanished.

The empress's mirror still stood in the same place, the height of a man—taller in fact, as the emperor realized when he walked up to it. He did not see in it the sturdy, stalwart figure of which he was so proud, or the room behind him; instead he saw a long-haired girl, stark naked, poised for flight like a frightened deer. He knew that, even though his wife's ghost had gone, her beautiful body remained in the mirror. But when he shut his eyes and pressed his face to the cold glass, he realized that apart from his wife there was only a dark abyss inside.

By night the emperor watched his wife's ghost comb her hair; by day he involved himself in various government matters in an attempt to assuage his grief. Worryingly, he refused to go anywhere near his concubines, and even his closest ministers did not detect what was in the depths of his heart. Finally one night, K locked his bedroom door to punish his wife. He lay down on the bed, turned onto his side, and closed his eyes, pretending not to hear the empress's constant knocking at the door. For a dozen years, Emperor K shared his bed with no one. He campaigned and plundered and extended his nation's frontiers north, south, east, and west. Nobody knew that every single night he still heard the soft but persistent knocking of his wife just outside the door.

The ministers took the opportunity of a banquet celebrating a successful campaign to petition the emperor to take a new wife.

The emperor found the topic of the nation's future boring, but their words touched him in a different way: he wanted to know whether the knocking he heard came from inside his own head or from the lingering presence of his wife. He left his door unlocked. In the depth of night, he was surprised to see his wife seated once more in front of her mirror, combing her hair. Even more astonishingly, her face was as youthful as ever.

After so many years of abstinence, he became intensely aroused and embraced the ghost from behind. He felt as if his body was on fire and gave a disgusting belch. As he kissed his wife's body passionately, he found she no longer cowered in shame as she used to. Instead, she put down the comb and looked at K with a mocking smile, as if she found the whole business faintly comical.

The emperor took the girl's face between his hands, and then suddenly pushed her away as if he had been punched. The girl's body was warm; he suddenly realized that what he was embracing so passionately was no ghost but his grown-up daughter. He had spent so long drunk with memories of his wife that he had neglected his growing daughter; in fact, he had failed even to look at her.

It was long after the empress's death when the emperor finally summoned a palace concubine to his room one night. The ministers in charge of choosing the concubine were very uneasy. After all this time, the concubines had grown old. A minister decided to sneak his own unmarried daughter into the emperor's room instead, in the hope that she might, by some lucky chance, win the emperor's heart as the late empress had done. However, when the girl emerged the next day, she admitted red-faced to her father that she was still a virgin.

"It's not unknown for emperors to marry their own daughters," whispered a minister, as if reading the emperor's thoughts. Emperor K felt the minister's filthy spittle lodge in his ear. He said nothing, but he knew, inside himself, that he would have to tie himself up that night, to keep from rushing to his daughter's bedroom. The sorcerer remembered later that it was only after many sleepless nights that K walked into his room. "If fate decrees that I cannot marry my daughter, then make her disappear from my sight forever," K said.

And now, to escape from his daughter's shadow, here he was knocking at the sorcerer's door again. The sorcerer seemed to have been expecting him. Without bothering to pick a card from the table, he pronounced his conclusion, "A very long journey is needed before K can appear again."

"Tomorrow, exactly at midday, I will point you to where the shadow of the national flag falls. That is where you must go."

◦ ◦ ◦

Only when the emperor's wedding drew near did the ministers seem to realize that Emperor J's disappearance was a problem that needed to be solved. But even though they repeatedly cast poker cards onto the outspread map to divine where he might be, the guards they sent to find him returned to the palace bringing with them only desolate, white snow.

As the day to welcome the new empress approached, people remembered the ant holes in the palace walls. The ministers ordered serving women to plug them using mud mixed with dried grass. Strangely, however, the holes would reappear the very same evening; at nighttime, the wind could be heard whistling through tiny apertures all over the palace. When the serving women bent down to peer through the holes, they could not help laughing, not at the ants (they could not see any of those) but at one another's buttocks, which stuck up awkwardly in the air.

No one knew it was the emperor's eyes that were everywhere in the palace, not ants. He had been an expert at spying in his own palace since boyhood. He made tiny holes in the walls with the sharp point of a bayonet and, by gluing his eyes to the holes and listening, he was able to find out the most unexpected things. He saw his ministers, stark naked, getting out of their own mothers' beds and then climbing on top of the concubines and serving women. Every time they bowed low before him, he could not help seeing those episodes of carnal intercourse in his mind's eye.

In the months before and after the first empress gave birth, he had hidden behind the wall every day observing the changes in her body through the ant holes. He had felt curiously alienated as he saw her belly swell like a frog's. When the bloody infant had emerged from between her legs, the emperor felt a combination of fear and excitement. He had hastily stopped up the tiny holes and hugged himself, panting.

This palace is a depraved place, the emperor thought in shame. It was only when he reminded himself that he was a poet that he felt comforted again. His staff in his hand, J stood in the snow nearby and looked at the crumbling palace. It occurred to him that what the people needed was not divination but poetry. However, he had a strong sense of duty. Unable simply to abandon his imperial responsibilities, he continued to pace back and forth outside the palace like a ghost. Now, before leaving forever, J decided to discharge his responsibilities once and for all by welcoming a new empress. As he drew nearer to the palace, the familiar aroma of roasting meat reawakened a sense of smell that had been numbed by the intense cold.

The smell of meat wafted from the overgrown palace garden. The trees had long since shriveled. Under one tree, there was a stout guard, who squatted there on his own all year round. He held a torch in his hand, and his hair and body were covered with a mantle of snow. In front of him was a mountainous pile of bodies.

"There are too many, I can't burn them all," he protested.

On the steps that led up to the palace, Snow waited for him like a rabbit hiding in the grass: motionless, staring at him from afar.

The guard had a moon-shaped face with somewhat unremarkable features. From a distance, all that could be seen was a pair of dark nostrils. His arms and legs were short and chubby and his body wobbled like a blancmange encased within the old army uniform he wore. Snow did not know the guard's name; in fact, no one in the palace did. He was just called Dumbo, a name that he accepted as stolidly as he did everything.

Snow's eyes moved from Dumbo's face to the pile of corpses. She noted their color as she squatted down, prodding their flesh to test its firmness and pulling back their eyelids. After a while, she stood up again and shook her head.

"These people have been dead too long," she said regretfully.

"It doesn't matter." Dumbo pointed outside the palace walls. "There are so many of them, we'll never finish burning them all."

Snow followed Dumbo's pointing finger, but could only see a black figure that had just climbed over the snow-capped, somber wall, and the dark, sunless sky behind it.

◦ ◦ ◦

When Shadow arrived, the nation's ministers and people felt they were welcoming a real princess.

The train of her wedding dress spread out behind her like a peacock's feathers. Every time she moved, a dozen female attendants lifted her train and rushed frantically around the great hall after her. There was much twinkling, too—Shadow's gown was woven of pure gold thread and encrusted with priceless gems. The crowds gazing at this elegant princess were amazed by the exotic display of wealth, and felt sincere admiration for its wearer, Shadow.

"Look at how gracefully she moves!"

At the evening's banquet, those who sat at the table with her were impressed by her bearing. Seated at her side, Snow was making slurping noises over her green bean soup (she was vegetarian), while Shadow had a knack for eating all sorts of animal heads without spilling a drop on her clothes. This was the first wedding banquet in the palace in a very long time. The only slightly embarrassing thing was the naked girl in the mirror that Shadow had ordered to be placed in the center of the hall. But the naked girl looked so beautiful as she brushed her hair that hardly anyone wanted her expelled from the banquet.

Instead it was the emperor, looking lonely and grief-stricken, who struck people as an outsider. J, who seemed to appear and disappear quite suddenly, had turned up in his old bridegroom's outfit, like a wanderer from beyond the Great Wall, clutching an ancient nine-stringed *qin* and plucking some tune he had just made up. His ill-fitting, long black gown gave off a musty smell. And no matter how hard J tried to create a celebratory atmosphere, his music made those present remember the softly floating snow outside the palace walls, and the nation's drifting prospects. During the performance, the *qin* strings broke three times; finally Emperor J stopped playing and declared that this was his gift to his newly wedded wife.

"Q can bring our nation a new future, just as in the princess we have finally been given a new empress," he pronounced.

The ministers hastened to make public their auguries as a way of wishing the new couple happiness. No one could quite remember how the banquet drew to a close, and afterwards no one could say if the auguries proved to be accurate, because Shadow did not actually become empress on her bridal night. Amid the bustle of guests leaving, someone saw Shadow's peacock dress on the ground. It looked as dull as a sloughed snakeskin. Shadow had fled from the banquet, and locked herself in the palace's sixty-fourth room, saying that she was following an old tradition from her homeland. "Only the man who finds the key and succeeds in opening the door can become my true husband," she said.

That chaotic night, the exhausted serving women resembled fireflies as they flitted around the palace carrying oil lamps, frantically searching for the key to the room. Peering through the keyhole at the greenish lights bobbing around in the darkness outside, Shadow gave way to helpless laughter.

"I hope they never find the key," said the girl in the mirror. "I just want to carry on combing my hair."

No one noticed Emperor J as he snuck through the darkness toward his new wife's room. He looked through one of his secret holes in the wall into the sealed room. He could see two naked girls, almost indistinguishable. As far as he was concerned, it was scarcely important who was the real empress and who was the image in the mirror; the world he saw through the keyhole seemed as unattainable as the world in the mirror. J had long known that it was only with this distance that he could bear to observe his wife.

◦ ◦ ◦

The nation's springtime did not come any sooner just because the emperor had married again. The freezing weather and the heaps of corpses continued to make the roads hard going. One evening after the snow stopped, the princess went in search of Dumbo. Her feet got soaked and she could not avoid treading on stiffened corpses as she went. But Dumbo had vanished without a trace that afternoon, leaving behind scorched bones in a burned-out fire, and human ashes that floated away with the wind. The princess stumbled along the road from the palace to the forest, nearly tripping over snow-covered corpses, pursing her lips and whistling for the beasts.

Dumbo had turned up under the trees in the garden as

usual that day, staring blankly at the bones. He felt unusually warm, as the sun's rays crept up his back. Slush from the tree branches dripped onto the fire, causing the bones to hiss and leap as if provoked to fury. By the time Dumbo came to his senses and became aware of the tolling bell, lunchtime was long over. Still, he threw down his rake and went, as usual, down the dark passage to the palace basement.

The basement rooms were the domain of the serving women and guards. After the midday meal, a haze of cheap grain liquor permeated the room and everyone in it, and the serving women fed the fire with a constant supply of logs.

Today Dumbo arrived late. The food had been cleared away, leaving only a large bowl of baked potatoes on the table. As Dumbo reached for one, the tipsy guards lounging on the floor thought of a game. They threw themselves on Dumbo, grabbed his potato, and stuffed it into one of their own pockets. Then they roared with laughter, their faces flushed blood-red from drink.

Dumbo made no sound. He simply retreated from the assault until he found his back against the wall and all he could see in front of him were bony hands and squashed potatoes. The guards egged on one of the serving women, and she snatched a handful of ash from the stove and stuffed it into Dumbo's mouth. Two guards pinioned Dumbo's hefty limbs with their claw-like arms, while others took turns shoving ash into his mouth until it was completely stopped up. The guards in the back, disappointed to be left out of the fun, quickly thought up a new game: his ears were tempting, for a start. They pulled off his clothes and plugged every orifice in his body...

When Snow finally found Dumbo, he was tied to a tree, stark naked, at the entrance to the forest, and his eyes resembled those of a wounded animal. Snow tried to hoist him over her shoulder, as she would have done with any forest animal, but Dumbo was as heavy as an elephant.

Snow rolled his eyelids up. There were no tears and his eyes looked completely dried out. And though his limbs seemed unharmed, his body was purple with cold. Snow inspected his huge body minutely, and then climbed nimbly onto his belly and spread herself over him like a blanket. She shut her eyes and felt as if she were a soft skin that had been sewn onto another body. Just then, Dumbo's body began to emit warmth and, when she opened her eyes, she saw a bloated red face in front of her. At the same moment, Dumbo's organ suddenly stiffened. This, Snow remembered, was what the books talked about: it was what sometimes happened to the bodies of male animals.

Just then she saw a flock of what she took to be the dark, flesh-eating birds common all over the country, flying backwards towards them. Then she realized that they were not birds but beetles. They were heading—hundreds of thousands of them—straight for the palace. It looked as though they were bringing nightfall with them and would fly right into the new empress's chamber.

° ° °

"So now the game begins," said one girl to another, in a thoroughly bored voice.

That evening, almost all the serving women had been called

into the chamber and were waiting for the game to begin. They had no idea what the game was about. But they remembered the tug-of-war that the empress had made them play not long ago. One unfortunate serving woman had stood at the center of the circle, her long hair fanned out in the hands of the women around her, as they gripped their "rope" and pulled the woman's head every which way until the empress burst into gales of laughter.

This time, they watched as the empress put her hands against the wall. The wall looked as if it had been eaten away by sulfuric acid and was about to collapse—the wind whistled through a huge jagged hole, making everyone shiver. Through the hole, they could see a dark sky looming over the tranquil, snow-covered ground.

At first, they thought it was a black cloud, but then they realized a swarm of beetles was flying directly toward the palace. Before the stunned serving women could react, they were surrounded; panic broke out. They felt the beetles thumping against them and heard the high-pitched whining in their ears. The beetles soon flew off and the women sighed with relief, until they noticed one middle-aged serving woman whose entire right arm was covered in a swarm. The beetles, their carapaces gleaming, scurried to and fro. Then, just as suddenly, they disappeared through the holes in the wall, taking the woman's arm with them. The armless woman gave a dull shriek, and fell to the ground in a faint.

At this moment, Snow walked into the empress's room. She produced some herbal anesthetic ointment from her pocket and applied it to the wound where the woman's arm used to be. She sent the servants to fetch a frozen pig's trotter from her room and then skillfully sewed it onto the woman's shoulder. The operation was almost perfect except that, some days later, when the woman tried using it to wash her face, the "hand" mischievously tipped over a bowl full of water.

Empress Shadow was so impressed by Snow's operation that she burst out clapping. Even the girl in the mirror put down her comb and looked on curiously.

"Is this magic? Can you teach me?" asked Shadow.

"No, it's not magic at all," Snow shook her head. "It's medicine." And she stalked off back to her own room.

Shadow wanted to learn this magic that Snow called "medicine." So every day she ordered a serving woman's arm to be cut off, after which she would clumsily sew a pig's trotter onto the shoulder in its place. But her implants either dropped off as soon as the thread came loose, or caused gangrene. The women gave off a nauseating stink as they walked around the palace, and eventually had to be thrown out by the ministers. By the time Shadow woke up one morning and realized she was tired of the game, she had hardly any serving women left.

The bored empress prowled the palace, in and out of every room, discovering ant holes everywhere. Through one of these holes, she saw Snow just waking up and clambering out from a pile of corpses. Snow performed no medical miracles that day—she just stepped over the bodies and deposited more grass-green vomit at the base of the ancient palace wall.

∘ ∘ ∘

Before he left the palace, Emperor J secretly gave Dumbo the ancient key to the empress's bedchamber.

"Get the empress pregnant, just as you got the previous empress pregnant."

The key spun through the air like a metal bird as Dumbo tossed it up into the tree branches. J heaved a long sigh; although the nation's future remained unpredictable, at least he had discharged all his responsibilities as emperor. Dumbo's eyes were fixed unwaveringly on the bright flames of his fire, but the emperor had already transformed himself into a beggar and, leaning on his staff, he was off. As he walked away through the snow and toward the city where his subjects lived, he was unaware that the pregnant Snow was taking quite a different road—the one into the forest.

For the first time in many years, those hidden forest-dwellers, the dwarves, followed the girl they now found stumbling through the forest on swollen feet. But when she finally tripped and fell unconscious to the ground, they realized that they had no idea what to do with this strange prey. Eventually, they treated her like any other animal that they were not going to eat immediately, and they tied her up and took her home.

The dwarves reared all kinds of deformed animals in their forest shacks. Snow practiced transplants on these creatures, with the result that they began to experience feelings of indignation just as humans do. One day, Snow woke up to see the dwarves throwing a deer with a human face into a large pot; she buried her head in her hands and was reduced to tears. The dwarves were astonished at Snow's pathetic behavior. Tears were incomprehensible to forest-dwellers. All they understood was taking a life for a life. Every morning, they piled the leftover meat and bones in front of Snow, but the girl refused to put anything in her mouth except the melting snow that dripped from the roof.

The empress, bored in the empty palace, went to bed very early one night. However, she had left the door ajar, and a fat palace guard stumbled in. It took him a long time to take off his boots, socks, and tatty old army uniform. He looked wearily at the empress sitting on the bed, and then glanced at the girl in the mirror.

He brooded for a while, and then said, "I can't make both of you pregnant."

Shadow exchanged amused looks with the girl in the mirror. Then she suddenly thought of a game to play on this stout guard.

The next day, everyone saw the empress riding a naked Dumbo around the palace. Since no one had the temerity to try and stop her, she even rode him out into the streets. The starving populace stared from a distance, and a few sporadic laughs were heard. The ministers, however, only said, "Dumbo's just a toy to her. She's a young girl, after all." The empress took no notice. Laughing and brandishing a gleaming metal fork, she placed a basket of apples on Dumbo's head and demanded that he keep up a steady pace. Everyone thought that the fork was for eating the apples, but in fact the empress was using it to prod Dumbo's now-swollen, now-flaccid penis.

° ° °

One night, when the dwarves returned from hunting, they discovered the girl lying curled up like a caterpillar, stiff and cold on the snowy ground. One dwarf poked her with a dead branch. The sharp end made a rent in the filthy old rags she wore, exposing a large expanse of white thigh. However, Snow lay there, her eyes unfocused, as if gazing at a tranquil sea, apparently absorbed in picking up distant sounds.

The dwarves tore off her clothes and bound her hands. Then they hauled her over to a tall tree outside the door and hung her from it, as they would the carcass of an animal. After all, dealing with carcasses was the only thing they knew. Anyone looking out from the palace window would have thought she had just been executed. But the dwarves made her an object of reverence. She was the demon woman whose beautiful white body they came to admire every day. The weather was so cold that Snow was soon encased in ice like a silkworm chrysalis.

It became an unspoken promise that the dwarves, when they went out to forage for food each day, would only bring back sound animals and would leave behind any beasts that Snow had operated on. They knew that soon only the dysmorphic ones would be left in the forest—after all, these were probably closer to the forest's essential nature. They lay in wait, their tiny bodies hidden under trees, spying on the animals' activities. The forest paths meandered mysteriously hither and thither but the dwarves were convinced that they led to survival, to the real exit from the world. By contrast, Snow's white body, hanging like some alien object in the tree, eventually made them doubt that this girl had ever really existed. Soon they began to see her as a spirit: they arranged decapitated animal heads around the tree roots and worshipped her before going out to hunt.

The dwarves heard the sound of ice cracking in their dreams. It gave them the illusion that winter had passed, but when they pushed their doors open, they discovered the world was still blanketed in snow and sword-like icicles hung from the trees. They really had heard the ice cracking, however, and when they looked up, they saw that it was Snow's icy carapace that had shattered. Her body showed no signs of decay but was clearly swollen. They did not realize that this was what happened in pregnancy and were terrified at the change in their demon goddess.

One night, they sensed a dark presence in the forest. With the thudding of hooves, a burly man appeared. When the dwarves woke up the next morning, the man was still waiting outside. "Why don't you sell her to me?" he said, pointing to Snow's ice-encased body. The dwarves looked at him; he must have come from a far-off country because, by then, only mutant animals remained in the forest. "I'll pay you whatever you want," the man went on. But the dwarves did not say a word; they just retreated deep into the undergrowth.

The man could not understand how the dwarves had managed to get Snow up into such a tall tree. He only knew that there was no way he could get her down by himself. Every day, he patrolled the base of the tree until one day he fell asleep. He was awakened by a great crash; the tree branch could bear Snow's weight no longer and she had fallen like a ripe fruit to the ground.

"It's always winter in the forest," said the dwarves as they extracted a bloody infant from between Snow's legs. "But perhaps this is a sign that the seasons are changing."

They carried the infant deep into the forest. In the early dawn, the man put Snow's stiffened body onto his horse and rode away along the winding path.

° ° °

When Emperor K returned to his country after his travels, what struck his people was not the fact that he had finally taken a new wife, but the astonishing news that the new empress had taken refuge in an enormous block of ice.

The country had a warm climate and had never experienced snowstorms, so people flocked to the lozenge-shaped square in the hope of seeing this extraordinary sight. However, even those who succeeded in pushing their way to the front could not help being a little disappointed. "That's not a block of ice, it's just glass!" they complained. Regardless of what it was made of, the woman sealed up inside of it was no more interesting than the woman in the mirror—her arms hung rigid, and she didn't even comb her hair.

Emperor K seemed very pleased with his new empress. When the ministers suggested various ways of releasing her from the "ice," perhaps with explosives or a blowtorch, he merely smiled and said, "She's fine as she is."

The ministers took this as a sign that he had fallen madly in love again, but to their surprise, K called for the disgraced concubines on his wedding night. "Aging bodies have their own charms," as he put it. So, just when he was past his prime, Emperor K began to throw himself into bodily pleasures.

Most of the women stepped into the emperor's room with a tremor of fear. It was filled with mirrors; in each of them, they could clearly make out the body of the empress in her ice block. Her flesh appeared to be frostbitten. Only her eyes seemed alive, watching every movement of the people in the room.

The real Snow was gazing towards her distant home. There, the snow had not stopped, the wind whistled, the country was showing no signs of decline. The ministers running the country's affairs had undergone a metamorphosis, as cells do, but their essence had not changed. They carried on just as before—no better, no worse.

Emperor J skulked in hidden corners, his legs turning to ice and death devouring him from the feet up. Still, this did not stop the emperor's poetry from being disseminated among the people, who used it to express their grief and their anger at the country.

The happy news was that the empress had finally produced a male heir. His body was white as snow—symbolic, perhaps, of the palace and the country into which he had been born. No one knew that a dwarf had snuck the infant out of the forest, and that it was probably the progeny of Dumbo, just like Princess Snow.

There were many lonely days of celebration for the royal family. As the empress and the baby rode in their horse-drawn carriage, hungry hands reached out to them. Among these stick-like appendages, there was one shaped like a pig's trotter that reduced the infant prince to fits of laughter. The carriage clip-clopped into the palace, the *suonas* sounded, and fireworks filled the sky.

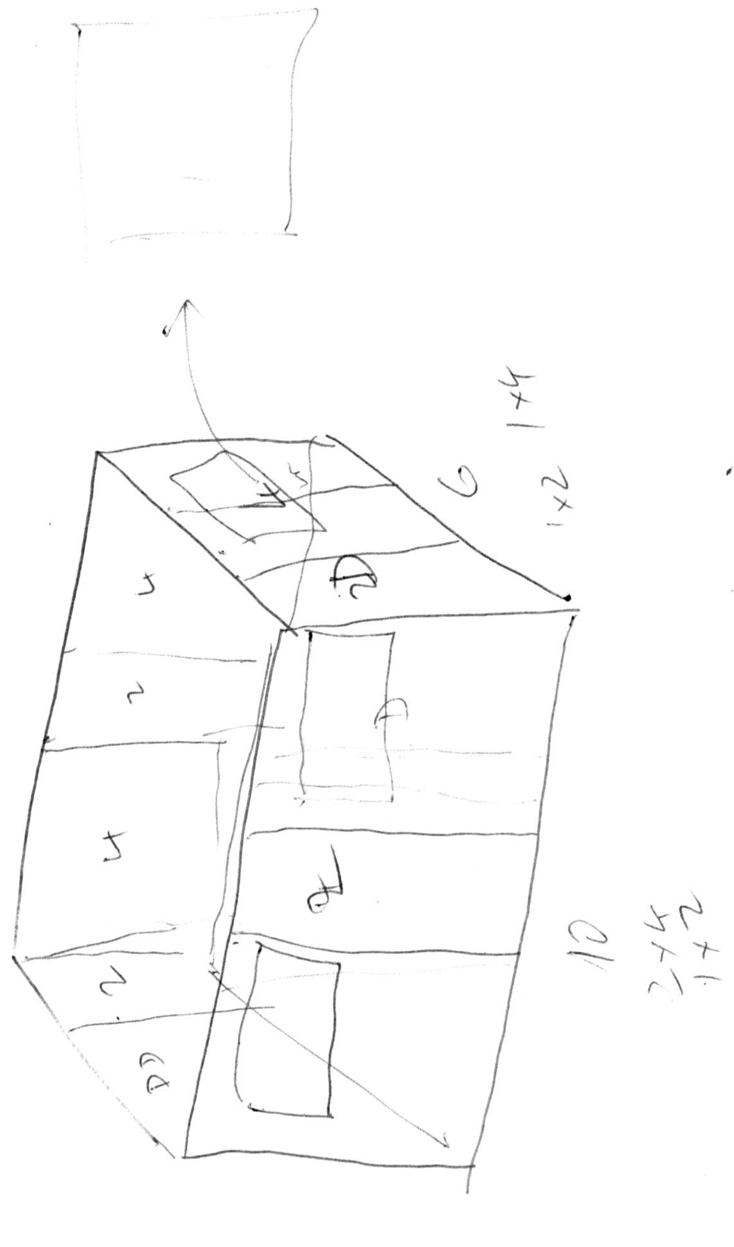